Transnational Due Process and Article V(1)(b) of the New York Convention

International Arbitration Law Library

VOLUME 72

Editors

Professor Julian D.M. Lew QC has been involved with international arbitration for more than forty years as counsel, as arbitrator and as an academic. He is the founder and has been the Head of the School of International Arbitration, Centre for Commercial Law Studies, Queen Mary University of London since its creation in 1985. He is now an independent international arbitrator at 20 Essex Street, London.

Stavros Brekoulakis is the Michael & Laura Hwang Professor in International Arbitration at the National University of Singapore and a member of 3 Verulam Buildings (Gray's Inn). He is a leading academic in international arbitration and has led, or been involved in, several projects with ICCA, ICC Commission and ILA. He also acts as an independent arbitrator and has been appointed as a chairman, sole arbitrator, co-arbitrator and emergency arbitrator under all the major arbitration rules.

Introduction

Since its first volume published in 1993, this authoritative practitioner-oriented series has published in-depth and analytical works on niche aspects of international arbitration, authored by specialists in the field.

Objective

This authoritative and established series covering in-depth analyses of niche areas appeals to both practitioners and academics. The series includes specific monographs and PhD dissertations of high quality, which are practical and cover issues not fully explored in general texts.

Frequency

A volume is published whenever an interesting topic presents itself.

The titles published in this series are listed at the end of this volume.

Transnational Due Process and Article V(1)(b) of the New York Convention

Grounding Interpretation and Application of the Due Process Defence in the Public International Law Framework for Treaty Interpretation

Dan Xie

Wolters Kluwer

Published by:
Kluwer Law International B.V.
PO Box 316
2400 AH Alphen aan den Rijn
The Netherlands
E-mail: lrs-sales@wolterskluwer.com
Website: www.wolterskluwer.com/en/solutions/kluwerlawinternational

Sold and distributed by:
Wolters Kluwer Legal & Regulatory U.S.
920 Links Avenue
Landisville, PA 17538
United States of America
E-mail: customer.service@wolterskluwer.com

ISBN 978-94-035-2437-5

e-Book: ISBN 978-94-035-2447-4
web-PDF: ISBN 978-94-035-2457-3

Table of Contents

Foreword

The 1958 United Nations Convention on the Recognition and Enforcement of Foreign Arbitral Awards, commonly referred to as the New York Convention, is the cornerstone of international commercial arbitration. Within its provisions, Article V(1)(b) delineates the due process defence, recognized as a pivotal ground for refusal under the Convention. Nevertheless, the interpretation and application of this defence are applied variability across State Parties, reflecting their diverse legal traditions and practices.

Against this backdrop, Dr Dan Xie's book *Transnational Due Process and Article V(1)(b) of the New York Convention* is profoundly insightful. The book undertakes a meticulous examination of the due process defence under the New York Convention. Dr Xie advocates for a comprehensive interpretative framework that is consistent with the principles outlined in the Vienna Convention on the Law of Treaties (VCLT), the fundamental principle of *audiatur et altera pars* and the practices of State Parties to the New York Convention. Central to her argument is the assertion that the due process standard within the New York Convention should transcend national legal systems, embodying a genuinely transnational standard.

In the pages of this book, Dr Xie meticulously constructs her argument, drawing upon foundational principles of international law and legal theory. Through carefully integrated sequence of chapters, she guides the reader through her comprehensive analysis. Chapter 2 lays the groundwork for a transnational approach, rooted in the interpretative rules of the VCLT. Chapters 3 through 7 delve into the application of the principle of *audiatur et altera pars* and subsequent state practice, offering a salutary understanding of their role in interpreting the due process defence.

Dr Xie's work makes three significant contributions to the discourse on transnationalism in arbitration. First, she delineates the scope and analytical potential for an autonomous approach, grounded in the VCLT, that provides a structured framework for domestic courts to take account of material legal sources in other jurisdictions. Second, by aligning arbitration scholarship with principles of public international law, she enriches ongoing debate on decentralized treaty interpretation in a climate in which treaty localization undermines transnationalization. Third, her sophisticated understanding of the need to revitalize the cohesive framework for a transnational due process standard provides clarity and potential unity in this complex legal terrain.

In conclusion, *Transnational Due Process and Article V(1)(b) of the New York Convention* represents a seminal contribution to the field of international arbitration. Dr Xie's rigorous scholarship, informed by principles of international law, offers valuable insights. Her book will undoubtedly have a significant influence on the discourse and practice of international commercial arbitration for years to come.

Dr Leon Trakman, LLM, S.J.D. (Harvard)
UNSW Emeritus Professor and Former Dean of Law
Faculty of Law
University of New South Wales

Acknowledgements

This book, an expansion of my doctoral thesis, embodies the generous contributions of many respected individuals and institutions. It is a personal accomplishment that also reflects a shared academic journey.

My profound appreciation goes to my supervisors: Professor Lucas Lixinski, Professor Leon Trakman, Associate Professor Jonathan Bonnitcha at the University of New South Wales, and Associate Professor Jeanne Huang from the University of Sydney. Their insightful supervision, constructive criticism, and professional ethos have been fundamental to this book's fruition.

I am equally grateful to my panel members of annual reviews, Professor Colin Picker, Professor Dimity Kingsford Smith, and Associate Professor Kun Fan, for their sage advice and ongoing support. Acknowledgement is also due to my external examiners, Professor Thomas Schultz of King's College London and Associate Professor Joshua Karton of Queen's University, for their insightful assessments and feedback that were vital in enhancing my thesis.

My journey was further enriched by the early guidance of Professor Patricia Shaughnessy and Professor Yong Wang, who were instrumental during the inception of my research at the University of New South Wales. I must also extend my thanks to the Australian Government Research Training Program Scholarship, which provided invaluable financial support.

The metamorphosis from thesis to book owes much to Professor Julian Lew and Professor Stavros Brekoulakis, co-editors of the Kluwer Law International's International Arbitration Law Library Series, who honoured me by including my work in this eminent collection. I also extend heartfelt thanks to Eleanor Taylor, the Acquisition Manager, whose editorial acumen and support have been indispensable.

Lastly, my deepest thanks go to my family, whose unyielding love and support have been my anchor throughout this endeavour.

To all who have been a part of this book's creation, through guidance, support, or encouragement, please accept my heartfelt thanks. This book is not just a work of scholarship but a testament to our shared dedication to furthering knowledge in the field of international commercial arbitration.

CHAPTER 1

Transnational Due Process and Article V(1)(b) of the New York Convention

§1.01 INTRODUCTION

The 1958 United Nations Convention on the Recognition and Enforcement of Foreign Arbitral Awards (hereinafter 'New York Convention' or 'Convention') is the most important convention in the field of international commercial arbitration.[1] It provides for the international recognition and enforcement of arbitration agreements and arbitral awards, which makes it much easier for a successful party to enforce an arbitral award internationally than a court judgment. The most esteemed feature of arbitration, as per statistics, is the enforceability of awards.[2]

In order to promote the recognition and enforcement of foreign arbitral awards, Article V of the New York Convention exhaustively outlines grounds that can result in refusal of recognition or enforcement. Under Article V(1)(b) of the New York Convention, recognition and enforcement of an arbitral award may be refused if the opposing party establishes that:

> [...]
>
> (b) The party against whom the award is invoked was not given proper notice of the appointment of the arbitrator or of the arbitration proceedings or was otherwise unable to present his case;
>
> [...].[3]

1. Albert Jan van den Berg, *The New York Arbitration Convention of 1958: Towards a Uniform Judicial Interpretation* (Kluwer Law and Taxation Publishers, 1981) 1.
2. *See* School of International Arbitration at Queen Mary University of London and White & Case, '2015 International Arbitration Survey: Improvements and Innovations in International Arbitration' (Queen Mary University of London and White & Case, 2015) 6, which suggests that 65% of respondents regard 'enforceability of awards' as the most valuable characteristic of arbitration compared with 'avoiding specific legal systems' (64%), 'flexibility' (38%) and other characteristics.
3. *Convention on the Recognition and Enforcement of Foreign Arbitral Awards*, open for signature 10 June 1958, 330 UNTS 3 (entered into force 7 June 1959) Art. V(1)(b).

This provision is widely regarded as 'the most important ground for refusal under the New York Convention'.[4] Ensuring a fair arbitral procedure is crucial for instilling confidence in parties from diverse legal systems in arbitration as a method of dispute resolution. Article V(1)(b) ensures the minimum requirements for a fair arbitral procedure and integrates the fundamental concept of due process into the New York Convention.

Article V(1)(b) specifies a universally accepted ground for refusal, which is not only due to the widespread acceptance of the New York Convention but also because the UNCITRAL Model Law on International Commercial Arbitration (hereinafter 'UNCITRAL Model Law') encompasses the same ground for refusing to recognise and enforce an arbitral award and for setting aside an arbitral award by the national court of the seat of arbitration.[5] In most respected commentaries on the New York Convention and authoritative textbooks on international commercial arbitration, the term 'due process' is commonly used in reference to Article V(1)(b).[6] Consequently, this book will use the term 'due process defence' as a synonym for Article V(1)(b).

It is usually the courts of the State Parties to the New York Convention that determine whether to recognise an arbitral award or allow or deny its enforcement. There is significant diversity across nations in the concretisation of the due process defence.[7] At a fundamental level, Chapter 2 of this book illustrates that national courts in different states have adopted three distinct approaches to interpreting the notion of due process under the New York Convention: (a) the *lex arbitri* – the law of the seat of the arbitration; (b) the *lex fori* – the law of the forum state where the recognition or enforcement of the award is sought; or (c) a uniform transnational standard that is independent of any specific national jurisdiction and is rooted more in an interpretation

4. Nigel Blackaby et al., *Redfern and Hunter on International Arbitration* (Oxford University Press, 6th ed., 2015) 627.
5. *UNCITRAL Model Law on International Commercial Arbitration*, UN GAOR, 40th sess., Supp No. 17, UN Doc. A/40/17 (adopted 21 June 1985) annex I, as amended by UN GAOR, 61st sess., Supp No. 17, UN Doc. A/61/17 (7 July 2006), annex I ('*UNCITRAL Model Law*') Arts 34, 36.
6. van den Berg (n. 1) 296–311; Maxi Scherer, 'New York Convention: Violation of Due Process, Article V(1)(b)' in Reinmar Wolff (ed.), *New York Convention: Convention on the Recognition and Enforcement of Foreign Arbitral Awards of 10 June 1958: Commentary* (C.H. Beck • Hart • Nomos, 2012) 279, 279–309; Andrés Jana, Angie Armer and Johanna Klein Kranenberg, 'Article V(1)(b)' in Herbert Kronke et al. (eds), *Recognition and Enforcement of Foreign Arbitral Awards: A Global Commentary on the New York Convention* (Kluwer Law International, 2010) 231, 231–256; Herman Verbist, 'Challenges on Grounds of Due Process Pursuant to Article V(1)(B) of the New York Convention' in Emmanuel Gaillard and Domenico Di Pietro (eds), *Enforcement of Arbitration Agreements and International Arbitral Awards: The New York Convention in Practice* (Cameron May, 2008) 679, 679–728; ICCA, 'ICCA's Guide to the Interpretation of the 1958 New York Convention: A Handbook for Judges' (International Council for Commercial Arbitration, 2011) 89–93; United Nations Commission on International Trade Law, *Secretariat Guide on the Convention on the Recognition and Enforcement of Foreign Arbitral Awards* (2016) 155–170; Blackaby et al. (n. 4) 627–629; Emmanuel Gaillard and John Savage (eds), *Fouchard Gaillard Goldman on International Commercial Arbitration* (Kluwer Law International, 1999) 985–987; Julian D M Lew, Loukas A Mistelis and Stefan M Kröll, *Comparative International Commercial Arbitration* (Kluwer Law International, 2003) 711.
7. For more details, *see* §2.02–§2.04 of Chapter 2, §5.03–§5.05 of Chapter 5, Chapters 6 and 7.

of Article V(1)(b).[8] Scholarship has duly identified and analysed the variances between these three approaches.[9]

Under both the *lex arbitri* and *lex fori* approaches, discrepancies among states regarding the interpretation and scope of the due process defence could be deemed justifiable. In both approaches, the contours of due process are determined by reference to a set of national laws that may differ from one jurisdiction to another. There are various policy factors that render both approaches problematic. First, the *lex fori* approach diminishes the predictability and legal certainty for arbitrators and parties.[10] Furthermore, the absence of certainty regarding the due process defence can give rise to a sense of 'due process paranoia'. In return, arbitrators' apprehension of enforcing courts' reactions unavoidably leads to excessively cautious procedural management in arbitral proceedings, leading to amplified cost and duration.[11] These concerns are magnified by the fact that a specific award may be enforced in several jurisdictions, making it arduous for the parties involved and arbitrators to anticipate beforehand where enforcement or recognition of the award will subsequently be sought. The *lex arbitri* approach could potentially lead to the enforcement of awards that significantly deviate from commonly held expectations regarding the fundamental prerequisites of a fair arbitration.

The author presents a particular understanding of the transnational approach to the due process defence in this book. This understanding is grounded in the interpretative framework of the Vienna Convention on the Law of Treaties (VCLT), specifically the general principle of *audiatur et altera pars* and subsequent practice of State Parties

8. For more details, *see* §2.02–§2.04 of Chapter 2.
9. In support of the *lex arbitri* approach, *see* Marike R P Paulsson, *The 1958 New York Convention in Action* (Kluwer Law International, 2016) 182–183; Osamu Inoue, 'The Due Process Defense to Recognition and Enforcement of Foreign Arbitral Awards in United States Federal Courts: A Proposal for a Standard' (2000) 11 *The American Review of International Arbitration* 247, 270–274; in support of the *lex fori* approach, *see* Jan Paulsson, *The Idea of Arbitration* (Oxford University Press, 2013) 36; Jan Paulsson, 'Arbitration in Three Dimensions' (2011) 60(2) *International and Comparative Law Quarterly* 291, 298 DOI: 10.1017/s0020589311000054; Jan Paulsson, 'Delocalisation of International Commercial Arbitration: When and Why It Matters' (1983) 32 *International and Comparative Law Quarterly* 53 10.1093/iclqaj/32.1.53; Jan Paulsson, 'Arbitration Unbound: Award Detached from the Law of Its Country of Origin' (1981) 30(2) *International and Comparative Law Quarterly* 358 DOI: 10.1093/iclqaj/30.2.358; in support of a uniform transnational standard, *see* Gaillard and Savage (n. 6) 986; Jean-François Poudret and Sébastien Besson, *Comparative Law of International Arbitration* (Sweet & Maxwell, 2nd ed., 2007) 835; Gary B Born, *International Commercial Arbitration* (Kluwer Law International, 2nd ed., 2014) 3504–3506; Scherer (n. 6) 285–286.
10. For more details, §2.03[D] of Chapter 2, Chapter 8.
11. In the Queen Mary and White & Case International Arbitration Survey (2015), the fear that the award could eventually be set aside or refused enforcement for violation of a party's due process rights is referred to as 'due process paranoia': *see* School of International Arbitration at Queen Mary University of London and White & Case, '2015 International Arbitration Survey: Improvements and Innovations in International Arbitration' (Queen Mary University of London and White & Case, 2015). *See also* Michael Polkinghorne and Benjamin Ainsley Gill, 'Due Process Paranoia: Need We Be Cruel to Be Kind' (2017) 34(6) *Journal of International Arbitration* 935; Lucy Reed, 'Ab(use) of Due Process: Sword vs Shield' (2017) 33 *Arbitration International* 361; Klaus Peter Berger and J Ole Jensen, 'Due Process Paranoia and the Procedural Judgment Rule: A Safe Harbour for Procedural Management Decisions by International Arbitrators' (2016) 32(3) *Arbitration International* 415.

to the New York Convention. It is argued that domestic courts ought to interpret Article V(1)(b) based on the premise that the due process defence maintains a uniform meaning and scope across all countries. The book puts forth three specific contributions towards theorising and developing the transnational approach. First, it maintains that the transnational approach can and should be based upon the framework of public international law governing treaty interpretation. The New York Convention is a treaty that binds Contracting States. Article III establishes a binding obligation under international law to enforce foreign arbitral awards, subject only to the narrowly defined exceptions in Article V. The interpretation of Article V(1)(b) should thus adhere to international law. The legal framework for interpreting treaties provides a set of techniques and tools that offer superior guidance for interpreting the due process defence when compared to an unstructured appeal to transnationalism. Furthermore, it reveals how much of the arbitration scholarship on transnationalism can be recast within the framework of public international law. In doing so, it contributes to debates within the field of international law on the decentralised interpretation of international law by domestic courts. Third, it shows how the author's preferred understanding of the transnational approach - one grounded in the public international law framework for treaty interpretation - resolves a range of practical questions about the precise content of the due process defence.

§1.02 PUBLIC INTERNATIONAL LAW AS A FRAMEWORK FOR THE INTERPRETATION AND APPLICATION OF THE DUE PROCESS DEFENCE

The VCLT establishes the appropriate framework for interpreting treaties under international law.[12] Since the provisions on treaty interpretation contained in Articles 31–33 of the VCLT are pre-existing customary international law, all parties to the New York Convention are bound by them when interpreting the due process defence.[13] Domestic courts, as independent actors whose decisions affect a nation's compliance with treaty obligations, may also be considered as part of the audience of the VCLT, extending beyond international courts and tribunals.[14]

Enforcing courts should view the New York Convention as an instrument that operates on the international plane.[15] Its international origin remains unchanged despite its incorporation into domestic law.[16] Enforcing courts should interpret and apply international rights and obligations that originate from treaties consistently with their international source, even when these rights and obligations are implemented

12. Richard Gardiner, *Treaty Interpretation* (Oxford University Press, 2nd ed., 2015) 142.
13. *See* §2.05[B] of Chapter 2.
14. For a detailed discussion of the applicability of the Vienna Convention by international courts, or tribunals, and national courts, *see* Gardiner (n. 12) 123–158; Michael Waibel, 'Principles of Treaty Interpretation Developed for and Applied by National Courts?' in Helmut Philipp Aust and Georg Nolte (eds), *The Interpretation of International Law by Domestic Courts* (Oxford University Press, 2016) 13.
15. For more details, *see* §2.04[B] and §2.05 of Chapter 2.
16. *See* §2.05 of Chapter 2.

through domestic legislation.[17] Essentially, there exists only one accurate interpretation of a treaty provision. Although the term 'due process' as used in the New York Convention may be derived from concepts applied in national legal systems,[18] once it is included in the Convention, it assumes a single meaning that cannot be altered according to nation-related variations, unless the Convention states otherwise.[19] In this regard, it is noteworthy that Article V(1)(b) is the singular basis for the decline of enforcement in the New York Convention, which is not explicitly tethered to the domestic law of a particular jurisdiction.[20]

It is necessary to ensure an independent interpretation of the due process defence under the New York Convention, as with other multilateral treaties. This can be achieved through utilising the techniques of treaty interpretation set out in Articles 31–33 of the VCLT. Enforcing courts should give any implementing legislation the same meaning as the treaty it incorporates and examine the underlying treaty to support interpretation of implementing legislation.[21] In doing so, enforcing courts should strive to identify the true autonomous meaning of the New York Convention's due process defence, uninfluenced by domestic legal concepts, terminology, or domestic interpretative techniques themselves.[22] This method aligns with the overall goal of uniformly applying the New York Convention.[23]

The fundamental principle of treaty interpretation, as outlined in Article 31 of the VCLT, is that a 'treaty shall be interpreted in good faith in accordance with the ordinary meaning to be given to the terms of the treaty in their context and in the light of its object and purpose'. According to this principle, treaty interpretation involves the search for a single meaning that applies to the legal relationships between all parties to the treaty; it is not for each State Party to ascribe to the treaty text a different interpretation that best suits its own legal tradition or broader policy objectives.

Based on the VCLT interpretation approach, the author contends that Article V(1)(b) should be construed as an autonomous rule. Nonetheless, this provision is

---

17. Hersch Lauterpacht, 'Decisions of Municipal Courts as a Source of International Law' (1929) 10 *British Yearbook of International Law* 65, 76–77; Francis Geoffrey Jacobs, 'Introduction' in Francis Geoffrey Jacobs and Shelley Roberts (eds), *The Effects of Treaties in Domestic Law* (Sweet & Maxwell, 1987) xxix.
18. Due process has been recognised as a general principle of law derived from the principal national legal systems: *see* Chapter 3.
19. Gardiner (n. 12) 33.
20. For more details, *see* §2.06[A][2] of Chapter 2.
21. David L Sloss, 'Domestic Application of Treaties' in Duncan B Hollis (ed.), *The Oxford Guide to Treaties* (Oxford University Press, 2nd ed., 2020) 358; Mathias Forteau, 'The Role of the International Rules of Interpretation for the Determination of Direct Effect of International Agreements' in Helmut Philipp Aust and Georg Nolte (ed.), *The Interpretation of International Law by Domestic Courts* (Oxford University Press, 2016) 109.
22. Michael P Van Alstine, 'Dynamic Treaty Interpretation' (1998) 146(3) *University of Pennsylvania Journal Law Review* 687, 730–731. *See also* Maren Heidemann and Andreas Knebel, 'Double Taxation Treaties: The Autonomous Interpretation Method in German and English Law; as Demonstrated by the Case of the Silent Partnership' (2010) 38(3) *Intertax* 136 DOI: 10.54648/taxi2010015.
23. For the objectives of the New York Convention, *see* UNCITRAL's website at https://uncitral.un.org/en/texts/arbitration/conventions/foreign_arbitral_awards. For commentaries, *see* van den Berg (n. 1) 4; Born (n. 9) 3504.

worded generically. Therefore, how can the broad language of Article V(1)(b) be interpreted as an independent norm able to offer practical direction on the wide array of specific questions arising in enforcement and recognition proceedings before national courts? One of the central contributions of the author in this book is to specify a transnational-informed approach that draws upon the general principle of due process and subsequent state practice in implementing and interpreting the New York Convention.

When interpreting the meaning of the due process defence, enforcing courts may refer to general principles of law as 'relevant rules of international law', following Article 31(3)(c) of the VCLT. *Audiatur et altera pars* is widely accepted as a general principle of international law, as outlined in Article 38(1)(c) of the Statute of the International Court of Justice (hereinafter 'ICJ Statute').[24] Not only in arbitration but also in other areas of international law, *audiatur et altera pars* converges at a high level of abstraction on the fundamental elements: (a) due notice of arbitrators' appointment and proceedings, (b) equality of arms, (c) the right to be heard, and (d) the impartiality and independence of arbitrators.[25] These fundamental elements of due process are widely recognised in national legal systems and have been transposed into international legal regimes.

The addressee of Article 38 of the ICJ Statute encompasses not only international lawyers but also national ones.[26] The author contends that the due process defence within the New York Convention embodies *audiatur et altera pars* in the realm of international commercial arbitration. Accordingly, in order to concretise the content of the due process defence under the New York Convention, enforcing courts can apply the core elements of *audiatur et altera pars* developed in other international law regimes, in particular international human rights law and international investment arbitration law. Moreover, the search for the general principle of due process in Article V(1)(b), and the comparative law exercise it entails,[27] can legitimise enforcing courts, particularly in states without a strong due process tradition, such as China,[28] in implementing, interpreting, and developing Article V(1)(b) of the New York Convention in a manner consistent with international practice.

The subsequent practice of State Parties in interpreting and applying the due process defence, specifically through domestic judicial decisions among State Parties, can also aid in specifying the meaning and operation of due process in more particular contexts. Accordingly, Chapters 5–7 of this book perform a comparative analysis of domestic judicial decisions among State Parties to pinpoint the similarities and differences in interpreting and applying the due process defence under the New York Convention. The similarities in domestic judicial decisions, such as the policies for the interpretation of the due process defence discussed in Chapter 5, may constitute

24. *See* §3.02 of Chapter 3.
25. For more details, *see* §3.03 of Chapter 3.
26. Ole Spiermann, 'The History of Article 38 of the Statute of the International Court of Justice: "A Purely Platonic Discussion"?' in Samantha Besson and Jean d'Aspremont (eds), *The Oxford Handbook of the Sources of International Law* (Oxford University Press, 2017) 167.
27. *See* §1.04[A] of Chapter 1.
28. *See* §2.02[A] of Chapter 2.

subsequent practice establishing agreements within the meaning of Article 31(3)(b) of the VCLT and thus should be considered by enforcing courts. With regard to discrepancies, the author argues that enforcing courts should use normative criteria, such as predictability, compatibility with the parties' legal expectations, and balance with efficiency, to determine which approaches to these issues are more appropriate. These normative criteria are relevant to the interpretation under the VCLT framework both because they are elements of the 'object and purpose' of the New York Convention and, more specifically, because the decisions of courts in different jurisdictions clarifying these criteria and the way in which they relate to one another may constitute the subsequent practice of State Parties within the meaning of Article 32 of the VCLT, and thus have the persuasive authority for enforcing courts.

The notion of general principles of law and subsequent practice of State Parties requires comparative analysis. Accordingly, the quest for the general principle of due process and subsequent practice regarding Article V(1)(b) contributes to comparative law through cross-regime comparisons between international commercial arbitration and other international legal regimes, cross-national comparisons of arbitration laws regarding due process, and comparative case studies of domestic judicial applications of Article V(1)(b) by State Parties. Section 1.04 below explains the comparative methods used in this book.

§1.03 GENERAL PRINCIPLES OF LAW AND SUBSEQUENT PRACTICE AMONG STATE PARTIES AS GATEWAYS FOR INTERPRETING TRANSNATIONAL MATERIALS

The international nature of the obligations under the New York Convention calls for international rather than domestic rules of interpretation.[29] Nevertheless, neither the methods of interpretation under Article 31(1) nor the *travaux préparatoires* under Article 32 of the VCLT shed any decisive light on the meaning of the due process defence under the New York Convention.[30] General principles of law, as an important source of international law, may serve as one of the bases for the interpretation and application of Article V(1)(b) of the New York Convention through Article 31(3)(c) of the VCLT ('any relevant rules of international law applicable in the relations between the parties').[31] Chapter 2 establishes an explicit connection between 'general principles of law' as defined in Article 38(1)(c) of the ICJ Statute and the customary law of treaty interpretation reflected in Article 31(3)(c) of the VCLT.[32] It is well established that the 'relevant rules of international law' in Article 31(3)(c) of the VCLT can be construed as referring to the sources of public international law contained in Article 38 of the ICJ

29. *See* §2.05[B][1] of Chapter 2.
30. *See* §2.06[A] and §2.06[C][1] of Chapter 2.
31. While the inclusion of Article V(1)(b) in the New York Convention constitutes the formal source of the international obligation in question, general principles of law can be used to interpret the vague treaty standards of 'proper notice' and 'unable to present his case' within Article V(1)(b).
32. *See* §2.06[B][2] of Chapter 2.

Statute.[33] These general principles of international law are integral to the body of international law[34] and may serve as 'relevant rules' for interpreting the New York Convention and are applicable in the relations between the parties to that Convention.

The general principle of *audiatur et altera pars*, which serves as a synonym for 'due process' in this book, can concretise the normative content of Article V(1)(b) of the New York Convention in terms of its core elements. As detailed in Chapter 3, §3.02, *audiatur et altera pars* is a widely recognised general principle of law within the meaning of Article 38(1)(c) of the ICJ Statute. This is due to its recognition in the national laws of the world's principal legal systems and compatibility with fundamental principles of international law.

General principles of law are regarded in Article 38(1)(c) of the ICJ Statute as an important source of international law and the source par excellence of international standards of procedure.[35] The author argues that 'proper notice' and 'being unable to present his case' in Article V(1)(b) of the New York Convention can be seen as a reflection of the general principle of international law, *audiatur et altera pars*, in international commercial arbitration.[36] Accordingly, enforcing courts may utilise the fundamental components of the general principle of *audiatur et altera pars* to concretise the normative substance of Article V(1)(b), with some adaptations to the peculiarities of international commercial arbitration.[37] While these fundamental components of due process are acknowledged in the major national legal systems, international human rights treaties, and international investment arbitration,[38] they can still assist enforcing courts in states that lack a tradition of due process – like China discussed in Chapter 2 – to establish and develop notions of due process that comply with international standards.

The subsequent practice of State Parties – referred to in Articles 31(3)(b) and 32 of the VCLT – may further refine and concretise the application of Article V(1)(b) of the New York Convention in specific factual cases. Regarding grounds for refusing to recognise or enforce foreign arbitral awards, the New York Convention endeavours to provide a uniform interpretation while also granting domestic courts some discretion. The interpretation and application of Article V(1)(b) could be better understood as achieving the universality of the principle of due process at an abstract level in relation to its fundamental elements while preserving differences between states at a more

33. Campbell Mclachlan, 'The Principle of Systemic Integration and Article 31(3)(c) of the Vienna Convention' (2005) 54(2) *International and Comparative Law Quarterly* 279, 290, 293–309 DOI: 10.1093/iclq/lei001.
34. Alain Pellet and Daniel Müller, 'Article 38' in Andreas Zimmermann (ed.), *The Statute of the International Court of Justice: A Commentary* (Oxford University Press, 3rd ed., 2019) 812–832; Malgosia Fitzmaurice, 'The History of Article 38 of the Statute of the International Court of Justice: The Journey from the Past to the Present' in Samantha Besson and Jean d'Aspremont (eds), *The Oxford Handbook of the Sources of International Law* (Oxford University Press, 2017) 182; Wolfgang Friedmann, 'The Uses of "General Principles" in the Development of International Law' (1963) 57(2) *American Journal of International Law* 279, 279 DOI: 10.2307/2195982.
35. *See* §3.02[B] of Chapter 3.
36. *Ibid.*
37. *See* §3.03 of Chapter 3.
38. *See ibid.*

concrete level. Legal interpretation establishes systemic relationships between rules and principles.[39] The above proposition implies that understanding Article V(1)(b) entails an analysis not only of the fundamental elements of the due process principle but also of the way national judges apply the law. Thus, Chapters 5, 6 and 7 use case studies to compare the decisions made by domestic courts in order to identify the differences and similarities between State Parties regarding the application of the due process defence and to assess the different solutions normatively in terms of their predictability, their degree of compatibility with legal expectations, and their degree of balance with efficiency.[40] The cases concern the content, form, address, addressee, language, and timing of due notice;[41] the right to make submissions;[42] the right to comment on the submissions;[43] the right to make the submissions considered;[44] and equality of arms.[45]

Domestic court decisions indicating agreement among all State Parties to the New York Convention as to the interpretation of Article V(1)(b) may constitute subsequent practice under Article 31(3)(b) of the VCLT.[46] As part of the General Rule of Interpretation, such agreements should be considered by enforcing courts.[47] To this end, enforcing courts should search for such agreements by examining and comparing the judicial decisions of other State Parties and assign greater weight to such agreements in similar cases. It may be relevant to use the judicial practice of one or more State Parties in the application of Article V(1)(b) as a complementary means of interpretation in accordance with Article 32 of the VCLT, even if it does not establish the agreement of all parties.[48] When confronted with discrepancies between State Parties, enforcing courts may evaluate the predictability of due process practice, its degree of compatibility with legal expectations, and its equilibrium with efficiency in a particular case.

§1.04 COMPARATIVE LAW METHODS

In order to provide a basis for the following chapters, this section elucidates the methodology implemented in this book. A comparative methodology is employed to ascertain the law applicable to the due process defence,[49] the existence and content of *audiatur et altera pars*,[50] the sources of due process rules,[51] and the application of the

39. Mclachlan (n. 33) 286–287.
40. They are understood as among the Article V's purposes, *see* §2.02[C], §2.02[E], §2.03[C], §2.03[D], and §2.06[A] of Chapter 2; Chapter 8.
41. *See* Chapter 6.
42. *See* §7.02 of Chapter 7.
43. *See* §7.03 of Chapter 7.
44. *See* §7.04 of Chapter 7.
45. *See* §7.05 of Chapter 7.
46. *See* §2.06[B][1] of Chapter 2.
47. *Ibid.*
48. *See* §2.06[C][2] of Chapter 2.
49. *See* Chapter 2.
50. *See* Chapter 3.
51. *See* Chapter 4.

due process defence in more specific scenarios.[52] It utilises insights and methods from comparative law to identify, analyse, and explain the similarities and differences in the interpretation and application of a specific international treaty provision, namely Article V(1)(b) of the New York Convention, by various national and international actors.[53]

In particular, the functional comparative method is employed to explore the fundamental elements of the due process principle as outlined in Article V(1)(b) of the New York Convention. A functional comparison is made not only between national legal systems but also between international commercial arbitration and other international legal regimes. In examining the application of the due process principle in concrete cases, national judicial decisions are compared to identify and analyse similarities and differences in how State Parties interpret and implement Article V(1)(b). A normative preference for a particular approach to due process in a specific scenario is then identified, considering pro-enforcement policy, predictability, the legal expectations of parties, and the balance between efficiency and due process.

[A] The Functional Method of Comparative Law

Scholars of comparative law have suggested that any comparative analysis requires a *tertium comparationis*, which is a common point of departure.[54] Chapter 3 draws broadly on the functional method of comparative law. At least eight different concepts of the functional method of comparative law are summarised by Ralf Michaels.[55] For the purposes of this book, the traditional functional method, based on equivalence functionalism, is adopted. This is a way of understanding differences and similarities in law by focusing not on the labels that the system attributes to legal solutions in its own internal organisation but on the role (function) that different legal doctrines play in responding to the same problems observed in different legal systems.[56] According to

52. *See* Chapters 5–7.
53. Some scholars define the study identifying, analysing, and explaining similarities and differences in how actors in different legal systems understand, interpret, apply, and approach international law as 'comparative international law': *see* Anthea Roberts et al., 'Conceptualizing Comparative International Law' in Anthea Roberts et al. (eds), *Comparative International Law* (Oxford University Press, 2018) 3, 6.
54. John C Reitz, 'How to Do Comparative Law' (1998) 46(4) *American Journal of Comparative Law* 617, 623 DOI: 10.2307/840981.
55. They are finalism, adaptionism, constructivism, classical functionalism, instrumentalism, refined functionalism, epistemological functionalism, and equivalence functionalism: *see* Ralf Michaels, 'The Functional Method of Comparative Law' in Mathias Reimann and Reinhard Zimmermann (eds), *The Oxford Handbook of Comparative Law* (Oxford University Press, 2nd ed., 2019) 346, 349–367.
56. Konrad Zweigert and Hein Kötz, *An Introduction to Comparative Law* (Tony Weir trans, Oxford University Press, 3rd ed., 1998) 39; Michaels (n. 55) 362–365, 372–375; Gerhard Dannemann, 'Comparative Law: Study of Similarities or Differences?' in Mathias Reimann and Reinhard Zimmermann (eds), *The Oxford Handbook of Comparative Law* (Oxford University Press, 2nd ed., 2019) 391, 394–395; Roberts et al. (n. 53) 12. For a summary of criticism of functional method, *see* Mathias Siems, *Comparative Law* (Oxford University Press, 2nd ed., 2018) 39–47.

this approach, a common function is the *tertium comparationis*,[57] which justifies, for example, a comparison between legal systems in different countries that share the function of providing compensation to accident victims (which may be tort law in some jurisdictions and insurance law in others).[58]

In this book, the basis for comparison is articulated in the challenge posed by Article V(1)(b) itself – i.e., determining when a domestic court should refuse enforcement of a foreign award on due process grounds. This is a function which is common to all the domestic legal systems considered in the book. Where the comparisons go beyond the standards of due process that are specifically tied to Article V(1)(b), the *tertium comparationis* is the objective of ensuring minimum standards of procedural fairness to the disputing parties in decentralised, consent-based adjudication systems. The principle of *audiatur et altera pars* in international law, Article V(1)(b) of the Convention, and the specific standards articulated by domestic courts in refusing to enforce awards based on due process violations all share this common function.

[1] The Role of Comparative Methods Within a Framework for Interpretation of Public International Law

Cross-national comparisons are deeply embedded in the very definition of what constitutes a general principle of law. To prove the existence of a general principle of law, an international lawyer must demonstrate its recognition by 'civilised nations', which implies that the principle can be identified in diverse legal families. The functional comparative method offers direction to international lawyers by addressing where to search within national legal systems for a given principle.

The identification of general principles of law may also involve cross-regime comparisons with other international legal regimes, guided by the functional method of comparative law.[59] In the case of the due process principle, this book draws on Article 6 of the European Convention on Human Rights (ECHR) as well as comparable provisions found in other human rights instruments including the Universal Declaration of Human Rights,[60] the International Covenant on Civil and Political Rights (ICCPR),[61] and the EU Charter of Fundamental Rights (EUCFR).[62] These sources are particularly relevant to the extent that they concern due process in civil adjudicative proceedings in a forum where the parties have given prior consent. This is distinct from due process in criminal proceedings or in regulatory action by a public authority.

57. Michaels (n. 55) 351, 372–375.
58. *Ibid.*, 372.
59. Marcelo Vázquez-Bermúdez, Special Rapporteur, *First Report on General Principles of Law*, UN Doc. A/CN.4/741 (5 April 2019) [190]–[230]; Pellet and Müller (n. 34) 924. For more details on the ascertainment of transposition to the international legal system, *see* §3.02[B][2] of Chapter 3.
60. *Universal Declaration of Human Rights*, adopted 10 December 1948, UNGA Res 217 A (III), Art. 10.
61. *International Covenant on Civil and Political Rights*, opened for signature 19 December 1966, 999 UNTS 171 (entered into force 23 March 1976) Art. 14.
62. Charter of Fundamental Rights of the European Union (entered into force 1 December 2009) Art. 47.

Comparative recourse could be made to the Fair and Equitable Treatment (FET) principle in international investment arbitration, particularly with regard to appropriate standards of due process in consent-based civil adjudication, as due process is commonly considered to be one of the elements of the FET principle.[63]

Having identified *audiatur et altera pars* as a general principle of law, Chapter 3 examines the fundamental elements of *audiatur et altera par* through a functional comparative methodology, with a focus on the comparison of national arbitration laws across countries, as well as an analysis of other international legal regimes. Through this approach, the book concretises and clarifies the normative content of Article V(1)(b) by assessing what commonalities exist at the level of national legal systems and other international regimes in the treatment of *audiatur et altera par*. It shows that at least four clusters of normative principles can be identified as fundamental elements of *audiatur et altera par* – due notice, equality of the parties, the right to be heard, and impartiality and independence.[64]

[2] The Selection of Comparative Legal Systems

A key issue in determining whether the principle of due process has been well accepted as a general principle of law is how to decide which legal systems should be included in a comparative study. There may be concerns that the general principle of due process is highly dependent on the subjective assessments of judges or arbitrators and that there is a lack of rigorous conditions for the development and application of the principle. As Sornarajah has observed, there exists a tendency to select a proposition from a handful of national systems and assert that it represents a general principle by continuously repeating it.[65]

Article 38(1)(c) of the ICJ Statute refers to 'the general principles of law recognised by civilized nations'. The term 'civilized nations' should not be interpreted as a cultural determination.[66] At least since the UN Charter came into force in 1945, it has become clear that all nations are equal sovereigns and must be considered to be 'civilized'.[67] Marcelo Vázquez-Bermúdez, the Special Rapporteur of the International Law Commission (ILC), suggested that 'community of nations' is the most appropriate

63. Fulvio Maria Palombino, *Fair and Equitable Treatment and the Fabric of General Principles* (TMC Asser, 2018) 60; 2012 US Model BIT, Art. 5(2)(a); *Fraport AG Frankfurt Airport Servs Worldwide v. Republic of the Philippines (Annulment)* (ICSID Arbitral Tribunal, Case No. ARB/03/25, 23 December 2010) [197]–[247].
64. *See* §3.03 of Chapter 3.
65. M Sornarajah, *The International Law on Foreign Investment* (Cambridge University Press, 3rd ed., 2010) 418.
66. Fitzmaurice (n. 34) 193.
67. Marcelo Vázquez-Bermúdez, Special Rapporteur, *Second Report on General Principles of Law*, UN Doc. A/CN.4/741 (9 April 2020) [2]; Pellet and Müller (n. 34) 927; Giacinto della Cananea, *Due Process of Law Beyond the State: Requirements of Administrative Procedure* (Oxford University Press, 2016) 188; Géza Herczegh, *General Principles of Law and the International Legal Order* (International Publications Service, 1969) 731.

term.[68] This term is also used in Article 15(2) of the ICCPR, which is widely accepted, with 173 signatories.[69]

It is also well accepted that 'recognition' is the crucial prerequisite for establishing a general principle of law.[70] Determining the 'recognition of a principle by civilized nations' does not necessitate a quantitative study of all national legal systems throughout the world. Instead, it requires focusing on the most representative legal systems.[71] For example, specialists in European Court law observe that the Court of Justice of the European Union (CJEU) typically does not require the presence of a principle in all Member States' legal systems when formulating general principles of law.[72] Instead, it has been confirmed by states and other international courts and tribunals that a principle, as defined in Article 38(1)(c) of the ICJ Statute, must be present in the 'principal' or 'major' legal systems, or in 'many' or the 'majority' of legal systems.[73]

The author argues that the comparative cross-national research should be representative and wide, covering diverse legal families and regions of the world, reflecting what may be called the 'principal legal systems of the world'[74] or the 'main legal systems of the world'.[75] The classification of legal families in comparative law can facilitate the identification of a common principle across different legal families. Although not absolute, the national legal systems within a legal family typically adhere to a shared set of rules and principles. Pellet and Müller argued that 'all modern domestic laws can be gathered into a few families or systems of law which, insofar as general principles are concerned, are coherent enough to be considered as "legal systems"'.[76] The classification of the national legal systems around the world into a handful of legal families based on the underlying common features of their laws has traditionally been the primary method used in comparative law.[77]

68. Vázquez-Bermúdez (n. 67) [2]. *See also* Stephan W Schill, 'General Principles of Law and International Investment Law' in Tarcisio Gazzini and Eric De Brabandere (eds), *International Investment Law: The Sources of Rights and Obligations* (Brill, 2012) 147; Antonio Cassese, *International Law* (Oxford University Press, 2nd ed., 2005) 188.
69. *International Covenant on Civil and Political Rights*, opened for signature 19 December 1966, 999 UNTS 171 (entered into force 23 March 1976) Art. 15(2).
70. Vázquez-Bermúdez (n. 67) [2]; Vladimir-Djuro Degan, 'General Principles of Law' (1992) 3 *Finnish Yearbook of International Law* 1, 46; Friedmann (n. 34) 280–281.
71. Vázquez-Bermúdez (n. 67) [28]; Patrick Dumberry, *A Guide to General Principles of Law in International Investment Arbitration* (Oxford University Press, 2020) 11.
72. Koen Lenaerts and Kathleen Gutman, 'The Comparative Law Method and the Court of Justice of the EU Courts and Comparative Law' in Mads Andenas and Duncan Fairgrieve (eds), *Courts and Comparative Law* (Oxford University Press, 2008) 158.
73. Vázquez-Bermúdez (n. 67) [27]; Friedmann (n. 34) 284–285.
74. Vázquez-Bermúdez (n. 67) [54]; Pellet and Müller (n. 34) 930–931.
75. Jaye Ellis, 'General Principles and Comparative Law' (2011) 22 *European Journal of International Law* 949, 954 DOI: 10.1093/ejil/chr072; Friedmann (n. 34) 284–285.
76. Pellet and Müller (n. 34) 928. *See also* Daniel Costelloe, 'The Role of Domestic Law in the Identification of General Principles of Law under Article 38(1)(c) of the Statute of the International Court of Justice' in Mads Andenas et al. (eds), *General Principles and the Coherence of International Law* (Brill, 2019) 177, 183.
77. Mariana Pargendler, 'The Rise and Decline of Legal Families' (2012) 60(4) *The American Journal of Comparative Law* 1043, 1043 DOI: 10.5131/ajcl.2012.0010; H Patrick Glenn, 'Comparative

Such classifications, however, are dynamic and subject to change. There has been considerable debate about the merging of the civil law and common law.[78] In light of this situation, it has been proposed by some academics that the term 'legal traditions' is more appropriate than 'legal families'. These scholars have identified the principal legal traditions globally as the Chthonic, Talmudic, Civil Law, Common Law, Hindu, Islamic and Asian traditions.[79] For a comparative analysis to identify a general principle of law, it is crucial to include representative common law and civil law legal systems.[80] These two traditions have a significant influence worldwide,[81] and therefore their inclusion is essential. Thus, to establish due process as a general principle of law, this book examines the national arbitration laws and judicial decisions of Germany, France, Italy, the Netherlands, Sweden, Switzerland, the United Kingdom, and the United States due to their influence on the Romanistic-Germanic, Scandinavian, and Anglo-American legal traditions.

However, an excessive dependence on the comparative studies of common and civil law jurisdictions would pose difficulties in determining the general principle of law – due process – as it would be limited to an investigation of national legal systems in Western Europe and North America. To address this issue, and taking into account the author's Asian background, this book will also examine the Asian perspective by drawing comparisons between Mainland China, Hong Kong SAR, Singapore, and Japan.

Furthermore, greater significance will be attributed to jurisdictions with extensive judicial experience arising from a higher volume of cases concerning due process in arbitration. Such jurisdictions are typically those in which arbitrations are commonly seated and where enforcement is often sought. For instance, the Queen Mary survey has identified London, Paris, Singapore, Hong Kong, Geneva, New York, and Stockholm as the most commonly chosen seats for arbitration due to their 'general reputation and recognition' and 'formal legal infrastructure'.[82] Therefore, a comprehensive analysis of the arbitration legislations and judicial decisions concerning due process will be conducted in these jurisdictions.

Legal Families and Comparative Legal Traditions' in Mathias Reimann and Reinhard Zimmermann (eds), *The Oxford Handbook of Comparative Law* (Oxford University Press, 2nd ed., 2019) 425.

78. John Henry Merryman, 'On the Convergence (and Divergence) of the Civil Law and the Common Law' (1981) 17 *Stanford Journal of International Law* 357.
79. H Patrick Glenn, *Legal Traditions of the World: Sustainable Diversity in Law* (Oxford University Press, 2nd ed., 2004) 410.
80. Raimondo suggested using the term 'Romano-Germanic' as 'it pays tribute to the efforts made by the universities of Latin and German countries to develop legal studies after the 12th century', which includes but not limited within 'continental Europe, Latin America, a large part of Africa, the Near East, Japan, Indonesia and China': *see* Fabián O Raimondo, *General Principles of Law in the Decisions of International Criminal Courts and Tribunals* (Martinus Nijhoff, 2008) 50–57.
81. *Ibid.*; Ellis (n. 75) 953–959.
82. School of International Arbitration at Queen Mary University of London and White & Case, '2018 International Arbitration Survey: The Evolution of International Arbitration' (Queen Mary University of London and White & Case, 2018) 9.

[B] Comparison of the Interpretation and Application of Article V(1)(b) by State Parties: Subsequent Practice in the Law Applicable to the Due Process Defence and Specific Standards

Comparison traditionally requires an invariant element: one compares with regard to something - *tertium comparationis.*[83] For this book, the benchmark for comparison will be an international legal rule itself - specifically Article V(1)(b) - as it is common to the legal systems. Domestic cases involving Article V(1)(b) have been selected for comparison in this book, as they can be considered 'subsequent state practice', providing another potential source of evidence for the interpretation of due process applied by State Parties, thus elucidating Article V(1)(b) in instances of ambiguity.[84] It is imperative to carefully analyse the reasoning of courts in other jurisdictions that have dealt with the due process defence. Considerable weight should be afforded to an interpretation that has gained general acceptance in other jurisdictions, while a nuanced approach is necessary when conflicting decisions or ambiguity arise.

Accordingly, this book compares decisions made by national courts in different State Parties, aiming to identify, analyse, and explain similarities and deviations in the interpretation and application of Article V(1)(b) of the New York Convention. Such similarities and differences primarily pertain to two areas: the law applicable to Article V(1)(b) and specific standards in particular cases.[85] Comparative case studies concerning the applicable law and specific standards entail two key stages: first, the description of similarities and differences in judicial decisions regarding both applicable law and specific standards; second, the analysis and explanation of such similarities and differences through normative analysis under certain values.

Chapters 2, 5, 6, and 7 shift attention from the comparative functions of laws to provide parties with fundamental procedural fairness to the distinct approaches taken in achieving this goal, including the applicable law and specific standards in concrete cases, which at times necessitates normative evaluation. The functional approach to comparative law illustrates that different legal systems may employ alternative means to address the same issues while their solutions remain functionally equivalent. However, the functional method provides neither the criteria for evaluation nor the yardstick for determining the 'better law' since functionally equivalent institutions are,

83. Michaels (n. 55) 372; Reitz (n. 54) 623.

84. *Vienna Convention on the Law of Treaties*, opened for signature 23 May 1969, 1155 UNTS 331 (entered into force 27 January 1980) Arts 31(3)(b) and 32; International Law Commission, 'Draft Conclusion on Subsequent Agreements and Subsequent Practice in Relation to the Interpretation of Treaties' (2018) 2 *Yearbook of the International Law Commission*, Part Two, Conclusion 5(1) (subsequent practice under Article 31(3)(b) 'may consist of any conduct of a party in the application of a treaty, whether in the exercise of its executive, legislative, judicial or other functions'). For more details, *see* §2.06[B][1] and §2.06[C][2] of Chapter 2.

85. Regarding different approaches to the law applicable to the due process defence by State Parties, *see* Chapter 2. For similarities and differences in concrete standards in representative scenarios under the categories of proper notice, right to be heard and equality between parties, *see* Chapters 5–7.

by definition, of equal value with respect to that function.[86] This inability to select the 'better law' may pose a challenge in situations where there is no unanimity of judicial decisions on the law applicable to Article V(1)(b), and there are no specific standards for concrete cases between legal systems. Fortunately, the interpretative framework set out in the VCLT provides guidance by situating recourse to subsequent practice within a wider framework for interpreting treaty texts, considering 'their context and in light of [the treaty's] object and purpose'.[87] In the case of the New York Convention, achieving predictability, compatibility with the legal expectations of parties and tribunals, and a balance between due process and efficiency are understood as being some of the purposes of Article V.[88] Chapter 2 evaluates different approaches to the law applicable to the due process defence with regard to these purposes. Chapters 5, 6 and 7 examine due process standards in particular cases and incorporate them into a broader interpretive exercise. This exercise evaluates the significance of judicial practices that align with parties' legal expectations or achieve a desirable balance between due process and efficiency.

In comparative research, it is imperative to approach and interpret legal sources in the same manner as the practitioners of the chosen system to ensure that they carry the same content and meaning as those understood in that system.[89] Civil law jurisdictions rely on legislation as source of laws, whereas statutes and case law are the sources of law in common law systems. Domestic arbitration statutes that implement the New York Convention may also form part of the 'subsequent practice' of State Parties for the due process defence.[90] Chapters 2, 5, 6 and 7 specifically focus on domestic court practice since domestic statutes with respect to the due process defence typically follow the phrasing of the New York Convention and lack detailed guidance. However, judicial decisions may clarify the meaning and application of the due process defence in specific cases. Moreover, there is an increasing availability of foreign court decisions. The *Yearbook Commercial Arbitration* from International Council for Commercial Arbitration (ICCA) that provides translations of important judgments on Article V(1)(b),[91] official or unofficial reporting series of original cases,[92] and New York

86. For a summary of the limits of functional method on evaluation, *see* Michaels (n. 55) 379–381. For the opposite views, *see* Mathias Siems, 'Bringing in Foreign Ideas: The Quest for "Better Law" in Implicit Comparative Law' (2014) 9 *Journal of Comparative Law* 119, 119–136 DOI: 10.2139/ssrn.2586732.
87. *Vienna Convention on the Law of Treaties*, opened for signature 23 May 1969, 1155 UNTS 331 (entered into force 27 January 1980) Art. 31(1).
88. *See* §2.02[C], §2.02[E], and §2.06[A]; Chapter 8.
89. Stefan Vogenauer, 'Sources of Law and Legal Method in Comparative Law' in Mathias Reimann and Reinhard Zimmermann (eds), *The Oxford Handbook of Comparative Law* (Oxford University Press, 2nd ed., 2019) 879.
90. International Law Commission (n. 84) Conclusion 5(1).
91. A Consolidated Index of Cases applying the New York Convention reported in the Yearbook since 1976 is available online on the ICCA website at www.arbitration-icca.org. An annotated List of Topics, which follows the Index of Cases, is available at www.newyorkconvention.org.
92. All official or unofficial reporting series of original cases in this book are sourced from common law jurisdictions and China.

Convention case databases[93] have been growing in both quantity and quality. Such a development allows for the identification of instances where domestic judges can utilise foreign law as a persuasive source.[94] Given the author's proficiency in both English and Mandarin and the significance of these languages in the development of international commercial arbitration, this book focuses on jurisdictions using either English or Mandarin when examining national court decisions on the interpretation of Article V(1)(b).

§1.05 CHAPTER STRUCTURE AND OUTLINE

The book contains eight chapters. This chapter provides a brief overview of the different approaches employed by State Parties in relation to the applicable law for Article V(1)(b) of the New York Convention, along with their limitations. The chapter elucidates the theoretical framework upon which the book is based, the merits of the transnational due process based on this theoretical framework, and the methodology adopted in this book.

Chapter 2 builds on existing research on international arbitration, exploring the *lex arbitri*, *lex fori*, and transnational approaches to the applicable law for the due process defence. A particular understanding of the transnational approach is presented based on VCLT's international interpretative rules. The chapter examines the interpretative techniques outlined in Articles 31–32 of the VCLT and their potential relevance to the interpretation of due process within the New York Convention. It concludes that 'relevant rules of international law', with particular reference to 'general principles of law' and 'subsequent practice', could offer insight into the meaning of Article V(1)(b).

Chapter 3 shows that *audiatur et altera pars* is a well-accepted general principle of law and argues that Article V(1)(b) of the New York Convention is an expression of this general principle of law in the field of international commercial arbitration. On this basis, it maintains that the general principle of *audiatur et altera pars* is applicable to the interpretation of Article V(1)(b). The chapter examines fundamental components of *audiatur et altera pars* – due notice, equality of arms, the right to be heard, and the impartiality and independence of arbitrators – that have been developed in international arbitration and other international regimes, which concretise the normative content of the due process defence under the New York Convention.

Chapter 4 analyses the structure of international arbitration procedure, identifying the diverse sources of law pertinent to the due process defence in the New York Convention. Chapter 5 explores the common policies that State Parties follow while interpreting the due process defence, including pro-enforcement policy, no review of the merits, judicial deference to the procedural discretion of arbitrators and institutional arbitration rules, and due regard to the international nature of international arbitration. Chapters 4 and 5 show the importance of these sources and policies as

93. *See, e.g.*, case databases at http://newyorkconvention1958.org/?opac_view=-1, http://www.newyorkconvention.org/.
94. H Patrick Glenn, 'Persuasive Authority' (1987) 32(2) *McGill Law Journal* 261.

forms of 'subsequent practice' in interpreting the due process defence within the interpretative framework established by international law. Chapter 5 also considers several factors that could restrict the application of Article V(1)(b) of the New York Convention. The above encompasses the threshold requirements for the due process defence, party waiver, and the deference granted by enforcing courts during the recognition and enforcement stage to the discretion of arbitral tribunals and the decisions of courts at the seat of the arbitration.

Chapters 6 and 7 develop the ideas presented in Chapters 4 and 5, taking into account analytical insights from Chapters 2 and 3. The aim is to examine how courts apply the legal sources of transnational due process and jurisprudential principles in concrete cases. Chapters 6 and 7 compare the case law on 'proper notice', 'the opportunity to present its case', and 'equal treatment' among the representative State Parties. The focus is on identifying commonly adopted interpretations and critiquing disparities based on their policy implications, including predictability, compatibility with legal expectations, and balance with efficiency. These two chapters analyse the tension between universality and diversity and address the question of how transnational due process can guarantee legal certainty for universal standards while maintaining a level of flexibility and national diversity in specific instances.

The book concludes with Chapter 8. In this concluding chapter, the author briefly summarises her argument that the content of the due process defence under the New York Convention can be concretised by the general principle of law and subsequent practice of State Parties through the application of the VCLT. On this basis, due process under the New York Convention should be understood as a form of transnational due process detached from domestic concepts in a particular national legal system. This understanding of transnational due process, which is grounded in the interpretative framework mandated by international law, can contribute to the uniform interpretation and application of Article V(1)(b) and protect the interests of the relevant stakeholders: parties, arbitrators, the seat of the arbitration, and the enforcing forum.

CHAPTER 2

The Law Applicable to the Due Process Defence

§2.01 INTRODUCTION

When enforcing courts are confronted with opposition to the recognition or enforcement of foreign arbitral awards based on the due process defence under Article V(1)(b) of the New York Convention, judges must first clarify the law governing the due process defence. However, the plain text of Article V(1)(b) and the *travaux préparatoires* of the New York Convention do not specify the applicable law.[1] This ambiguity as to the law applicable to the due process defence leads to divergent interpretations by State Parties, which undermines legal certainty and the main objectives of the New York Convention, which are harmonisation and unification.

National courts and scholars have adopted three different approaches to the law applicable to the due process defence: (a) the *lex arbitri* – the law of the arbitral seat;[2] (b) the *lex fori* – the law of the forum where the recognition or enforcement of the award is sought;[3] or (c) a uniform transnational standard derived from an autonomous interpretation of Article V(1)(b).).[4] One of the purposes of this chapter is to explore

1. United Nations Economic and Social Council, *Recognition and Enforcement of Foreign Arbitral Awards: Report by the Secretary-General*, 21st sess., Agenda Item 8, UN Doc. E/2822 (31 January 1956) annex I, 20–26.
2. The law of the place or seat of the arbitration is referred to as the '*lex arbitri*': *see* Nigel Blackaby et al., *Redfern and Hunter on International Arbitration* (Oxford University Press, 6th ed., 2015) 166. In addition to the seat's arbitration legislation, other laws of the seat may also be relevant, such as laws concerning public policy: *see* §2.02[B].
3. In addition to the forum's arbitration legislation, other laws of the forum may also be relevant, such as laws concerning public policy: *see* §2.03.
4. For proponents of this approach, *see* Maxi Scherer, 'New York Convention: Violation of Due Process, Article V(1)(b)' in Reinmar Wolff (ed.), *New York Convention: Convention on the Recognition and Enforcement of Foreign Arbitral Awards of 10 June 1958: Commentary* (C.H. Beck • Hart • Nomos, 2012) 279, 285; Gary B Born, *International Commercial Arbitration* (Kluwer Law International, 2nd ed., 2014) 3505–3506.

which approach is more appropriate in terms of the interpretative rules on treaties. Specifically, it examines the way in which each approach is implemented by representative jurisdictions and analyses the underlying policies that appear to have influenced each approach.

This chapter shows that jurisdictions that adopt the *lex arbitri* or *lex fori* approach apply, in essence, the enforcing forum's domestic interpretative rules to interpret the due process defence prescribed in a treaty. Under the domestic rules of interpretation, enforcing courts tend to rely on the choice-of-law method to find an appropriate domestic law (the *lex arbitri*, or their own national notions of due process – the *lex fori*) to interpret Article V(1)(b). As shown in Chapters 6 and 7, national courts applying these two approaches have reached different conclusions with respect to questions arising under Article V(1)(b).

In contrast to domestic interpretation, the uniform transnational approach adopted in this book argues that Article V(1)(b) is a truly transnational rule and should be interpreted according to the uniform standard derived directly from an autonomous interpretation of the New York Convention. Unlike the other two approaches, the uniform transnational approach is mainly supported by academics, with few jurisdictions expressly adopting it. Nevertheless, case law in selected jurisdictions, such as France, Sweden, and the United Kingdom, shows that courts sometimes apply the due process defence with reference to other sources beyond their own domestic law, such as international human rights treaties, UNCITRAL instruments (the UNCITRAL Model Law and the UNCITRAL Rules), decisions on Article V(1)(b) by foreign courts, and commentaries by foreign jurists, in order to identify the well-accepted criteria of due process standards common to most State Parties.[5]

However, scholars advocating the uniform transnational approach do not identify the sources of this uniform transnational due process. This chapter argues that a uniform transnational approach to the due process defence can be achieved through the international rules of treaty interpretation contained primarily in the VCLT. This chapter argues that enforcing courts should apply the international rules of interpretation grounded in the VCLT to the due process defence, thereby ensuring that due process under the New York Convention is a truly transnational standard independent of any particular national legal system.

Accordingly, this chapter is structured as follows. Section 2.02 examines the *lex arbitri* approach, identifying those jurisdictions that appear to have adopted this approach and explaining why they have done so. Section 2.03 assesses the *lex fori* approach. Section 2.04 analyses the uniform transnational approach. Section 2.05 argues that the uniform transnational approach can be placed on a sturdier theoretical footing by grounding it in the framework of treaty interpretation under international law. Section 2.06 then specifies the range of techniques and sources relevant to the interpretation of Article V(1)(b) under this framework. Section 2.07 concludes the chapter.

---

5. *See* §2.06[E].

§2.02 THE LAW OF THE ARBITRAL SEAT: *LEX ARBITRI*

A few State Parties consider that the applicable law for determining whether there has been a breach of due process should be the law of the arbitral seat. They argue that the law of the seat is the law most closely connected with the arbitral proceedings in terms of choice-of-law rules; it is therefore the applicable law for notice and due process under the New York Convention. The *lex arbitri* approach is also supported by the 'territorial view' that the legal force of an award is derived from the law of the seat and that the courts of that country have a supervisory function over the arbitral proceedings and primary jurisdiction over the validity of the award. The *lex arbitri* approach recognises the supportive role of the law of the arbitral seat in arbitral proceedings, the predictability and certainty of the law for parties and arbitrators, and the interest of the seat in ensuring that its mandatory rules are observed by the parties and arbitrators. However, as shown in §2.03, some enforcing states are unwilling to allow their legal machinery to be used to enforce awards made in arbitrations that did not meet that enforcing state's own minimum due process requirements in international commercial arbitration.

[A] Jurisdictions Adopting the Law of the Arbitral Seat

China is one of the few jurisdictions in the world to adopt the *lex arbitri* approach to determining the due process defence under the New York Convention. In their decisions handed down over the past twenty years, Chinese courts have consistently stated that they apply due process standards under the law of the seat of arbitration. With respect to 'proper notice', the Supreme People's Court (SPC) and local courts have confirmed that reference should be made to the parties' agreement, or to the arbitration rules chosen by the parties,[6] or, in the absence of any indication, to the law of the country in which the award was made, which is analogous to the applicable law prescribed in Article V(1)(d) of the New York Convention.[7] In Chinese courts, there is little controversy as to the applicable law for the due process defence owing to China's unique 'prior-reporting mechanism'. Essentially, this mechanism requires the higher level courts to review the decisions of lower courts on foreign arbitral awards before a negative decision can be made by a lower court in order to ensure uniform application and interpretation of the law and to prevent local protectionism.[8] This mechanism was introduced by the SPC in 1995 in response to widely criticised decisions refusing

6. *See* below nn. 11, 13.
7. *See* below n. 14.
8. Zheng Sophia Tang, 'Chapter 5: Country Report: China' in Friedrich Rosenfeld, Dietmar Czernich and Franco Ferrari (eds), *Due Process as a Limit to Discretion in International Commercial Arbitration* (Kluwer Law International, 2020) 115, 117; Jingzhou Tao and Mariana Zhong, 'Resolving Disputes in China: New and Sometimes Unpredictable Developments' in Peter Quayle and Xuan Gao (eds), *International Organizations and the Promotion of Effective Dispute Resolution* (Brill & Nijhoff, 2019) vol 2, 62; José Alejandro Carballo Leyda, 'A Uniform, Internationally Oriented Legal Framework for the Recognition and Enforcement of Foreign Arbitral Awards in Mainland China, Hong Kong and Taiwan?' (2007) 6(2) *Chinese Journal of International Law* 345,

recognition or enforcement of foreign arbitral awards based on public policy.[9] These responses by the SPC to lower courts constitute judicial interpretation and are a de facto source of law in China.[10]

As discussed below, Chinese practice illustrates the impact of national interpretative rules on domestic courts that have no concept or tradition of due process in arbitration. Chinese courts have consistently held that the content and manner of notice should be determined by the parties' agreement or the applicable arbitration rules and that the requirements of judicial service are irrelevant and inapplicable to the due process defence under the New York Convention. One of the landmark decisions is *Angfohuapin v. Henan Harvest*, which concerned the enforcement of a default award made by the Belarusian Chamber of Commerce and Industry (BelCCI).[11] In this case, the Intermediate People's Court of Zhengzhou held that the service of arbitration documents should be in accordance with the parties' agreement or the arbitration rules chosen by the parties. As the notice was served in accordance with Article 20 of the BelCCI Arbitration Rules, the court concluded that the award met the requirements of Article V(1)(b) and should therefore be enforced.[12] This doctrine has been confirmed by Chinese courts in subsequent cases.[13] The court also clarified that the Hague Service Convention and the Bilateral Treaty on Civil and Criminal Matters between China and Belarus were irrelevant to the standards of due notice in arbitration.

In the absence of a reference to the parties' agreement or the applicable arbitration rules, Chinese courts have consistently relied on the law of the seat of the arbitration to determine 'proper notice' under Article V(1)(b).[14] The SPC judges, who

---

352 DOI: 10.1093/chinesejil/jmm021; Randall Peerenboom, 'The Evolving Regulatory Framework For Enforcement of Arbitral Awards in the People's Republic of China' (2011) 1(2) *Asian-Pacific Law and Policy Journal* 1, 1.

9. 《最高人民法院关于人民法院处理与涉外仲裁及外国仲裁事项有关问题的通知》 [Notice on the Issues Concerning Foreign-Related or Foreign Arbitration] Supreme People's Court, Fa Fa [1995] No. 18, promulgated on 28 August 1995 and amended on 16 December 2008 (Fa Shi [2008] No. 18); Lei Zhu and Yongping Xiao, 'Article V(1)(b) of the New York Convention in China: Applying the Due Process Defense Without the Doctrine of Due Process' (2019) 49 *Hong Kong Law Journal* 57, 62.
10. Zhu and Xiao (n. 9) 63.
11. 《昂佛化品合资有限责任公司申请承认白俄罗斯工商会国际仲裁院仲裁裁决民事裁定书》 [*Angfohuapin Co Ltd v. Henan Harvest Chemical Co – Enforcement of A Foreign Arbitral Award*], 郑州市中级人民法院 [Intermediate People's Court of Zhengzhou] (2013) 郑民三初字第37号 [Zheng Min San Chu Zi No. 37], 26 June 2013, English translation available at http://cicc.court.gov.cn/html/1/219/199/204/665.html.
12. *Ibid.*
13. 《来宝资源有限公司申请承认执行外国仲裁裁决民事裁定书》 [*Noble Resources Pte Ltd v. Xiongsheng Co Ltd – Enforcement of A Foreign Arbitral Award by International Cotton Association*], 绍兴市中级人民法院 [Intermediate People's Court of Shaoxing] (2014) 浙绍仲确字第1号 [Zhe Shao Zhong Que Zi No. 1], 12 June 2016 (holding that notice should accord to the Rules of International Cotton Association chosen by parties); 《嘉能可国际股份有限公司申请承认和执行外国仲裁裁决民事裁定书》 [*Glencore International AG v. Qiying Energy Chemical Engineering Co Ltd – Enforcement of A Foreign Arbitral Award by London Court of International Arbitration*], 宁波市中级人民法院 [Intermediate People's Court of Ningbo] (2014) 浙甬仲确字第1号 [Zhe Yong Zhong Que Zi No. 1], 24 June 2016 (holding that 'proper notice' should be determined by parties' agreement and LCIA Arbitration Rules).
14. 《最高人民法院关于是否裁定不予承认和执行英国伦敦 "ABRA轮2004年12月28日租约" 仲裁裁决的请示的复函》 [*Cosmos Marine v. Kaiqiang Commercial Co Ltd – the Reply of SPC on the*

are responsible for responding to lower courts when they refuse to recognise or enforce foreign arbitral awards, reaffirmed this:

> Whether proper notice has been given to the parties should be determined in accordance with the *parties' agreement*, or, in the absence of such an agreement, by reference to the *arbitration rules* agreed by the parties. In the absence of any indication, *the law of the seat of the arbitration* should be applied.[15]

Partly because of the lack of a tradition of due process in China[16] and partly because Chinese courts consider that the notice, as part of the arbitral process, should be governed by the law applicable to arbitral proceedings, as required by Article V(1)(d) of the New York Convention,[17] Chinese courts rely on the *lex arbitri* to determine whether an award violates the due process defence under the New York Convention. First, there is no principle of due process in the Chinese Constitution, nor does the Constitution expressly refer to the right to a fair hearing.[18] Similarly, the Chinese Arbitration Law only recognises the substantive fairness of arbitral awards as one of the principles of arbitration and makes no express reference to procedural fairness and the principle of due process.[19]

Recognition of a Foreign Award concerning a Charter Party rendered in London], 最高人民法院 [Supreme People's Court] (2006) 民四他字第34号 [Min Si Ta Zi No. 34], 10 January 2006; 《关于辽宁省高级人民法院就不予承认与执行德国汉堡交易所商品协会仲裁法庭2/11号仲裁裁决请示一案的答复》 [Reply of the SPC on the Refusal of Recognition and Enforcement of an Award rendered by Hamburg Exchange Commodity Association] 最高人民法院 [Supreme People's Court] (2014) 民四他字第31号[Min Si Ta Zi No. 31], 30 June 2014; 《德国舒乐达公司与中国丹东君澳食品有限公司申请承认和执行外国仲裁裁决民事裁定书》 [*Schroeder KG GmbH (Germany) v. China Dandong Junao Food Co Ltd – Recognition and Enforcement of an Award rendered by Hamburg Exchange Commodity Association*] 辽宁省丹东市中级人民法院 [Intermediate People's Court of Dandong] (2012) 丹民三特字第00001号[Dan Min San Te Zi No. 00001], 14 October 2014, English translation of the decision issued by Intermediate People's Court of Dandong available at http://cicc.court.gov.cn/html/1/219/199/204/714.html; 《Ecom公司与国泰华投资有限公司关于承认和执行外国仲裁裁决民事裁定书》 [*Ecom Agroindustrial Co Ltd v. Guotaihua Investment Co Ltd – Recognition and Enforcement of a Foreign Award by International Cotton Association*], 深圳市中级人民法院 [Intermediate People's Court of Shenzhen] (2014) 深中法涉外初字第60号 [Shen Zhong Fa She Wai Chu Zi No. 60], 25 May 2015.

15. 刘贵祥，沈红雨 [Guixiang Liu and Hongyu Shen] 《我国承认和执行外国仲裁裁决的司法实践述评》 [Judicial Practice of the Recognition and Enforcement of Foreign Arbitral Awards in China] (2002) 79(1) 《北京仲裁》 *Beijing Arbitration* 1, 16–17 (emphasis added). *See also* another article by the Judge of the SPC, 高晓力[Gao Xiaoli] 《中国法院承认和执行外国仲裁裁决的积极实践》 [Positive Practice of Chinese Courts in Recognizing and Enforcing Foreign Arbitral Awards] (2018) 5 《法律适用》 *Journal of Law Application* 2, 6.
16. Zhu and Xiao (n. 9); Weixia Gu, 'When Local Meets International: Mediation Combined with Arbitration in China and Its Prospective Reform in a Comparative Context' (2015) 10(2) *Journal of Comparative Law* 84, 94; Shijian Mo, 'Interpretation and Application of the New York Convention in China' in George A Bermann (ed.), *Recognition and Enforcement of Foreign Arbitral Awards – The Interpretation and Application of the New York Convention by National Courts* (Springer, 2017) 199.
17. Liu and Shen (n. 15) 16–17.
18. 《中华人民共和国宪法》(2018修正) [Constitution of the People's Republic of China] (2018 Amendment) National People's Congress, promulgated and effective on 11 March 2018.
19. 《中华人民共和国仲裁法》 [Arbitration Law of the People's Republic of China] Standing Committee of the National People's Congress, Order of the President of the People's Republic of China [2017] No. 76, promulgated on 1 September 2017, effective on 1 January 2018, Arts 1, 7 (Article 7 of Chinese Arbitration Law stresses the substantive aspect of 'fairness' and explicitly

Moreover, the SPC's jurisprudence on the due process defence under the New York Convention is consistent with its approach to setting aside arbitral awards seated in Mainland China ('domestic awards'). The due process defence is not a separate ground for setting aside domestic awards under the Chinese Arbitration Law and the Chinese Civil Procedure Law.[20] Rather, for domestic awards, procedural irregularities are considered to fall within the scope of 'arbitral proceedings not in accordance with the agreed procedural rules or the *lex arbitri*', which is similar in wording to Article V(1)(d) of the New York Convention.[21] It is therefore perhaps not surprising that the SPC has not distinguished between Article V(1)(b) and Article V(1)(d) in its jurisprudence.[22] China's approach shows that 'judges, when confronted with treaties, were at least as strongly influenced by [domestic] rules with which they were much more familiar, and accordingly formulated maxim on the basis of their own domestic principles which they believed to be of universal application'.[23]

Very few academics support the *lex arbitri* approach based on the following arguments.[24] Marike Paulsson argued that enforcing courts should apply the notion of due process of the country of the seat of the arbitration since the application of the *lex fori* is expressly dealt with in a separate article – Article V(2)(b) of the New York Convention.[25] Osamu Inoue suggested that the role of the *lex arbitri* should be taken into account in the interpretation and application of Article V(1)(b). Inoue suggested a two-step process. First, enforcing courts should determine whether the requirements of due process under the law chosen by the parties and, in the absence of a choice, the law of the seat of the arbitration have been satisfied. If these requirements have been met, the next step is to examine the requirements under the 'minimal fairness standard' of the country in which the recognition or enforcement is sought.[26]

explains that 'disputes shall be fairly and reasonably settled by arbitration based on facts and law').

20. 《中华人民共和国民事诉讼法》 [Civil Procedure Law of the People's Republic of China] Standing Committee of the National People's Congress, Order of the President of the People's Republic of China No. 71, promulgated on 24 December 2021, effective on 1 January 2022, Art. 244; 《中华人民共和国仲裁法》 [Arbitration Law of the People's Republic of China] Standing Committee of the National People's Congress, Order of the President of the People's Republic of China [2017] No. 76, promulgated on 1 September 2017, effective on 1 January 2018, Art. 58.
21. *Ibid.* According to 'Interpretation of the SPC', 'violation of statutory procedures' means a violation of arbitration procedures as stipulated in the Arbitration Law or arbitration rules chosen by parties, which may influence the result of an award: *see* 《最高人民法院关于适用<中华人民共和国仲裁法>若干问题的解释》 [Interpretation of the Supreme People's Court on Certain Issues Concerning the Applicability of the Arbitration Law of PRC] Supreme People's Court, Fa Shi [2006] No. 7, promulgated on 16 December 2008 and effective on 31 December 2008, Art. 20.
22. Zhu and Xiao (n. 9) 67.
23. Christoph Schreuer, 'The Interpretation of Treaties by Domestic Courts' (1971) 45 *British Yearbook of International Law* 255, 299.
24. Marike R P Paulsson, *The 1958 New York Convention in Action* (Kluwer Law International, 2016) 182–183; Osamu Inoue, 'The Due Process Defense to Recognition and Enforcement of Foreign Arbitral Awards in United States Federal Courts: A Proposal for a Standard' (2000) 11 *The American Review of International Arbitration* 247, 270–274.
25. Paulsson (n. 24) 183.
26. Inoue (n. 24) 270–275. For the meaning of 'minimal fairness standard' and the way to use it, *see* §2.03[A].

[B] The Application of the Law of the Seat and Choice-of-Law Rules

As explained above, the reason why Chinese courts apply the *lex arbitri* to the due process defence under the New York Convention is that they consider proper notice to be notice that complies with the law governing the arbitration. The following choice-of-law rules may be used to support this contention.

[1] The Content of the Lex Arbitri

The *lex arbitri* refers to the law of the country on the territory of which the arbitration takes place.[27] The seat of arbitration is not just a matter of geography. It is the legal seat of the arbitration, which means that the arbitration will be conducted within the legal framework of the law of the seat.[28] Thus, the seat of the arbitration is not necessarily the place of physical hearings, as a tribunal may hold hearings and meetings anywhere it deems appropriate in consultation with the parties.[29]

The *lex arbitri* comprises the rules, including but not limited to those governing arbitrability, the constitution of arbitral tribunals, any grounds for challenging arbitrators, interim measures, default proceedings, judicial assistance where necessary (e.g., filling a vacancy in the constitution of the arbitral tribunal if there is no other mechanism), the supervisory jurisdiction over the arbitration (setting aside an award or removing an arbitrator for misconduct), arbitral hearings and equal treatment between parties.[30] Although the *lex arbitri* is mainly concerned with procedural law and in some jurisdictions (e.g., France and Germany) is part of a civil procedural code, it is much more than a procedural law. It includes the determination of arbitrability and public policy, both of which concern the substantive law.

---

27. Blackaby et al. (n. 2) 166.
28. Born (n. 4) 1530–1531; Gabrielle Kaufmann-Kohler, 'Identifying and Applying the Law Governing the Arbitration Procedure – The Role of the Law of the Place of Arbitration' in Albert Jan van den Berg (ed.), *Improving the Efficiency of Arbitration Agreements and Awards: 40 Years of Application of the New York Convention* (Kluwer Law International, 1999) 336; William W Park, 'The Lex Loci Arbitri and International Commercial Arbitration' (1983) 32(1) *The International and Comparative Law Quarterly* 21 DOI: 10.1093/iclqaj/32.1.21.
29. International Chamber of Commerce, *Arbitration Rules* (adopted 1 January 2021) ('*ICC Arbitration Rules*') Art. 18(2); London Court of International Arbitration, *LCIA Arbitration Rules* (adopted 1 October 2014) ('*LCIA Arbitration Rules*') Art. 16(3); Arbitration Institute of the Stockholm Chamber of Commerce, *SCC Arbitration Rules* (adopted 1 January 2023) ('*SCC Arbitration Rules*') Art. 25(2); Hong Kong International Arbitration Centre, *Administered Arbitration Rules* (adopted 1 November 2018) ('*HKIAC Arbitration Rules*') Art. 14(2); Singapore International Arbitration Centre, *SIAC Arbitration Rules* (adopted 1 August 2016) ('*SIAC Arbitration Rules*') Art. 21(2); United Nations Committee on International Trade Law, *UNCITRAL Arbitration Rules* (2nd ed., 2010), GA Res 65/22, 6th Comm A/65/465, 66th sess., Agenda Item 77, UN Doc. A/RES/65/22 (6 December 2010) ('*UNCITRAL Arbitration Rules*') Art. 18(2); *UNCITRAL Model Law on International Commercial Arbitration*, UN GAOR, 40th sess., Supp No. 17, UN Doc. A/40/17 (adopted 21 June 1985) annex I, as amended by UN GAOR, 61st sess., Supp No. 17, UN Doc. A/61/17 (7 July 2006), annex I ('*UNCITRAL Model Law*') Art. 20(2).
30. Blackaby et al. (n. 2) 168–169.

[2] *Arbitral Proceedings and the* Lex Arbitri

Based on the principle of sovereignty, the seat of the arbitration, where the arbitral proceedings take place, has the authority to regulate the manner in which the arbitral proceedings are to be conducted on its territory. It is generally accepted that the law applicable to the arbitral proceedings is the law of the seat of arbitration,[31] which links the conduct of the arbitral proceedings to the national legal system of the seat of arbitration.

The national arbitration laws at the seat generally ensure that the arbitral procedure provides each party with an equal opportunity to present its case.[32] In other words, issuing proper notice and affording each party an opportunity to present its case as stipulated in Article V(1)(b) of the New York Convention are also required by the law of the arbitral seat.

The New York Convention, by referring to 'the law of the country where the arbitration took place'[33] or, synonymously, 'the law of the country where the award is made', recognises the territorial link between the seat of arbitration and the law governing that arbitration.[34] In particular, Article V(1)(d) provides that recognition or enforcement of an award may be refused on the ground that the arbitral procedure, including the composition of the arbitral tribunal, 'was not in accordance with the agreement of the parties, or, failing such agreement, was not in accordance with the law of the country where the arbitration took place'.[35] This suggests that the sources of the procedural rules of arbitration include the agreement of the parties (including institutional arbitration rules approved by the parties) and the law of the seat of arbitration.[36]

The UNCITRAL Model Law also strengthens the legal link between the seat and the law governing the arbitration in Article 1(2), which provides that '[t]he provisions of this Law, except Articles 8, 9, 35 and 36, apply only if the place of arbitration is in the

31. *Ibid.*, 166–185; Lord Collins of Mapesbury and Jonathan Harris (eds), *Dicey, Morris and Collins on the Conflict of Laws* (Sweet & Maxwell, 15th ed., 2012) 840–849; Jean-François Poudret and Sébastien Besson, *Comparative Law of International Arbitration* (Sweet & Maxwell, 2nd ed., 2007) cha 2; Georgios Petrochilos, *Procedural Law in International Arbitration* (Oxford University Press, 2004) [3.31]–[3.72].
32. *See, e.g.*, *UNCITRAL Model Law*, UN Docs A/40/17 and A/61/17 (n. 29) Art. 18; UK: *Arbitration Act 1996* (UK) c 23, s. 33(1)(a); France: *Code de procédure civile* [Code of Civil Procedure] (France) 13 January 2011, Art. 1510 [Emmanuel Gaillard et al., Code of Civil Procedure, http://parisarbitration.com/wp-content/uploads/2017/02/EN-French-Law-on-Arbitration.pdf]; Sweden: *Swedish Arbitration Act* (Sweden) SFS No. 1996:116, s. 24 [Joel Dahlquist Cullborg trans, *The Swedish Arbitration Act* (2019), https://sccarbitrationinstitute.se/sites/default/files/2022-11/the-swedish-arbitration-act_1march2019_eng-2.pdf]; Switzerland: *Federal Act on Private International Law* (Switzerland) 18 December 1987, Art. 182(3) [Andreas Bucher trans, *The English translations of Federal Act on Private International Law*, http://www.andreasbucher-law.ch/images/stories/pil_act_1987_as_from_1st_july_2022.pdf].
33. *Convention on the Recognition and Enforcement of Foreign Arbitral Awards*, open for signature 10 June 1958, 330 UNTS 3 (entered into force 7 June 1959) Art. V(1)(d).
34. *Ibid.*, Arts V(1)(a), V(1)(e).
35. *Ibid.*, Art. V(1)(d).
36. Blackaby et al. (n. 2) 156; Collins and Harris (n. 31) 841.

territory of this State'.[37] The UNCITRAL Model Law makes the seat of arbitration the primary connecting factor for the application of its provisions, in particular its mandatory arbitration rules, which must be observed in order to obtain a valid award.

The provisions of the *lex arbitri* relating to the content of the notice and the manner of its delivery may be regarded as default rules rather than mandatory rules. This is the case where the parties have not explicitly chosen their own rules of notice, either through specific rules in their agreement or by opting for standard rules of procedure, such as those of the International Chamber of Commerce (ICC) or the UNCITRAL. However, the requirements of the *lex arbitri* relating to the equality of the parties and the right of each party to present its case are generally mandatory. The arbitral award may be set aside by the courts of the seat of the arbitration if the arbitral proceedings violate these mandatory provisions.[38]

[C] The Relationship Between Article V(1)(b), Article V(1)(d) and Article V(1)(e)

Although the link between the arbitral procedure and the law of the arbitral seat is evident in Article V(1)(d) of the New York Convention, its wording indicates that priority is given to party autonomy. Only in the absence of parties' agreement is the law of the seat to be considered. However, the exercise of party autonomy is subject to the mandatory rules governing due process at the arbitral seat; otherwise, the rendered award may be set aside. This is particularly true for jurisdictions under the UNCITRAL Model Law. Article 18 of the UNCITRAL Model Law requires arbitrators to treat all parties equally and to give each party a full opportunity to present its case. This provision is considered as a mandatory rule in the sense that parties may not derogate from it.[39] Article 19 further confirms the mandatory nature of Article 18 by establishing a hierarchy of considerations in which the right to be heard and equal treatment, together with other mandatory rules, are paramount. The autonomy of the parties and the discretion of arbitrators rank second and third, respectively.[40] The drafting history

37. Articles 8 and 9 are concerned with enforcement of arbitral agreements and interim measures, respectively; Articles 35 and 36 are related with recognition and enforcement of the award.
38. *UNCITRAL Model Law*, UN Docs A/40/17 and A/61/17 (n. 29) Art. 34(2)(a)(ii); UK: *Arbitration Act 1996* (UK) c 23, s. 68; Sweden: Swedish Arbitration Act (Sweden) SFS No. 1996:116, s. 34(6) [Joel Dahlquist Cullborg trans, The Swedish Arbitration Act (2019), https://sccarbitrationinstitute.se/sites/default/files/2022-11/the-swedish-arbitration-act_1march2019_eng-2.pdf]; Switzerland: *Federal Act on Private International Law* (Switzerland) 18 December 1987, Art. 190(2)(d) [Andreas Bucher trans, The English translations of Federal Act on Private International Law, http://www.andreasbucher-law.ch/images/stories/pil_act_1987_as_from_1st_july_2022.pdf]; France: Code de procédure civile [Code of Civil Procedure] (France) 13 January 2011, Art. 1492(4) [Emmanuel Gaillard et al., Code of Civil Procedure, http://parisarbitration.com/wp-content/uploads/2017/02/EN-French-Law-on-Arbitration.pdf].
39. Howard M Holtzmann and Joseph E Neuhaus, *A Guide to the 2006 Amendments to the UNCITRAL Model Law on International Commercial Arbitration: Legislative History and Commentary* (Kluwer Law International, 2015) 550; Peter Binder, *International Commercial Arbitration and Mediation in UNCITRAL Model Law Jurisdictions* (Kluwer Law International, 4th ed., 2019) 330.
40. Binder (n. 39) 337.

of Article 18 of the UNCITRAL Model Law confirms that Article 18 applies not only to the arbitrators in their conduct of arbitral proceedings but also to the parties in the design of the arbitral procedure:

> The fundamental precepts of Article 18 were intended to apply both to actions taken by the *arbitral tribunal* and to procedural agreements reached by the *parties*. The drafting history is absolutely clear on this point. In some of the early drafts of what became Article 18, the provision was apparently a limitation only on the discretion of the arbitral tribunal and not on the parties. At its fifth and final session on the Model Law, however, the Working Group directed that the text be amended to emphasize that the principle of equality and the right to present one's case '*should be observed not only by the arbitral tribunal but also by the parties when laying down any rules of procedure*'.[41]

Even in jurisdictions that have not implemented the UNCITRAL Model Law, such as the United Kingdom, parties may be prevented from waiving their right to due process guarantees because such due process rights are mandatory.[42] The New York Convention also tends to protect the interests of the arbitral seat and provides, in Article V(1)(e), that the court where the recognition or enforcement is sought may refuse to recognise or enforce an award that has been set aside by the courts in the seat of the arbitration. Given that the interests of the arbitral seat in seeing its mandatory rules observed and the legal expectations of arbitrators and parties as to the mandatory rules of due process in the seat of the arbitration have been recognised by the New York Convention in Articles V(1)(d) and V(1)(e), these interests and legal certainty may have some weight in the consideration of the standards of due process set out in Article V(1)(b) of the New York Convention.

[D] Seat Theory and Delocalisation

As discussed above, the concept that an arbitration is governed by the law of the place in which it takes place, which is the 'seat' of the arbitration, has been well established in both the theory and practice of international arbitration. As to whether and to what extent the arbitral seat plays a role in international arbitration, the territorial and delocalised theories provide different views. The territorial view argues that the legal force of an award derives from the law of the seat and that the courts of that country have a supervisory function over arbitral proceedings and primary jurisdiction over the validity of the award.[43] In the second half of the 20th century, however, there was considerable debate between the proponents of seat control of arbitration and those who favoured 'delocalised arbitration'. The delocalised arbitration view gives the

41. UN Doc. A/CN.9/246 (6 March 1984) [62] (emphasis added).
42. *Arbitration Act 1996* (UK) c 23, s. 68.
43. Francis Mann, 'The UNCITRAL Model Law - Lex Facit Arbitrum' (1986) 2(3) *Arbitration International* 241; Michael Reisman, *Systems of Control in International Adjudication and Arbitration* (Duke University Press, 1992) 113–120; Roy Goode, 'The Role of the *Lex Loci Arbitri* in International Commercial Arbitration' (2001) 17(1) *Arbitration International* 19; Bruno Leurent, 'Reflections on the International Effectiveness of Arbitration Awards' (1996) 12(3) *Arbitration International* 269.

greatest possible scope for party autonomy by removing international arbitration from the control of the laws of the seat and the supervisory control of its courts.[44] Consequently, some international arbitrators have argued that an international arbitral tribunal has no *lex fori* as a court, either substantively or procedurally.[45]

Proponents of the delocalisation theory acknowledge that the legal force of the award cannot derive exclusively from party autonomy and contend that the legal force of the award derives either from the legal systems in which it is enforced[46] or from a transnational legal system that is independent of all national legal systems.[47] There are two developments in relation to delocalisation. First, the notion that the role of national courts should be more supportive rather than interventionist has been established by the modern national arbitration laws,[48] notably the UNCITRAL Model Law.[49] Second, it is proposed that the dual system of control (first by the law of the arbitral seat and then by the law of the enforcing forum) should be replaced with the end system of control by the law of the enforcing forum. One of the most important progressive steps taken by the New York Convention was the abandonment of the doctrine of double exequatur prescribed by the 1927 Geneva Convention, which required the award-creditor to first obtain the final confirmation of an award at the seat before seeking the recognition or enforcement of the award.[50]

---

44. Collins and Harris (n. 32) 841. *See also* Emmanuel Gaillard, 'Sociology of International Arbitration' (2015) 31(1) *Arbitration International* 1; Emmanuel Gaillard, 'The Emerging System of International Arbitration: Defining System' (2012) 106(1) *American Society of International Law Proceedings of Annual Meetings* 287; Emmanuel Gaillard, *Legal Theory of International Arbitration* (Martinus Nijhoff Publishers, 2010); Jan Paulsson, *The Idea of Arbitration* (Oxford University Press, 2013); Jan Paulsson, 'Delocalisation of International Commercial Arbitration: When and Why It Matters' (1983) 32 *International and Comparative Law Quarterly* 53; Jan Paulsson, 'Arbitration Unbound: Award Detached from the Law of Its Country of Origin' (1981) 30(2) *International and Comparative Law Quarterly* 358 DOI: 10.1093/iclqaj/30.2.358; Loukas Mistelis, 'Delocalization and Its Relevance in Post-Award Review' in Fabien Gelinas and Frederic Bachand (eds), *25 Years of the UNCITRAL Model Law* (Juris, 2013); Loukas Mistelis, 'Setting Aside of Arbitral Awards and Forum Shopping in International Arbitration: Delocalization, Party Autonomy and National Courts in Post-Award Review' in Franco Ferrari (ed.), *Forum Shopping in the International Commercial Arbitration Context* (Sellier, 2013); Gabrielle Kaufmann-Kohler, 'Globalization of Arbitral Procedure' (2003) 36 *Vanderbilt Journal of Transnational Law* 1313; Julian D M Lew, 'Is There a Global Free-standing Body of Substantive Arbitration Law' in Albert Jan van den Berg (ed.), *International Arbitration: The Coming of a New Age*, ICCA Congress 17 (Kluwer Law International, 2013) 53; Julian D M Lew, 'Achieving the Dream: Autonomous Arbitration' (2006) 22 *Arbitration International* 179.
45. *Insurer (US) v. Manufacturer (Italy)*, Interim Award, ICC Case No. 11333 (2002), reported in (2006) XXXI *Yearbook Commercial Arbitration* 117, 119–120.
46. Arthur von Mehren, *Limitations on Party Choice of the Governing Law: Do They Exist for International Commercial Arbitration* (Tel Aviv University, 1986) 19; Paulsson, 'Delocalisation of International Commercial Arbitration' (n. 44) 53; Paulsson, 'Arbitration Unbound' (n. 44) 358.
47. Gaillard, *Legal Theory of International Arbitration* (n. 44) 35.
48. For the regulations on the supportive role rather than supervision in modern arbitration law in the major jurisdictions, *see* the discussion in Lew, 'Achieving the Dream' (n. 44) 192–193.
49. *UNCITRAL Model Law*, UN Docs A/40/17 and A/61/17 (n. 29) Art. 5 ('[i]n matters governed by this Law, no court shall intervene except where so provided in this Law').
50. *Convention on the Execution of Foreign Arbitral Awards*, open for signature 26 September 1927, 92 LNTS 301 (entered into force 25 July 1929) Art. I(d). For commentaries, *see also* Christoph Liebscher, 'Non-Binding Award, Article V(1)(e)' in Reinmar Wolff (ed.), *New York Convention:*

France is one of the jurisdictions in favour of delocalisation. The French Cour de Cassation, for instance, enforced an award set aside by the English High Court and held that:

> [A]n international arbitral award, which is not anchored in any national legal order, is a decision of international justice whose validity must be examined according to the rules applicable in the country where its recognition and enforcement are sought.[51]

In addition to French courts, courts in the United States have occasionally been willing to recognise and enforce arbitral awards that have been set aside by the courts of the arbitral seat. For instance, the District Court in Washington DC granted the enforcement of an award that had been set aside by the Egyptian court.[52] Similarly, the District Court in the Southern District of New York enforced an award that had been set aside in Mexico City.[53] The District Court held that giving effect to the setting-aside decision by the Mexican court would be contrary to United States public policy and 'repugnant to fundamental notions of what is decent and just in the State where enforcement is sought'.[54] The Supreme Court of Canada also supported the delocalisation theory, holding that:

> Arbitration is part of no state's judicial system ... The arbitrator has no allegiance or connection to any single country ... In short, arbitration is a creature that owes its existence to the will of the parties alone.[55]

Nevertheless, it appears that the arguments in favour of total delocalisation, in the sense of freeing an international arbitration from the control of the legal system of the arbitral seat, remain for the time being aspirational and are therefore supported by very few authorities.[56] As discussed in §2.02[B][1], the law of the arbitral seat still performs irreplaceable and vital functions: supplementing the procedural rules chosen by the parties when they are incomplete; supporting interim measures where coercive state powers are necessary; and providing a forum for challenging arbitral awards based on the grounds of excess of jurisdiction, procedural irregularities, and violation of arbitrability and public policy. Significantly, it is the law of the arbitral seat that confers nationality on an arbitral award so that it can be recognised or enforced under the New York Convention to which its country of origin is a party.

Convention on the Recognition and Enforcement of Foreign Arbitral Awards of 10 June 1958: Commentary (C.H. Beck • Hart • Nomos, 2012) 357–358.

51. *PT Putrabali Adyamulia (Indonesia) v. Rena Holding*, Cour de Cassation [Supreme Court], First Civil Chamber, 29 June 2007 reported in (2007) XXXII *Yearbook Commercial Arbitration* 299, 302.
52. *Chromalloy Aeroservices Inc v. Arab Republic of Egypt*, 937 F Supp 907 (D DC, 1996).
53. *Corporación Mexicana de Mantenimiento Integral, S de RL de CV v. PEMEX-Exploration y Produccin* (2nd Cir, No. 13-4022, 2 August 2016).
54. *Ibid.*, slip op 28, quoting *Tahan v. Hodgson*, 662 F 2d 862, 864 (DC Cir, 1981).
55. *Dell Computer Corp v. Union des consommateurs* 2007 SCC 34 (2007) 284 DLR (4th) 577, [51].
56. Maxi Scherer, 'Effects of Foreign Judgments Relating to International Arbitral Awards: Is the "Judgment Route" the Wrong Road?' (2013) 4(3) *Journal of International Dispute Settlement* 587, 619 DOI: 10.1093/jnlids/idt013.

Moreover, as discussed above, the country in which the arbitration takes place has its own conception of normatively appropriate levels of procedural fairness to protect and therefore has the authority to regulate procedural rules of arbitration. If a state voluntarily relinquishes this authority, parties may believe that they will lose the remedies provided by the courts of the seat in the event that arbitral awards violate the principle of procedural fairness and may therefore be unlikely to choose that country as the seat of arbitration. As a result of these concerns, Belgium, which had delocalised international arbitration, has changed its position.[57]

[E] Conclusion

In sum, the connection between the arbitral procedure and the law of the arbitral seat has been recognised by Article V(1)(d) of the New York Convention, which deals with the violation of the agreed procedure or the procedure prescribed by the law of the seat. Further, the interest of the seat in ensuring that its mandatory rules are observed by the parties and the arbitral tribunal is confirmed by Article V(1)(e) of the New York Convention.

On the one hand, for the parties and the arbitral tribunal, the law applicable to the arbitral proceedings is the law of the arbitral seat. They must obey the mandatory rules of the arbitral seat, which require each party to have an equal opportunity to present its case in order to avoid the setting aside of awards. Also, where neither the parties nor the institutional arbitration rules provide for specific rules on notice of arbitral proceedings, Article V(1)(d) of the New York Convention provides that such notice shall comply with the relevant arbitration law of the seat. On the other hand, parties and tribunals cannot anticipate all potential forums for recognition or enforcement of awards and thus cannot comply with the laws of the enforcing forum regarding due process during the arbitration.

The question arises as to the extent to which the enforcing courts should take into account the law governing the arbitral procedure when determining the standards of due process under the New York Convention. In other words, the question is whether enforcing courts should consider legal certainty and predictability for parties and tribunals, and the seat's own conception of normatively appropriate levels of procedural fairness, as discussed in more detail in §2.06[A][2] and Chapter 8.

However, the application of the law of the seat alone may overlook the normatively appropriate level of procedural fairness that the enforcing forum seeks to protect. Some states where recognition or enforcement is sought are unwilling to allow their legal machinery to be used to enforce awards that were obtained in arbitrations that

---

57. By its law of 27 March 1985, a provision was added to Article 1717 of the Belgian Code Judiciaire to the effect that a losing party was unable to challenge an award made in an international arbitration held in Belgium before the Belgian courts, unless at least one of the parties had a place of business or other connection with Belgium. However, this provision seems to discourage parties from choosing Belgium as the arbitral seat. Finally, by its law of 19 May 1998, it has since been changed and now allows parties to an international arbitration to be outside of local control if they agree but no longer provides for compulsory delocalisation.

have not met that state's own notions of the minimum standard of procedural fairness expected in international commercial arbitration. Thus, they apply their own national law to determine whether there has been a violation of due process under the New York Convention and treat serious procedural irregularities as violations of public policy, as discussed in the next section. Consequently, as shown in the next section, it is not surprising to see that most State Parties apply the law of the forum of enforcement in determining whether the due process defence under the New York Convention has been satisfied. It seems reasonable to assume that countries, such as China, prefer the *lex arbitri* mainly because they have weak domestic due process guarantees – in terms of both conceptualisation and application of functional, applicable standards. Under these circumstances, unlike countries with stronger due process safeguards, Chinese courts have few domestic notions and doctrines to refer to. Another reason that Chinese courts are willing to acknowledge the weakness of domestic legal regimes regarding due process and relinquish some sovereignty in this regard is that they fear widespread criticism if they refuse to recognise or enforce foreign arbitral awards based on their domestic notions, such as public policy.[58] Thus, in part because of the lack of domestic guarantees for due process and in part because of China's current pro-arbitration policy, Chinese judges are inclined to apply the *lex arbitri* rather than its domestic law to determine the due process defence under the New York Convention.

§2.03 THE LAW OF THE FORUM WHERE THE RECOGNITION OR ENFORCEMENT IS SOUGHT: *LEX FORI*

In practice, a significant number of courts have applied their own national standards to determine whether there has been a violation of due process under Article V(1)(b). For instance, national courts in Germany,[59] Italy,[60] Spain,[61] Switzerland,[62] the United States,[63] the United Kingdom,[64] and elsewhere,[65] in both common law and civil law

58. 《最高人民法院关于人民法院处理与涉外仲裁及外国仲裁事项有关问题的通知》[Notice on the Issues Concerning Foreign-related or Foreign Arbitration] Supreme People's Court, Fa Fa [1995] No. 18, promulgated on 28 August 1995 and amended on 16 December 2008 (Fa Shi [2008] No. 18); Zhu and Xiao (n. 9) 62.
59. Hanseatisches Oberlandesgericht Hamburg [Hanseatic Higher Regional Court of Hamburg], 27 July 1978 reported in (1979) IV *Yearbook Commercial Arbitration* 266.
60. Corte Di Appello Di Napoli [Court of Appeal of Naples], 20 February 1975 reported in (1979) IV *Yearbook Commercial Arbitration* 275, 276; Corte Di Appello Di Napoli [Court of Appeal of Naples], 18 May 1982 reported in (1985) X *Yearbook Commercial Arbitration* 461, 462.
61. Supreme Court of Spain, First Civil Law Chamber, No. 332 of 2000, 31 July 2000 reported in (2007) XXXII *Yearbook Commercial Arbitration* 532, 537.
62. Tribunal Fédéral [Federal Supreme Court of Switzerland, First Civil Law Chamber], No. 4A 374/2014, 26 February 2015 reported in (2016) XLI *Yearbook Commercial Arbitration* 567, [8] [35].
63. *Generica Ltd v. Pharmaceutical Basics Inc*, 125 F 3d 1123, 1129 (7th Cir, 1997); *Iran Aircraft Indus v. Avco Corp*, 980 F 2d 141, 145 (2nd Cir, 1992); *Parsons & Whittemore Overseas Co v. Societe Generale De L'Industrie Du Papier (RAKTA)*, 508 F 2d 969, 975–976 (2nd Cir, 1974); *Sonera Holding BV v. Cukurova Holding AS*, 895 F Supp 2d 513, 521 (SD NY, 2012); *Laminoirs v. Southwire Co*, 484 F Sup 1063, 1067 (ND Ga, 1980); *Biotronik Mess-und Therapiegeraete GmbH & Co v. Medford Med Instrument Co*, 415 F Supp 133, 140 (D NJ, 1976); *Karaha Bodas Co v. Perusahaan Pertambangan Minyak Dan Gas Bumi Negara*, 364 F 3d 274, 298–299 (5th Cir,

jurisdictions, have held that the law of the forum where recognition or enforcement is sought should be applied in determining whether a party has been denied the opportunity to present its case. This approach indicates that judges, who are bound to conform to the rules of interpretation of the country where they sit, are inclined to look to the notions of due process in their own law for inspiration.[66] This approach, however, ignores the rules of interpretation embodied in the New York Convention, the mandatary rules of procedural fairness of the seat, and the need of parties and arbitrators for legal certainty.

[A] Jurisdictions Applying the *Lex Fori*

The most representative jurisdictions applying the *lex fori* in common law systems are the United States and the United Kingdom. Since the United States ratified the New York Convention in 1970, US courts have consistently held that the New York Convention awards are subject to review under the forum state's standards of due process (i.e., the due process standards of the Fifth and Fourteenth Amendments to the US Constitution).[67] The Second Circuit Court has recognised that the exception provided for in Article V(1)(b) 'essentially sanctions the application of the forum state's standards of due process' and that the due process rights of the forum are 'entitled to full force under the Convention as defences to enforcement'.[68] An arbitral award 'should be denied or vacated if the party challenging the award proves that he was not given a meaningful opportunity to be heard as our due process jurisprudence defines it'.[69] Under US law, the enquiry underlying the due process exception is 'limited to determining whether the procedure used was fundamentally unfair'[70] and 'the fundamental requirement of due process is the opportunity to be heard at a meaningful time and in a meaningful manner'.[71] A fundamentally fair hearing is the one that 'meets the minimal requirements of fairness – adequate notice, a hearing on the evidence, and an

2004); *Employers Insurance of Wausau v. Banco de Seguros del Estado*, 199 F 3d 937, 942 (7th Cir, 1999); *Telenor Mobile Commc'ns AS v. Storm LLC*, 524 F Supp 2d 332, 368 (SD NY, 2007); *Geotech Lizenz AG v. Evergreen Sys Inc*, 697 F Supp 1248, 1253 (ED NY, 1988).

64. *Cukurova Holding AS v. Sonera Holding BV* [2014] UKPC 15 (13 May 2014) [32].
65. *See, e.g.*, Hong Kong: *Paklito Investment Ltd v. Klockner East Asia Ltd* [1993] 2 HKLR 39, 47.
66. Albert Jan van den Berg, *The New York Arbitration Convention of 1958: Towards a Uniform Judicial Interpretation* (Kluwer Law and Taxation Publishers, 1981) 298.
67. *See Karaha Bodas Co v. Perusahaan Pertambangan Minyak Dan Gas Bumi Negara*, 364 F 3d 274, 298–299 (5th Cir, 2004).
68. *Parsons & Whittemore Overseas Co v. Société Générale De L'Industrie Du Papier (RAKTA)*, 508 F 2d 969, 975–976 (2nd Cir, 1974); *Iran Aircraft Indus v. Avco Corp*, 980 F 2d 141, 145 (2nd Cir, 1992).
69. *Generica Ltd v. Pharmaceutical Basics Inc*, 125 F 3d 1123, 1129–1130 (7th Cir, 1997).
70. *Tempo Shain Corp v. Bertek Inc*, 120 F 3d 16, 20 (2nd Cir, 1997); *BSH Hausgeräte GmbH v. Jak Kamhi* (SD NY, No. 17 Civ 5776, 2 March 2018) slip op 10.
71. *Parsons & Whittemore Overseas Co v. Société Générale De L'Industrie Du Papier (RAKTA)*, 508 F 2d 969, 975–976 (2nd Cir, 1974). *See also Matthews v. Eldridge*, 424 US 319, 333 (1976); *Iran Aircraft Indus v. Avco Corp*, 980 F 2d 141, 145 (2nd Cir, 1992); *Hispasat SA v. Bantel Telecom LLC* (SD Fla, No. 17-20534-CV, 2 August 2017) slip op 8.

impartial decision by the arbitrator'.[72] Albert Jan van den Berg, in his insightful commentaries on the New York Convention, considered that the US approach, namely the law of the forum state, 'stated concisely what Article V(1)(b) is all about'.[73]

Likewise, English courts generally apply their own notion of 'natural justice' to determine whether there has been a breach of due process.[74] Sections 100–103 of the Arbitration Act 1996 give effect to the New York Convention in the United Kingdom.[75] Section 103(2)(c) reproduces almost exactly the text of Article V(1)(b) of the New York Convention and cannot provide more detailed guidance on the application of the due process defence under the Convention. In the United Kingdom, the concept and application of the due process defence are largely governed by case law. In *Minmetals*, the English court held that the due process defence requires that the award-debtor be prevented from presenting its case by circumstances beyond its control, which will normally cover the case where the procedure followed was contrary to the rules of natural justice.[76] In *Kanoria*, the Court of Appeal held that according to the ordinary meaning of section 103(2)(c), a party to an arbitration is unable to present its case if it is never informed of the case to be heard.[77] The court in *Cukurova* referred to the principles in *Minmetals* and *Kanoria* and emphasised that, in applying those principles, the enforcing court must apply its own concept of natural justice, that is, the concept of natural justice as understood and applied in the forum where enforcement is sought.[78] The courts in Hong Kong, another Commonwealth jurisdiction, also follow the *lex fori* approach to interpreting the due process defence under the Convention.[79]

In civil law jurisdictions, such as Germany and Switzerland, it is not uncommon for courts to apply their domestic law to determine the due process defence under the New York Convention. The prevailing view in Germany is that the standard of the protection afforded by Article V(1)(b) is determined by German law.[80] In deciding whether to apply the due process defence of the Convention, German courts have held that 'the question [of] whether the requirements of due process have been satisfied

72. *Slaney v. International Amateur Athletic Federation*, 244 F 3d 580, 592 (7th Cir, 2001); *Dastime Group Ltd, et al., v. Moonvale Investments Ltd, et al.* (ND Cal, No. 17-CV-01859-JSW, 11 October 2017) slip op 12.
73. van den Berg (n. 66) 297.
74. For the opposite position, *see Tesco Ltd v. William Moffett, Richard Mclaughlin, James Mclaughlin & Anson Logue* [2015] NIQB 68 (1 July 2015) [15] (the Northern Ireland High Court used the *lex arbitri* – Arbitration Act 1954 of the Republic of Ireland – to judge the standard of 'proper notice' and considered 'the proper notice to be notice that is compliant with the applicable law as to the notice of proceedings').
75. The New York Convention was first given domestic effect by the Arbitration Act 1975.
76. *Minmetals Germany GmbH v. Ferco Steel Ltd* [1999] CLC 647, 658.
77. *Ajay Kanoria, Esols Worldwide Ltd & Indekka Software PVT Ltd v. Tony Francis Guinness* [2006] EWCA Civ 222 (21 February 2006) [32].
78. *Cukurova Holding AS v. Sonera Holding BV* [2014] UKPC 15 (13 May 2014) [32].
79. *Paklito Investment Ltd v. Klockner East Asia Ltd* [1993] 2 HKLR 39, 47.
80. Karl-Heinz Böckstiegel, Stefan Michael Kröll and Patricia Nacimiento (eds), *Arbitration in Germany: The Model Law in Practice* (Kluwer Law International, 2nd ed., 2015) 469; Dennis Solomon, 'Interpretation and Application of the New York Convention in Germany' in George A Bermann (ed.), *Recognition and Enforcement of Foreign Arbitral Awards – The Interpretation and Application of the New York Convention by National Courts* (Springer, 2017) 355.

must be considered under the German law, which is the law of the enforcing state'.[81] The German courts further clarified that the applicable law governing due process under Article V(1)(b) was irrelevant to the *lex arbitri*, which merely provided the relevant standard for the 'correctness of the procedure' under Article V(1)(d).[82] Similarly, since the Swiss courts considered the 'right to be heard' to be one of the procedural public policy claims, they applied the standard of Article V(2)(b), which is the law of the forum where recognition or enforcement is sought, to the due process defence.[83] As the Swiss Federal Supreme Court stated:

> A foreign award may be incompatible with the Swiss legal system not only because of its substantive content but also because of the proceedings in which it was rendered. In this respect, Swiss public policy requires that the fundamental procedural rules derived from the *Constitution*, such as *the right to a fair process and the right to be heard*, be complied with.[84]

[B] The Application of *Lex Fori*

Some of the jurisdictions that have adopted the *lex fori* approach apply, in essence, the same procedural standards as those required by domestic constitutional law.[85] As a corollary to this, they sometimes refer to the standards of procedural irregularities for domestic arbitral awards in set-aside proceedings when determining the due process defence under the New York Convention.

[1] Constitutional Due Process

In the US, the courts apply their own constitutional concept of due process to both set-aside proceedings and the recognition and enforcement of foreign arbitral awards.[86] In other words, US courts consider the sources of such due process standards to be the Due Process Clauses contained in the Fifth and Fourteenth Amendments, which generally provide that the state (national or local) may not deprive a 'person' of 'property' without 'due process of law'.[87] Both amendments, however, are limited by

81. Hanseatisches Oberlandesgericht Hamburg [Hanseatic Higher Regional Court of Hamburg], 27 July 1978 reported in (1979) IV *Yearbook Commercial Arbitration* 266, 267.
82. BayObLG (16.03.2000, 4Z Sch 50/99), NJW-RR 2001, 431[20]; Böckstiegel, Kröll and Nacimiento (n. 80) 471.
83. Tribunal Fédéral [Federal Supreme Court of Switzerland, First Civil Law Chamber], No. 4A 374/2014, 26 February 2015 reported in (2016) XLI *Yearbook Commercial Arbitration* 567, [11].
84. *Ibid.*, [8] (emphasis added).
85. *See* the discussion of the US, Germany, and the UK below.
86. *Research and Development Center 'Teploenergetika' LLC v. EP International LLC & Worldwide Vision LLC* (ED Va, Civ No. 2:15-CV-362) slip op 13 ('A participation defence corresponds to a constitutional due process defence').
87. *Karaha Bodas Co v. Perusahaan Pertambangan Minyak Dan Gas Bumi Negara*, 364 F 3d 274, 298–299 (5th Cir, 2004); *Iran Aircraft Indus v. Avco Corp*, 980 F 2d 141, 145–146 (2nd Cir, 1992). *See also* Ina C Popova and Duncan Pickard, 'Chapter 20: Country Report: The United States of America' in Friedrich Rosenfeld, Dietmar Czernich and Franco Ferrari (eds), *Due Process as a Limit to Discretion in International Commercial Arbitration* (Kluwer Law International, 2020)

the 'state action doctrine', which means that they apply only to actions taken by the government against individuals. Federal courts have consistently held that, in the absence of sate action, the due process requirements of the Fifth and Fourteenth Amendments do not apply directly to arbitral proceedings.[88] This means that arbitrators are not directly bound by the due process standards set forth in these two Amendments. Nevertheless, US courts apply constitutional due process principles when reviewing arbitral awards in set-aside and enforcement proceedings.[89] Moreover, US courts have held that the standards of the Federal Arbitration Act (FAA) for domestic arbitral awards apply to recognition and enforcement of New York Convention awards to the extent that they are 'not in conflict' with those of the Convention.[90] For instance, the FAA sets forth that a court may set aside an arbitral award 'where the arbitrators were guilty of misconduct... in refusing to hear evidence pertinent and material to the controversy; or of any other misbehaviour by which the rights of any party have been prejudiced'.[91] These standards of due process in set-aside proceedings can be applied to the recognition or enforcement of foreign arbitral awards.[92]

Similarly, German courts have applied their constitutional standards to the due process exception under the New York Convention.[93] They held that '[n]o comparison between German law and the foreign law can be made in respect of the application of the basic principles of due process'.[94] Relevant due process provisions include Articles 3(1) and 103(1) of the Basic Law of the Federal Republic of Germany (hereinafter 'German Constitution'). Article 3(1) provides that 'all persons shall be equal before the law', while Article 103(1) sets forth that 'every person shall be entitled to a hearing in accordance with the law'.[95] In applying the due process defence under the New York Convention, German courts have emphasised that the fundamental rights which

429; Louis Del Duca and Nancy A Welsh, 'Interpretation and Application of the New York Convention in the United States' in George A Bermann (ed.), *Recognition and Enforcement of Foreign Arbitral Awards – The Interpretation and Application of the New York Convention by National Courts* (Springer, 2017) 995, 1022.

88. *Desiderio v. Nat'l Ass'n of Sec Dealers Inc*, 191 F 3d 198, 206 (2nd Cir, 1999); *FDIC v. Air Fla Sys Inc*, 822 F 2d 833, 842 (9th Cir, 1987); *Elmore v. Chi & Ill Midland Ry Co*, 782 F 2d 94, 96 (7th Cir, 1986).
89. *Iran Aircraft Indus v. Avco Corp*, 980 F 2d 141, 146 (2nd Cir, 1992); *Parsons & Whittemore Overseas Co v. Societe Generale De L'Industrie Du Papier (RAKTA)*, 508 F 2d 969, 975 (2nd Cir, 1974).
90. 9 USC § 208 (2012); *Alghanim & Sons v. Toys R Us*, 126 F 3d 15, 16 (2nd Cir, 1997); *Zeiler v. Deitsch*, 500 F 3d 157, 164 (2nd Cir, 2007).
91. 9 USC § 10(a)(3) (2012).
92. Duca and Welsh (n. 87) 1020.
93. Oberlandesgericht Munich [Court of Appeal Munich], 34 Sch 26/08, 22 June 2009 reported in (2010) XXXV *Yearbook Commercial Arbitration* 371, [18]; Solomon (n. 80) 355; Friedrich Jakob Rosenfeld, 'Chapter 8: Country Report: Germany' in Friedrich Rosenfeld, Dietmar Czernich and Franco Ferrari (eds), *Due Process as a Limit to Discretion in International Commercial Arbitration* (Kluwer Law International, 2020) 177, 179.
94. Oberlandesgericht Munich [Court of Appeal Munich], 34 Sch 26/08, 22 June 2009 reported in (2010) XXXV *Yearbook Commercial Arbitration* 371, [18].
95. Grundgesetz für die Bundesrepublik Deutschland [Basic Law of the Federal Republic of Germany] (Germany) Arts 3(1), 103(1).

Article 103(1) of the German Constitution is intended to protect are the party's right to defend himself and the right to be able to influence the shaping of the procedure.[96]

[2] *Due Process Standards for Setting Aside Domestic Arbitral Awards and the International Character of Convention Arbitral Awards*

The courts' preference for the *lex fori* approach may be reinforced by the fact that national arbitration laws usually include the violation of due process as one of the grounds for setting aside arbitral awards. Courts have accumulated a wealth of experience in applying their domestic due process standards to the setting aside of arbitral awards. These domestic rules of procedural fairness in the setting aside of arbitral awards seated in its jurisdiction constitute one of the sources of the forum's due process standards, to some extent, which may influence judges in the interpretation and application of the due process defence under the Convention.

Any discussion of the violation of due process as a ground both for setting aside arbitral awards and for refusing recognition or enforcement of foreign arbitral awards would be incomplete without mention of the UNCITRAL Model Law. Originally promulgated in 1985 and revised in 2006, the UNCITRAL Model Law has been adopted in whole or in part by 87 states in a total of 120 jurisdictions, including Australia, Austria, Belgium, Hong Kong, Denmark, Germany, Egypt, India, Ireland, Japan, New Zealand, Norway, the Republic of Korea, Spain, Singapore, and South Africa.[97] One of the main objectives of establishing the UNCITRAL Model Law was to harmonise and limit the grounds for setting aside arbitral awards.[98] Early in the drafting process of the UNCITRAL Model Law, it was suggested that the grounds for setting aside an arbitral award should be consistent with the grounds for refusing recognition and enforcement of foreign arbitral awards under the New York Convention:

> Ideally, one should aim at a list [...] that would contain only those reasons on which recognition and enforcement may be refused under the 1958 New York Convention, i.e., article V(1), (a)-(d) and (2) [...] It would help to prevent that an international award falls victim to local particularities of law although the case at hand bears no substantive connection with that respective state.[99]

Accordingly, the UNCITRAL Model Law includes the violation of due process not only as a ground for non-recognition or non-enforcement of foreign arbitral awards but also as a ground for setting aside arbitral awards seated in the territory of the state.[100]

---

96. Oberlandesgericht Munich [Court of Appeal Munich], 34 Sch 26/08, 22 June 2009 reported in (2010) XXXV *Yearbook Commercial Arbitration* 371, [18].
97. The implementation of the Model Law in different states is available at https://uncitral.un.org/en/texts/arbitration/modellaw/commercial_arbitration/status.
98. Toms Krumiņš, *Arbitration and Human Rights: Approaches to Excluding the Annulment of Arbitral Awards and Their Compatibility with the ECHR* (Springer, 2020) 108; Holtzmann and Neuhaus (n. 39) 10–11.
99. Report of the Secretary-General: Possible Features of a Model Law on International Commercial Arbitration, A/CN.9/207, 14 May 1981, [110].
100. *UNCITRAL Model Law*, UN Docs A/40/17 and A/61/17 (n. 29) Arts 34(2)(a)(ii), 36(1)(a)(ii).

Article 18 of the UNCITRAL Model Law defines the requirements of due process as '[t]he parties shall be treated with equality, and each party shall be given the full opportunity of presenting his case',[101] which are applicable to both setting-aside and enforcement proceedings.

Take the example of one of the Model Law jurisdictions, Hong Kong, which has adopted the *lex fori* approach.[102] The Hong Kong Arbitration Ordinance clarifies the abstract definition of 'equal treatment of parties' contained in Article 18 of the UNCITRAL Model Law as 'the parties must be treated with equality; and the arbitral tribunal is required to be independent and to act fairly and impartially as between the parties, giving them a reasonable opportunity'.[103] In addition, the Hong Kong Arbitration Ordinance uses the same wording as that in the UNCITRAL Model Law, providing for breach of due process as one of the grounds both for setting aside arbitral awards seated in Hong Kong and for refusing recognition and enforcement of foreign arbitral awards.[104] Some of the national arbitration laws that do not adopt the UNCITRAL Model Law, such as those of the United Kingdom, France, and Switzerland, also include the standards of procedural fairness for arbitrations seated in the national territory,[105] and the violation of such standards may lead to the setting aside of arbitral awards.[106]

Although these national arbitration laws provide for the violation of due process as one of the grounds for annulment of arbitral awards by the courts of the seat, this discussion shows that these jurisdictions applying the *lex fori* generally recognise the distinctions between the due process standards of Article V(1)(b) and those of purely

101. *UNCITRAL Model Law*, UN Docs A/40/17 and A/61/17 (n. 29) Art. 18.
102. *Paklito Investment Ltd v. Klockner East Asia Ltd* [1993] 2 HKLR 39, 47.
103. *Arbitration Ordinance* (Hong Kong) cap 609, ss 46(2)–(3). Hong Kong has its own procedural rules and court system: *see Basic Law of the Hong Kong Special Administrative Region of the People's Republic of China* Arts 1, 2, 8. Although the Hong Kong Special Administrative Region (Hong Kong SAR) is an inalienable part of the People's Republic of China, Hong Kong SAR enjoys legislative and independent judicial power including that of final adjudication. The laws previously in force in Hong Kong, that is, the common law, rules of equity, ordinances, subordinate legislation, and customary law, shall be maintained, except for any that contravene the Basic Law of Hong Kong and subject to any amendment by the legislature of the Hong Kong SAR.
104. *Ibid.*, ss 81(1)(2)(a)(ii), 89(2)(c).
105. *See Arbitration Act 1996* (UK) c 23, s. 33(1)(a) ('the tribunal shall act fairly and impartially as between the parties, giving each party a reasonable opportunity of putting his case and dealing with that of his opponent'); *Code de procédure civile* [Code of Civil Procedure] (France) Art. 1520(4); *Federal Act on Private International Law* (Switzerland), 1 January 1989, Art. 182(3) [Andreas Bucher trans, *The English translations of Federal Act on Private International Law*, http://www.andreasbucher-law.ch/images/stories/pil_act_1987_as_from_1st_july_2022.pdf] ('[a]rbitral tribunal shall ensure equal treatment of the parties and the right of the parties to be heard in adversarial proceedings').
106. *Arbitration Act 1996* (UK) c 23, s. 68(2)(a); *Code de procédure civile* [Code of Civil Procedure] (France) Arts 1520(4), 1525; *Federal Act on Private International Law* (Switzerland), 1 January 1989, Art. 190(2)(d) [Andreas Bucher trans, *The English translations of Federal Act on Private International Law*, http://www.andreasbucher-law.ch/images/stories/pil_act_1987_as_from_1st_july_2022.pdf].

domestic procedural law. They generally recognise the international character of foreign arbitral awards and apply domestic due process standards specifically for international arbitration.[107]

Accordingly, courts in the United States and Switzerland have confirmed that what may be a violation of procedural fairness under domestic law is not necessarily a breach of due process under Article V(1)(b) of the New York Convention.[108] For instance, the US shows deference to the international character of Convention awards when applying American standards of due process. Under section 208 of the FAA, provisions relating to domestic arbitration may apply to foreign arbitration to the extent that they are 'not inconsistent with' the New York Convention.[109] As discussed above, US courts apply a so-called minimal requirements of fairness standard, which differs from their domestic due process standards reserved for domestic awards.[110] These 'minimal requirements of fairness' are interpreted by US courts as 'standards of fundamental fairness'.[111] These standards 'do not include the complete set of procedural rights guaranteed by the Federal Rules of Civil Procedure'. Instead, they require a fundamentally fair hearing, which is one that 'meets "the minimal requirements of fairness" - adequate notice, a hearing on the evidence, and an impartial decision by the arbitrator…'.[112] Similarly, Swiss courts have held that a procedural defect in the foreign arbitral proceedings will not necessarily lead to a refusal of enforcement, even if the

107. *See Generica Ltd v. Pharm Basics Inc*, 125 F 3d 1123, 1129–1130 (7th Cir, 1997) (arbitral award would be denied enforcement if challenging party proves it was 'not given a meaningful opportunity to be heard as our due process jurisprudence defines it. … [But] [p]arties that have chosen to remedy their disputes through arbitration … should not expect the same procedures they would find in the judicial arena'); *Parsons & Whittemore Overseas Co v. Societe Generale De L'Industrie Du Papier (RAKTA)*, 508 F 2d 969, 975–976 (2nd Cir, 1974); *Employers Insurance of Wausau v. Banco de Seguros del Estado*, 199 F 3d 937, 942–943 (7th Cir, 1999).
108. *See, e.g.*, the US: *Karaha Bodas Co v. Perusahaan Pertambangan Minyak Dan Gas Bumi Negara*, 364 F 3d 274, 299 (5th Cir, 2004); *Slaney v. International Amateur Athletic Federation*, 244 F 3d 580, 591 (7th Cir, 2001); *Employers Insurance of Wausau v. Banco de Seguros del Estado*, 199 F 3d 937, 944 (7th Cir, 1999); *Generica Ltd v. Pharm Basics Inc*, 125 F 3d 1123, 1130 (7th Cir, 1997); *Parsons & Whittemore Overseas Co v. Societe Generale De L'Industrie Du Papier (RAKTA)*, 508 F 2d 969, 975 (2nd Cir, 1974); Switzerland: Canton Tessin Camera di Esecuzione e Fallimenti [Court of Appeal of the Canton of Ticino, Execution and Bankruptcy Chamber], 19 June 1990 reported in (1995) XX *Yearbook Commercial Arbitration* 762, 763–764 [4].
109. 9 USC § 208 (1970) provides that 'Chapter 1 [9 USC §§ 1–16] applies to actions and proceedings brought under this chapter [9 USC §§ 201–208 (1970)] to the extent that chapter [9 USC §§ 1–16] is not in conflict with this chapter [9 USC §§ 201–208 (1970)] or the [New York] Convention as ratified by the United States'.
110. *Iran Aircraft Indus v. Avco Corp*, 980 F 2d 141, 146 (2nd Cir, 1992); *Generica Ltd v. Pharm Basics Inc*, 125 F 3d 1123, 1130 (7th Cir, 1997); *Karaha Bodas Co v. Perusahaan Pertambangan Minyak Dan Gas Bumi Negara*, 364 F 3d 274, 298–299 (5th Cir, 2004).
111. *Jorf Lasfar Energy Company v. AMCI Export Corporation* (WD Pa, Civ No. 05-0423, 22 December 2005) slip op 6.
112. *Karaha Bodas Co v. Perusahaan Pertambangan Minyak Dan Gas Bumi Negara*, 364 F 3d 274, 298–299 (5th Cir, 2004). *See also Slaney v. International Amateur Athletic Federation*, 244 F 3d 580, 592 (7th Cir, 2001); *Dastime Group Ltd, et al., v. Moonvale Investments Ltd, et al.* (ND Cal, No. 17-CV-01859-JSW, 11 October 2017) slip op 12; *Generica Ltd v. Pharm Basics Inc*, 125 F 3d 1123, 1130 (7th Cir, 1997).

procedural defect would have led to the setting aside of a Swiss award, unless it violates the fundamental principles of the Swiss legal system and sense of justice.[113]

Similarly, German courts hold that the due process requirements of the New York Convention constitute only a minimum standard and that this does not mean that such arbitral proceedings must conform in all respects with German Arbitration Law.[114] As discussed above, German courts consider that the due process defence overlaps to some extent with procedural public policy. Both academics and German courts have emphasised that the due process requirements of the New York Convention must be applied under the international rather than the national public policy.[115] Thus, it is not necessarily a breach of public policy for a foreign arbitration to depart from mandatory rules of domestic procedure, unless it is contrary to international public policy.[116] They would only refuse to recognise or enforce a foreign award 'where the foreign decision was rendered in proceedings that are so different from the *fundamental* principles of German procedural law that the decision cannot be deemed to have been rendered in proper, legally correct proceedings'.[117]

Accordingly, the requirements of the judicial due process under German domestic procedural law, such as clarification and indication, do not apply to international arbitration.[118] German courts have held that the constitutionally protected right to due process that is applicable to the New York Convention requires arbitrators only to take cognisance of and evaluate the parties' arguments and to allow the parties to present their case with respect to all the considerations on which the award will be based.[119] Arbitrators are not required to deal with every detail of the parties' arguments in the award, nor does silence on an argument necessarily mean that it has been ignored, unless that argument is essential to the making of the award.[120] In contrast to the requirements of domestic procedural law, there is no general obligation on an arbitral tribunal to provide references and explicit reasons for its decisions in respect of each

---

113. Canton Tessin Camera di Esecuzione e Fallimenti [Court of Appeal of the Canton of Ticino, Execution and Bankruptcy Chamber], 19 June 1990 reported in (1995) XX *Yearbook Commercial Arbitration* 762, 763–764 [4].
114. Böckstiegel, Kröll and Nacimiento (n. 80) 29 [81].
115. *Ibid.*, 29 [80]–[81]; Hanseatisches Oberlandesgericht [Hanseatic Court of Appeal] (2) Sch 04/99, 30 September 1999 reported in (2006) XXXI *Yearbook Commercial Arbitration* 640, 647–651.
116. Oberlandesgericht Celle [Court of Appeal Celle], 8 Sch 06/06, 31 May 2007 reported in (2008) XXXIII *Yearbook Commercial Arbitration* 524, [23]. *See also* Oberlandesgericht Thuringia [Higher Regional Court of Thuringia], 1 Sch 7/13, 20 November 2013 reported in (2015) XL *Yearbook Commercial Arbitration* 422, [33].
117. Oberlandesgericht [Higher Regional Court of Brandenburg], 8 Sch 01/99, 2 September 1999 reported in (2004) XXIX *Yearbook Commercial Arbitration* 697, 699 (emphasis added).
118. Oberlandesgericht Munich[High Regional Court of Munich], 34 Sch 21/11, 11 April 2012 reported in (2014) XXXIX *Yearbook Commercial Arbitration* 389, [8].
119. *Ibid.*; Oberlandesgericht Munich [Higher Regional Court of Munich], 34 Sch 10/11, 14 November 2011 reported in (2012) XXXVII *Yearbook Commercial Arbitration* 231, [10]; Oberlandesgericht Naumburg [Higher Regional Court of Naumburg], 10 Sch 04/10, 4 March 2011 reported in (2012) XXXVII *Yearbook Commercial Arbitration* 226, [6]–[7].
120. Oberlandesgericht Frankfurt [Court of Appeal Frankfurt], 26 SchH 03/09, 12 October 2009 reported in (2010) XXXV *Yearbook Commercial Arbitration* 377, [20].

party's arguments, nor is there any obligation to discuss the law with the parties concerned.[121]

In summary, jurisdictions that apply the *lex fori* confirm, either explicitly or implicitly, that they take into account the international character of Convention awards in determining a breach of due process under Article V(1)(b). Thus, what may constitute a breach of due process under their domestic law is not necessarily a breach of due process under the New York Convention. This approach mitigates to some extent the potential parochialism of the *lex fori* approach and is also consistent with the pro-enforcement spirit of the New York Convention.

[C] The Relationship Between Article V(1)(b) and Article V(2)(b)

Article V(2)(b) of the New York Convention denies recognition and enforcement if the granting of enforcement would violate the public policy of the country where recognition or enforcement is sought. Although commentators often see public policy as a concept being subject to divergent interpretations by domestic courts in different jurisdictions, case law in the New York Convention jurisdictions tends to confine public policy within core values and the most basic notions of morality and justice.[122] In applying the public policy defence, some courts review not only the substantive matters of awards but also the procedural aspects.[123] Thus, they may refuse to recognise or enforce an award where the arbitral procedure contradicts their understanding of basic procedural fairness in the state where recognition or enforcement is sought. Some courts in the jurisdictions that adopt the *lex fori* approach, such as Germany, Switzerland, and Spain, treat procedural irregularities – if serious enough – as amounting to violations of public policy. In these cases, they usually concur that the due process defence under Article V(1)(b) may overlap, to some extent, with the public policy exception under Article V(2)(b) of the New York Convention.[124] Some courts acknowledge the duplication between Article V(1)(b) and Article V(2)(b),[125] while others take the view that a proper distinction between these two provisions is

121. Oberlandesgericht Munich [Higher Regional Court of Munich], 34 Sch 10/11, 14 November 2011 reported in (2012) XXXVII *Yearbook Commercial Arbitration* 231, [9]; Oberlandesgericht Düsseldorf [Court of Appeal Düsseldorf], I-4 Sch 10/09, 15 December 2009 reported in (2010) XXXV *Yearbook Commercial Arbitration* 386, [16].
122. United Nations Commission on International Trade Law, *Secretariat Guide on the Convention on the Recognition and Enforcement of Foreign Arbitral Awards* (2016) 240.
123. van den Berg (n. 66) 300.
124. *See, e.g.*, Germany: Oberlandesgericht Munich [Court of Appeal Munich], 34 Sch 26/08, 22 June 2009 reported in (2010) XXXV *Yearbook Commercial Arbitration* 371, [18]; Oberlandesgericht Frankfurt [Court of Appeal Frankfurt], 26 SchH 03/09, 12 October 2009 reported in (2010) XXXV *Yearbook Commercial Arbitration* 377, [20]; Switzerland: Tribunal Fédéral [Federal Supreme Court of Switzerland, 1st Civil Law Chamber], 8 December 2003 reported in (2004) XXIX *Yearbook Commercial Arbitration* 834, 840; Spain: Supreme Court of Spain, First Civil Law Chamber, No. 332 of 2000, 31 July 2000 reported in (2007) XXXII *Yearbook Commercial Arbitration* 532.
125. *See, e.g.*, Spain: Supreme Court of Spain, First Civil Law Chamber, No. 332 of 2000, 31 July 2000 reported in (2007) XXXII *Yearbook Commercial Arbitration* 532.

necessary.[126] It is therefore worth examining the relationship between Article V(1)(b) and Article V(2)(b).

[1] *Public Policy under the New York Convention: Domestic or International?*

Although some scholars argue that public policy under the New York Convention should be an international public policy rather than a domestic public policy with national connotations,[127] the wording of the New York Convention, 'the public policy of *that country* [the country where recognition or enforcement is sought]' (emphasis added), indicates that the Convention does not intend to exclude national notions of public policy. In private international law, states may invoke public policy, which reflects their national values, as a ground for refusing the recognition or enforcement of foreign judgments and arbitral awards or for opposing the application of foreign law that is considered contrary to their public policy.[128] This public policy is referred to as external public policy – *ordre public externe* – and is much narrower than the concept of public policy that states may apply internally.[129]

Although states generally make a distinction between *ordre public externe* and *internal public policy*, both are based on the state's own concepts. For instance, French courts have adopted *ordre public externe* in the context of the New York Convention and defined it as 'the body of rules and values whose violation the *French legal order* cannot tolerate even in situations of international character'.[130] Similarly, German courts have defined the public policy defence under the New York Convention as the basis of German public and economic life or the German perception of justice.[131] In common law jurisdictions, the Second Circuit of the United States Court of Appeals held that '[e]nforcement of foreign arbitral awards may be denied [on the basis of public policy] only where enforcement would violate the forum state's *most basic notions of morality and justice*'.[132] In the UK, the courts held that it is English public

126. Bundesgerichtshof [Federal Supreme Court], 15 May 1986 reported in (1987) XII *Yearbook Commercial Arbitration* 489, 490 [2]–[3].
127. Born (n. 4) 2838; Anton G Maurer, *The Public Policy Exception under the New York Convention: History, Interpretation, and Application* (JurisNet, 2013) 346.
128. Collins and Harris (n. 31) 735–740, 896–900.
129. Monique Hazelhorst, *Free Movement of Civil Judgments in the European Union and the Right to a Fair Trial* (Springer, 2017) 67.
130. *Agence pour la sécurité de la navigation aérienne en Afrique et à Madagascar v. M N'DOYE Issakha*, Court of Appeal of Paris, France, 16 October 1997 (emphasis added).
131. Oberlandesgericht [OLG] München, Germany, 34 Sch 019/05, 28 November 2005; Oberlandesgericht [OLG] Düsseldorf, Germany, VI Sch (Kart) 1/02, 21 July 2004; Hanseatisches Oberlandesgericht [Hanseatic Court of Appeal] (2) Sch 04/99, 30 September 1999 reported in (2006) XXXI *Yearbook Commercial Arbitration* 640; Bundesgerichtshof [BGH] Germany, III ZR 269/88, 18 January 1990.
132. *Parsons & Whittemore Overseas Co v. Societe Generale De L'Industrie Du Papier (RAKTA)*, 508 F 2d 969, 974 (2nd Cir, 1974) (emphasis added).

policy that is meant when determining whether to recognise or enforce the New York Convention awards.[133] The Hong Kong courts also held that the public policy under Article V(2)(b) refers to Hong Kong's notions of justice.[134]

In the area of public policy, some scholars have distinguished between 'international public policy' and 'transnational public policy'.[135] As shown above, it has been suggested that 'international public policy' is, in fact, no more than domestic public policy applied to foreign arbitral awards, and its content and application remain subject to each state.[136] In contrast, the 'transnational public policy' has a different meaning, signifying an international consensus on universal standards and accepted norms of conduct that must be applied in all fora.[137] As shown above, some courts may interpret Article V(2)(b) of the New York Convention as international public policy, which is still subject to that state's own concepts. In contrast, a transnational public policy, defined as norms agreed upon by all civilised nations, is not what the drafters envisaged when they drafted the language of Article V(2)(b), and thus it is not adopted by the courts in practice. The current consensus seems to be that the domestic law of the enforcing state is the primary source of public policy under Article V(2)(b).[138] Nevertheless, as discussed in Chapter 3, a transnational public policy, referring to norms recognised by all civilised nations, aligns with one of the book's central arguments that the due process defence under the New York Convention should be based on the general principle of *audiatur et altera pars*. Also, this transnational perspective can encourage enforcing courts to consider how other foreign courts deal with the due process defence, which is the core requirement of subsequent practice under the VCLT.[139]

133. Collins and Harris (n. 31) 896.
134. *Hebei Import & Export Corp v. Polytek Engineering Co Ltd* [1999] 2 HKLRD 665, 676.
135. Leon E Trakman, 'Aligning State Sovereignty with Transnational Public Policy' (2018) 93(2) *Tulane Law Review* 207; Jean-Michel Marcoux, 'Transnational Public Policy as an International Practice in Investment Arbitration' (2019) 10(3) *Journal of International Dispute Settlement* 496; Catherine Kessedjian, 'Transnational Public Policy' in Albert Jan van den Berg (ed.), *International Arbitration 2006: Back to Basics?*, ICCA Congress Series (Kluwer Law International, 2007) 857, 857–870; Pierre Lalive, 'Transnational (or Truly International) Public Policy and International Arbitration' in Pieter Sanders (ed.), *Comparative Arbitration Practice and Public Policy in Arbitration: ICCA International Arbitration Congress*, ICCA Congress Series No. 3 (Kluwer Law International, 1986) 257, 257–320.
136. *World Duty Free Co Ltd v. Kenya* (ICSID Arbitral Tribunal, Case No. ARB/00/7, 4 October 2006) [138]; Margaret L Moses, 'Chapter 11: Public Policy under the New York Convention: National, International, and Transnational' in Katia Fach Gomez and Ana M Lopez-Rodriguez (eds), *60 Years of the New York Convention: Key Issues and Future Challenges* (Kluwer Law International, 2019) 169, 173; Kessedjian (n. 135), 859–860.
137. *World Duty Free Co Ltd v. Kenya* (ICSID Arbitral Tribunal, Case No. ARB/00/7, 4 October 2006) [139]. For definitions of transnational public policy, *see* Marcoux (n. 135) 498; Paulsson, *The Idea of Arbitration* (n. 44) 208; Kessedjian (n. 135), 858–862; Michael Pryles, 'Reflections on Transnational Public Policy' (2007) 24(1) *Journal of International Arbitration* 1, 2 DOI: 10.54648/joia2007002.
138. Moses (n. 136) 182; George A Bermann, *International Arbitration and Private International Law* (Hague Academy of International Law, 2017) 331.
139. For more details, *see* §2.06[B], §2.06[C][2].

[2] Substantive and Procedural Public Policy

Courts in some jurisdictions, in both common law and civil law jurisdictions, hold that the public policy under Article V(2)(b) not only is limited to cases involving the substance of the award but also applies to procedural irregularities. If the arbitral procedure contains serious irregularities (e.g., fraud, bribery, the violation of res judicata, the violation of the right to be heard), the courts in Canada, UK and US may refuse to recognise or enforce the award based on the violation of Article V(2)(b).[140]

Also, the Swiss Federal Supreme Court held that a foreign award may be incompatible with the Swiss legal system not only because of its substance but also because of the procedure by which the award was made. In its words:

> There is a difference between *substantive* and *procedural public policy* [...] procedural public policy guarantees parties the right to an independent judgment on their submissions and the facts submitted to the arbitral tribunal, in accordance with the applicable procedural law; substantive public policy is breached when fundamental and generally recognised principles are breached, leading to an untenable contradiction with the notion of justice, so that the decision appears incompatible with the values recognised in a state governed by the rule of law.[141]

Further, it emphasised that Swiss public policy requires that the recognition and enforcement of foreign arbitral awards should comply with the fundamental procedural principles laid down in the Constitution, such as the right to a fair trial and the right to be heard.[142] German courts have taken a similar approach. For example, the Higher Regional Court of Thuringia held that 'public policy concerns, not only the decision, but also the proceeding that precedes that arbitral award'.[143] According to German law, public policy constitutes 'the basic principles of social and economic life' in Germany.[144] Accordingly, the procedural public policy encompasses the basic principles of German procedural law or the 'minimum standards of procedural justice'.[145]

The Report of the UNCITRAL Commission on the Model Law on International Commercial Arbitration also considers that the term 'public policy' used in the New

---

140. *See, e.g.*, Canada: *Karaha Bodas Company, LLC v. Perusahaan Pertambangan Minyak Dan Gas Bumi Negara and PT PLN (Persero)* [2007] ABQB 616 (24 October 2007); UK: *Gater Assets Ltd v. Nak Naftogaz Ukrainiy* [2008] EWHC 237 (15 February 2008); *Westacre Investments Inc v. Jugoimport-SPDR Holding Ltd & others* [2000] 1 QB 288; US: *Karaha Bodas Co v. Perusahaan Pertambangan Minyak Dan Gas Bumi Negara*, 364 F 3d 274 (5th Cir, 2004).
141. *X SpA v. Y Srl*, Federal Tribunal, Switzerland, 8 March 2006, Arrêts du Tribunal Fédéral (2006) 132 III 389, 392 (emphasis added).
142. Tribunal Fédéral [Federal Supreme Court of Switzerland, First Civil Law Chamber], 8 December 2003 reported in (2004) XXIX *Yearbook Commercial Arbitration* 834, 840 [13]; Tribunal Fédéral [Federal Supreme Court of Switzerland, First Civil Law Chamber], No. 4A 374/2014, 26 February 2015 reported in (2016) XLI *Yearbook Commercial Arbitration* 567, [8], [35].
143. Oberlandesgericht Thuringia [Higher Regional Court of Thuringia], 1 Sch 7/13, 20 November 2013 reported in (2015) XL *Yearbook Commercial Arbitration* 422, [27].
144. Oberlandesgericht Thuringia [Thuringia Court of Appeal], 4 Sch 04/03, 8 November 2004 reported in (2008) XXXIII *Yearbook Commercial Arbitration* 500, [7].
145. Oberlandesgericht Cologne [Cologne Court of Appeal], 9 Sch 01-03, 23 April 2004 reported in (2005) XXX *Yearbook Commercial Arbitration* 557, [5].

York Convention covers the fundamental principles of law and justice in substantive as well as procedural respects.[146] Thus, the New York Convention does not preclude certain grounds of procedural irregularity from being raised as public policy grounds under Article V(2)(b).[147] In cases where there has been a violation of procedural fairness in the arbitral procedure, the opposing party could invoke a breach of due process under Article V(1)(b) or Article V(2)(b) or both.[148] Both case law and scholarship in Germany and Switzerland have acknowledged that the distinction between these two grounds for challenge has little or no relevance in practice since in many cases the breach of due process also constitutes a breach of public policy under Article V(2)(b).[149]

[3] The Distinction Between Due Process and Procedural Public Policy

Others, however, highlighted the distinction between Article V(1)(b) and Article V(2)(b). Even though, to a large extent, the concept of due process under Article V(1)(b) defines procedural public policy, the two concepts are not identical. First, procedural public policy has functioned as a 'catch-all' provision, which is capable of addressing a diversity of fundamental procedural values. Procedural public policy includes not only the right to be heard and the equal treatment of parties as required by Article V(1)(b) but also res judicata, fraud, bribery, corruption, and other serious procedural irregularities.

Another notable difference between these two provisions is that Article V(2)(b) allows a claim to be examined by the court ex officio, whereas a claim under Article V(1)(b) can only be made by the party seeking to refuse the recognition or enforcement

146. Report of the United Nations Commission on International Trade Law on the Work of Its 18th Session, UN GAOR, 40th sess., Supp 17, UN Doc. A/40/17 (21 August 1985) [297].
147. *See, e.g.*, Hong Kong: *Hebei Import & Export Corp v. Polytek Engineering Co Ltd* [1999] 2 HKLRD 665, 691; Canada: *Louis Dreyfus SAS v. Holding Tusculum BV* [2008] QCCS 5903 (the court has found a violation of public policy where the tribunal had granted a remedy not requested by the parties and the court considered that the right to be heard has been breached); France: *Soc Excelsior Film TV v. Soc UGC-PH*, Court of Cassation, France, 24 March 1998 (the French Court of Cassation found a breach of procedural public policy where arbitrators had acted in a manner that breached the principles of independence and impartiality).
148. Germany: Oberlandesgericht Frankfurt [Court of Appeal Frankfurt], 26 SchH 03/09, 12 October 2009 reported in (2010) XXXV *Yearbook Commercial Arbitration* 377, [20]; Switzerland: Tribunal Fédéral [Federal Supreme Court of Switzerland, First Civil Law Chamber], No. 4A 374/2014, 26 February 2015 reported in (2016) XLI *Yearbook Commercial Arbitration* 567; Spain: Supreme Court of Spain, First Civil Law Chamber, No. 332 of 2000, 31 July 2000 reported in (2007) XXXII *Yearbook Commercial Arbitration* 532, 537 [15].
149. Oberlandesgericht Frankfurt [Court of Appeal Frankfurt], 26 SchH 03/09, 12 October 2009 reported in (2010) XXXV *Yearbook Commercial Arbitration* 377, [20]; Tribunal Fédéral [Federal Supreme Court of Switzerland], 12 January 1989, reported in (1990) XV *Yearbook Commercial Arbitration* 509; Andrea Bonomi and Elza Reymond-Eniaeva, 'Interpretation and Application of the New York Convention in Switzerland' in George A Bermann (ed.), *Recognition and Enforcement of Foreign Arbitral Awards – The Interpretation and Application of the New York Convention by National Courts* (Springer, 2017) 929; Elliott Geisinger, 'Implementing the New York Convention in Switzerland' (2008) 25(6) *Journal of International Arbitration* 691, 699 DOI: 10.54648/joia2008056; Solomon (n. 80) 355.

of an award.[150] This distinction, however, does not preclude parties from arguing that their procedural rights have been violated on public policy grounds.[151]

Also, some courts have generally adopted a more restrictive interpretation of the public policy defence and are unlikely to uphold it when other specific grounds in Article V of the New York Convention are satisfied. This conservative approach to public policy is reasonable, given that it involves the most basic values of morality and justice. Conversely, the due process defence is not subject to such a restrictive interpretation. In the well-known case of *Parsons*, the New York District Court held that the Convention's public policy defence should be construed narrowly and that the enforcement of foreign arbitral awards should be refused only 'where enforcement would violate the forum state's most basic notions of morality and justice'.[152] The Court of Appeal of England and Wales also held that the public policy defence 'should be approached with extreme caution'.[153]

Apropos of 'public policy', it is worth recalling the sceptical observation of an English Judge that 'it is never argued at all but when other points fail'.[154] This position is reflected in another Commonwealth case in which the Hong Kong High Court was reluctant to apply public policy to refuse enforcement of foreign arbitral awards despite a breach of due process. The court held that public policy was to be interpreted narrowly and refused to apply it in all occasions.[155] The court was of the view that the case in question was decided solely on the basis of the due process defence (the breach of the requirement of an opportunity to present a case), which was a sufficiently serious irregularity to justify refusal of enforcement, and did not involve public policy issues.[156] In Singapore, the Singapore High Court has made it clear that the threshold for the public policy grounds for setting aside or refusing recognition or enforcement is even higher than the grounds for the due process defence.[157] Similarly, the Highest Arbitrazh Court of the Russian Federation endorsed the practice of Russian lower courts that Article V(1)(b) constitutes an independent defence to recognition and enforcement and that, in view of its exceptional nature, there is no need to apply the public policy defence contained in Article V(2)(b).[158]

In the EU, the European Court of Justice (ECJ) has also confirmed that the public policy exception in the European instruments has a residual function: it applies only in

150. *Convention on the Recognition and Enforcement of Foreign Arbitral Awards*, open for signature 10 June 1958, 330 UNTS 3 (entered into force 7 June 1959) Arts V(1)-(2).
151. *See travaux préparatoires*, Report of the Committee on the Enforcement of International Arbitral Awards, E/AC42/4/Rev 1,10; Comments of the Representative of the Egyptian Government, Mr Osman: Summary Record of the Sixth Meeting, E/AC42/SR6, 4.
152. *Parsons & Whittemore Overseas Co v. Société Générale De L'Industrie Du Papier (RAKTA)*, 508 F 2d 969, 974 (2nd Cir, 1974).
153. *Deutsche Schachtbau-und Tiefbohrgesellschaft mbH v. Shell International Petroleum Co Ltd* [1990] 1 AC 295.
154. Peregrine Bingham, *Reports of Cases Argued and Determined in the Court of Common Pleas, and Other Courts: With Tables of the Cases and Principal Matters* (J Butterworth, 1825) 252.
155. *Paklito Investment Ltd v. Klockner East Asia Ltd* [1993] 2 HKLR 39, 50.
156. *Ibid.*
157. *ADG and another v. ADI and another matter* [2014] 3 SLR 481, [116].
158. Presidium of the Highest Arbitrazh Court, Russian Federation, Information Letter No. 156 of 26 February 2013.

cases where the other, more specific, grounds for refusal do not apply.[159] As discussed below in §2.06[B][2], §3.02, and §3.03, the notion of due process in the New York Convention may refer to Article 6(1) of the ECHR. The European Court of Human Rights (ECtHR) has considered that Article 6(1) is subject to *extensive* interpretation, as opposed to *restrictive* interpretation of public policy and has held:

> In a democratic society within the meaning of the Convention, the right to a fair administration of justice holds such a prominent place that a restrictive interpretation of Article 6 para 1 would not correspond to the aim and the purpose of that provision [...][160]

The underlying reason for the restrictive application and residual function of public policy is that states generally apply their own concept of public policy (including national public policy and international public policy) and restrict its application as they deem necessary. As shown above, the notion of transnational public policy in the context of Article V(2)(b) remains a largely academic rather than practical one. However, as discussed in Chapter 3, due process embodies procedural principles shared by states and constitutes a general principle of international law rather than pertaining only to the notion of public policy adopted by a particular state. This notion that due process draws on the general principle of law provides a common standard and reduces the possibility for states to adopt an excessively divergent national concept of public policy.

[D] Conclusion

Several courts adopting the *lex fori* approach treat serious procedural irregularities as violations of public policy. This indicates that enforcing states also have an interest in ensuring that their mandatory rules are observed as a matter of domestic public policy. However, a tribunal in an international arbitration cannot predict where a successful party might seek recognition or enforcement of the award and therefore cannot apply the standards of due process of each potential forum state. The application of the *lex fori* could jeopardise the legal certainty of parties and tribunals and make it more difficult for them to predict the effects of their actions on the arbitral proceedings. It is assumed that one of the obligations of arbitrators is to render an enforceable award.[161] Certain institutional arbitration rules provide that arbitrators should make every effort to render a 'legally enforceable' award.[162] In this sense, the *lex fori* approach will

159. *Hoffman v. Krieg* (European Court of Justice, C-145/86, ECLI:EU:C:1988:6).
160. *Delcourt v. Belgium* (European Court of Human Rights, Grand Chamber, Application No. 2689/65, 7 January 1970) [25].
161. Günther J Horvath, 'The Duty of the Tribunal to Render an Enforceable Award' (2001) 18(2) *Journal of International Arbitration* 135, 136 DOI: 10.54648/317806; William W Park, 'Arbitration in Autumn' (2011) 2(2) *Journal of International Dispute Settlement* 287, 292 DOI: 10.1093/jnlids/idr001; Born (n. 4) 1993.
162. For institutional arbitration rules providing that the arbitrators shall make every effort to make sure that the award is enforceable *'at law'*, *see ICC Arbitration Rules* (n. 29) Art. 42; *LCIA Arbitration Rules* (n. 29) Art. 32(2); *SCC Arbitration Rules* (n. 29) Art. 2(2); *SIAC Arbitration*

complicate the arbitrator's investigation of due process standards in each potential recognition or enforcement forum, which would make the arbitrator's task more burdensome and impractical.

In essence, the *lex fori* approach adopts the domestic concept of due process in the enforcing forum to interpret the due process defence under the international convention. However, the application to international conventions, such as the New York Convention, of domestic standards of due process that may be appropriate in setting aside proceedings results in State Parties perpetuating pre-existing state law rather than adapting it to the broader context of the international convention. Indeed, it is arguable that the state is adopting the substance of the Convention but failing to adapt domestic rules or approaches to due process in response to this international law. Admittedly, each state has the authority to regulate the standards of procedural fairness for arbitral awards sitting within its jurisdiction. The question is whether states should continue to adhere to their domestic concepts and constructs of the meaning and scope of due process, which are based on the sovereignty of states, even if those states have surrendered or shared some of their sovereignty as parties to the New York Convention.

Once a state has acceded to the New York Convention, as discussed below in §2.05 and §2.06, it is obliged to interpret and apply the Convention in accordance with the rules of interpretation contained in the Convention and not in accordance with the state's domestic rules of interpretation. Unlike the public policy defence, which expressly allows the enforcing state to use its own law to interpret the New York Convention, the due process defence does not explicitly refer to the rules and standards of due process in a particular national legal system. In this context, it is arguable that the law of the state where recognition or enforcement is sought could be directly applicable to the determination of the due process defence under the New York Convention, which is an international body of law endorsed by multiple states with divergent due process rules. As shown in §2.05 and §2.06 below, the transnational due process approach based on the VCLT may provide a more protective solution for predictability and more guarantees of fundamental procedural fairness than the domestic approach based on the concept of due process of the enforcing forum.

§2.04 THE UNIFORM TRANSNATIONAL APPROACH DERIVED FROM THE NEW YORK CONVENTION

Some scholars argue that the due process defence under the New York Convention should be interpreted as an autonomous and transnational due process independent of any individual State Party. The *lex arbitri* and *lex fori* approaches are grounded in national rules of interpretation. Accordingly, in both approaches, the contours of due process are defined by reference to some body of national law through their national choice-of-law rules, which will vary between states. In contrast, the uniform and

Rules (n. 29) Art. 41(2). For scholars who argue that the arbitrators have the duty to make an enforceable award, *see* Horvath (n. 161) 292; Park (n. 161) 292.

transnational approach that I argue for is based on an international interpretative framework for treaties, which helps to ensure consistency.

[A] Academic Scholars in Favour of the Uniform Transnational Approach

Some scholars have argued that Article V(1)(b) constitutes a truly transnational rule and should be interpreted according to the uniform standard derived directly from an autonomous interpretation of the New York Convention, that is, independently of the distinct features of a particular Member State's legal system.[163] Unlike the *lex arbitri* and *lex fori* approaches, this uniform transnational approach is mainly supported by academics, with few jurisdictions explicitly adopting it.[164]

In their eminent treatise, Fouchard, Gaillard and Goldman considered that Article V(1)(b) 'is expressed in terms of substantive rules, and not in choice of law terms...In fact, the New York Convention creates an international substantive rule and considers a breach of that rule to be sufficient in itself to warrant the refusal of recognition or enforcement'.[165] Similarly, Poudret and Besson highlighted that, unlike Article V(1)(a) and Article V(1)(d) with explicit choice-of-law rules, Article V(1)(b) contains standard and uniform requirements.[166]

Further, Scherer and Born argued that only the uniform transnational standards of due process derived directly from Article V(1)(b) are most consistent with the overall objectives of the New York Convention, which are to establish uniform standards to facilitate the recognition and enforcement of foreign arbitral awards and to prevent the application of parochial rules that would obstruct the recognition and enforcement.[167] Scherer argued that it would be burdensome for a tribunal to comply with the standards of due process established by all potential forums. She also argued that jurisdictions applying their own standards of due process sometimes have different views on the same issue arising under Article V(1)(b), which undermines certainty and predictability in the application of the Convention.[168]

This approach emphasises that the New York Convention defines the meaning of due process and that it is this definition that an enforcing court must take into account. This uniform, text-based approach ensures international consistency in the interpretation of the New York Convention. It encourages courts to refrain from relying on parochial definitions of due process that are confined by localised legal usage.

163. Emmanuel Gaillard and John Savage (eds), *Fouchard Gaillard Goldman on International Commercial Arbitration* (Kluwer Law International, 1999) 986; Poudret and Besson (n. 31) 835; Born (n. 4) 3504–3506; Scherer (n. 4) 285–286.
164. Nevertheless, case law in a few states, such as France, Sweden, and the UK, demonstrates that courts sometimes apply sources of law beyond their national law, including the rules of other international conventions (e.g., Article 6(1) of the European Convention of Human Rights), the UNCITRAL documents, decisions by foreign courts on the New York Convention, and commentary by foreign jurists: *see* §2.06[E].
165. Gaillard and Savage (eds) (n. 163) 986.
166. Poudret and Besson (n. 31) 835.
167. Scherer (n. 4) 286; Born (n. 4) 3505.
168. Scherer (n. 4) 286.

However, academics do not explain what this uniform transnational due process entails, or what sources courts can draw upon to interpret such transnational due process. Sections 2.05 and 2.06 below attempt to fill this gap by examining the rules of treaty interpretation, in particular the general principles of law and subsequent practice.

The leading commentator on the New York Convention, van den Berg, has suggested that the difference between the *lex fori* approach and the transnational approach may be merely a matter of academic taste without pragmatic impacts.[169] As discussed above, jurisdictions that adopt their own law to assess the due process exception generally consider the international element of arbitral awards and distinguish the due process standards under the New York Convention from the purely domestic standards. This judicial attitude would mitigate the potentially parochial standards of the *lex fori* approach and produce effects similar to those of the uniform transnational approach.[170]

However, as discussed in §2.04[B], §2.05 and §2.06, there is a marked difference in sources of law between the concept of uniform transnational due process and the domestic approach (either the law of the seat or the law of the enforcing forum). If the due process defence is determined by domestic law, then enforcing courts would use the sources of municipal law to interpret it. However, if the due process defence is understood as an international rule, the courts may look to sources of international law to decide.

[B] Domestic Rules of Interpretation Versus International Rules of Interpretation for the New York Convention

Both the *lex arbitri* and *lex fori* approaches use the domestic rules of interpretation of the forum state to interpret the meaning and scope of the due process defence under the New York Convention. The difference between them is that states, such as China, which adopt the *lex arbitri* approach, apply the law of the arbitral seat to interpret the notion of due process under the New York Convention in accordance with their domestic rules of interpretation. Conversely, states that adopt the *lex fori* approach use their own concepts to interpret the due process defence after consulting their domestic rules of interpretation.

Under domestic rules of interpretation, it is not uncommon for State Parties to apply national legal concepts and terminology to due process under the New York Convention, either under the law of the arbitral seat or the law of the enforcing forum, when determining whether the requirements of the due process defence under the Convention have been satisfied.

Even though the term 'due process' used in the New York Convention may be drawn from concepts applied in national legal systems, once it is included in the

169. van den Berg (n. 66) 298.
170. *Ibid.*

Convention, it assumes a single meaning that cannot be altered according to nation-related variations, unless the Convention states otherwise.[171] In principle, there can be only one true interpretation of a treaty provision. Enforcing courts should seek the true autonomous international meaning of the treaty. It follows that, as in the case of other multilateral treaties, the New York Convention should be given an independent meaning derivable from the sources mentioned in Articles 31 and 32 of the VCLT. It has been indicated that 'autonomous and international interpretation', free from any individual national legal culture, has a particular application to private law treaties:

> ...interpretation of a private law convention must proceed on the basis of its 'international character'. This directive serves a separating and elevating function. That is, it suggests an 'autonomous' interpretation free from the influence of national legal concepts and terminology, and even from the domestic interpretive techniques themselves. In doing so, this mandate amounts to an express direction to interpreters to view a convention as occupying an entirely different, elevated international dimension.[172]

In this sense, by applying international interpretative rules based on the VCLT, the concept of 'due process' in the New York Convention can be given an autonomous meaning separate from the distinct features of the legal system of any individual State Party.

§2.05 TREATY INTERPRETATION BY NATIONAL COURTS

International treaties have their own rules or principles of interpretation, which are mainly set out in Articles 31–33 of the VCLT.[173] As discussed below, the Vienna Convention's approach to interpretation is generally considered to be customary international law and therefore applies to all treaties and to all states in the world, unless the treaty in question contains its own rules on interpretation. Thus, the Vienna Convention's approach is applicable to the interpretation and application of the due process defence under the New York Convention. Unlike national rules of interpretation, the VCLT offers a good means of creating an autonomous meaning of due process under the New York Convention, free from the influence of national legal concepts and terminology. Nevertheless, since both the New York Convention and the VCLT will inevitably continue to be interpreted by domestic judges, it is necessary to discuss the interpretation of treaties by domestic courts and whether it is desirable to expect these courts to produce an autonomous interpretation of international legal instruments, divorced from domestic traditions of statutory interpretation.

171. Richard Gardiner, *Treaty Interpretation* (Oxford University Press, 2nd ed., 2015) 33.
172. Michael P Van Alstine, 'Dynamic Treaty Interpretation' (1998) 146(3) *University of Pennsylvania Journal Law Review* 687, 730–731. *See also* Maren Heidemann and Andreas Knebel, 'Double Taxation Treaties: The Autonomous Interpretation Method in German and English Law; as Demonstrated by the Case of the Silent Partnership' (2010) 38(3) *Intertax* 136.
173. Helmut Philipp Aust, 'Between Universal Aspiration and Local Application' in Helmut Philipp Aust and Georg Nolte (eds), *The Interpretation of International Law by Domestic Courts* (Oxford University Press, 2016) 336.

This section starts with an examination of the status and reception of the New York Convention by State Parties. It argues that although the Convention has been implemented by some State Parties, this does not change the international origin of the implemented statutes. Accordingly, national courts should apply the rules of interpretation specific to treaties when interpreting Article V(1)(b) of the Convention or implemented legislation. Given that Articles 31–33 of the VCLT constitute the usual and generally accepted method of treaty interpretation by states and are considered to be customary international law, this section considers the Vienna Convention Rules to explore the meaning of, and the law applicable to, the due process defence prescribed in Article V(1)(b) of the New York Convention.

[A] The Status and Reception of the New York Convention by State Parties

[1] Monism and Dualism

Differences between countries in terms of the relationship between international law and domestic legal systems may have an impact on the status and reception of the New York Convention by State Parties and on the interpretation and application of the due process defence and should therefore be examined at the outset. The different relationships between international and domestic law are often explained in terms of the distinction between monism and dualism.

There is no consensus on the definition of 'monism' and 'dualism'. Some scholars use the terms to describe contrasting perspectives on the relationship between international and domestic law.[174] Other scholars use the terms to describe different types of domestic legal systems,[175] as used in this chapter. In this sense, dualist states are states in which 'the constitution...accords no special status to treaties; the rights and obligations created by them have no effect in domestic law unless legislation is in force to give effect to them'.[176] In other words, dualist countries generally require a treaty to be incorporated into domestic law before it enters into force, and courts have no authority to apply treaties directly as law.[177] In these dualist states, the domestic implementing provision, analogous to Article V(1)(b) of the New York Convention, is subject to interpretation by domestic judges, and the laws interpreted by the courts are domestic laws. As a result, domestic judges are more prone to statutory interpretation

174. James Crawford (ed.), *Brownlie's Principles of Public International Law* (Oxford University Press, 8th ed., 2012) 48–50 (used in this sense, dualism 'emphasises the distinct and independent character of the international and national legal systems', while monism 'postulates that national and international law form one single legal order, or at least a number of interlocking orders which should be presumed to be coherent and consistent').
175. Anthony Aust, *Modern Treaty Law and Practice* (Cambridge University Press, 3rd ed., 2013) 159–177.
176. *Ibid.*, 167.
177. David L Sloss, 'Domestic Application of Treaties' in Duncan B Hollis (ed.), *The Oxford Guide to Treaties* (Oxford University Press, 2nd ed., 2020) 358.

using domestic rules of interpretation to interpret and apply the implementing provision of the due process defence.

In contrast, monist countries consider that a treaty can be directly applied without domestic implementation once it has been concluded in accordance with the Constitution and has entered into force for the state.[178] In this case, it is the treaty rather than domestic law that is interpreted by domestic courts. Accordingly, it is more likely that judges in monist countries will interpret Article V(1)(b) in accordance with the international rules of interpretation found in the VCLT and thus construe the meaning and scope of due process independently of their domestic notions.[179]

However, the monism-dualism divide has fundamental limitations as a means of explaining the full relationship between international law (e.g., treaties and customary international law) and domestic legal orders (e.g., constitution, statutes and common law). The reality in many states is not nearly as dichotomous, and many countries 'contain both dualist and monist elements'.[180] First, monist states often distinguish between treaties that are directly applicable as law (self-executing) and treaties that are indirectly applicable (non-self-executing).[181] Most monist states give their courts some discretion in determining whether a treaty is self-executing.[182] In the United States, for instance, when a court decides that a treaty is not self-executing, it sometimes acts as if the treaty has not been incorporated into domestic law, even though the Constitution expressly states that 'all treaties' are 'the supreme Law of the Land'.[183] This distinction between self-executing and non-self-executing treaties in monist states has blurred the traditional monist and dualist divide. It is therefore necessary to examine the position of domestic judges who consider the New York Convention to be non-self-executing in order to determine whether they tend to implement the international or the domestic rules of interpretation. Second, a state's relationship with treaties may diverge from customary international law. According to Verdier and Versteeg's research, more than eighty percent of dualist states apply customary international law directly, as opposed to their approach to treaties.[184] It appears that these dualist states apply customary international law in the same way as monist states. As discussed in more detail below, the VCLT is deemed to be customary international law and should therefore be applied by all parties to the New York Convention. There should not be much divergence between dualist and monist states in applying the VCLT to the interpretation of the New York Convention.

178. Aust (n. 175) 163.
179. For different positions on interpretative rules found in the VCLT between monist countries and dualist countries, *see* Chang-fa Lo, *Treaty Interpretation under the Vienna Convention on the Law of Treaties: A New Round of Codification* (Springer, 2017) 133.
180. Aust (n. 175) 162.
181. Sloss (n. 177) 363–364, 373–375; Pierre-Hugues Verdier and Mila Versteeg, 'International Law in National Legal Systems: An Empirical Investigation' (2015) 109(3) *American Journal of International Law* 514, 522 DOI: 10.5305/amerjintelaw.109.3.0514.
182. Sloss (n. 177) 373; Verdier and Versteeg (n. 181) 522.
183. David Sloss, 'United States' in David Sloss (ed.), *The Role of Domestic Courts in Treaty Enforcement: A Comparative Study* (Cambridge University Press, 2009) 509–514, 527–529, 534–539.
184. Verdier and Versteeg (n. 181) 529–530.

[2] Implementation or Self-Execution of the Convention

Given the limitations of the monist-dualist dichotomy, this part examines how the New York Convention has been received by State Parties to determine whether it has been implemented in legislation or whether it has been deemed to be self-executing. According to Bermann's 2017 comparative study, only a minority of jurisdictions, such as China,[185] consider the New York Convention to be self-executing and therefore apply it directly and without legislative implementation.[186] As a result, most countries have incorporated the Convention by means of statutes that either reproduce the text of the Convention as such (e.g., Sweden, the United Kingdom, Singapore, Australia, Hong Kong and France)[187] or refer to the Convention for the recognition and enforcement of foreign arbitral awards (e.g., Germany, Switzerland and the United States).[188]

The way in which treaties are given effect in domestic law can play a significant role in shaping the approach of courts to treaty interpretation. Both those jurisdictions that regard the New York Convention as being self-executing and those that merely refer to it in domestic law when recognising or enforcing awards focus on interpreting the text of the New York Convention itself.[189] These jurisdictions may be more receptive to the applicability of international rules of interpretation found in the VCLT with respect to the meaning of the due process defence under the Convention. The situation is complicated in jurisdictions that have reproduced or rephrased the text of the New York Convention in their domestic law.[190] In these jurisdictions, the New York

185. 《中华人民共和国民事诉讼法》 [Civil Procedure Law of the People's Republic of China] Standing Committee of the National People's Congress, Order of the President of the People's Republic of China No. 71, promulgated on 27 June 2017, effective on 1 July 2017, Art. 260.
186. George A Bermann, 'Recognition and Enforcement of Foreign Arbitral Awards: The Interpretation and Application of the New York Convention by National Courts' in George A Bermann (ed.), *Recognition and Enforcement of Foreign Arbitral Awards – The Interpretation and Application of the New York Convention by National Courts* (Springer, 2017) 7.
187. Sweden: *Swedish Arbitration Act* (Sweden) SFS No. 1996:116 ss 54–60 [Joel Dahlquist Cullborg trans, The Swedish Arbitration Act (2019), https://sccarbitrationinstitute.se/sites/default/files/2022-11/the-swedish-arbitration-act_1march2019_eng-2.pdf]; the UK: *Arbitration Act 1996* (UK) c 23, ss 100–104; Singapore: *International Arbitration Act* (Singapore, cap 143 A, 2002 rev ed) ss 27–33; Australia: *International Arbitration Act (No 136) 1974* (Cth) ss 3–14; Hong Kong: *Arbitration Ordinance* (Hong Kong) cap 609, ss 87–91; France: *Code de procédure civile* [Code of Civil Procedure] (France) 13 January 2011, Art. 1525 [Emmanuel Gaillard et al., Code of Civil Procedure, http://parisarbitration.com/wp-content/uploads/2017/02/EN-French-Law-on-Arbitration.pdf].
188. Germany: *Zivilprozessordnung* [Code of Civil Procedure](Germany) § 1030 (1); Switzerland: *Federal Act on Private International Law* (Switzerland), 1 January 1989, Art. 194 [Andreas Bucher trans, *The English translations of Federal Act on Private International Law*, http://www.andreasbucher-law.ch/images/stories/pil_act_1987_as_from_1st_july_2022.pdf]; the US: 9 USC §§ 201–208 (1970).
189. China: *see* above nn. 11–15; Germany: *see* above n. 59; the US: *see* above n. 63.
190. *See, e.g.*, the UK: *see* above n. 64; Hong Kong: *see* above n. 65; Singapore: *Newspeed International Limited v. Citus Trading Pte Ltd* [2001] SGHC 126; Sweden: *Lenmorniiproekt OAO v. Arne Larsson & Partner Leasing Aktiebolag*, Högsta Domstolens [Supreme Court], Ö 13-09, 16 April 2010 reported in (2010) XXXV *Yearbook Commercial Arbitration* 456 [3]; Australia: *Uganda Telecom Limited v. Hi-Tech Telecom Pty Ltd* [2011] FCA 131 (22 February 2011); France: Cour d'appel de Paris [Paris Court of Appeal], 27 November 1987 reported in (1989) *Revue de l'Arbitrage* 62.

Convention, including Article V(1)(b), is applied indirectly rather than directly.[191] As Professor Bermann rightly observed, 'it is that implementing legislation – not the text of the Convention – that will be given direct application by national courts'.[192] In such circumstances, domestic judges are more likely to use their domestic rules of interpretation to determine the meaning and scope of the due process defence.

However, the difference between the direct and indirect application of the New York Convention should not be exaggerated. International rights and obligations arising from treaties are still to be applied as *international* rather than domestic law, even after they have been incorporated into domestic law.[193] Implementing legislation must therefore be interpreted in the light of the Convention and cannot be construed as purely domestic law.

There has been some movement towards interpreting treaties as treaties rather than statutes. Some states prefer to give the incorporating statute the same meaning as the treaty that it incorporates, and frequently consult the underlying treaty to help construe the meaning of the implementing statute.[194] In almost all British Commonwealth jurisdictions, treaties, including the New York Convention, have no formal legal status in the domestic legal system unless the legislature enacts a statute incorporating the treaty into domestic law.[195] For example, the English courts have relaxed some of the English rules of statutory interpretation where the statute gives effect to an international convention.[196] They have interpreted the implementing statute in a normal manner appropriate to the interpretation of an international convention, unconstrained by technical rules of English law or by English case law, but based on broad principles of general acceptation.[197] Although their application remains inconsistent and sometimes piecemeal, some progress is being made towards a more direct application of the VCLT as a substitute for the previous mixture of domestic precedents and the intermittent selection of rules.[198]

191. Bermann (n. 186) 7; Michael Waibel, 'Principles of Treaty Interpretation Developed for and Applied by National Courts?' in Helmut Philipp Aust and Georg Nolte (eds), *The Interpretation of International Law by Domestic Courts* (Oxford University Press, 2016) 20.
192. Bermann (n. 186) 7.
193. Hersch Lauterpacht, 'Decisions of Municipal Courts as a Source of International Law' (1929) 10 *British Yearbook of International Law* 65, 76–77; Francis Geoffrey Jacobs, 'Introduction' in Francis Geoffrey Jacobs and Shelley Roberts (eds), *The Effects of Treaties in Domestic Law* (Sweet & Maxwell, 1987) xxix.
194. Sloss (n. 177) 358; Mathias Forteau, 'The Role of the International Rules of Interpretation for the Determination of Direct Effect of International Agreements' in Helmut Philipp Aust and Georg Nolte (ed.), *The Interpretation of International Law by Domestic Courts* (Oxford University Press, 2016) 109.
195. Aust (n. 175) 194–195.
196. For a detailed account of the English case law on interpretation of treaties, *see* Shaheed Fatima QC, *Using International Law in Domestic Courts* (Hart Publishing, 2005).
197. *Stag Line Ltd v. Foscolo, Mango & Co Ltd* [1932] AC 328, 350; *Ulster-Swift Ltd v. Taunton Meat Haulage Ltd* [1977] 1 WLR 625, 628; *Fothergill v. Monarch Airlines Ltd* [1981] AC 251, 282, 293; *Owners of Cargo on Board the Morviken v. Owners of the Hollandia* [1983] 1 AC 565, 572.
198. *Adams v. Secretary of State for Justice* [2011] UKSC 18; *R (ST) v. Secretary of State for the Home Department* [2012] UKSC 12 (21 March 2012).

In relation to the New York Convention, courts in the UK and Australia have held that the incorporating statute must be interpreted in the light of the Convention.[199] For instance, in *Hiscox v. Outhwaite*, which concerned the interpretation of where an arbitral award was 'made' under the New York Convention, the judge at first instance interpreted the issue by explicitly referring to the Vienna Rules.[200]

In other words, even states that require the New York Convention to be incorporated into a statute before it comes into force are still under an international obligation to give the due process defence the same meaning as that under the New York Convention when implementing the statute. Whether a State Party requires domestic implementation or considers the Convention to be self-executing should not affect the meaning of the due process defence. The issue is to decide which rules of interpretation – international or domestic – are preferable as a means of arriving at the true meaning of Article V(1)(b).

[B] Rules of Treaty Interpretation: Domestic or International?

At the outset, it is necessary to discuss whether domestic courts can be independent actors in the application of treaties. The role of domestic courts in the application of treaties varies greatly depending on the nature of the treaty. Generally, states enter into treaties to regulate three different types of relations: 'horizontal relations between and among states, vertical relations between states and private actors, and transnational relations between private actors who interact across national boundaries'.[201] With respect to treaty provisions, such as those in the New York Convention, that regulate transnational relations between private actors, the judiciary plays a central role in ensuring compliance with treaty provisions, and the executive is marginalised.[202] Accordingly, domestic courts are the primary decision-makers whose rulings determine whether the nation complies with its treaty obligations.

The sources of rules of treaty interpretation binding on national courts may be either domestic or international.[203] The international rules on treaty interpretation are contained in the VCLT[204] and can be applied by international courts and tribunals as

199. *Uganda Telecom Limited v. Hi-Tech Telecom Pty Ltd* [2011] FCA 131 (22 February 2011) [21]; Collins and Harris (n. 31) 15–16.
200. *Hiscox v. Outhwaite* [1992] 1 AC 562.
201. Sloss (n. 177) 364.
202. *Ibid.*, 375–377.
203. André Nollkaemper, 'Grounds for the Application of International Rules of Interpretation in National Courts' in Helmut Philipp Aust and Georg Nolte (eds), *The Interpretation of International Law by Domestic Courts* (Oxford University Press, 2016) 34–48. This book does not distinguish between the terms 'rules of interpretation' and 'principles of interpretation' and uses both terms as synonymous throughout the book.
204. *Vienna Convention on the Law of Treaties*, opened for signature 23 May 1969, 1155 UNTS 331 (entered into force 27 January 1980). Regarding whether the Vienna Rules are 'rules', *see* Gardiner, *Treaty Interpretation* (n. 171) 38–41 (stating that practice in the application of Articles 31–3 of the VCLT indicates that courts and tribunals habitually refer to these provisions as 'rules' while often applying them more as 'principles').

well as national courts.[205] In Gardiner's words, '[i]n interpretation of treaties, the Vienna Rules are the "proper law", to borrow a term from private international law'.[206] Notwithstanding the fact that some states may apply national rules of interpretation to construe the meaning of the due process defence, this book examines the concept of the due process defence under the Convention by relying on international rules of treaty interpretation, namely, the VCLT. It does so on the basis that such rules of interpretation are widely regarded as customary international law for treaty interpretation and should be applied to all parties to the New York Convention.[207] Also, the adoption of international interpretative rules is consistent with the international scope of the New York Convention and contributes to its uniform interpretation and application.

[1] The International Quality of the New York Convention

The international quality of the obligations under the New York Convention requires national courts to apply international rather than domestic rules of interpretation.[208] Only where the New York Convention makes explicit or implicit reference to domestic law may national courts apply domestic rules of interpretation, which is not the case for the due process defence. This is because the rules of international law should be interpreted in the same way as they are interpreted in the international legal system that created them.[209] '[I]t is a major premise of treaty interpretation that there is no reason for different application of the [international] rules within a national legal system from their application in an international setting.'[210] The VCLT was designed specifically for the interpretation of international treaties, in contrast to national rules of interpretation which focus mainly on domestic statutes. National rules for the interpretation of statutes may not be appropriate for the interpretation of treaties because international conventions are drafted in a very different way from domestic

205. For a detailed discussion of the applicability of Vienna Convention by international courts and tribunals and national courts, *see* Gardiner, *Treaty Interpretation* (n. 171) 123–158; Waibel (n. 191) 13 (stating that even in the absence of the explicit consideration of national courts as a central audience of the VCLT's interpretative provisions, national courts were at least implicitly a potential audience. During the drafting of VCLT, International Law Commission consulted the interpretative practice of national courts).
206. Gardiner, *Treaty Interpretation* (n. 171) 142.
207. Richard Gardiner, 'The Vienna Convention Rules on Treaty Interpretation' in Duncan B Hollis (ed.), *The Oxford Guide to Treaties* (Oxford University Press, 2nd ed., 2020) 459, 460.
208. Friedrich Rosenfeld, Dietmar Czernich and Franco Ferrari, 'General Report' in Friedrich Rosenfeld, Dietmar Czernich and Franco Ferrari (eds), *Due Process as a Limit to Discretion in International Commercial Arbitration* (Kluwer Law International, 2020) 6.
209. *See* International Law Commission, Conclusions of the Work of the Study Group on the Fragmentation of International Law: Difficulties Arising from the Diversification and Expansion of International Law, UN Doc. A/61/10 (2006) 407 (stating that '[i]nternational law is a legal system. Its rules and principles (*i.e.*, its norms) act in relation to and should be interpreted against the background of other rules and principles. As a legal system, international law is not a random collection of such norms. There are meaningful relationships between them. Norms may thus exist at higher and lower hierarchical levels, [and] their formulation may involve greater or lesser generality and specificity and their validity may date back to earlier or later moments in time').
210. Gardiner, *Treaty Interpretation* (n. 171) 125.

statutes. Awareness of the peculiarities of the interpretation of international treaties might also prevent national judges from applying parochial constructions of international rules.

[2] Uniform Interpretation of the New York Convention

As noted above, the purpose of the New York Convention is to provide common legislative standards both for the recognition of arbitration agreements and for the judicial recognition and enforcement of foreign and non-domestic arbitral awards.[211] If uniform interpretation fails, then one of the main goals of the New York Convention – the establishment of common rules – will be jeopardised.[212] It is therefore very important that the interpretation of the New York Convention should, as far as possible, be uniform in the applicable laws of all State Parties.[213] The uniform interpretation of the New York Convention can facilitate enforcement by providing predictable enforcement results and reducing enforcement 'shopping'.[214] Accordingly, State Parties should ensure that their national courts promote uniformity as an important interpretative objective in order to maintain consistency and predictability in the application of the New York Convention.[215] This objective has been confirmed by several national courts. For instance, in a case involving the interpretation of the New York Convention, an Iranian court held that account must be taken of its international character and of the need to promote uniformity in its application and the observance of good faith in international trade.[216]

The best way for courts to achieve this legal unification objective of the New York Convention is to commit themselves to following the uniform rules of interpretation set out in the VCLT.[217] A single set of international rules on treaty interpretation could provide consistent methods of interpretation and a common interpretative ground,[218] which could facilitate the uniform interpretation of the due process defence by different judges. This is in contrast to the adoption of national rules of interpretation, which may vary from one jurisdiction to another and lead to different interpretations of the due process defence under the New York Convention.

---

211. For the objectives of the New York Convention, *see* UNCITRAL's website, https://uncitral.un.org/en/texts/arbitration/conventions/foreign_arbitral_awards.
212. Andrea Bonomi, 'Chapter 13: The Concept of Public Policy under the 1958 New York Convention: An Autonomous Interpretation?' in Franco Ferrari and Friedrich Jakob Rosenfeld (eds), *Autonomous Versus Domestic Concepts under the New York Convention* (Kluwer Law International, 2021) 315, 325.
213. Collins and Harris (n. 31) 15; Nollkaemper (n. 203) 41.
214. Filip JM De Ly, 'Chapter 2: Uniform Interpretation: What Is Being Done?' in Franco Ferrari and Friedrich Jakob Rosenfeld (eds), *Autonomous Versus Domestic Concepts under the New York Convention* (Kluwer Law International, 2021) 13, 15.
215. Frederic Bachand, 'Court Intervention in International Arbitration: The Case for Compulsory Judicial Internationalism Symposium' (2012) 2012(1) *Journal of Dispute Resolution* 83, 95.
216. Farshad Rahimi Dizgovin, 'Enforcement of International Treaties by Domestic Courts of Iran: New Developments' (2018) 58(1) *Virginia Journal of International Law* 227, 252.
217. Bachand (n. 215) 95.
218. Lo (n. 179) 35–36.

[3] Performance of International Obligations from Customary International Law

The application of the VCLT by national courts is intrinsic to the fulfilment of international obligations.[219] At the time of writing, there are 116 parties to the VCLT.[220] States that are parties to both the VCLT and the New York Convention are obliged to apply the international principles of treaty interpretation set out in the VCLT when construing the meaning of the New York Convention, even though the breach of such obligations would not give rise to the international responsibility.[221] Article 26 of the VCLT, concerning the binding force of agreement treaties (*pacta sunt servanda*), provides that '[e]very treaty in force is binding upon the parties to it and must be performed by them in good faith'[222] – including the VCLT itself.

In drafting Articles 31–33 of the VCLT, the ILC sought to codify the comparatively few general principles which appear to constitute the general rules governing the interpretation of treaties.[223] It is well established that the provisions for the interpretation of treaties contained in Articles 31–32 of the VCLT reflect pre-existing customary international law and apply to all states, regardless of whether or not they are parties to the VCLT.[224] As the ICJ has stated:

219. Nollkaemper (n. 203) 37.
220. The status of the VCLT is available at https://treaties.un.org/pages/ViewDetailsIII.aspx?src=TREATY&mtdsg_no=XXIII-1&chapter=23&Temp=mtdsg3&clang=_en (last visited on 15 July 2023).
221. Waibel (n. 191) 21; Nollkaemper (n. 203) 37 (stating that the performance of the VCLT is an obligation that does not belong to the category of obligations breached, which will lead to international responsibility). Also, as discussed before, for the dualist states, they deem that they are not obliged to treaties until the implementation of treaties into domestic law.
222. *Vienna Convention on the Law of Treaties*, opened for signature 23 May 1969, 1155 UNTS 331 (entered into force 27 January 1980) Art. 26.
223. 'Reports of the International Law Commission on the Second Part of Its Seventeenth Session and on Its Eighteenth Session' (1966) 2 *Yearbook of the International Law Commission* 169, 218–219.
224. Arbitral Award of 31 July 1989 (*Guinea-Bissau v. Senegal*) (Judgment) [1991] ICJ Rep 53, 70 [48]; Appellate Body Report, *European Communities – Customs Classification of Frozen Boneless Chicken Cuts*, WTO Doc. WT/DS269/AB/R, WT/DS286/AB/R, WT/DS269/AB/R/Corr.1, WT/DS286/AB/R/Corr.1 (27 September 2005) [176] (confirming the status of Art. 31 of the VCLT as rules of customary international law); Appellate Body Report, *Japan–Taxes on Alcoholic Beverages*, WTO Doc. WT/DS8/AB/R, WT/DS10/AB/R, WT/DS11/AB/R (1 November 1996) [10] (confirming the status of Arts 31(1) & 32 of the VCLT as rules of customary international law); Appellate Body Report, *United States – Countervailing Duties on Certain Corrosion-Resistant Carbon Steel Flat Products from Germany*, WTO Doc. WT/DS213/AB/R, WT/DS213/AB/R/Corr.1 (19 December 2002) [61] (confirming the status of Articles 31 & 32 of the VCLT as rules of customary international law); Appellate Body Report, *United States – Final Countervailing Duty Determination with Respect to Certain Softwood Lumber from Canada*, WTO Doc. WT/DS257/AB/R (17 February 2004) [59] (confirming the status of Article 33 of the VCLT as rules of customary international law). For commentaries in favour of this position, *see* Gardiner, 'The Vienna Convention Rules on Treaty Interpretation' (n. 207) 477; 'Draft Conclusion on Subsequent Agreements and Subsequent Practice in Relation to the Interpretation of Treaties' (2018) 2 *Yearbook of the International Law Commission*, Part Two, Conclusion 2(1); Gardiner, *Treaty Interpretation* (n. 171) 14–20; Waibel (n. 191) 9; Yves le Bouthillier, 'Commentary on Article 32 of the Vienna Convention' in Olivier Corten and Pierre Klein (eds), *The Vienna Conventions on the Law of Treaties: A Commentary* (Oxford University Press, 2011)

> It is now well established that the provisions on interpretation of treaties contained in Articles 31 and 32 of the Convention reflect *pre-existing customary international law*, and thus may be (unless there are particular indications to the contrary) applied to *treaties concluded before* the entering into force of the 1969 [VCLT] in 1980. The International Court of Justice has applied customary rules of interpretation, now reflected in Articles 31 and 32 of the 1969 [VCLT], to a treaty concluded in 1955 ... and to a treaty concluded in 1890, bearing on rights of States that even on the day of Judgment were still *not parties to* the 1969 [VCLT] ... There is no case after the adoption of the [1969 VCLT] in which the International Court of Justice or any other leading tribunal has failed so to act.[225]

Since the rules of interpretation set out in Articles 31–32 of the VCLT are rules of customary international law that bind all states in the interpretation of treaties, they apply to treaties, such as the New York Convention, which were concluded before the VCLT entered into force.[226]

[4] Consideration of National Rules for Treaty Interpretation under the Internationalist Approach

The application of the VCLT to the interpretation of the New York Convention does not exclude the application of national rules of interpretation, provided that they do not conflict with the Vienna Rules. The line between the international and national rules of interpretation may be blurred to some extent where the national rules reflect the international rules. It is generally accepted that the customary international law is derived from the practice and *opinio juris* of states.[227] Also, the principles laid down in the VCLT were inspired by the interpretative practice of national courts. In particular, the ILC based its discussion of treaty interpretation on the reports of interpretative practice within international courts, international tribunals, and national courts.[228] Thus, it is not very different for national courts to apply the rules of the VCLT directly when their domestic rules of interpretation reflect international rules.

Nor is the application of the rules of treaty interpretation an end in itself. It is a means to another end: to establish and apply the correct meaning of due process under the New York Convention. '[T]he obligation to apply international rules of treaty interpretation is an obligation of result.'[229] Accordingly, a state will not be in breach of its obligations under international law as long as it correctly interprets and applies the

---

841, 843–846; Campbell Mclachlan, 'The Principle of Systemic Integration and Article 31(3)(c) of the Vienna Convention' (2005) 54(2) *International and Comparative Law Quarterly* 279, 293 DOI: 10.1093/iclq/lei001.

225. Arbitration regarding the *Iron Rhine ('Ijzeren Rijn') Railway (Belgium v. Netherlands)* (Award) (2005) XXVII *RIAA* 35, 62 [45] (emphasis added).
226. Lo (n. 179) 33; Gardiner, *Treaty Interpretation* (n. 171) 7. *See also Ben Nevis (Holdings) Ltd v. Revenue and Customs Commissioners* [2013] EWCA Civ 578 (23 May 2013) [17].
227. Alain Pellet and Daniel Müller, 'Article 38' in Andreas Zimmermann (ed.), *The Statute of the International Court of Justice: A Commentary* (Oxford University Press, 3rd ed., 2019) 904.
228. Waibel (n. 191) 13.
229. Nollkaemper (n. 203) 39.

treaty.[230] In this respect, there is nothing necessarily wrong with applying national rules in interpreting the New York Convention, as long as the outcome of interpretation is consistent with the state's treaty obligations.

It is acknowledged that, for the time being, national courts are likely to be more familiar with the means of interpreting the New York Convention under their domestic law than they are with the VCLT, given their limited experience in treaty interpretation. As discussed above, under domestic rules of interpretation, State Parties apply the law of the arbitral seat or the law of the enforcing forum to determine the due process defence. Neither the *lex arbitri* nor the *lex fori* approaches go beyond the limits of traditional choice-of-law rules; they are still required to find an 'appropriate national law' for the due process defence. National laws, whether the law of the seat of arbitration or the law of the enforcing forum, may have different notions of due process from one state to another, which is not appropriate for the interpretation and application of a treaty provision. However, by applying the international rules of interpretation embodied in the VCLT, as shown in Chapters 3 to 7, they are more likely to arrive at the intended true meaning of due process under international law and, in particular, under the New York Convention, and to reach a consensus on uniform interpretations based on the general principle of due process and the subsequent practice of State Parties.

§2.06 THE INTERPRETATION OF THE DUE PROCESS DEFENCE UNDER THE VCLT

In Article 31 (entitled 'General Rule of Interpretation'), Article 32 (entitled 'Supplementary Means of Interpretation'), and Article 33 (entitled 'Interpretation of Treaties Authenticated in Two or More Languages'), the VCLT provides rules for the interpretation of treaties.[231] The role of the Vienna Rules is to provide a loose framework from which the elements relevant to a particular case need to be selected.[232] It is not the intention in this section to review all the elements of the above Articles; rather, only those elements relevant to the interpretation of Article V(1)(b) of the New York Convention will be examined. As there are no significant differences in the meaning of the due process defence in all authentic texts in English, French, Chinese, Russian, and Spanish, Article 33 of the VCLT and its implications will not be analysed in this section.[233] In the absence of an agreement among all State Parties or an instrument made by one or more parties in connection with the conclusion of the New York Convention concerning Article V(1)(b), this section will not analyse Article 31(2) of the

230. Waibel (n. 191) 22.
231. *Vienna Convention on the Law of Treaties*, opened for signature 23 May 1969, 1155 UNTS 331 (entered into force 27 January 1980) Arts 31–33.
232. Gardiner, *Treaty Interpretation* (n. 171) 56.
233. The English, French, Chinese, Russian, and Spanish texts of the New York Convention have been decided to be equally authentic: *see Convention on the Recognition and Enforcement of Foreign Arbitral Awards*, open for signature 10 June 1958, 330 UNTS 3 (entered into force 7 June 1959) Art. XVI(1). The certified true copy of the New York Convention is available at, https://treaties.un.org/doc/Treaties/1959/06/19590607%2009-35%20PM/Ch_XXII_01p.pdf.

VCLT and its application in the New York Convention.[234] Accordingly, this section examines the general rules of interpretation (Articles 31(1) and 31(3)) and the supplementary means of interpretation (Article 32) under the VCLT.

[A] The General Rule of Interpretation: Article 31(1) of the VCLT

It should be noted that Article 31, as a whole, forms the 'general rule of interpretation'.[235] Thus, both Article 31(1) and Article 31(3), which are explicated in §2.06[A][1] and §2.06[A][2] below, are part of provisions that constitute a single general rule.

Article 31(1) of the VCLT provides that:

> A treaty should be interpreted in good faith in accordance with the ordinary meaning to be given to the terms of the treaty in their context and in the light of its object and purpose.[236]

The VCLT's crucible rule in Article 31(1) has four elements: (1) good faith; (2) ordinary meaning; (3) context; and (4) object and purpose. Article 31(1) is silent as to the weight that interpreters should give to each element, except that the ILC has envisaged the weight of these four elements as 'a single combined operation'.[237] Although these elements can only be considered one at a time, they must be evaluated together.[238] Consideration of the elements does not follow a hierarchical sequence, but is a crucible and recursive process that requires weighing the elements and allowing them to work together.[239] As the ILC's Commentary states, 'all the various elements, as they were present in any given case, would be thrown into the *crucible*, and their *interaction* would give the legally relevant interpretation'.[240]

While the application of the Vienna Rules is mandatory in the interpretation of treaties, the manner in which they are applied is intended to serve as appropriate principles and guidelines. The Vienna Rules provide a loose framework from which the elements relevant to a particular case need to be selected, but the application of these elements requires evaluation and balancing in particular circumstances. This evaluation and balancing is a core element of judgment that no rules can fully capture.[241] As one of the Special Rapporteurs of the ILC's preparatory work for the VCLT stated, '[i]n a sense all "rules" of interpretation have the character of "guidelines" since their

234. The reservations, declarations and notifications of State Parties regarding the New York Convention are available at, https://uncitral.un.org/en/texts/arbitration/conventions/foreign_arbitral_awards/status2. For general commentaries on Article 31(2) of the VCLT, *see* Gardiner, *Treaty Interpretation* (n. 171) 240–242.
235. *See* the title of Article 31 of the VCLT.
236. *Vienna Convention on the Law of Treaties*, opened for signature 23 May 1969, 1155 UNTS 331 (entered into force 27 January 1980) Art. 31(1).
237. 'Reports of the International Law Commission' (n. 223) 219–220.
238. Gardiner, *Treaty Interpretation* (n. 171) 32.
239. Julian Davis Mortenson, 'Is the Vienna Convention Hostile to Drafting History' (2013) 107(4) *American Journal of Comparative Law* 780, 781 DOI: 10.5305/amerjintelaw.107.4.0780; Gardiner, *Treaty Interpretation* (n. 171) 39.
240. 'Reports of the International Law Commission' (n. 223) 219–220 (emphasis added).
241. Gardiner, *Treaty Interpretation* (n. 171) 56.

application in a particular case depends so much on the appreciation of the context and the circumstances of the point to be interpreted'.[242]

[1] Good Faith

Although it is difficult to give a precise definition of the concept of good faith, it does include the principle of 'effectiveness'.[243] One meaning of the principle of effectiveness is that an interpretation of a term should be preferred when it provides a meaning that can be effectively applied in comparable cases rather than being subject to multiple different meanings. Indeed, it is better for that meaning to have an effect rather than to be a meaning that is devoid of effect; hence, the effectiveness (*ut res magis valeat quam pereat*).[244] Another aspect of the principle of effectiveness is the adoption of an interpretation that achieves the objectives of the treaty[245] rather than circumventing or marginalising them, which is explained in §2.06[A][2] below.

International tribunals have suggested that the meaning of the principle of effectiveness should include the effectiveness of all applicable provisions of a treaty in a harmonised way.[246] In the case of the New York Convention, judges should not interpret Article V(1)(b) in isolation from the other grounds for refusal of recognition and enforcement under the New York Convention. Rather, they should consider the relationship between these grounds and the due process defence. Article V(1)(d) deals with non-compliance with the agreed procedure or, in the absence of such an agreement, with the procedure prescribed by the law of the seat.[247] As shown in §2.02[A], Chinese courts have considered that the notice and other procedural issues that may affect the parties' right to present their case are part of the arbitral proceedings and should therefore be governed by the law applicable to the arbitral proceedings as prescribed in Article V(1)(d) of the New York Convention.[248] Accordingly, they have not distinguished between these two grounds for refusal in their case law and have held that the violation of due process may well be covered by Article V(1)(d) of the New York Convention.[249]

---

242. 'Sixth Report on the Law of Treaties, by Sir Humphrey Waldock, Special Rapporteur' (1966) 2 *Yearbook of the International Law Commission* 51, 94 [1].
243. Gardiner, *Treaty Interpretation* (n. 171) 168.
244. *Ibid.*, 168–169, 179–181.
245. *Ibid.*, 168–169.
246. Appellate Body Report, *Korea - Definitive Safeguard Measure on Imports of Certain Dairy Products*, WT/DS98/AB/R (14 December 1999) [80]–[81] ('It is the duty of any treaty interpreter to read all applicable provisions of a treaty in a way that gives meaning to all of them, harmoniously...a treaty should be interpreted as a whole, and, in particular, its sections and parts should be read as a whole').
247. *Convention on the Recognition and Enforcement of Foreign Arbitral Awards*, open for signature 10 June 1958, 330 UNTS 3 (entered into force 7 June 1959) Art. V(1)(d) ('The composition of the arbitral authority or the arbitral procedure was not in accordance with the agreement of the parties, or, failing such agreement, was not in accordance with the law of the country where the arbitration took place').
248. *See* above n. 17.
249. *See* above nn. 11–15.

However, Article V(1)(b) has independent value and effectiveness and cannot be replaced by Article V(1)(d). As discussed in §2.02[C], Article V(1)(d) provides that the agreement of the parties takes precedence over other considerations, underlining the importance of party autonomy. It is only in the absence of agreement between the parties that the arbitration law of the place of arbitration is to be taken into account. In contrast, the procedural fairness required by Article V(1)(b) acts as a limitation on party autonomy in arbitral proceedings in order to ensure equal treatment of the parties and reasonable opportunities to present their respective cases.[250] This distinction has been accepted by several enforcing courts. For example, German courts have consistently held that Article V(1)(b) covers only violations of the right to present one's case and not issues relating to the arbitral proceedings, which could be addressed under Article V(1)(d).[251] Thus, circumstances that violate due process, but not the parties' agreement, are not covered by Article V(1)(d). In this sense, the law applicable to the due process defence has its own significance and should be determined independently of the applicable law under Article V(1)(d).

[2] Ordinary Meaning, Context, Object and Purpose

First and foremost, as a starting point, 'ordinary meaning' cannot be considered in isolation when applying general rules of interpretation. Rather, it should be applied in conjunction with the context, object and purpose. 'It has to be accepted that there is commonly no single "ordinary" meaning of a word and thus there is the need for a direct link to the context and the treaty's object and purpose.'[252] The ordinary meaning may be determinative, but only if it is confirmed by an examination of the context, object and purpose.[253]

Second, as Waldock (the ILC Special Rapporteur) observed, 'the natural and ordinary meaning of terms is not to be determined in the abstract but by reference to the context in which they occur'.[254] The context directs the interpreter to take account of many elements. These range from those that are fairly immediate, such as the wording of surrounding provisions, article headings, and punctuation. The context also extends to more remote factors such as: comparison with other related and contrasting provisions on similar matters; the use of similar wording; the adoption of a structure or scheme underlying a provision; or the treaty as a whole.[255]

The New York Convention lists seven exclusive grounds for non-recognition or non-enforcement of a foreign arbitral award. With respect to the wording of all the

250. Blackaby et al. (n. 2) 356.
251. CLOUT Case No. 457 [Hanseatisches Oberlandesgericht Hamburg, Germany, 1 Sch 02/99, 14 May 1999], http://www.dis-arb.de/de/47/datenbanken/rspr/hanseat-olg-hamburg-az-1-sch-02-99-datum-1999-05-14-id30; CLOUT Case No. 371 [Hanseatisches Oberlandesgericht Bremen, Germany, 2 Sch 04/99, 30 September 1999], http://www.dis-arb.de/de/47/datenbanken/rspr/hanseat-olg-bremen-az-2-sch-04-99-datum-1999-09-30-id28.
252. Gardiner, 'The Vienna Convention Rules on Treaty Interpretation' (n. 207) 465.
253. Gardiner, *Treaty Interpretation* (n. 171) 185.
254. 'Sixth Report on the Law of Treaties' (n. 242) 56.
255. Gardiner, *Treaty Interpretation* (n. 171) 197–210.

grounds for non-recognition or non-enforcement, the text of Article V(1)(b) does not prescribe any applicable law for the 'proper notice' and 'right to present its case', unlike the other six grounds that explicitly provide for the applicable law. The wording of Article V(1)(b) suggests that it may be intended to establish a substantive rule rather than a choice-of-law approach to finding an appropriate 'national law' for the due process defence, as opposed to the other six grounds for refusal.

In its structure, the New York Convention distinguishes the first five grounds for refusal in Article V(1) from the remaining two grounds in Article V(2) in terms of applicable law. Article V(2) provides for two grounds for refusal, arbitrability and public policy, both of which should be determined by the law of the forum in which enforcement is sought. In contrast, Article V(1) provides for different applicable laws for each ground of refusal, which clearly takes into account the characteristics of international arbitration and the specific purposes of each ground of refusal.[256] The structure of Article V suggests that the New York Convention intends to bring together the grounds under the law of the forum of enforcement in Article V(2), as distinct from the other five grounds for refusal, including the due process defence, in Article V(1). This suggests that the applicable law for Article V(1)(b) is unlikely to be the law of the forum of enforcement. If this were not the case, the due process defence should have been included in Article V(2) and not in Article V(1).

The distinction between applicable law in Article V(1) and Article V(2) leads to different applications. Since 'arbitrability' and 'public policy' generally concern the fundamental interests of the enforcing forum, enforcing courts are required to apply the grounds for refusal under Article V(2) ex officio. By contrast, enforcing courts may apply the other five grounds for refusal in Article V(1) only at the request of the party resisting enforcement. In other words, the opposing party can waive the grounds for refusal in Article V(1) but not those in Article V(2). This means that the enforcing courts would apply the grounds in Article V(2) ex officio if these grounds are satisfied, even if the opposing party does not raise them. However, enforcing courts may not apply the grounds for refusal in Article V(1) ex officio if the opposing party does not raise them.

Lastly, the notion of 'object and purpose' in Article 31(1) of the VCLT functions mainly as a means of determining the ordinary meaning of terms; it is not intended to provide independent sources of meaning contrary to the plain language of the treaty. This is because the object and purpose cannot be considered in isolation from the terms of the treaty and is inherent in the treaty text.[257] As stated above, the object and purpose of the New York Convention is to establish a uniform set of standards for the recognition and enforcement of arbitration agreements and foreign or non-domestic

---

256. The first five refusal grounds are concerned with capacity of parties and validity of arbitration agreement, proper notice and due process, jurisdictional issues, composition of tribunal or procedure and award suspended or set aside. For commentaries on the applicable laws for these grounds, *see* van den Berg (n. 66) 275–358; Reinmar Wolff (ed.), *New York Convention: Convention on the Recognition and Enforcement of Foreign Arbitral Awards of 10 June 1958 Commentary* (C.H. Beck • Hart • Nomos, 2012) 225–385.
257. *USA, Federal Reserve Bank v. Iran, Bank Markazi* Case A28 (2000–02) 36 Iran–US Claims Tribunal Reports 5, 22 [58].

arbitral awards in the greatest number of cases possible and to prevent the application of parochial rules that would impede the recognition and enforcement of arbitral awards.[258] As explained above, the wording of Article V(1)(b) does not contain a choice-of-law provision, either as to the law of the arbitral seat or as to the law of the forum in which enforcement is sought, unlike other grounds for refusal contained in explicitly applicable laws. National rules of treaty interpretation, which usually refer to the choice-of-law rules of one state, may differ significantly from those applied in another state, which may lead to divergent understandings of the New York Convention's due process defence among State Parties. This diversity of interpretation is contrary to the original purpose of the State Parties to the New York Convention: to ensure uniformity.

The purpose of Article V(1)(b) is not only to protect the due process rights of the parties but also to ensure efficiency. As shown in §3.03, the core concepts of due process under the New York Convention include proper notice of the appointment of the arbitrators and of the proceedings, equality of arms, a reasonable opportunity to be heard, and the impartiality and independence of the arbitrators. The terms 'proper' and 'reasonable' indicate that the requirements of due process must be balanced with efficiency. It is not advisable to sacrifice efficiency in order to accommodate unreasonable procedural demands.[259] Thus, both due process and efficiency are the purposes of Article V(1)(b). With respect to specific standards of due process in concrete cases, Chapters 5, 6 and 7 integrate consideration of these purposes into a wider interpretative exercise that assesses the weight to be given to judicial practices that achieve a good balance with efficiency.

The interpretation of context and purpose also requires enforcing courts to coordinate Article V(1)(b) with the purposes of other provisions of the New York Convention. Article VII of the New York Convention establishes the pro-enforcement policy by providing that the provisions of the Convention shall not deprive the parties of any right they may have to avail themselves of an arbitral award in the manner and to the extent allowed by the law of the enforcing country.[260] Thus, if states adopt idiosyncratic but deferential approaches to due process that do not deny enforcement to some awards that could be refused enforcement under Article V(1)(b), this will not be contrary to their obligations under international law. Article III also implies the

258. For the objectives of the New York Convention, *see* UNCITRAL's website, https://uncitral.un.org/en/texts/arbitration/conventions/foreign_arbitral_awards; van den Berg (n. 66) 4; Born (n. 4) 3504.

259. *See* the official comment on Article 18 of the UNCITRAL Model Law, Seventh Secretariat Note - Analytical Comments on Draft Text, A/CN.9/264 (25 March 1985) 559.

260. *Convention on the Recognition and Enforcement of Foreign Arbitral Awards*, open for signature 10 June 1958, 330 UNTS 3 (entered into force 7 June 1959) Art. VII ('The provisions of the present Convention shall not affect the validity of multilateral or bilateral agreements concerning the recognition and enforcement of arbitral awards entered into by the Contracting States nor deprive any interested party of any right he may have to avail himself of an arbitral award in the manner and to the extent allowed by the law or the treaties of the country where such award is sought to be relied upon').

pro-enforcement policy,[261] which enforcing courts should consider when interpreting and applying the due process defence under the New York Convention. Accordingly, as shown in §5.02[A], enforcing courts apply the due process defence restrictively, and most courts consider that they have discretion to recognise or enforce awards even if the due process defence is satisfied.

The context and purpose interpretation also requires enforcing courts to protect the predictability and legal expectations of parties and tribunals when interpreting and applying the due process defence. As noted in §2.02[C] and §2.06[A][1], Article V(1)(d) guarantees the priority of the parties' freedom to agree on the procedure to be followed by the tribunal, subject to due process. The parties' agreement on procedural rules includes the institutional or ad hoc arbitration rules chosen by the parties and the discretionary powers of the arbitral tribunal in procedural matters. Article V(1)(d) emphasises the freedom of the parties to facilitate the proper functioning of international commercial arbitration according to their expectations, which allows the parties to tailor the 'rules of the game' to their specific needs. Accordingly, in the absence of a serious breach of due process, State Parties are obliged to respect the parties' agreement, their choice of arbitration rules, and the arbitral tribunal's discretion regarding the conduct of the arbitral proceedings in determining due process issues in specific cases.[262] Chapters 5–7 below analyse the similarities and differences in the interpretation and application of the due process defence by State Parties and propose a normative preference for one particular due process practice over another based on pro-enforcement policy objectives, predictability, parties' legal expectations, and the balance between efficiency and due process.

[B] The General Rule of Interpretation: Article 31(3) of the VCLT

Article 31(3) of the VCLT sets forth:

> There shall be taken into account, together with the context:
>
> (a) any subsequent agreement between the parties regarding the interpretation of the treaty or the application of its provisions;
> (b) any subsequent practice in the application of the treaty which establishes the agreement of the parties regarding its interpretation;
> (c) any relevant rules of international law applicable in the relations between the parties.[263]

---

261. *Convention on the Recognition and Enforcement of Foreign Arbitral Awards*, open for signature 10 June 1958, 330 UNTS 3 (entered into force 7 June 1959) Art. III ('Each Contracting State shall recognise arbitral awards as binding and enforce them in accordance with the rules of procedure of the territory where the award is relied upon, under the conditions laid down in the following articles. There shall not be imposed substantially more onerous conditions or higher fees or charges on the recognition or enforcement of arbitral awards to which this Convention applies than are imposed on the recognition or enforcement of domestic arbitral awards').
262. For more details, *see* §5.02[C].
263. *Vienna Convention on the Law of Treaties*, opened for signature 23 May 1969, 1155 UNTS 331 (entered into force 27 January 1980) Art. 31(3).

[1] Subsequent Agreement and Subsequent Practice

According to the ILC, a 'subsequent agreement' under Article 31(3)(a) is 'an agreement between the parties, reached *after the conclusion of a treaty*, regarding the interpretation of the treaty or the application of its provisions'.[264] However, a 'subsequent practice' under Article 31(3)(b) refers to 'conduct in the application of a treaty, *after its conclusion*, which *establishes the agreement* of the parties *regarding the interpretation of the treaty*'.[265] An 'agreement' under Article 31(3)(a) and (b) requires a 'common understanding regarding the interpretation of a treaty which the parties are aware of and accept'.[266]

The distinction between 'subsequent agreement' under Article 31(3)(a) and 'subsequent practice' under Article 31(3)(b) is not always clear. According to the ILC commentaries, 'subsequent agreement' and 'subsequent practice' are distinguished by 'whether an agreement of the State Parties can be identified as such, in *a common act or undertaking*, or whether it is necessary to identify an agreement through *separate acts* that in combination demonstrate a common position'.[267] Some international tribunals have argued that the term 'subsequent agreement' under Article 31(3)(a) is limited to 'a common act or undertaking' between all the parties.[268] By contrast, different subsequent agreements between a limited number of State Parties, which together constitute an agreement between all State Parties as to the interpretation of a treaty, may constitute subsequent practice under Article 31(3)(b).[269] Used in this sense, there is no clear agreement among all State Parties to the New York Convention as to 'a common act or undertaking' in interpreting Article V(1)(b) of the New York Convention. This book therefore focuses on 'subsequent practice' in order to identify an agreement among State Parties on the interpretation of Article V(1)(b) through separate acts which, taken together, demonstrate a common understanding.

'Subsequent practice' under Article 31(3)(b) of the VCLT 'may consist of any conduct of a party in the application of a treaty, whether in the exercise of its executive, legislative, judicial or other functions'.[270] Under the New York Convention, the implementing legislation and domestic judicial application of Article V(1)(b), which creates a consensus among all State Parties, are part of such 'subsequent practice'

264. 'Draft Conclusion on Subsequent Agreements and Subsequent Practice' (n. 224) Conclusion 4(1) (emphasis added).
265. *Ibid.*, Conclusion 4(2) (emphasis added).
266. *Ibid.*, Conclusion 10(1).
267. International Law Commission, 'Draft Conclusion on Subsequent Agreements and Subsequent Practice in Relation to the Interpretation of Treaties with Commentaries' (2018) https://legal.un.org/ilc/texts/instruments/english/commentaries/1_11_2018.pdf Commentary to Conclusion 4, [10] (emphasis added).
268. *See* Appellate Body Report, *United States – Measures Concerning the Importation, Marketing and Sale of Tuna and Tuna Products*, WT/DS381/AB/R (13 June 2012) [371]; Gardiner, *Treaty Interpretation* (n. 171) 248-249.
269. International Law Commission, 'Draft Conclusion on Subsequent Agreements and Subsequent Practice with Commentaries' (n. 267) Commentary to Conclusion 4 [12].
270. 'Draft Conclusion on Subsequent Agreements and Subsequent Practice' (n. 224) Conclusion 5(1). *See also* Hugh Thirlway, *The Sources of International Law* (Oxford University Press, 2nd ed., 2019) 73.

under Article 31(3)(b), which will be examined in Chapters 3 and 5. Specifically, Chapter 3 will focus on the core elements of due process reflected in the implementing legislation relating to the New York Convention,[271] and Chapter 5 will examine the common practice of all State Parties with respect to the interpretation and application of Article V(1)(b) in relation to pro-enforcement policy, no review of merits, judicial deference to the procedural discretion of arbitrators and institutional arbitration rules, and due regard for the international character of Convention awards.[272]

[2] Relevant Rules of International Law

Of great importance in determining the meaning and scope of due process under the New York Convention is Article 31(3)(c) of the VCLT, which states that the interpretation of treaties should include 'relevant rules of international law'. First, in the context of international treaties, including the New York Convention, the establishment of obligations between State Parties in 'international law' can be understood as referring to public international law.[273] One of the most widely accepted sources of international law is contained in Article 38 of the Statute of the ICJ. It states that treaties, customary law, and general principles of law are the sources of international law, while judicial decisions and academic writings are subsidiary sources.[274] Therefore, 'relevant rules of international law' in Article 31(3)(c) of the VCLT can be construed as referring to the sources of international law contained in Article 38 of the ICJ Statute.[275] For the purposes of this book, as discussed in more detail in Chapter 3, general principles of law play an important role in the interpretation and application of the due process defence under the New York Convention, as due process has been widely recognised as a general principle of international law.

'The general principles of law recognised by civilised nations' place the treaty provision on due process within a principled framework for the purposes of interpretation under Article 31(3)(c) of the VCLT.[276] In *Golder v. United Kingdom*, the ECtHR established a clear connection between 'general principles of law' within the meaning of Article 38(1)(c) of the ICJ Statute and Article 31(3)(c) of the VCLT when interpreting Article 6(1) of the ECHR concerning the right of access to justice.[277] The court based its

271. *See* §3.03.
272. *See* §5.02.
273. Gardiner, *Treaty Interpretation* (n. 171) 299.
274. Pellet and Müller (n. 227) 812–832; Malgosia Fitzmaurice, 'The History of Article 38 of the Statute of the International Court of Justice: The Journey from the Past to the Present' in Samantha Besson and Jean d'Aspremont (eds), *The Oxford Handbook of the Sources of International Law* (Oxford University Press, 2017) 182; Wolfgang Friedmann, 'The Uses of "General Principles" in the Development of International Law' (1963) 57(2) *American Journal of International Law* 279, 279 DOI: 10.2307/2195982.
275. Mclachlan (n. 224) 290, 293–309.
276. Martti Koskenniemi, Report of the Study Group of the International Law Commission on Fragmentation of International Law: Difficulties Arising from the Diversification and Expansion of International Law, UN Doc. A/CN.4/L.682 (13 April 2006) [469].
277. *Golder v. United Kingdom* (European Court of Human Rights, Grand Chamber, Application No. 4451/70, 21 February 1975) [35].

interpretation on Article 31(3)(c) of the VCLT and held that 'relevant rules of international law' included 'general principles of law recognised by civilised nations'.[278] Accordingly, the ECtHR considered that a right of access to the civil courts was a general principle of law and could be relied upon in interpreting the meaning of Article 6 of the ECHR.[279]

As discussed in more detail in Chapter 3, when interpreting the New York Convention, judges may look to sources of international law, in particular the general principle of *audiatur et altera pars*, to interpret the meaning of due process under the New York Convention. Significant reliance on the internationally recognised principle of *audiatur et altera pars*, in the sense of general principles of law, would prevent State Parties from reverting to a purely domestic situation where traditional local concepts are imposed on the meaning of due process in international cases. Moreover, the application of general principles of law to the due process defence may free judges from the constraints, rigidities or deficiencies of their own legal systems and allow them to adopt elements of other legal systems, such as national legal systems in the case of Article 38(1)(c) of the ICJ Statute, or other branches of international law.[280]

Second, it seems reasonable to infer that 'relevant' rules of international law are those which deal with the same subject matter as Article V(1)(b) of the New York Convention being interpreted or those which in any way affect that interpretation. As explained in more detail in Chapter 3, due process is provided for not only in the New York Convention but also in other international human rights treaties, such as the Universal Declaration of Human Rights,[281] the ICCPR,[282] the ECHR,[283] the EUCFR,[284] the American Convention on Human Rights,[285] and the African Charter on Human and Peoples' Rights.[286] The word 'relevant' also includes the due process provisions of these treaties.

In essence, Article 31(3)(c) expresses a more general principle of treaty interpretation – systemic integration into the international legal system – because treaties themselves are creatures of international law.[287] The subject matter of due process in

278. *Ibid.*
279. *Ibid.*
280. Jan Wouters, 'Conclusions: The Role of General Principles in a Multi-layered Legal Setting' in Mads Andenas et al. (eds), *General Principles and the Coherence of International Law* (Brill, 2019) 200.
281. *Universal Declaration of Human Rights*, adopted 10 December 1948, UNGA Res 217 A (III) Art. 10.
282. *International Covenant on Civil and Political Rights*, opened for signature 19 December 1966, 999 UNTS 171 (entered into force 23 March 1976) Art. 14.
283. *Convention for the Protection of Human Rights and Fundamental Freedoms*, opened for signature 4 November 1950, 213 UNTS 221 (entered into force 3 September 1953) Art. 6(1).
284. *Charter of Fundamental Rights of the European Union* (entered into force 1 December 2009) Art. 47.
285. *American Convention on Human Rights*, opened for signature 22 November 1969, 1144 UNTS 123 (entered into force 18 July 1978) Art. 8(1).
286. *African Charter on Human and Peoples' Rights*, adopted 27 June 1981, 1520 UNTS 217 (entered into force 21 October 1986) Art. 7(1).
287. Mclachlan (n. 224) 280.

the New York Convention is recognised as part of and operating within the international legal system. Thus, the due process defence of the New York Convention should be 'applied and interpreted against the background of the general principles of international law',[288] and these principles should be applied when issues arise that cannot be resolved by the due process defence.

In the real world, it is inevitable that there will be inconsistent decisions concerning the rules that states adopt in applying the concept of due process, as explained in Chapters 6 and 7. However, the sources of international law, in particular the general principles of law, would go a long way towards establishing a consensus on the conceptual and principled nature of due process, as discussed in Chapter 3.

[C] Supplementary Means of Interpretation

Article 32 of the VCLT sets forth:

> Recourse may be had to supplementary means of interpretation, including the preparatory work of the treaty and the circumstances of its conclusion, in order to *confirm* the meaning resulting from the application of article 31, or to *determine* the meaning when the interpretation according to article 31:
>
> (a) leaves the meaning ambiguous or obscure; or
> (b) leads to a result which is manifestly absurd or unreasonable.[289]

[1] Preparatory Work of the New York Convention

The text of Article 32 identifies two functions of supplementary means: the first is to 'confirm' a meaning resulting from the application of the general rule in Article 31, and the second is to 'determine' the meaning when the interpretation according to Article 31 leaves the meaning ambiguous, obscure, or leads to a manifestly absurd or unreasonable result.

Under Article 32 of the VCLT, recourse may be had to supplementary means of interpretation, 'including preparatory works of the treaty'. It is reasonable to limit the preparatory works to permanent records (*travaux préparatoires*) since it is not possible for treaty interpreters to have the live testimony of all those who participated in the drafting of a treaty.[290] In drafting the VCLT, the ILC accepted the suggestion of the Special Rapporteur (Waldock) that:

> They [*travaux préparatoires*] are not, except in the case mentioned [agreements, instruments, and other documents ultimately covered elsewhere in the Vienna rules], an authentic means of interpretation. They are simply evidence to be weighed against any other relevant evidence of the intentions of the parties, and their cogency depends on the extent to which they furnish proof of the *common*

288. Arnold Mcnair, *The Law of Treaties* (Oxford University Press, 1961) 466.
289. *Vienna Convention on the Law of Treaties*, opened for signature 23 May 1969, 1155 UNTS 331 (entered into force 27 January 1980) Art. 32 (emphasis added).
290. Gardiner, 'The Vienna Convention Rules on Treaty Interpretation' (n. 207) 472.

> understanding of the parties as to the meaning attached to the terms of the treaty. Statements of individual parties during the negotiations are therefore of small value in the absence of evidence that they were assented to by the other parties.[291]

The *travaux préparatoires* help to ascertain the consensus of the State Parties to the New York Convention.[292] According to the *travaux préparatoires*, the drafters of the New York Convention rejected the proposal of the New Zealand delegation that Article V(1)(b) should expressly provide that the law of the place where the award was made shall apply.[293] This shows that the drafters of the Convention did not intend to exclusively apply the law of the arbitral seat to the due process defence under Article V(1)(b).

[2] Subsequent Practice as a Supplementary Means of Interpretation

In addition to the preparatory works on the treaty, Article 32 of the VCLT provides for 'subsequent practice' as a supplementary means of interpretation, consisting of 'conduct by *one or more* parties in the application of the treaty, *after its conclusion*'.[294] First, the term 'subsequent' refers to acts occurring 'after the conclusion of a treaty'.[295] Second, 'subsequent practice' under Article 32 is distinguishable from 'subsequent practice' under Article 31(3)(b) of the VCLT. A 'subsequent practice' under Article 32 refers to a practice of one or more (but not all) parties that does not presuppose an agreement of all parties, but which nevertheless may be relevant as a subsidiary means of interpretation.[296] Third, similar to 'subsequent practice' under Article 31(3)(b), 'subsequent practice' as a supplementary means of interpretation under Article 32 may include 'any conduct of a party in the application of a treaty, whether in the exercise of its executive, legislative, judicial or other functions'.[297]

'Subsequent practice' under Article 32 does not require that all State Parties have a uniform practice. Thus, subsequent practice 'in the vast majority' of State Parties, 'in many jurisdictions', or 'in several member States', may be sufficient to constitute 'subsequent practice' within the meaning of Article 32 of the VCLT.[298] From this perspective, Chapters 6 and 7 discuss the application of Article V(1)(b) of the New York Convention by national courts and examine the similarities and differences between

291. 'Sixth Report on the Law of Treaties' (n. 242) 54 [5]–[6] (emphasis added).
292. *Travaux préparatoires* of the New York Convention is available at http://www.uncitral.org/uncitral/en/uncitral_texts/arbitration/NYConvention_travaux.html.
293. United Nations Economic and Social Council, Recognition and Enforcement of Foreign Arbitral Awards: Comments by Governments on the Draft Convention on the Recognition and Enforcement of Foreign Arbitral Awards, UN Doc. E/CONF. 26/3 (10 March 1958) 2.
294. 'Draft Conclusion on Subsequent Agreements and Subsequent Practice' (n. 224) Conclusion 4(3) (emphasis added).
295. 'Reports of the International Law Commission' (n. 223) 221[14].
296. International Law Commission, 'Draft Conclusion on Subsequent Agreements and Subsequent Practice with Commentaries' (n. 267) Commentary to Conclusion 4 [16].
297. 'Draft Conclusion on Subsequent Agreements and Subsequent Practice' (n. 224) Conclusion 5(1).
298. International Law Commission, 'Draft Conclusion on Subsequent Agreements and Subsequent Practice with Commentaries' (n. 267) Commentary to Conclusion 4 [27], [29], [31].

State Parties. As stated in Chapter 1, this book argues that domestic courts should take into account the judicial decisions of other State Parties on the application of Article V(1)(b) when these decisions are more predictable and consistent with the legal expectations of parties, or strike a good balance with efficiency. This book also argues that courts should actively engage in a 'judicial dialogue' even if no agreement can be reached among State Parties on certain aspects of the due process defence. Apart from the application of Article 32, these references to foreign decisions may encourage the development of subsequent practice.[299]

[D] Reservations

As is well known, Article I(3) of the New York Convention allows for certain reservations:

> When signing, ratifying or acceding to this Convention, or notifying extension under article X hereof, any State may on the basis of reciprocity declare that it will apply the Convention to the recognition and enforcement of awards made only in the territory of another Contracting State. It may also declare that it will apply the Convention only to differences arising out of legal relationships, whether contractual or not, which are considered as commercial under the national law of the State making such declaration.[300]

With regard to reservations, Article 19 of the VCLT provides that:

> A State may, when signing, ratifying, accepting, approving or acceding to a treaty, formulate a reservation unless:
>
> (a) the reservation is prohibited by the treaty;
> (b) the treaty provides that only specified reservations, which do not include the reservation in question, may be made; or
> (c) in cases not falling under subparagraphs (a) and (b), the reservation is incompatible with the object and purpose of the treaty.

According to the UN Treaty Collection, of the State Parties, only the Republic of Argentina made national law reservations.[301] However, the New York Convention only permits 'reciprocity' and 'commercial' reservations, not national law reservations. According to Article 19 of the VCLT, if a treaty expressly permits certain reservations, only these may be lawfully made. Although Article 19 of the VCLT is not widely accepted as customary international law applicable to all states,[302] the Final Act of the

299. Antonios Tzanakopoulos, 'Judicial Dialogue as a Means of Interpretation' in Helmut Philipp Aust and Georg Nolte (eds), *The Interpretation of International Law by Domestic Courts* (Oxford University Press, 2016) 72, 94.
300. *Convention on the Recognition and Enforcement of Foreign Arbitral Awards*, open for signature 10 June 1958, 330 UNTS 3 (entered into force 7 June 1959) Art. I(3).
301. The Argentine Republic declared that 'the Convention will be interpreted in accordance with the principles and clauses of the National Constitution in force or those resulting from modification made by virtue of the Constitution': *see* the UN Treaty Collection, https://treaties.un.org/Pages/ViewDetails.aspx?src=TREATY&mtdsg_no=XXII-1&chapter=22&clang=_en.
302. *See* above n. 224.

New York Convention has endorsed the idea of Article 19(b) of the VCLT.[303] Thus, the making of national law reservations to the New York Convention may be considered impermissible. In the absence of lawful national law reservations, national courts should interpret the due process defence of the New York Convention in the light of international law rather than their national law.

[E] The Feasibility of Transnational Interpretation Based on the VCLT

National judges are, to a considerable extent, products of their own culture, training, and professional experience.[304] Thus, national judges may tend to interpret the New York Convention through a national lens.[305] Nevertheless, of the states that are parties to the New York Convention, some courts, such as the Dutch Supreme Court, have explicitly referred to Articles 31–33 of the VCLT when interpreting Article V of the New York Convention.[306] In addition, a handful of jurisdictions, including France and Sweden, have to some extent adopted a transnational interpretation of the due process defence. As discussed in §2.06[B][2] and Chapter 3, *audiatur et altera pars* has been widely accepted as a general principle of law, as confirmed by international human rights conventions (e.g., the ECHR) and other international arbitration documents (e.g., the UNCITRAL Model Law and the UNCITRAL Arbitration Rules). Courts in France and Sweden have used sources beyond their national law, including Article 6(1) of the ECHR, the UNCITRAL Model Law and the UNCITRAL Arbitration Rules, to interpret the meaning of due process under the New York Convention. In doing so, the French and Swedish courts interpret the due process defence in the light of general principles of law. As for the Model Law jurisdictions, given their international origin and the need for uniformity, they are more likely to accept transnational due process.

[1] France and the ECHR

In France, the fundamental procedural guarantees do not derive directly from the Constitution of the French Republic.[307] Hence, the standards of due process to which

303. *Final Act and Convention on the Recognition and Enforcement of Foreign Arbitral Awards*, E/CONF.26/8Rev.1 (10 June 1958) 5 ('the Conference decided that, without prejudice to the provisions of its articles I(3), X, XI and XIV, no reservation shall be admissible').
304. Waibel (n. 191) 17.
305. Anthea Roberts, 'Comparative International Law? The Role of National Courts in Creating and Enforcing International Law' (2011) 60(1) *International and Comparative Law Quarterly* 57, 75 DOI: 10.1017/s0020589310000679.
306. *Viktorovich Maximov v. OJSC Novolipetsky Metallurgichesky*, Netherlands Supreme Court, ECLI:NL:HR:2017:2992, 24 November 2017. Although this case is mainly concerned with the interpretation of Article V(1)(e), it is relevant since it shows how the VCLT may impact issues as to uniform interpretation of the New York Convention in general. For more analysis of this case, *see* Ly (n. 214) 21–24.
307. François-Xavier Train, 'Interpretation and Application of the New York Convention in France' in George A Bermann (ed.), *Recognition and Enforcement of Foreign Arbitral Awards – The Interpretation and Application of the New York Convention by National Courts* (Springer, 2017) 299.

foreign arbitral awards are subject are not judged by the standards of domestic law. Rather, they find international sources in general principles of law, jurisprudence and international conventions, in particular the ECHR.[308] French scholars argue that France has adopted a more international notion of due process under the New York Convention, which in many respects borrows from Article 6(1) of the ECHR.[309] Similarly, the Swiss Federal Tribunal, while adopting the *lex fori* approach, has also held that the ECHR, and in particular Article 6(1) thereof, applies to arbitral proceedings.[310]

The now-defunct European Commission of Human Rights explicitly confirmed that the ECHR is indirectly applicable to arbitration and that the courts of State Parties have a responsibility to ensure the fairness and correctness of arbitral proceedings. In *Jakob v. the Federal Republic of Germany*, the Commission applied Article 6(1) of the ECHR in deciding whether the applicant's right to be heard had been violated during the arbitral proceedings and held that:

> Applicant company had voluntarily entered into an arbitration agreement and thereby renounced its right to have its civil rights determined in court proceedings for the conduct of which the State is responsible under the Convention [...] This does not mean, however, that the respondent State's responsibility is completely excluded [...] as the arbitration award had to be recognised by [...] courts and be given executory effect by them. The courts thereby exercised a certain control and guarantee as to *the fairness and correctness of the arbitration proceedings* which they considered to have been carried out in conformity with *fundamental rights* and in particular with *the right* of the applicant company *to be heard*.[311]

In addition, the case law of the ECtHR and most scholars recognise that the ECHR is indirectly applicable to arbitration through the obligations imposed on courts in ECHR State Parties to ensure that the rights and freedoms of the ECHR are observed in arbitral proceedings.[312] An arbitration agreement constitutes a waiver by the parties of their right of access to the courts, but it cannot be regarded as a blanket waiver of the procedural safeguards contained in Article 6(1) of the ECHR.[313] Domestic courts are obliged to exercise some control over arbitral proceedings and to ensure that fundamental human rights are applied in such proceedings. In other words, State Parties are still responsible for violations of the ECHR whenever they are involved in arbitral proceedings, either by helping to facilitate interim measures or by setting-aside, and recognition and enforcement proceedings.[314] Thus, when considering a challenge to

308. *Ibid.*
309. *Ibid.*
310. *Egemetal v. Fuchs*, 28 April 2000, ATF 126 III 249 (2000); *Hitachi v. SMS* 30 June 1994, ATF, 15 *ASA Bulletin* 99 (1997).
311. *Jakob Boss Söhn KG v. the Federal Republic of Germany* (European Court of Human Rights, Grand Chamber, Application No. 18479/91, 2 December 1991) (emphasis added). This finding was echoed in England following the entry into force of the Human Rights Act 1998, which implemented the ECHR: *see* [2001] 2 Lloyd's Rep 657.
312. Massimo V Benedettelli, 'Human Rights as a Litigation Tool in International Arbitration: Reflecting on the ECHR Experience' (2015) 31(4) *Arbitration International* 631, 640–642 DOI: 10.1093/arbint/aiv036; Aleksandar Jaksic, *Arbitration and Human Rights* (Peter Lang, 2002) 183–187.
313. Petrochilos (n. 31) [4.51].
314. Krumiņš (n. 98) 46–47; Aleksandar Jaksic, 'Procedural Guarantees of Human Rights in

the recognition or enforcement of an award on the grounds of a violation of due process under the New York Convention, courts in Europe may well be obliged to apply the procedural guarantees contained in the ECHR.

[2] Sweden and the UNCITRAL Documents

Swedish courts also refer to sources beyond their municipal law when interpreting and applying the due process defence under the New York Convention. In the *Belaya Ptitsa* case, the Swedish Supreme Court held that neither Article V(1)(b) nor the available preparatory works to section 54(2) of the Swedish Arbitration Act[315] provide guidance on the meaning of due process.[316] Although the UNCITRAL Model Law has not been adopted by Sweden,[317] the Swedish Supreme Court referred to the corresponding provisions of the UNCITRAL Model Law and the UNCITRAL Arbitration Rules to ascertain the meaning of the due process defence under the New York Convention. In particular, it referred to Article 18 of the UNCITRAL Model Law ('a full opportunity of presenting his case') and Article 17 of the UNCITRAL Arbitration Rules ('a reasonable opportunity of presenting its case') to emphasise the equal treatment of the parties in presenting their cases and concluded that this requires the tribunal to provide the parties with sufficient time and opportunity to present their respective cases.[318]

[3] Model Law Jurisdictions, the UK and Subsequent Practice

An internationalist approach to the interpretation of the due process defence is more likely to be accepted in the Model Law jurisdictions. Article 2A(1) of the Amendment to the UNCITRAL Model Law provides that '[i]n the interpretation of this [Model] Law, regard is to be had to its *international origin* and to the need to promote *uniformity* in its application and the observance of good faith'.[319]

The requirements of 'international origin' and 'uniform application' increase the influence of transnational arbitration principles and practice on due process. The term 'international origin' should be an indication of the Model Law's strong preference for an internationalist interpretation based on internationally accepted application and practice of the principle of due process by the community of international commercial arbitration. The second requirement, to promote the uniform application of due

Arbitration Proceedings: A Still Unsettled Problem?' (2007) 24(2) *Journal of International Arbitration* 159, 162 DOI: 10.54648/joia2007013; Petrochilos (n. 31) 154.

315. Section 54(2) is the counterpart to Article V(1)(b) of the New York Convention, reproducing the text of the Convention.
316. *Belaya Ptitsa – Kursk v. Robot Grader AB*, Högsta Domstolens [Supreme Court], Ö 3626-17, 04 May 2018 reported in the Arbitration Institute of the Stockholm Chamber of Commerce, 5 [14], https://www.arbitration.sccinstitute.com/Swedish-Arbitration-Portal/Supreme-Court/The-Supreme-Court2/The-Supreme-Court/d_3259325-judgment-in-the-swedish-supreme-court-4-may-2018.-case-no.-o-3626-17 ('*Belaya Ptitsa*').
317. For the status of the UNCITRAL Model Law, *see* https://uncitral.un.org/en/texts/arbitration/modellaw/commercial_arbitration/status.
318. *Belaya Ptitsa* (n. 316) 6 [16].
319. *UNCITRAL Model Law*, UN Docs A/40/17 and A/61/17 (n. 29) Art. 2(A)(1) (emphasis added).

process, is nothing more than an aspect of the internationalist approach to interpretation. The second requirement falls within the scope of the comparative analysis proposed by the first requirement. As Justice Croft of Australia states, the term 'promotion of uniformity' requires interpreters to have regard to the decisions of foreign courts which have applied and interpreted the provisions of the Model Law.[320] In another Model Law jurisdiction, Japan, the Tokyo High Court held that courts should adopt the interpretations which are commonly adopted in other countries or which would be accepted in the international community and avoid the temptation to follow the usual path that they would take in domestic litigation when interpreting the Japanese Arbitration Act.[321] As shown in §2.06[B][1] and §2.06[C][2], these cases of other State Parties involving the due process defence under the New York Convention constitute 'subsequent practice' of State Parties within the meaning of Articles 31 and 32 of the VCLT.

The United Kingdom has not adopted the UNCITRAL Model Law, and English courts have held that they must apply the country's own concept of natural justice to determine the due process defence. However, they usually refer to non-domestic sources, such as studies conducted by commentators on the New York Convention, as well as case law of other State Parties. In *Anthony*, for instance, the Court of Appeal held that the statutory language of the Arbitration Act 1996, which directly enacts the New York Convention, must be given an autonomous meaning, which may be informed by the *travaux préparatoires*, the decisions of foreign courts on it and the views of foreign jurists on it – *la jurisprudence* and *la doctrine*.[322]

§2.07 CONCLUSION

Although the main addressees of Article V(1)(b) are the domestic judges of the State Parties, for the sake of the rights of defence of the parties, their expectation of legal certainty should also be considered when determining the law applicable to the due process defence. Since the main implementers of due process are the arbitrators conducting the arbitral proceedings, it is necessary for arbitrators to know the law and standards of due process that should be applied under Article V(1)(b). The *lex arbitri* approach can protect the legal expectations of the parties and arbitrators, as well as the interests of the arbitral seat in ensuring compliance with its mandatory rules. Nevertheless, the *lex arbitri* approach may lead to the enforcement of awards that fall far short of widely shared expectations as to the essential requirements of fair arbitration. The *lex fori* approach protects the interests of the forum state and has been supported by many State Parties. However, the *lex fori* approach jeopardises the legal certainty for

320. Clyde Croft, 'Recent Developments in Arbitration in Australia' (2011) 28(6) *Journal of International Arbitration* 599, 604.
321. The decision of the Supreme Court on 12 December 2017 (reported in 民集 (Minshû) vol 71-10, 2016).
322. *Anthony Lombard-Knight & Jakob Kinde v. Rainstorm Pictures Inc* [2014] EWCA Civ 356 (27 March 2014) [3] [35] (the court even referred to the *ICCA Guide to the Interpretation of the 1958 New York Convention: A Handbook for Judges* as an aid to interpret the 'pro-enforcement basis of the New York Convention').

parties and tribunals. It also makes it difficult to predict the impact of arbitral proceedings on the judicial recognition and enforcement of ensuing awards.

Both the *lex arbitri* and *lex fori* approaches are based on the forum state's domestic rules of treaty interpretation, which inevitably favours domestic concepts of due process and results in states having divergent understandings of due process. This chapter has argued that the due process defence should be interpreted as a transnational due process based on the international rules of interpretation prescribed by the VCLT. The incorporation of the New York Convention into domestic law does not affect the international obligations of State Parties to give the due process defence in the Convention the same meaning domestically. It is also important to note that the international rules of interpretation in the VCLT are closer to the true meaning of Article V(1)(b) than the variety of interpretations that might be given to it by different domestic laws. Moreover, since Articles 31–32 of the VCLT constitute customary international law applicable to all countries, State Parties to the New York Convention are obliged to apply these rules in interpreting the due process defence.

According to Article 31(1) of the VCLT (the general rule of interpretation), in particular with regard to systematic interpretations of the New York Convention, the applicable law for Article V(1)(b) is not intended to be national law. It is evident that Article V(1)(b) deliberately omits any reference to national law, whereas Articles V(1)(a), V(1)(d) and V(2) expressly refer to national law.

Moreover, the structure and wording of Article V suggest that the applicable law for Article V(1)(b) is not likely to be the law of the enforcing forum. The New York Convention distinguishes the first five grounds for refusal in Article V(1) from the remaining two grounds in Article V(2) in terms of applicable law. The structure of Article V suggests that the New York Convention intends to group together the grounds based on the law of the forum of enforcement in Article V(2), as distinct from the other five grounds for refusal, including the due process defence, in Article V(1). Also, according to the *travaux préparatoires* of the Convention, the drafters of the Convention did not intend to apply the law of the arbitral seat exclusively to the due process defence.

Article 31(1) and the *travaux préparatoires* prescribed in Article 32 of the VCLT shed no decisive light on the meaning of the due process defence under the New York Convention. Guidance in interpreting the meaning of the due process defence can be found in the 'relevant rules of international law', in particular, the general principles of international law in which due process has acquired a well-accepted meaning. The next chapter explores the general principle of *audiatur et altera pars* and its core elements, which can be used to concretise the meaning and scope of the due process defence under the New York Convention.

CHAPTER 3

The Principle of *Audiatur Et Altera Pars* in International Commercial Arbitration

§3.01 INTRODUCTION

Chapter 2 explored three approaches to the law governing the due process defence under the New York Convention. It contended that the international nature of the obligations under the New York Convention requires national courts to employ the international interpretative framework outlined in the VCLT. Recourse to other 'relevant rules of international law' is one of the interpretative techniques enunciated in the VCLT. As discussed in Chapter 2, general principles of law constitute integral components of the 'relevant rules of international law' and can thus be employed in interpreting the due process defence under the New York Convention. The identification of general principles of law exceeds the ad hoc use of comparative legal authorities and entails the abstraction of domestic rules into a set of principles that hold a transnational character.

This chapter explores the function of general principles of law in interpreting Article V(1)(b) of the New York Convention. Section 3.02 demonstrates that *audiatur et altera pars*, which the thesis equates with 'due process', enjoys broad recognition as a general principle of law under Article 38(1)(c) of the Statute of the ICJ. The principle of *audiatur et altera pars* has been recognised in the principal legal systems of the world through their domestic legislation and case law and is in line with the fundamental principles of international law.[1]

In this chapter, it is argued that Article V(1)(b) of the New York Convention should be considered as a transnational due process that reflects the general principle of *audiatur et altera pars* in the field of international arbitration. The general principle of *audiatur et altera pars* embodies the conceptualised and principled nature of

1. *See* §3.02[B].

procedural fairness, which is commonly adopted in major national legal systems.[2] The acceptance of this principle as a general principle of law is evident by the incorporation of corresponding rules in treaties and other international instruments.[3] Interpreting Article V(1)(b) of the New York Convention in line with this general principle enables a precise definition of the provision, without being limited to any specific jurisdiction's practice or jurisprudence, whether it be *lex arbitri* or *lex fori*.

The purpose of this chapter is to exhibit that the notion of transnational due process can be considered as a general principle of law, which harmonises with the objective and interpretative rules of the New York Convention that are based on the VCLT. The chapter is organised in the following manner, where §3.02 scrutinises the general principles of law as sources of international law and the fundamental methodologies for their identification. Furthermore, it is demonstrated in §3.02 that *audiatur et altera pars* can be identified as a general principle of law using a two-step analysis. In §3.03, the key components of *audiatur et altera pars*, as found in both national legal systems and international legal regimes such as human rights law, international investment law and international arbitration, are examined. The chapter is concluded in §3.04.

§3.02 *AUDIATUR ET ALTERA PARS* AS A GENERAL PRINCIPLE OF LAW

General principles of law are recognised by Article 38(1)(c) of the Statute of the ICJ as a crucial source of international law and are widely acknowledged as the source par excellence of international procedural norms.[4] This chapter contends that the New York Convention's requirement for due process may be viewed as an embodiment of the general principle of law – *audiatur et altera pars* –which is adapted for international commercial arbitration specifically. This section examines theories behind general principles of law and the method used for establishing due process as a general principle of law within the international legal system.

[A] General Principles of Law and *Audiatur Et Altera Pars*

[1] General Principles of Law

Article 38(1)(c) of the Statute of the ICJ identifies 'the general principles of law recognised by civilised nations' as a source of international law that the ICJ must adhere to, alongside international customs and treaties. Upon its adoption, Article 38 of the Statute of the ICJ did not aim to embody the doctrine of sources of international law 'in the contemporary sense of a finite list of abstract forms that determine law-creation

2. *See* §3.02[B][1].
3. *See* §3.02[B][2].
4. *Ibid.*

and law-ascertainment'.[5] Nevertheless, in the years following its inception, Article 38 has assumed significance and interpretation beyond that envisioned by its initial drafters and is now used to refer to the doctrine of the sources of international law.[6] It has been suggested that Article 38 is considered a customary rule of international law.[7] As a result, the sources of international law prescribed in Article 38 are generally deemed relevant before the ICJ and other international courts and tribunals, subject to any particular rules set out in their respective statutes.[8]

While some scholars have argued that general principles of law are subordinate to treaties and customary international law in practice,[9] they remain an autonomous and formal source of international law. Like treaties and customs, they are distinct from 'subsidiary means for the determination of rules of law' – judicial decisions and doctrine.[10] General principles of law 'lie at the very foundation of the legal system and are indispensable to its operation'.[11] They 'constitute both the backbone of the body of law governing international dealings and the potent cement that binds together the various and often disparate cogs and wheels of the normative framework of the international community'.[12] However, the differentiation between customary international law and

---

5. Thomas Skouteris, The Notion of Progress in International Law Discourse (TMC Asser Press, 2010) 123.
6. Alain Pellet and Daniel Müller, 'Article 38' in Andreas Zimmermann (ed.), *The Statute of the International Court of Justice: A Commentary* (Oxford University Press, 3rd ed., 2019) 812–832; Malgosia Fitzmaurice, 'The History of Article 38 of the Statute of the International Court of Justice: The Journey from the Past to the Present' in Samantha Besson and Jean d'Aspremont (eds), *The Oxford Handbook of the Sources of International Law* (Oxford University Press, 2017) 182; Wolfgang Friedmann, 'The Uses of "General Principles" in the Development of International Law' (1963) 57(2) *American Journal of International Law* 279, 279 DOI: 10.2307/2195982.
7. Patrick Dumberry, A Guide to General Principles of Law in International Investment Arbitration (Oxford University Press, 2020) 14; Valentina Vadi, *Analogies in International Investment Law and Arbitration* (Cambridge University Press, 2015) 120.
8. Giacinto della Cananea, *Due Process of Law Beyond the State: Requirements of Administrative Procedure* (Oxford University Press, 2016) 158; Vadi (n. 7) 120; Michael Wood, Special Rapporteur, Second Report on Identification of Customary International Law, UN Doc. A/CN.4/672 (22 May 2014) 6; Michael Wood, Special Rapporteur, First Report on Formation and Evidence of Customary International Law, UN Doc. A/CN.4/663 (17 May 2013) 14.
9. Pellet and Müller (n. 6) 941 (general principles of law are 'without any doubt, a subsidiary or additional source of international law (...) in the sense that the Court will usually only resort to them for filling a gap in the treaty or customary rules available to settle a particular dispute, and, what is even more apparent, will decline to invoke them when such other rules exist'); Fitzmaurice (n. 6) 193–194; Vadi (n. 7) 40; Malcolm Shaw, *International Law* (Cambridge University Press, 7th ed., 2014) 70; Vladimir-Djuro Degan, 'General Principles of Law' (1992) 3 *Finnish Yearbook of International Law* 1, 53; Johan G Lammers, 'General Principles of Law Recognized by Civilized Nations' in Frits Kalshoven, Pieter Jan Kuyper and Johan G Lammers (eds), *Essays in the Development of the International Legal Order: In Memory of Haro F Van Panhuys* (Springer, 1980) 65–66.
10. Dumberry (n. 7) 17; Pellet and Müller (n. 6) 932–936; Charles T Kotuby and Luke A Sobota, *General Principles of Law and International Due Process: Principles and Norms Applicable in Transnational Disputes* (Oxford University Press, 2017) 9; James Crawford (ed.), *Brownlie's Principles of Public International Law* (Oxford University Press, 8th ed., 2012) 34; Arnold McNair, 'The General Principles of Law Recognized by Civilized Nations' (1957) 33 *British Yearbook of International Law* 1, 6.
11. Bin Cheng, *General Principles of Law as Applied by International Courts and Tribunals* (Cambridge University Press, 2nd ed., 2006) 390.
12. Vadi (n. 7) 120.

general principles of law can occasionally be unclear when the latter becomes integrated into the former.[13] Treaties may reflect general principles of law, in which case general principles of law appear as codification conventions in the strict sense. The transnational due process in the New York Convention exemplifies this relationship between treaties and general principles of law, which will be further explained below.

[2] Audiatur Et Alteram Pars

Article V(1)(b) of the New York Convention provides that recognition or enforcement of a foreign arbitral award may be refused if the opposing party proves that it was not given proper notice of the appointment of the arbitrator or of the arbitral proceedings or was otherwise unable to present its case. As van den Berg states, this provision 'concerns the fundamental principle of procedure, that of fair hearing and adversary proceedings, also referred to as *audiatur et alteram pars* (or *audi et alteram partem*)'.[14]

Audiatur et altera pars (or *audi alteram partem*) is a Latin phrase meaning 'listen to the other side', or 'may the other side also be heard',[15] derived from Augustine of Hippo's views on natural law, according to which all parties before an international tribunal must have the opportunity to be heard and be treated equally before the law.[16] It is '[a] principle of due process according to which parties before an authoritative tribunal must have an equal opportunity to be heard and their arguments considered under the law'.[17]

It has been suggested that *audiatur et altera pars* should be considered as a principle rather than a rule because of its constitutive procedural value.[18] There is no clear-cut distinction between principles and rules, although some consensus exists: a principle 'is a general normative proposition considered to be expressive of the ratio of a series of more detailed rules' and 'expresses an important or general legal value, or it is the hallmark of a legal idea that permeates different questions of law'.[19] Conversely, a rule 'is narrower and more limited in its reach; and its scope of application and its effects are spelled out much more clearly'.[20]

13. Attila Tanzi, 'Conclusions: Testing General Principles of Law in International Investment Law: Between Principles and Rules of International Law' in Mads Andenas et al. (eds), *General Principles and the Coherence of International Law* (Brill, 2019) 298–299; Giorgio Gaja, 'General Principles of Law' in Rüdiger Wolfrum (ed.), *The Max Planck Encyclopedia of Public International Law* (Oxford University Press, 2013) [24].
14. Albert Jan van den Berg, *The New York Arbitration Convention of 1958: Towards a Uniform Judicial Interpretation* (Kluwer Law and Taxation Publishers, 1981) 297.
15. Aaron X Fellmeth and Maurice Horwitz, *Guide to Latin in International Law* (Oxford University Press, 2009) 41.
16. *Ibid.*
17. *Ibid.*
18. Robert Kolb, 'General Principles of Procedural Law' in Andreas Zimmermann et al. (eds), *The Statute of the International Court of Justice: A Commentary* (Oxford University Press, 3rd ed., 2019) 965.
19. *Ibid.*, 964. *See also* Neil MacCormick, *Legal Reasoning and Legal Theory* (Clarendon, 1978) 152.
20. Kolb (n. 18) 965.

In terms of terminology, 'equality between parties' and 'the right to be heard' in adversarial proceedings are often referred to as 'due process' in common law[21] and as '*audi et alteram partem*' (no person shall be condemned unheard), '*principe de la contradiction*' (principle of adversarial proceedings), '*égalité des parties*' (principle of equality between parties), '*rechtliches Gehör*' (right to be heard) in civil law jurisdictions.[22] While it has been suggested by Born to use the more neutral term 'procedural fairness',[23] most prominent commentaries generally employ the term 'due process' in the context of Article V(1)(b) of the New York Convention.[24] Additionally, highly regarded treatises, which are commonly acknowledged as comparatively authoritative textbooks, refer to the 'due process' defence as a ground for non-recognition and non-enforcement of foreign arbitral awards under Article V(1)(b).[25] In the realm of administrative law, 'due process' aims to safeguard individuals from the capricious actions of the government by necessitating that it adhere to suitable procedures when its agents intend to deprive anyone of life, liberty, or property.[26] For the purposes of this book, the focus is on the definition of due process in the context of international adjudication, particularly international commercial arbitration, which mandates that both parties before an international tribunal must have an opportunity to be heard and be treated equally under the law. Therefore, in this book, the terms 'due process' and 'procedural fairness' are interchangeable and are used in conjunction with the notion of '*audiatur et altera pars*'.

---

21. *Parsons & Whittemore Overseas Co v. Societe Generale De L'Industrie Du Papier (RAKTA)*, 508 F 2d 969, 975 (2nd Cir, 1974); *Paklito Investment Ltd v. Klockner East Asia Ltd* [1993] 2 HKLR 39, 48; *Dallah Real Estate and Tourism Holding Co v. Ministry of Religious Affairs* [2010] UKSC 46 (3 November 2010) [102].
22. van den Berg (n. 14) 297; Herman Verbist, 'Challenges on Grounds of Due Process Pursuant to Article V(1)(B) of the New York Convention' in Emmanuel Gaillard and Domenico Di Pietro (eds), *Enforcement of Arbitration Agreements and International Arbitral Awards: The New York Convention in Practice* (Cameron May, 2008) 679; Georgios Petrochilos, *Procedural Law in International Arbitration* (Oxford University Press, 2004) 145.
23. Born considered that 'due process' usually has a specific meaning in the context of some domestic litigation procedure: *see* Gary B Born, *International Commercial Arbitration* (Kluwer Law International, 2nd ed., 2014) 3494.
24. van den Berg (n. 14) 296–311; Maxi Scherer, 'New York Convention: Violation of Due Process, Article V (1)(b)' in Reinmar Wolff (ed.), *New York Convention: Convention on the Recognition and Enforcement of Foreign Arbitral Awards of 10 June 1958: Commentary* (C.H. Beck • Hart • Nomos, 2012) 279–309; Andrés Jana, Angie Armer and Johanna Klein Kranenberg, 'Article V(1)(b)' in Herbert Kronke et al. (eds), *Recognition and Enforcement of Foreign Arbitral Awards: A Global Commentary on the New York Convention* (Kluwer Law International, 2010) 231–256; Verbist (n. 22) 679–728; ICCA, *ICCA's Guide to the Interpretation of the 1958 New York Convention: A Handbook for Judges* (International Council for Commercial Arbitration, 2011) 89–93; Emmanuel Gaillard and George A Bermann (eds), *The UNCITRAL Secretariat Guide on the New York Convention* (Brill, 2017) 161–179.
25. Nigel Blackaby et al., *Redfern and Hunter on International Arbitration* (Oxford University Press, 6th ed., 2015) 627–629; Emmanuel Gaillard and John Savage (eds), *Fouchard Gaillard Goldman on International Commercial Arbitration* (Kluwer Law International, 1999) 985–987; Julian D M Lew, Loukas A Mistelis and Stefan M Kröll, *Comparative International Commercial Arbitration* (Kluwer Law International, 2003) 711.
26. Cananea (n. 8) 1–14. *See also Daniels v. Williams*, 474 US 327, 331 (1986).

As shown in more detail below, international courts and tribunals have accepted that *audiatur et altera pars* 'may be regarded as *a general principle of law* translating into practice the fundamental requirement of *equality between the parties* in judicial proceedings'.[27] *Audiatur et altera pars* is a fundamental principle of adjudicative proceedings and is therefore applicable to all types of adjudication, including judicial and arbitral proceedings.[28] It is applicable to proceedings before the ICJ, standing international tribunals, as well as bodies such as the Human Rights Committee under the ICCPR.

However, these international bodies may not always derive the same requirements for the conduct of proceedings from the *audiatur et altera pars* principle due to significant distinctions between forms of adjudication, in particular variations in the extent of institutionalisation of adjudication. In general, a more institutionalised form of international adjudication, such as the ICJ, may have a more developed set of rules for the application of *audiatur et altera pars*. The ICJ handles mostly public law disputes but follows a procedure that is more in line with private law: the jurisdiction is established by the consent of the State Parties, and states confront each other on an equal footing, reflecting sovereign equality.[29] From this perspective, in particular the adversarial nature of ICJ proceedings, states can be compared to transnational private parties before an international arbitral tribunal. Accordingly, international commercial arbitration proceedings can benefit from the theory and practice of *audiatur et altera pars* developed in international courts and tribunals.[30] Notably, the rules guaranteeing procedural fairness in international commercial arbitration may differ from those applied in international judicial proceedings. For instance, the principle of *audiatur et altera pars* is not disproportionately prejudiced when an arbitral tribunal orders paper-based proceedings only if both parties consent, which is not generally permitted in international judicial proceedings. The concept of party autonomy enables international commercial arbitration to depart from the *audiatur et altera pars* safeguards found in judicial proceedings. Efficiency and flexibility are highly valued in international arbitration, even if this comes at the expense of certain procedural fairness rules. It is assumed that parties fully comprehend the advantages and disadvantages of arbitration over litigation in a mature commercial market.[31]

27. Cheng (n. 11) 291 (emphasis added). *See also* Dumberry (n. 7) 145–149; Kolb (n. 18) 969–983; Kotuby and Sobota (n. 10) 54–86; Friedmann (n. 6) 290.
28. Kolb (n. 18) 969–976; Malcolm N Shaw (ed.), *Rosenne's Law and Practice of the International Court: 1920-2015* (Brill, 5th ed., 2016) vol. 3, Chapter 16, [258]; Hugh Thirlway, 'The Law and Procedure of the International Court of Justice 1960-1989: Part Eleven' (2001) 71(1) *British Yearbook of International Law* 71, 128–134 DOI: 10.1093/bybil/71.1.71; Cheng (n. 11) 290–298.
29. Kolb (n. 18) 984.
30. Regarding the jurisprudence and practice of *audiatur et altera pars* developed by international courts and tribunals, *see* §3.03.
31. Ilias Bantekas, 'Equal Treatment of Parties in International Commercial Arbitration' (2020) 69(4) *The International and Comparative Law Quarterly* 991, 994 DOI: 10.1017/s0020589320000287.

[B] The Way to Ascertain *Audiatur Et Altera Pars* as a General Principle of Law Derived from National Legal Systems

It would be useful to give a brief account of the categories of general principles of law and the approaches to identifying them before determining the most appropriate category for due process. The reason for discussing these categories is that the methodology used to identify them is distinct. International lawyers have never reached agreement on the categories of general principles of law. Marcelo Vázquez-Bermúdez (Special Rapporteur of the International Law Commission on General Principles of Law) observed that while various categories of general principles of law have been proposed in the literature, two appear to be supported by practice and widely accepted by scholars: the first category consists of general principles of law derived from national legal systems and the second includes those that have emerged within the international legal system.[32]

Not all members of the ILC have endorsed the notion of general principles of law derived exclusively from the international legal system and have expressed concerns about the approach to identifying such principles and their relationship with customary international law.[33] The drafters of Article 38 of the ICJ Statute, including Lord Phillimore, may not have envisaged the possibility of general principles of law existing solely in the international legal system. Nevertheless, practical illustrations elucidate that the ICJ has applied the general principles of law that derive from and are fundamental to the international legal order, such as the principle of sovereign equality.[34] The methodology used to identify general principles of law derived from the international legal order is to identify those principles that are recognised by the community of nations. These principles may be those that: (a) are widely recognised by international instruments, in particular treaties; (b) underpin the general rules of conventional or customary international law; or (c) are inherent in the fundamental requirements and basic characteristics of the international legal order.[35]

Both international lawyers and members of the ILC unanimously endorsed the first category and agreed on the general methodology for ascertainment. This involves identifying the existence of a common principle among the principal legal systems of the world, coupled with determining its transposition into the international legal

32. Marcelo Vázquez-Bermúdez, Special Rapporteur, *First Report on General Principles of Law*, UN Doc. A/CN.4/741 (5 April 2019) paras 188–253. The general principles of law can also be subdivided into two categories according to its content: (1) norms that regulate substantive conduct, and therefore apply to both private parties and states and (2) norms that regulate the exercise of sovereign or adjudicative powers, and therefore apply only to states and international tribunals: *see* Kotuby and Sobota (n. 10) 1.
33. Marcelo Vázquez-Bermúdez, Special Rapporteur, *Second Report on General Principles of Law*, UN Doc. A/CN.4/741 (9 April 2020) para. 2.
34. *See, e.g.*, *Corfu Channel Case (United Kingdom v. Albania) (Merits)* [1949] ICJ Rep 4; Reservations to the Convention on Genocide (Advisory Opinion) [1951] ICJ Rep 15. *See also* Samantha Besson, 'General Principles in International Law – Whose Principles?' in Samantha Besson and Pascal Pichonnaz (eds), *Les principes en droit européen–Principles in European Law* (Schulthess, 2011) 33.
35. Vázquez-Bermúdez, Second Report on General Principles of Law (n. 33) [119].

order.[36] As Lord Phillimore, one of the authors of the proposal for the Statute of the ICJ that was finally adopted, clearly explained, the general principles of law referred to in Article 38(1)(c) are those 'which were accepted by *all nations in foro domestico*'.[37]

The general principles of law derived from national legal systems demand a well-structured comparative analysis of national legal systems. International courts and tribunals frequently proclaim the existence of a general principle without adequately explaining the methodology used to extract it.[38] The ICJ, for example, rarely publishes its process for comparing states' practices in applying a particular legal principle. Instead, it simply asserts that the principle is 'widely accepted as having been assimilated into the catalogue of general principles of law'[39] or that it is 'admitted in all systems of law'.[40] The ICJ's assertion of a general principle of law, whether or not it finds a parallel in national legal systems, is rarely accompanied by an adequate demonstration of its existence in international law.[41] International courts and tribunals appear to heavily rely on previous decisions of other international courts and tribunals, as these judicial decisions are a supplementary means of establishing rules and principles of law according to Article 38(1)(d) of the ICJ Statute.[42]

Despite little guidance from the ICJ, the ILC and scholars have provided insight into the method of determining general principles of law. They have proposed a two-step analysis to identify general principles of law derived from national legal systems: first, to determine the existence of a principle common to the major legal systems of the world and, second, to ascertain the transposition of that principle into the international legal order.[43] The first step is to establish that there is a general legal principle recognised by the community of nations and to determine the content of this general principle of law.[44] Through this analysis, the existence and essential content of a general principle of law derived from national legal systems can be objectively

36. Vázquez-Bermúdez, *First Report on General Principles of Law* (n. 32) [190]–[230]; Pellet and Müller (n. 6) 924.
37. Advisory Committee of Jurists, Procès-verbaux of the Proceedings of the Advisory Committee of Jurists, June 16th–July 24th, 1920, with Annexes (Van Langenhuysen Brothers, 1920) 335 (emphasis added).
38. *See, e.g., Corfu Channel Case (United Kingdom v. Albania) (Merits)* [1949] ICJ Rep 4. *See also* Johann R Leiss, 'The Juridical Nature of General Principles' in Mads Andenas et al. (eds), *General Principles and the Coherence of International Law* (Brill, 2019) 79, 80–81; Stephan W Schill, 'General Principles of Law and International Investment Law' in Tarcisio Gazzini and Eric De Brabandere (eds), *International Investment Law: The Sources of Rights and Obligations* (Brill, 2012) 141; Fabián O Raimondo, *General Principles of Law in the Decisions of International Criminal Courts and Tribunals* (Martinus Nijhoff, 2008) 57–58.
39. *Sea-Land Servs, Inc v. Islamic Republic of Iran*, 6 Iran-US Cl Trib Rep 149, 168 (1984).
40. *Corfu Channel Case (United Kingdom v. Albania)* (Merits) [1949] ICJ Rep 4.
41. Gaja (n. 13) para. 20.
42. Leiss (n. 38) 81; Raimondo (n. 38) 45.
43. Vázquez-Bermúdez, *Second Report on General Principles of Law* (n. 33) [19]–[106]; Pellet and Müller (n. 6) 925–31; Jan Wouter et al., *International Law: A European Perspective* (Hart Publishing, 2018) 154–155.
44. Vázquez-Bermúdez, *Second Report on General Principles of Law* (n. 33) [22]; Pellet and Müller (n. 6) 925–930.

determined.[45] According to Marcelo Vázquez-Bermúdez (the ILC's Special Rapporteur), in order to identify a general principle of law, 'one must carefully examine all the available evidence showing that a general principle of law has been "recognised by civilised nations"'.[46] This objective criterion is based on the existing legislation and case law of national legal systems, together with the relevant literature, as elaborated below. The second step of the analysis is to show, on the one hand, that these principles are compatible with the fundamental principles of international law and, on the other hand, that the conditions exist for their adequate application in the international legal system.[47]

According to the categories of general principles of law discussed above, *audiatur et altera pars* is not exclusively applicable to the international legal system. Instead, as explained below, it is a principle common to the principal national legal systems and is derived from the two-step analysis process.

[1] Determining the Existence of **Audiatur Et Altera Pars Common to the Principal National Legal Systems**

As mentioned above, it is possible to establish *audiatur et altera pars* as a general principle of law through a two-step analysis. Specifically, the first step involves comparing national legal systems to demonstrate the principle's common acceptance, thus gaining recognition from the community of nations.[48] This process requires both vertical and horizontal steps. The vertical step involves extracting a legal principle from national legal rules, while the horizontal step involves ascertaining its recognition among the principal nations.[49] This two-step analysis has to address three specific issues: how to determine a common principle among the principal legal systems; what materials are necessary for the comparative research; and which national legal systems should be consulted.[50]

(a) The Vertical Step: Extracting a Principle from Rules

The first question to be addressed in a comparative legal analysis is which national law to examine. National legal sources, including legislation and national court decisions, form the basis for identifying general principles of law that emerge from municipal laws. It is essential to consider the peculiarities of each jurisdiction in order to select relevant material.[51] In common law jurisdictions, some important rules for the due process defence are not explicitly established in statutes but are instead established through case law. Consulting binding case law is permissible and appropriate in

45. Vázquez-Bermúdez, Second Report on General Principles of Law (n. 33) [20].
46. *Ibid.*, [11].
47. *Ibid.*, [22]; Pellet and Müller (n. 6) 930–931.
48. F A Mann, 'Reflections on a Commercial Law of Nations' (1957) 20 *British Yearbook of International Law* 33, 36.
49. Raimondo (n. 38) 46–57.
50. For the selection of the national legal systems for the comparative study, *see* §1.04[A][2].
51. Vázquez-Bermúdez, *Second Report on General Principles of Law* (n. 33) [70]; Raimondo (n. 38) 48.

common law courts. Moreover, Article 38(1)(d) of the Statute of the ICJ considers 'judicial decisions and the teachings of the most highly qualified publicists of the various nations' as 'subsidiary means for the determination of rules of law'.[52] The term 'rules of law' unequivocally encompasses all three sources of international law stipulated in Article 38(1) of the Statute of the ICJ – international conventions, international custom, and general principles of law. As such, judicial decisions and the works of the most eminent legal scholars can be employed as auxiliary means of determining general principles of law. In international courts and tribunals, scholars' teachings are referenced to demonstrate the universality of certain legal principles among the major legal systems of the world.[53] While caution is necessary, academic literature can facilitate transcending linguistic obstacles encountered in comparative analyses of national legal systems.

Second, one must compare the rules currently applied in the national legal systems and extract a commonly shared principle. Alternatively, one can distil a principle from those rules via an inductive process of abstraction and generalisation. This process involves sufficiently generalising and abstracting legal principles from the national systems to transform them into general principles of law.[54] It is worth highlighting that the principles involved are of a general nature. A comprehensive set of detailed rules cannot be derived from the general principles of law, which is necessary to establish a common principle among the primary legal systems.[55] The broadening of the law's scope makes it less probable to discover detailed rules that apply to all states. Nevertheless, minor deviations in legal rules between different national legal systems do not hinder the identification of a general principle of law. Rather, it is crucial to ascertain if there is a shared legal principle that underpins those legal rules.[56]

(b) Horizontal Step – A Comparative Study of the Principle of Due Process in Major National Legal Systems

It is easy to distil the principle of due process from the specific rules in the principal national legal systems, as due process is firmly established in both constitutional and arbitration law in the major national legal systems. For example, the Fourteenth Amendment of the United States Constitution stipulates that no individual shall be

52. Statute of the International Court of Justice Art. 38 (1)(d).
53. Vázquez-Bermúdez, *Second Report on General Principles of Law* (n. 33) [179], *see also* the literature cited.
54. Dumberry (n. 7) 97–127; Pellet and Müller (n. 6) 930; Daniel Costelloe, 'The Role of Domestic Law in the Identification of General Principles of Law under Article 38(1)(c) of the Statute of the International Court of Justice' in Mads Andenas et al. (eds), *General Principles and the Coherence of International Law* (Brill, 2019) 177, 177–194; Brianna Gorence, 'The Constructive Role of General Principles in International Arbitration' (2018) 17(3) *The Law and Practice of International Courts and Tribunals* 455, 463 DOI: 10.1163/15718034-12341389; Eirik Bjorge, 'Public Law Sources and Analogies of International Law' (2018) 49(4) *Victoria University of Wellington Law Review* 533, 537 DOI: 10.26686/vuwlr.v49i4.5339; Kotuby and Sobota (n. 10) 19–21; Schill (n. 38) 148.
55. Pellet and Müller (n. 6) 927.
56. Raimondo (n. 38) 49.

deprived of 'life, liberty, or property, without due process of law'.[57] Various constitutions, not just throughout Europe[58] but also in Commonwealth countries including South Africa,[59] as well as in East Asian countries such as Japan[60] and South Korea,[61] incorporate principles of procedural fairness. These constitutional provisions bolster the courts' explication of the requirements of due process. As discussed in Chapter 2, certain jurisdictions such as Germany and the US apply their constitutional due process standards directly to the recognition and enforcement of foreign arbitral awards under the New York Convention.

Also, states have implemented arbitration legislation with procedural fairness guarantees. Both jurisdictions that have adopted the UNCITRAL Model Law and other national arbitration laws that are not based on the UNCITRAL Model Law have recognised that arbitral proceedings should comply with the principle of due process. According to Article 18 of the UNCITRAL Model Law, arbitrators must treat both parties equally and give each party a full opportunity to present its case.[62] Article 18 is renowned as the 'Magna Carta of Arbitral Procedure'[63] and must be adhered to by the parties.[64] Article 19 reaffirms the mandatory nature of Article 18 and establishes a hierarchy of sources with the right to be heard and the right to equal treatment taking precedence. This works as a limitation on other mandatory provisions, such as party autonomy and tribunal discretion, in arbitral proceedings.[65]

The arbitration laws of jurisdictions that follow the Model Law, including Germany, Singapore, Hong Kong, Japan and most Arab countries,[66] typically include regulations akin to Article 18 of the UNCITRAL Model Law. These laws typically recognise a breach of due process as a valid reason to set aside an award, as well as to

---

57. The Fourteenth Amendment to the Constitution of the United States, s. 1.
58. *See, e.g.*, Grundgesetz für die Bundesrepublik Deutschland [Basic Law of the Federal Republic of Germany] (Germany) Art. 103(1); *Constitution of the Italian Republic*, Art. 24 https://www.senato.it/documenti/repository/istituzione/costituzione_inglese.pdf.
59. *Constitution of the Republic of South Africa*, Art. 35, https://www.gov.za/documents/constitution/chapter-2-bill-rights.
60. *Constitution of Japan*, Art. 37, https://japan.kantei.go.jp/constitution_and_government_of_japan/constitution_e.html.
61. *Constitution of the Republic of Korea*, Art. 27, https://www.refworld.org/docid/3ae6b4dd14.html.
62. *UNCITRAL Model Law on International Commercial Arbitration*, UN GAOR, 40th sess., Supp No. 17, UN Doc. A/40/17 (adopted 21 June 1985) annex I, as amended by UN GAOR, 61st sess., Supp No. 17, UN Doc. A/61/17 (7 July 2006), annex I ('*UNCITRAL Model Law*') Art. 18.
63. United Nations Committee on International Trade Law, *Analytical Commentary on the Draft Text of the Model Law*, UN Doc. A/CN.9/264 (25 March 1985) 45.
64. Howard M Holtzmann et al. (eds), A Guide to the 2006 Amendments to the UNCITRAL Model Law on International Commercial Arbitration: Legislative History and Commentary (Kluwer Law International, 2015) 550; Peter Binder, International Commercial Arbitration and Mediation in UNCITRAL Model Law Jurisdictions (Kluwer Law International, 4th ed., 2019) 330.
65. *UNCITRAL Model Law*, UN Docs A/40/17 and A/61/17 (n. 62) Art. 19 (party agreement and discretion of arbitrators rank second and third separately). *See also* Binder (n. 64) 337.
66. Saudi Arabia, Bahrain, Egypt, Jordan, Qatar, Syria and the UAE have adopted the UNCITRAL Model Law. For more discussion of the due process in arbitration in the Middle East, *see* Nayla Comair-Obeid and Zeina Obeid, 'Chapter 13: Country Report: Middle East' in Friedrich Rosenfeld, Dietmar Czernich and Franco Ferrari (eds), *Due Process as a Limit to Discretion in International Commercial Arbitration* (Kluwer Law International, 2020) 265, 265–278.

refuse recognition and enforcement of foreign arbitral awards under the New York Convention. For example, the German law governing arbitration is found in the German Code of Civil Procedure ('Zivilprozessordnung' (ZPO)), which is based on the UNCITRAL Model Law. The ZPO mandates that '[t]he parties are to be accorded equal treatment' and '[e]ach party is to be given an effective and fair legal hearing', in accordance with section 1042 of the 'General Procedural Rules'.[67] German courts have described the right to be heard in arbitral proceedings as a fundamental guarantee ensuring procedural fairness,[68] a fundamental procedural right of every human being,[69] a protection linked to human dignity in which it enables the parties to actively influence the conduct of arbitral proceedings,[70] and a guarantee ensuring orderly proceedings based on the principle of the rule of law.[71]

Likewise, in Asia, section 24(b) of the Singapore International Arbitration Act (IAA) enables the opposing party to challenge an arbitral award if it demonstrates that 'a breach of the rules of *natural justice* occurred in connection with the *making of the award* by which the rights of any party have been prejudiced'.[72] Singaporean case law defines the rules of natural justice as encompassing 'the opportunity to be heard and the equality of treatment'.[73] Although Singapore has also adopted the UNCITRAL Model Law, the courts consider that section 24(b) of the IAA, which acknowledges national justice, is comparable to Article 34(2)(b)(ii) of the Model Law, rendering the two provisions equivalent.[74] Similarly, under sections 46(2) and 46(3) of the Hong Kong Arbitration Ordinance, which replaced Article 18 of the UNCITRAL Model Law, it is mandated that 'the parties must be treated with equality' and 'the tribunal is required to be independent and to act fairly and impartially as between the parties, giving them a reasonable opportunity to present their cases and to deal with the cases of their opponents'.[75] In another Model Law jurisdiction, Japan, the Japanese Arbitration Act mandates arbitrators to treat parties equally and to give each party a full opportunity to present its case according to Article 25.[76]

Similar due process guarantees are present in arbitration statutes of non-Model Law jurisdictions, including the United Kingdom,[77] the United States,[78] France,[79]

67. Zivilprozessordnung [Code of Civil Procedure] (Germany) § 1042, https://www.gesetze-im-internet.de/englisch_zpo/englisch_zpo.html#p3674.
68. Court of Appeals Frankfurt, 26 Sch H 3/09, 28 October 2010; Court of Appeals Cologne, 9 Sch 18/02, 26 November 2002.
69. Court of Appeals Cologne, 19 Sch 11/10, 28 June 2011; Bremen Court of Appeals, 2 Sch 02/03, 4 December 2003.
70. Court of Appeals Munich, SchiedsVZ 2010, 169.
71. Oberlandesgericht Cologne [Cologne Court of Appeal], 9 Sch 01-03, 23 April 2004 reported in (2005) XXX *Yearbook Commercial Arbitration* 557.
72. *International Arbitration Act* (Singapore, cap 143 A, 2002 rev ed) s. 24(b) (emphasis added).
73. *Soh Beng Tee & Co Pte Ltd v. Fairmount Development Pte Ltd* [2007] SGCA 28, [42].
74. *Government of the Republic of the Philippines v. Philippine International Air Terminals Co Inc* [2007] 1 SLR (R) 278, [18]; *ADG and another v. ADI and another matter* [2014] 3 SLR 481, [118], [127]–[151].
75. *Arbitration Ordinance* (Hong Kong) cap 609, ss 46(2)–46(3).
76. *Japanese Arbitration Act* (Japan), Art. 25 [Arbitration Law Follow-up Research Group trans, Arbitration Law, https://japan.kantei.go.jp/policy/sihou/arbitrationlaw.pdf] (implementing Article 18 of UNCITRAL Model Law).
77. *See* nn. 85–86 below.

Switzerland,[80] Italy,[81] Sweden,[82] the Netherlands,[83] and Lebanon.[84] For example, 'General Duty of the Tribunal' under section 33(1)(a) of the English Arbitration Act mandates the tribunal to act fairly and impartially between the parties and provide each party with a reasonable opportunity to present their case and counterarguments.[85] According to section 68 of the English Arbitration Act, parties may request the setting aside of an arbitral award due to a 'serious irregularity affecting the tribunal, the proceedings or the award', which can encompass the tribunal's failure to adhere to section 33.[86] English case law believes that this reflects the 'internationally accepted view that the court should be able to correct serious failure to comply with the "due process" of arbitral proceedings'.[87]

Article 1510 of the French Code of Civil Procedure states that 'the arbitral tribunal shall ensure that the parties are *treated equally* and shall uphold the principle of *due process*'.[88] What is translated as 'due process' is the '*principe du contradictoire*'. Some academics have proposed translating '*principe du contradictoire*' as 'principle of an adversarial process', highlighting the significance of affording both parties reasonable and equal opportunities to present their case.[89] Similar provisions regarding adversarial proceedings can be found in other non-Model Law arbitration statutes. For instance, Article 182(3) of the Swiss International Law Act,[90] Article 816 of the Italian Code of Civil Procedure,[91] and Article 24 of the Swedish Arbitration Act[92] share similar

78. *See* n. 93 below.
79. *See* n. 88 below.
80. *See* n. 90 below.
81. *See* n. 91 below.
82. *See* n. 92 below.
83. *See* n. 95 below.
84. *See* n. 94 below.
85. *Arbitration Act 1996* (UK) c 23, s. 33(1)(a).
86. *Arbitration Act 1996* (UK) c 23, ss 68(1)–68(2).
87. *U&M Mining Zambia Ltd v. Konkola Copper Mines* [2014] EWHC 2374 (Comm) (15 July 2014) [14].
88. *Code de procédure civile* [Code of Civil Procedure] (France) 13 January 2011, Art. 1510 [Emmanuel Gaillard et al., Code of Civil Procedure, https://sccinstitute.com/media/37105/french_law_on_arbitration.pdf] (emphasis added).
89. Friedrich Rosenfeld, Dietmar Czernich and Franco Ferrari, 'General Report' in Friedrich Rosenfeld, Dietmar Czernich and Franco Ferrari (eds), *Due Process as a Limit to Discretion in International Commercial Arbitration* (Kluwer Law International, 2020) 4. As shown in §3.03, in addition to the equal treatment and granting reasonable opportunities to present its case, the concept of due process also includes proper notice and impartiality and independence of arbitrators.
90. *Federal Act on Private International Law* (Switzerland) 18 December 1987, Art. 182(3) [Andreas Bucher trans, *The English translations of Federal Act on Private International Law*, http://www.andreasbucher-law.ch/images/stories/pil_act_1987_as_amended_until_1_7_2014.pdf] ('the arbitral tribunal shall ensure equal treatment of the parties and the right of both parties to be heard in adversarial proceedings').
91. *Italian Code of Civil Procedure*, Art. 816 (the arbitrators must 'respect in any case the principle of adversarial process by granting both parties reasonable and equivalent opportunities to present their case'). The violation of Article 816 constitutes a ground of setting aside awards: *see Italian Code of Civil Procedure*, Art. 829(1)(9).
92. *Swedish Arbitration Act* (Sweden) SFS No. 1996:116, s. 24 [Joel Dahlquist Cullborg trans, *The Swedish Arbitration Act* (2019) https://sccinstitute.com/media/408924/the-swedish-arbitration-act_1march2019_eng.pdf] ('[t]he arbitrators shall afford the parties, to the extent necessary,

principles. In the United States, the FAA sets forth the grounds for setting aside awards, which include violations of the impartiality and independence of arbitrators and the parties' right to be heard.[93] In the Middle East, Lebanese courts have held that arbitrators should adhere to due process safeguards detailed in Articles 371 and 372 of the Lebanese Code of Civil Procedure. These safeguards guarantee the rights of the defence and the proper administration of justice.[94] Similarly, in the Netherlands, the Dutch Arbitration Act outlines more detailed requirements for due process in arbitral proceedings:

> The Arbitral tribunal shall treat the parties equally. The arbitral tribunal shall give the parties the opportunity to set out and explain their positions and to comment on each other's positions and on all documents and other information brought to the attention of the arbitral tribunal during the proceedings. The arbitral tribunal shall not base its decision, where it is unfavourable for one party, upon documents and other information on which that party was not sufficiently able to comment.[95]

Moreover, the identification of a principle common to the world's major legal systems considers other forms of material, such as public and private codification initiatives. These international instruments attempt to deduce general principles through comparative analysis. For instance, the UNIDROIT Principles of Transnational Civil Procedure (hereinafter 'UNIDROIT Principles'), one of the modern soft law instruments, offer a more precise elucidation of due process as a general principle of law. The UNIDROIT Principles list 'impartiality and independence',[96] 'procedural equality of parties',[97] 'due notice' and 'right to be heard'[98] as fundamental procedural principles. As detailed in §3.03 below, these principles serve to establish and embody the concept of due process.

The generalisation and distillation of the underlying legal principles that shape the rules of procedural fairness in municipal law are not challenging, as this has been done in the national constitutions and arbitration laws of the major jurisdictions. Thus, this chapter does not examine the rules or standards that states adopt when applying the concept of due process to abstract common principles. As discussed in more detail in Chapters 6 and 7, various jurisdictions apply different rules when it comes to the concept of due process. Nevertheless, these variances do not hinder the identification of a general principle of law.

---

an opportunity to present their respective cases in writing or orally... A party shall be given an opportunity to review all documents and all other materials pertaining to the dispute which are supplied to the arbitrators by the opposing party or another person').

93. *Federal Arbitration Act*, 9 US Code § 10 (a)(1)–10 (a)(3) (2012).
94. Beirut Court of First Instance, No. 37, 27 October 2008, reported in (2009) 49 *Lebanese Review of Arab & International Arbitration* 28.
95. Wetboek van Burgerlijke Rechtsvordering [Dutch Code of Civil Procedure] (Netherlands) Art. 1036 (2).
96. *ALI/UNIDROIT Principles of Transnational Civil Procedure* (American Law Institute and International Institute for the Unification of Private Law, 2006) Art. 1.
97. *Ibid.*, Art. 3.
98. *Ibid.*, Art. 5.

[2] *Ascertainment of Transposition into the International Legal System*

The second stage of identifying the general principles of law in *foro domestico* involves determining whether a principle common to the main legal systems worldwide has been transposed into the international legal system.[99] The arbitral tribunal in the case of *El Paso Energy International Company v. The Argentine Republic* held that the general principles of law are 'rules largely applied in *foro domestico*, in private or public, substantive or procedural matters, provided that, *after adaptation*, they are suitable for application on the *level of public international law*'.[100] General principles of law that derive from national legal systems may need adaption in order to be applicable at an international level based on the characteristics specific to international law.[101]

Although the principle of due process derives from the major national legal systems, it cannot be conceptualised solely by reference to how it is understood in the context of a particular national procedural system when it is transposed into international instruments in order to function as a fundamental procedural norm for adjudicative proceedings. Instead, it must be conceptualised by reference to an international instrument.

The ILC Report indicates that for such transposition to be accepted, the principle must not contradict fundamental principles of international law, such as the principle of sovereignty and the concept of territorial sovereignty, and the conditions necessary for the adequate application of the principle in the international legal order must be present.[102] The practice of states and the jurisprudence of international courts and tribunals appear to suggest that international instruments, in particular treaties, may serve as evidence that a principle common to the major legal systems of the world has been *transposed* into the international legal system.[103] As illustrated further below, the principle of *audiatur et altera pars* is present not only in the major national legal systems but also in the international legal order, including international human rights law and international investment law. It is argued that this cross-fertilisation is essential for the proper functioning of the international justice system.[104] As Kolb stated:

> The application of the same principles across the legal order, in its most different branches, has the obvious effect of increasing its unity by a web of interrelationships and of interdependencies. This movement exists both on the plane of international law, within its branches, and on the level of the relation of international law to internal law: general principles of law permit to reach a great fluidity

99. Vázquez-Bermúdez, Second Report on General Principles of Law (n. 33) [73].
100. *El Paso Energy International Company v. The Argentine Republic* (ICSID Arbitral Tribunal, Case No. ARB/03/15, 11 October 2011) [622] (emphasis added).
101. Raimondo (n. 38) 70.
102. Vázquez-Bermúdez, *Second Report on General Principles of Law* (n. 33) [74]–[96]. *See also Rome Statute of the International Criminal Court*, opened for signature 17 July 1998, 2187 UNTS 3 (entered into force 1 July 2002) Art. 21(1)(c); Giorgio Gaja, 'General Principles in the Jurisprudence of the ICJ' in Mads Andenas et al. (eds), *General Principles and the Coherence of International Law* (Brill, 2019) 39.
103. Vázquez-Bermúdez, Second Report on General Principles of Law (n. 33) [97].
104. Kotuby and Sobota (n. 10) 15.

> of the main legal ideas, which can be transported by way of analogy from one branch to the other, from one legal system to the other. If an image be ventured, the general principles are the bees of law.[105]

In international human rights law, the principle of '*audiatur et altera pars*' is reflected in Article 6(1) of the ECHR. This article states that:

> In the determination of his civil rights and obligations or of any criminal charge against him, everyone is entitled to a fair and public hearing within a reasonable time by an independent and impartial tribunal established by law.[106]

Similar provisions can be found in other human rights instruments, including the Universal Declaration of Human Rights,[107] the ICCPR,[108] and the EUCFR.[109] In addition, the ECJ ruled that the principle of *audiatur et altera pars* is common to the legal orders of EU Member States and can be relied upon even in the absence of any applicable treaty.[110] For an international tribunal that adheres to the rule of law, it must ensure all the necessary guarantees of fairness, justice, and impartiality, in full conformity with internationally recognised human rights instruments.[111]

Article 6 of the ECHR has historically applied to criminal and civil proceedings. However, in recent years, it has also been extended to encompass commercial arbitration.[112] The ECtHR has acknowledged the relevance of arbitral proceedings in interpreting the ECHR's fair trial guarantees.[113] As discussed in Chapter 2, although the direct applicability of the ECHR to arbitral tribunals has been controversial, both ECtHR practice and certain scholars have agreed that Article 6(1) of the ECHR is applicable to arbitral proceedings. Consequently, national courts in the EU are obliged to ensure that arbitral proceedings observe this provision.

105. Robert Kolb, 'Principles as Sources of International Law (With Special Reference to Good Faith)' (2006) 53(1) *Netherland International Law Review* 1, 27 DOI: 10.1017/s0165070x06000015.
106. *Convention for the Protection of Human Rights and Fundamental Freedoms*, opened for signature 4 November 1950, 213 UNTS 221 (entered into force 3 September 1953) Art. 6(1).
107. *Universal Declaration of Human Rights*, adopted 10 December 1948, UNGA Res 217 A (III), Art. 10.
108. *International Covenant on Civil and Political Rights*, opened for signature 19 December 1966, 999 UNTS 171 (entered into force 23 March 1976) Art. 14.
109. Charter of Fundamental Rights of the European Union (entered into force 1 December 2009) Art. 47.
110. *Transocean Marine Paint Ass'n v. Commission* (C-17/74) [1974] ECR 1063.
111. *Prosecutor v. Duško Tadić a/k/a 'DULE' (Decision on the Defence Motion for Interlocutory Appeal on Jurisdiction)* (International Criminal Tribunal for the Former Yugoslavia, Appeals Chamber, Case No. IT-94-1-A, 2 October 1995) [43].
112. *See, e.g., Ferrara v. AG 1824*, judgment by the Brussels Court of Appeals in 2002, which, however, stressed that arbitrators have a duty to ensure that fair trial guarantees are met. *See also* Bantekas (n. 31); Cananea (n. 8) 196; Massimo V Benedettelli, 'Human Rights as A Litigation Tool in International Arbitration: Reflecting on the ECHR Experience' (2015) 31(4) *Arbitration International* 631, 642 DOI: 10.1093/arbint/aiv036; Petrochilos (n. 22) 153; Aleksandar Jaksic, *Arbitration and Human Rights* (Peter Lang, 2002) 186.
113. *See, e.g., Tabbane v. Switzerland* [2016] Eur Court HR 109, [27]; *Klausecker v. Germany* [2015] EHRR SE8, [69]–[77]; *Deweer v. Belgium* [1979–80] 2 EHRR 439, [49]; *Jakob Boss Söhn KG v. the Federal Republic of Germany* (European Court of Human Rights, Application No. 18479/91, 2 December 1991); *Lithgow and Others v. UK* [1986] 8 EHRR 329, [201].

In addition, due process has been introduced into international investment arbitration as a general principle of law. It is deemed as part of the applicable law, whether through explicit provision in choice-of-law clauses within international investment treaties or because arbitral tribunals rightfully interpret investment treaties in accordance with public international law and its sources, which include general principles of law.[114] In investment arbitration, due process is commonly regarded as a component of the FET standard.[115] The North American Free Trade Agreement (NAFTA) tribunals have affirmed that host states must not deny justice and should uphold due process as stipulated in Article 1105.[116] Similarly, Article 5(2)(a) of the 2012 US Model BIT states that:

> Fair and equitable treatment includes the obligation not to deny justice in criminal, civil, or administrative adjudicatory proceedings in accordance with *the principle of due process* embodied in the *principal legal systems of the world*.[117]

Similar provisions incorporating due process in the FET standard are prevalent in various investment treaties, such as the Comprehensive Economic and Trade Agreement.[118] International tribunals and scholars generally consider that 'the international law requirements of due process', in the sense of a general principle of law, must be observed in investor-state arbitration.[119] The test for the FET pertains to an international standard of 'justice' being met rather than simple compliance with local law.[120] Due process, within the context of investment arbitration, has two connotations. First, as a part of the FET principle, it places significant obligations on host states in relation to investments by foreign investors.[121] Due process extends beyond the judicial system of host states and encompasses all forms of governmental decision-making, such as executive and legislative measures taken by the government and administration.[122] Second, arbitral tribunals must meet obligations under the principle of due process when determining investor-state cases.[123] The second meaning and standards of due

114. Schill (n. 38) 142.
115. *Waste Management, Inc v. United Mexican States (Award)* (ICSID Arbitral Tribunal, Case No. ARB(AF)/00/3, 30 April 2004) [98] (defined a violation of fair and equitable treatment as 'involv[ing] a lack of due process leading to an outcome which offends judicial propriety – as might be the case with a manifest failure of natural justice in judicial proceedings or a complete lack of transparency and candour in an administrative process'); Dumberry (n. 7) 145–149; Fulvio Maria Palombino, *Fair and Equitable Treatment and the Fabric of General Principles* (TMC Asser, 2018) 58–82; Cananea (n. 8) 2–3, 47–53; Schill (n. 38) 170–174.
116. Palombino (n. 115) 60.
117. 2012 US Model BIT, Art. 5(2)(a) (emphasis added). For the discussion of the closely related concept of denial of justice in international law, *see* Dumberry (n. 7) 310–314; Jan Paulsson, *Denial of Justice in International Law* (Cambridge University Press, 2005).
118. Comprehensive Economic and Trade Agreement, Art 8.10.2(b).
119. *SD Myers, Inc v. Government of Canada (Partial Award)* (UNCITRAL Arbitration Tribunal, 13 November 2000) [134]; Schill (n. 38) 142.
120. Alex Mills, The Confluence of Public and Private International Law: Justice, Pluralism and Subsidiarity in the International Constitutional Ordering of Private Law (Cambridge University Press, 2009) 267.
121. Dumberry (n. 7) 146; Palombino (n. 115) 58–82.
122. Dumberry (n. 7) 310, citing Alexandra Diehl, *The Core Standard of International Investment Protection* (Wolters Kluwer, 2012) 431.
123. Dumberry (n. 7) 146.

process bear more relevance to this book and may be applicable to arbitral tribunals in international commercial disputes. To illustrate, ad hoc annulment committees scrutinise investor-state awards under the Convention on the Settlement of Investment Disputes between States and Nationals of Other States (ICSID Convention). ICSID awards may be invalidated if there has been 'a serious departure from a fundamental rule of procedure'.[124] The ICSID ad hoc annulment committee nullified the *Fraport AG v. Philippines* award as the tribunal depended on evidence submitted after the formal proceedings ended. This action denied the claimant its fundamental right to be heard.[125]

The relevance of general principles of law extends beyond the relations between states in public international law. Such principles also apply to interactions between states and private investors in investment law and in the context of purely international commercial arbitration.[126] Due process is a general principle of law that applies to all adjudicatory processes, including arbitration. However, there are some slight variations in the specific rules derived from the principle of due process between international commercial arbitration law and public international law. The fundamental international treaties governing modern international commercial arbitration, such as the European Convention on International Commercial Arbitration[127] and the New York Convention,[128] acknowledge the principle of due process. These provisions demonstrate a universal legal principle that governs the arbitral process, which mandates that both sides are granted a reasonable opportunity to present their case and receive equal treatment.

§3.03 CORE ELEMENTS OF *AUDIATUR ET ALTERA PARS* IN INTERNATIONAL COMMERCIAL ARBITRATION

As demonstrated above, *audiatur et altera pars* has been well accepted as a general principle of law, and Article V(1)(b) of the New York Convention embodies it in international commercial arbitration. Thus, the elements of *audiatur et altera pars* that have been established in international legal regimes can define and elucidate the normative substance of Article V(1)(b) of the New York Convention.

A principle is typically broad in scope and does not detail the specific conditions of its application or legal effects. Derivatives or related concepts can be extracted from a principle to give it substance.[129] Identifying the subsidiary principles of *audiatur et*

124. *Convention on the Settlement of Investment Disputes between States and Nationals of other States*, opened for signature 18 March 1965, 575 UNTS 159 (entered into force 14 October 1966) Art. 52(1)(d).
125. *Fraport AG Frankfurt Airport Servs Worldwide v. Republic of the Philippines (Annulment)* (ICSID Arbitral Tribunal, Case No. ARB/03/25, 23 December 2010) [197]–[247].
126. Schill (n. 38) 143–145; Friedmann (n. 6) 295.
127. *European Convention on International Commercial Arbitration*, opened for signature 21 April 1961, 484 UNTS 349 (entered into force 18 October 1965) Art. IX(1)(b).
128. *Convention on the Recognition and Enforcement of Foreign Arbitral Awards*, open for signature 10 June 1958, 330 UNTS 3 (entered into force 7 June 1959) Art. V(1)(b).
129. Kolb (n. 18) 964.

altera pars, the general working attributes, is helpful in converting a principle into an operational tool. In examining the guarantees of due process, this section considers not just national arbitration laws and institutional arbitration rules but also the fundamental principles of civil adjudication as prescribed by international treaties. Although the exact contours of due process cannot be defined, as set out in this section, it typically encompasses the following fundamental notions and elements: (a) due notice of the appointment of arbitrators and of the proceedings; (b) equality of arms; (c) the right to be heard; and (d) arbitrators' impartiality and independence.[130] In view of their general quality and importance, these attributes may be regarded as further principles derived from the principle of due process and constitute the precise content of the due process guarantees in Article V(1)(b) of the New York Convention.

[A] Due Notice

Due notice is a prerequisite for the right to be heard with equality by an impartial and independent tribunal. Justice requires that a person has notice of a decision before he can be conclusively bound by its result. Proper notice has long been a 'fundamental condition' that is 'universally prescribed in all systems of law established by civilised countries'.[131] Accordingly, this fundamental principle is a core component of due process in both international and national legal systems.[132]

Due notice is essential to judicial proceedings and is usually regarded as one of the grounds for refusing recognition or enforcement of foreign judgments, although the specific standards of proper service for foreign judgments may differ from those for foreign arbitral awards. For instance, the Convention on the Recognition and Enforcement of Foreign Judgments in Civil or Commercial Matters explicitly requires that the defendant be served with the document instituting the proceedings 'in sufficient time and in such a way as to enable them to arrange for their defence', and failure to serve properly may be a ground for refusing recognition or enforcement of foreign judgments.[133] In *Beer v. Austria*, the ECtHR held that a lack of service prevented a party from being aware of and responding to an appeal lodged by the other party, thereby

130. Rosenfeld, Czernich and Ferrari (n. 89) 19–38; Kotuby and Sobota (n. 10) 157–184; Lucy Reed, 'Ab(use) of Due Process: Sword vs Shield' (2017) 33 *Arbitration International* 361, 367–368; Cananea (n. 8) 52; Born (n. 23) 3505; Jeff Waincymer, *Procedure and Evidence in International Arbitration* (Kluwer Law International, 2012) 15–16; Willian W Park, 'The Procedural Soft Law of International Arbitration: Non-governmental Instruments' in Loukas A Mistelis and Julian D M Lew QC (eds), *Pervasive Problems in International Arbitration* (Kluwer Law International, 2006) 143–144; *ALI/UNIDROIT Principles of Transnational Civil Procedure* (American Law Institute and International Institute for the Unification of Private Law, 2006) Arts 1, 3, 5; Cheng (n. 11) 291.
131. *Twining v. New Jersey*, 211 US 78, 111 (1908).
132. Kotuby and Sobota (n. 10) 158–163; Charles T Kotuby, 'General Principles of Law, International Due Process, and the Modern Role of Private International Law' (2013) 23(3) *Duke Journal of Comparative & International Law* 411, 427; *ALI/UNIDROIT Principles of Transnational Civil Procedure* (American Law Institute and International Institute for the Unification of Private Law, 2006) Art. 5.
133. Convention on the Recognition and Enforcement of Foreign Judgments in Civil or Commercial Matters, concluded 2 July 2019, Art. 7(1)(a).

violating the principle of due process.[134] In this judgment, the ECtHR highlighted that 'what is at stake is the litigants' confidence in the workings of justice, which is based on, inter alia, the knowledge that they have had the opportunity to express their views on every document in the file'.[135] Furthermore, the Brussels Ibis Regulation enables courts to refuse recognition or enforcement of a judgment if the judgment was given in default of appearance and the defendant has been able to prove that there was a defect in the service of the judgment which rendered him incapable of defending himself effectively.[136]

Adequate notice is also a requirement for the recognition and enforcement of a foreign arbitral award, as reflected in the New York Convention, the European Convention on International Commercial Arbitration and the UNCITRAL Model Law. The requirement of 'proper notice' to the parties is intended to ensure the right of the parties to present their case and to have an impartial and independent tribunal. Proper notice of the appointment of arbitrators and of the arbitral proceedings ensures that the parties are informed so that they can participate in the arbitral proceedings, challenge the potential biased or partial arbitrators, or object to unfair arbitral proceedings. Although the New York Convention, national arbitration laws and related institutional arbitration rules allow for notice of arbitral proceedings to be given by different mechanisms, those mechanisms must, in the circumstances, adequately inform the interested parties of the appointment of arbitrators and of the arbitral procedure for responding to and challenging the procedural irregularities.[137]

[B] Equality of the Parties

Fundamental to the *audiatur et altera pars* principle discussed in §3.02[A][2] is the notion of equality of the parties.[138] As stated in Article 14(1) of the ICCPR, everyone 'shall be equal before the courts and tribunals'.[139] Procedural inequality under the ICCPR has typically been determined by the United Nations Human Rights Committee

134. *Beer v. Austria* (European Court of Human Rights, Application No. 30428/96, 6 February 2001).
135. *Ibid.*, [18].
136. Brussels Ibis Regulation, Art. 45(1)(b).
137. *See UNCITRAL Model Law*, UN Docs A/40/17 and A/61/17 (n. 62) Art. 24(2); United Nations Committee on International Trade Law, *UNCITRAL Arbitration Rules* (2nd ed., 2010), GA Res 65/22, 6th Comm A/65/465, 66th sess., Agenda Item 77, UN Doc. A/RES/65/22 (6 December 2010) ('*UNCITRAL Arbitration Rules*') Art. 28(1); International Chamber of Commerce, *Arbitration Rules* (adopted 1 January 2021) ('*ICC Arbitration Rules*') Art. 26(1); Singapore International Arbitration Centre, *SIAC Arbitration Rules* (adopted 1 August 2016) ('*SIAC Arbitration Rule*') Art. 24(2); London Court of International Arbitration, *LCIA Arbitration Rules* (adopted 1 October 2014) ('*LCIA Arbitration Rules*') Art. 19(3); Arbitration Institute of the Stockholm Chamber of Commerce, *SCC Arbitration Rules* (adopted 1 January 2017) ('*SCC Arbitration Rules*') Art. 32(2); Hong Kong International Arbitration Centre, *Administered Arbitration Rules* (adopted 1 November 2018) ('*HKIAC Arbitration Rules*') Art. 22(4).
138. Dumberry (n. 7) 145; Kotuby and Sobota (n. 10) 176–183; Fellmeth and Horwitz (n. 15) 41; Cheng (n. 11) 291.
139. *International Covenant on Civil and Political Rights*, opened for signature 19 December 1966, 999 UNTS 171 (entered into force 23 March 1976) Art. 14(1).

(UNHRC). The UNHRC developed its test for the principle of equality of the parties in General Comment No. 32 on Article 14 of the ICCPR:

> The right to equality before courts and tribunals also ensures equality of arms. This means that the *same* procedural rights are to be provided to all the parties unless *distinctions are based on law and can be justified on objective and reasonable grounds*, not entailing *actual disadvantage* or other *unfairness* to the defendant.[140]

Although the ECtHR has not provided an explicit definition of what constitutes a 'fair hearing' within the meaning of Article 6(1) of the ECHR, the court has held that a 'fair hearing' must include certain elements – the most fundamental of which are the principles of equality of arms and the right to be heard.[141] In applying Article 6(1) of the ECHR, the ECtHR has held that 'equality of arms' means that each party must be afforded a reasonable opportunity to present his case, including his evidence, under conditions which do not place him at a substantial disadvantage vis-à-vis his opponent.[142]

Although there is no explicit reference to it in the New York Convention, it is well accepted by scholars and domestic courts that the notion of equal treatment between parties permeates Article V(1)(b) of the New York Convention.[143] Unlike the New York Convention, the UNCITRAL Model Law guarantees equal treatment in a more explicit manner. As discussed above, Article 18 provides that '[t]he parties shall be treated with equality and each party shall be given a full opportunity of presenting his case'.[144] Equality of arms ensures that a party is not treated less favourably than its counterparty in arbitral proceedings. Following the adoption of the UNCITRAL Model Law, the UNCITRAL Arbitration Rules and all major rules of international arbitral institutions confirm the principle of equal treatment and the right to be heard.[145]

Equality of arms has been confirmed by national arbitration laws in both Model Law and non-Model Law jurisdictions. As discussed above, section 46(2) of the Hong Kong Arbitration Ordinance, similar to the Model Law, also explicitly states the requirement of equality of arms.[146] Similar provisions can be found in the German Code

140. United Nations Human Rights Council, *General Comment No 32, Article 14: Right to Equality Before Courts and Tribunals and to a Fair Trial*, CCPR/C/GC/32, 19th session, 23 August 2007, [13] (emphasis added).
141. Ola Johan Settem, Applications of the 'Fair Hearing' Norm in ECHR Article 6(1) to Civil Proceedings: With Special Emphasis on the Balance Between Procedural Safeguards and Efficiency (Springer, 2016) 96–118; Bernadette Rainey, Elizabeth Wicks and Clare Ovey, Jacobs, White and Ovey: The European Convention on Human Rights (Oxford University Press, 2014) 263–265; Petrochilos (n. 22) 144–149.
142. *Dombo Beheer BV v. the Netherlands* (European Court of Human Rights, Application No. 14448/88, 27 October 1993) [33].
143. Blackaby et al. (n. 25) 356; Scherer (n. 24) 298–299; Verbist (n. 22) 679; *Paklito Investment Ltd v. Klockner East Asia Ltd* [1993] 2 HKLR 39.
144. *UNCITRAL Model Law*, UN Docs A/40/17 and A/61/17 (n. 62) Art. 18.
145. *See UNCITRAL Arbitration Rules*, UN Doc. A/RES/65/22 (n. 137) Art. 17(1); *ICC Arbitration Rules* (n. 137) Art. 22(4); *SIAC Arbitration Rules* (n. 137) Art. 17(1); *LCIA Arbitration Rules* (n. 137) Art. 14(4)(i); *HKIAC Arbitration Rules* (n. 137) Art. 13(1); *SCC Arbitration Rules* (n. 137) Art. 23(2).
146. *Arbitration Ordinance* (Hong Kong) cap 609, s. 46(2).

of Civil Procedure (ZPO)[147] and the Japanese Arbitration Act.[148] Even non-Model Law jurisdictions, such as France, Switzerland, Italy, and the Netherlands, uphold the principle of equality of arms in arbitration.[149] French courts have highlighted that the objective of equality of arms is to ensure that no party is placed at a decisive disadvantage vis-à-vis its opponent:

> Equality of arms, which is an element of fair trial protected by international public policy, entails the obligation to give each party a reasonable opportunity to present its case, including its evidence, under conditions that do not place it at a *distinct disadvantage* in relation to its adversary.[150]

First, the above-mentioned jurisprudence of the UNHRC, the ECtHR, and the French courts emphasise that the essence of the principle of equality is to prevent one party from being placed at a substantial disadvantage vis-à-vis its opponent. Equality of arms defines the fundamental structure of the adjudicatory proceedings, which must be adversarial: each party must be accorded the same procedural rights, and there must be a constant effort to redress potential inequalities between the parties that may affect the fair outcome of the proceedings.[151] It requires that the opportunities afforded to the parties in adversarial proceedings be fairly balanced.[152] Thus, the court or the tribunal should treat the parties equally and ensure that they are as equal as possible in terms of overall power. It is worth noting that what equality of arms seeks to do is not to ensure that either party is given a particular procedural right. Instead, it simply ensures that when one party is given a procedural right, the other party should be granted the same treatment.[153]

Second, equality of arms requires that courts or tribunals give the parties an equal opportunity to present their cases, particularly their arguments. As stated in an investment award, equality of arms requires that 'each party is given the right to

147. *Zivilprozessordnung* [Code of Civil Procedure] (Germany) § 1042, https://www.gesetze-im-internet.de/englisch_zpo/englisch_zpo.html#p3674.
148. *Japanese Arbitration Act* (Japan), Art. 25 [Arbitration Law Follow-up Research Group trans, Arbitration Law, https://japan.kantei.go.jp/policy/sihou/arbitrationlaw.pdf] (implementing Article 18 of UNCITRAL Model Law).
149. France: *Code de procédure civile* [Code of Civil Procedure] (France) 13 January 2011, Art. 1510 [Emmanuel Gaillard et al., Code of Civil Procedure, https://sccinstitute.com/media/37105/french_law_on_arbitration.pdf] ('the arbitral tribunal shall ensure that the parties are treated equally and shall uphold the principle of due process'); Switzerland: *Federal Act on Private International Law* (Switzerland) 18 December 1987, Art. 182(3) [Andreas Bucher trans, *The English translations of Federal Act on Private International Law*, http://www.andreasbucher-law.ch/images/stories/pil_act_1987_as_amended_until_1_7_2014.pdf] ('the arbitral tribunal shall *ensure equal treatment* of the parties and the right of both parties to be heard in *adversarial proceedings*'); Italy: *Italian Code of Civil Procedure*, Art. 816 (the arbitrators must 'respect in any case the principle of adversarial process by granting both parties reasonable and equivalent opportunities to present their case'); the Neverlands: Wetboek van Burgerlijke Rechtsvordering [Dutch Code of Civil Procedure] (Netherlands) Art. 1036 (2).
150. Caroline Kleiner, 'Chapter 7: Country Report: France' in Friedrich Rosenfeld, Dietmar Czernich and Franco Ferrari (eds), *Due Process as a Limit to Discretion in International Commercial Arbitration* (Kluwer Law International, 2020) 166 (emphasis added).
151. Kolb (n. 18) 969.
152. Bantekas (n. 31) 1003.
153. John Henry Dingfelder Stone, *Court Interpreters and Fair Trials* (Springer, 2018) 110.

...state its [case] and to produce all *arguments* and *evidence* in support of it...on an *equal level*'.[154] In practice, it requires that 'both parties are entitled to submit evidence on equal terms, both have the same rights to inspect and analyse records, and both may present and question witnesses without procedural differences'.[155] An example of its application can be found in *Vojnovic v. Croatia*, where the UNHRC found that the trial court had violated Article 14(1) of the ICCPR by refusing, without giving reasons, to hear the complainant's witnesses after allowing the opposing party to present its evidence.[156]

Third, equality of arms emphasises the substantive rather than formal equality of the parties. On the one hand, the principle of equality of arms requires that both parties be given equal opportunities in the proceedings. It requires that the same remedies are equally available to both parties. Quantitatively, the equality of the parties is a constant factor in the sense that each party should be entitled to an identical amount of opportunity to present its case to the tribunal. This will normally mean, save in exceptional circumstances, the same time to prepare their written pleadings, the same number of written and oral pleadings, or a reasonable time to respond to new arguments.[157]

On the other hand, the principle of equality has a more fundamental constitutional aspect than specific procedural rules. Sometimes, it may indeed be necessary to deviate from or soften specific procedural rules in order to ensure effective rather than theoretical equality. It is worth noting that equal treatment of parties does not mean absolute equality between parties. As the Norwegian government commented in the *travaux préparatoires* to the 1976 UNCITRAL Arbitration Rules, 'absolute equality seems insufficient to prevent real inequality between the parties' and 'it is not sufficient that the same formal rules be applied to both parties'.[158] For the same reasons, the UNHRC has held that distinctions are permissible if they are based on law and can be justified on objective and reasonable grounds.[159]

Equality of parties may be interwoven with another two facets of due process – the right to be heard and the impartiality and independence of adjudicators, discussed below. When a party is treated unequally, this may raise reasonable doubts as to the impartiality and independence of the arbitrators. Unequal time for oral argument or opportunity to present evidence may also violate a party's right to present its case. Nevertheless, the equality of the parties continues to serve an independent purpose in the attributes of due process. A party that has been given full opportunity to present its case by impartial and independent arbitrators may still feel that it has been treated

154. *Wena Hotels Ltd v. Arab Republic of Egypt (Annulment)* (ICSID Arbitral Tribunal, Case No. ARB/98/4, 5 February 2002) [57] (emphasis added).
155. Stone (n. 153) 109.
156. Human Rights Committee, *Views: Communication No 1510/2006*, 95th sess., UN Doc. CCPR/C/95/D/1510/2006 (30 March 2009) [8.2]–[8.3] ('*Dusan Vojnovic v. Croatia*').
157. Shaw (n. 28) para. 258; Kolb (n. 18) 970.
158. *See* (1975) 6 *UNCITRAL Yearbook*, UN Doc. A/CN.9/97/Add.3 (Norway) 184; (1976) 7 *UNCITRAL Yearbook*, UN Doc. A/CN.9/112, 163.
159. United Nations Human Rights Council (n. 140) [13]; Human Rights Committee, *Views: Communication No 1347/2005*, 90th sess,. UN Doc. CCPR/C/90/D/1347/2005 (23 July 2007) [7.4] ('*Dudko v. Australia*').

unfairly and unjustly if the opposing party is given a greater opportunity to present its case.

[C] Right to Be Heard: Reasonable Opportunity to Present One's Case

The definition of *audiatur et altera pars* discussed in §3.02[A][2] indicates that another core notion of due process is to ensure the parties' right to be heard.[160] This is reflected in Article 18 of the UNCITRAL Model Law, which requires that 'each party shall be given a full opportunity of presenting his case'. In his seminal book on general principles of law, Professor Cheng has also stated:

> It may indeed be submitted that besides the fundamental idea of equality between the parties, another ratio of the principle *audiatur et altera pars* is that it ensures the *presentation of sufficient data concerning the case* for the judge to 'arrive at a judicial conclusion'.[161]

There is not only a striking similarity but also a connection between the development of the right to be heard and the jurisprudence of different international regimes. Although it pertains to administrative proceedings, the ECJ has held that the rights of the defence include that the person concerned must have been enabled to express his views effectively.[162] In the ECJ case of *Transocean Marine Paint Association*, Werner, as Advocate General, carried out a comparative analysis of the legal systems of the Member States and found that the maxim *audiatur et altera pars* was 'a rule embedded in the law of some of our countries' and could therefore be included among the rules of law to be respected by the ECJ.[163] He argued that *audiatur et altera pars* requires that an authority, before exercising a power that might adversely affect a particular person, must give that person an opportunity to be heard, which the ECJ must follow.[164] The ECtHR also held that while the tribunal has discretion to disregard what it considers irrelevant to the case, such an authority can only be considered effective if both parties have been heard.[165] Thus, a fundamental requirement in both courts and arbitral proceedings is that the parties must be able to present their cases effectively.[166]

First, the right to be heard requires tribunals to give each party a reasonable opportunity to present its case. At first sight, the word 'full' in Article 18 of the UNCITRAL Model Law can be misleading: it suggests that a party is entitled to present its case as much as it sees fit. In the context of Article 18, however, the word 'full' must

160. Dumberry (n. 7) 145; Kotuby and Sobota (n. 10) 176–83; Fellmeth and Horwitz (n. 15) 41; Cheng (n. 11) 291.
161. Cheng (n. 11) 298 (emphasis added).
162. *Michelin v. Commission of the European Communities* (European Court of Justice, C-322-81, ECLI:EU:C:1983:313, 9 November 1983) [8].
163. *Opinion of Advocate General Werner* (C-17/74) [1974] ECR 1082, 1087.
164. *Ibid.*
165. *Donadze v. Georgia* (European Court of Human Rights, Second Section, Application No. 74644/01, 7 March 2006) [35].
166. *H v. Belgium* [1987] 10 EHRR 339, [53].

be understood as meaning 'reasonable' – no more and no less than a right to have a reasonable opportunity to present its case.[167] Article 18 does not entitle a party to obstruct the proceedings by dilatory tactics, such as submitting objections, amendments, or evidence only on the eve of the award.[168] In practice, it seems unlikely that an enforcing court would refuse to recognise or enforce an award where the tribunal has taken a clearly reasonable and proportionate approach to limit the scope of the evidence that a party wishes to present. This is confirmed by the fact that most modern arbitration rules adopted after the UNCITRAL Model Law expressly provide that a party should be given a 'reasonable opportunity to present its case', which encourages arbitral tribunals to balance the right to be heard with efficiency in determining the appropriate arbitral procedure.[169]

Second, the right to be heard requires tribunals to give each party a reasonable opportunity to comment on both the evidence and the arguments of the other party.[170] The ECtHR, for example, sees the right to be heard essentially as a right to adversarial proceedings or a right to challenge the other side's evidence before the court.[171] The ECtHR has defined the right to adversarial proceedings as 'the opportunity for the parties to have knowledge of and comment on the observations filed or evidence adduced by the other party'.[172] As mentioned above, the Dutch Arbitration Act clarifies that the right to be heard includes the opportunity for the parties to comment on each other's positions and on all documents and other information brought to the attention of the arbitral tribunal.[173] Likewise, France also equates the right to be heard with the adversarial principle, according to which no evidence or argument may serve as a basis for a decision unless it has been subject to the possibility of comment and contradiction by the other party. In the context of arbitration, Article 1510 of the French Civil Code of Procedure requires that the 'arbitral tribunal shall ensure that the parties are treated equally and shall uphold the adversarial principle'.[174] French courts have also drawn

167. *JVL Agro Industries Ltd v. Agritrade International Pte Ltd* [2016] 4 SLR 768, [145]; *ADG and another v. ADI and another matter* [2014] 3 SLR 481, [104].
168. United Nations Committee on International Trade Law, *Analytical Commentary on the Draft Text of the Model Law*, UN Doc. A/CN.9/264 (25 March 1985) 46–47.
169. *UNCITRAL Arbitration Rules*, UN Doc. A/RES/65/22 (n. 137) Art. 17; *ICC Arbitration Rules* (n. 137) Art. 22(4); *LCIA Arbitration Rules* (n. 137) Art. 14(4)(i); *HKIAC Arbitration Rules* (n. 137) Art. 13(1); *SCC Arbitration Rules* (n. 137) Art. 23(2).
170. Settem (n. 141) 98–110.
171. Toms Krumiņš, Arbitration and Human Rights: Approaches to Excluding the Annulment of Arbitral Awards and Their Compatibility with the ECHR (Springer, 2020) 54; Stone (n. 153) 113; Stefan Trechsel, Human Rights in Criminal Proceedings (Oxford University Press, 2005) 89.
172. *See, e.g.*, *Sebahattin Evcimen v. Turkey* (European Court of Human Rights, Application No. 31792/06, 23 February 2010) [25]; *KS v. Finland* (European Court of Human Rights, Application No. 29346/95, 31 May 2001) [21].
173. Wetboek van Burgerlijke Rechtsvordering [Dutch Code of Civil Procedure] (Netherlands) Art. 1036 (2).
174. *Code de procédure civile* [Code of Civil Procedure] (France) 13 January 2011, Art. 1510 [Emmanuel Gaillard et al., Code of Civil Procedure, https://sccinstitute.com/media/37105/french_law_on_arbitration.pdf]. Although the English translation of Article 1510 made by Emmanuel Gaillard et al. is the expression 'due process' as the equivalent of '*principe de la contradiction*', the better translation is 'adversarial principle': *see* Kleiner (n. 150) 157.

the contours of the adversarial principle in arbitral proceedings according to the formula:

> The *adversarial principle* only requires that parties have been able to make known their allegations of fact and law and to discuss those of their opponent, so that nothing that served to base the decision of the arbitrators has escaped to the debate.[175]

Third, the right to be heard also entitles the party to present its witnesses and to examine witnesses against it. Although it is in the context of criminal proceedings, Article 14(3)(e) of the ICCPR explicitly entitles an accused to 'examine, or have examined, the witnesses against him', as well as 'to obtain the attendance and examination of witnesses on his behalf under the same conditions as witnesses against him'.[176] The ability to challenge and rebut evidence is necessary to preserve not only a party's right to present its case but also its right to adversarial proceedings.[177] In the context of international commercial arbitration, this means that the parties have the right to call before the arbitral tribunal the witnesses they consider relevant to their case and to examine witnesses called by the opposing party.

[D] Impartiality and Independence of the Arbitrators

It can be said that there are two cardinal features of an adjudicational process: the impartiality and independence of the tribunal and its corollary, the equality of the parties.[178] The principle of *nemo iudex in causa sua* (no one can be a judge in his own case) constitutes 'the most elementary and essential guarantee of impartiality in the administration of justice'.[179] Although applied in an investment arbitration, the tribunal applied a simple test of procedural fairness, requiring that the hearing be fair and that an adjudicator be unbiased and impartial.[180] The ECJ explicitly held that the right to an impartial tribunal constitutes the 'cornerstone' of the right to a fair trial, which is a general principle of EU law.[181] The impartiality and independence of arbitrators is also confirmed by the ICCPR in its Article 14(1), which requires that 'everyone shall be entitled to a fair and public hearing by a competent, independent and impartial tribunal established by law'.[182] Article 6(1) of the ECHR uses similar wording regarding the requirement of an independent and impartial tribunal.

175. Kleiner (n. 150) 162 (emphasis added).
176. *International Covenant on Civil and Political Rights*, opened for signature 19 December 1966, 999 UNTS 171 (entered into force 23 March 1976) Art. 14(3)(e).
177. Trechsel (n. 171) 292.
178. Cananea (n. 8) 35; Cheng (n. 11) 290; *AMZ v. AXX* [2015] SGHC 283.
179. Cheng (n. 11) 284.
180. *ADC Affiliate Limited and ADC & ADMC Management Limited v. Republic of Hungary (ADC)* (Award) (ICSID Arbitral Tribunal, Case No. ARB/03/16, 2 October 2006).
181. *Chronopost SA and La Poste v. Union française de l'express (UFEX) and Others* (European Court of Justice, C-341/06 P, C-342/06 P, ECLI:EU:C:2008:375, 1 July 2008) [46].
182. *International Covenant on Civil and Political Rights*, opened for signature 19 December 1966, 999 UNTS 171 (entered into force 23 March 1976) Art. 14(1).

Moreover, *nemo iudex in causa sua* has a wider scope than a literal interpretation of the Latin phrase would suggest: it applies in all cases where adjudicators have sufficient personal or pecuniary interests in the outcome of the proceedings to give rise to doubt as to their independence and impartiality.[183] It is therefore a fundamental principle of international arbitration that all arbitrators, including those appointed by the parties, must be and remain independent and impartial with respect to the parties and their dispute. Arbitration statutes and institutional arbitration rules usually provide for three instruments to safeguard impartiality and independence: the constant obligation of arbitrators to be impartial and independent, the disclosure by arbitrators of circumstances which may give rise to justifiable doubts as to their impartiality or independence before and during the arbitral proceedings, and the right of the parties to challenge a partial or dependent arbitrator.[184]

The concept of 'independence' is generally considered to relate to issues arising from the relationship, financial or otherwise, between an arbitrator and one of the parties.[185] Thus, 'independence' is generally subject to an objective test because it does not involve the state of mind of an arbitrator.[186] In contrast, 'impartiality' is considered to be concerned with an arbitrator's actual or apparent bias – either in favour of one of the parties or in relation to the issue(s) in dispute.[187]

The standards for disclosure of circumstances that may give rise to justifiable doubts as to an arbitrator's impartiality and independence and for challenges to arbitrators may be objective or subjective. The objective standard means that there are circumstances which may give rise to reasonable and justifiable doubts as to an arbitrator's impartiality or independence. Conversely, the subjective standard means that there are circumstances which may give rise to justifiable doubts in the mind of a party as to the impartiality or independence of the arbitrators. The ECtHR has held that impartiality 'normally denotes the absence of prejudice or bias and its existence or otherwise can be tested in various ways'.[188] The ECtHR generally applies both objective and subjective tests to determine whether arbitrators are impartial: 'a *subjective* test seeking to determine the personal conviction and behaviour of a particular judge; and on objective text seeking to ascertain whether the tribunal itself

183. Kotuby and Sobota (n. 10) 173.
184. International Bar Association, *IBA Guidelines on Conflicts of Interest in International Arbitration* (adopted 23 October 2014) General Standard 1 ('every arbitrator shall be impartial and independent of the parties at the time of accepting an appointment to serve and shall remain so until the final award has been rendered or the proceedings have otherwise finally terminated'); *ICC Arbitration Rules* (n. 137) Arts 11(1)–(3), 22(4); *LCIA Arbitration Rules* (n. 137) Arts 5(3)–(5), 10(1), 14(4)(i); *SCC Arbitration Rules* (n. 137) Arts 18(1), 18(4),19(1), 23(2); *SIAC Arbitration Rules* (n. 137) Arts 13(1), 13(4)–(5), 14(1); *HKIAC Arbitration Rules* (n. 137) Arts 11(1), 11(4), 11(6); *UNCITRAL Arbitration Rules*, UN Doc. A/RES/65/22 (n. 137) Arts 11, 12 (1); *UNCITRAL Model Law*, UN Docs A/40/17 and A/61/17 (n. 62) Art. 12.
185. Blackaby et al. (n. 25) 255.
186. *Ibid.*
187. *Ibid.*
188. *See, e.g., Micallef v. Malta* (European Court of Human Rights, Grand Chamber, Application No. 17056/06, 15 October 2009) [93]; *Morice v. France* (European Court of Human Rights, Grand Chamber, Application No. 29369/10, 23 April 2015) [73]; *Upite v. Latvia* (European Court of Human Rights, Fifth Section, Application No. 7636/08, 1 September 2016) [30].

offered sufficient guarantees to exclude any *legitimate doubt* in respect of its impartiality'.[189] A similar mechanism exists in international commercial arbitration. The UNCITRAL Model Law adopts an objective standard for the disclosure of impartiality and independence. It provides that the arbitrator 'shall disclose any circumstances likely to give rise to *justifiable doubts* as to his impartiality or independence'.[190] It appears to adopt an objective standard for the challenge of arbitrators by providing that a challenge can only be sustained if there are circumstances which give rise to justifiable doubts as to an arbitrator's impartiality or independence.[191] This objective approach to challenging arbitrators is followed by leading arbitral institutions such as London Court of International Arbitration (LCIA), Singapore International Arbitration Centre (SIAC), Hong Kong International Arbitration Centre (HKIAC) and Stockholm Chamber of Commerce (SCC) Arbitration Rules.[192] However, these leading arbitral institutions do not have a uniform approach to the standard of disclosure of circumstances relating to impartiality and independence. The UNCITRAL Arbitration Rules,[193] HKIAC Arbitration Rules,[194] SIAC Arbitration Rules,[195] and SCC Arbitration Rules[196] adopt an objective standard for disclosure, while the ICC Arbitration Rules and LCIA Arbitration Rules apply the subjective standard to varying degrees.[197]

It is noteworthy that transparency has recently become an additional safeguard for independence and impartiality. Some arbitral institutions have adopted guidelines to publicise the identity, role, and method of appointment of arbitrators, as well as decisions on challenges. For example, in February 2016, the ICC adopted the Guidance Note for the Disclosure of Conflicts by Arbitrators, which provides for the publication of information on arbitrators involved in ICC proceedings on its website.[198] These disclosure measures provide parties with more information about arbitrators and enable them to make more informed decisions about appointments, thereby enhancing the protection of due process in the constitution of an independent and impartial

189. *Upite v. Latvia* (European Court of Human Rights, Fifth Section, Application No. 7636/08, 1 September 2016) [30] (emphasis added). *See also Micallef v. Malta* (European Court of Human Rights, Grand Chamber, Application No. 17056/06, 15 October 2009) [93]–[94]; *Sahiner v. Turkey* (European Court of Human Rights, First Section, Application No. 29279/95, 25 September 2001) [36].
190. *UNCITRAL Model Law*, UN Docs A/40/17 and A/61/17 (n. 62) Art. 12(1) (emphasis added).
191. *Ibid.*, Art. 12(2).
192. LCIA Arbitration Rules (n. 137) Art. 10(1); SCC Arbitration Rules (n. 137) Art. 19(1); SIAC Arbitration Rules (n. 137) Art. 14(1); HKIAC Arbitration Rules (n. 137) Art. 11(6).
193. *UNCITRAL Arbitration Rules*, UN Doc. A/RES/65/22 (n. 137) Art. 11.
194. HKIAC Arbitration Rules (n. 137) Art. 11(4).
195. *SIAC Arbitration Rules* (n. 137) Art. 13(4)–(5).
196. *SCC Arbitration Rules* (n. 137) Art. 18(4).
197. ICC Arbitration Rules adopt the subjective disclosure standard for independence ('in the eyes of the parties') and the objective disclosure standard for impartiality ('reasonable doubts'): *see ICC Arbitration Rules* (n. 137) Art. 11(2)–(3). In contrast, LCIA Arbitration Rules adopt the subjective disclosure standard for both independence and impartiality ('in the mind of any party'): *see LCIA Arbitration Rules* (n. 137) Arts 5(4)–(5).
198. International Chamber of Commerce, *Note to Parties and Arbitral Tribunals on the Conduct of the Arbitration under the ICC Rules of Arbitration* (adopted 30 October 2017). *See also* the ICC Blog on the Note at https://iccwbo.org/media-wall/news-speeches/icc-court-adopts-guidance-note-on-conflict-disclosures-by-arbitrators/.

tribunal. In addition, the LCIA has published the Notes for Arbitrators on Independence and Impartiality, which require arbitrators to consider, among other things, the existence and nature of any past or present relationship, direct or indirect, with any of the parties or their counsel. Any doubt as to whether a relationship should be disclosed must be resolved in favour of disclosure.[199] Similarly, the SIAC and the HKIAC have also published the Code of Ethics for an Arbitrator.[200] In particular, the SIAC Code of Ethics requires an arbitrator to disclose the extent of his or her prior knowledge of the dispute.[201]

A breach of impartiality or independence is not in itself a ground for refusing recognition or enforcement of foreign arbitral awards under the New York Convention. However, such a violation may constitute grounds for challenging an arbitrator during the arbitral proceedings under institutional arbitration rules and the UNCITRAL Model Law.[202] For the purposes of this book, it is only where the breach of impartiality or independence renders a party unable to present its case or results in inequality between the parties that such a breach constitutes a procedural irregularity under the New York Convention. This line of reasoning was confirmed by the Katowice Court of Appeal, which held that an arbitrator's lack of impartiality violates Article 18 of the Model Law only if it results in inequality between the parties.[203] The lack of impartiality or independence may, however, satisfy the grounds for refusal to recognise or enforce arbitral awards under Article V(1)(d) of the New York Convention – 'the composition of the arbitral authority or the arbitral procedure was not in accordance with the agreement of the parties, or, failing such agreement, was not in accordance with the law of the country where the arbitration took place'. This book will not consider the breach of Article V(1)(d) in detail. Instead, it focuses on whether a lack of independence or impartiality results in one party being unable to present its case or in inequality between the parties.

§3.04 CONCLUSION

Chapter 2 explained why enforcing courts should use the VCLT rules of interpretation rather than their domestic rules of interpretation, to interpret the due process defence under the New York Convention. This chapter interpreted the due process defence from the perspective of general principles of law under the interpretative framework provided by the VCLT.

199. London Court of International Arbitration, *LCIA Notes for Arbitrators* (adopted 26 October 2017) Art. 8.
200. Singapore International Arbitration Centre, *Code of Ethics for An Arbitrator* (adopted 2015) Art. 2; Hong Kong International Arbitration Centre, *Code of Ethical Conduct*, Rule Two.
201. Singapore International Arbitration Centre, *Code of Ethics for An Arbitrator* (adopted 2015) Art. 2(2)(b).
202. *See, e.g., UNCITRAL Model Law*, UN Docs A/40/17 and A/61/17 (n. 62) Art. 12; *LCIA Arbitration Rules* (n. 137) Art. 10(1); *SCC Arbitration Rules* (n. 137) Art. 19(1); *SIAC Arbitration Rules* (n. 137) Art. 14 (1); *HKIAC Arbitration Rules* (n. 137) Art. 11(6).
203. *A. L. v. (…) Spółka Akcyjna v. P*, CLOUT Case 1465, available at https://www.uncitral.org/clout/clout/data/pol/clout_case_1465_leg-3091.html.

Section 3.02 showed that *audiatur et altera pars* has been accepted as a general principle of law within the meaning of Article 38(1)(c) of the Statute of the ICJ since it is recognised by the principal legal systems of the world and is compatible with the fundamental principles of international law. This is further confirmed by the fact that it is common to find expressions of *audiatur et altera pars* in international instruments relating to international human rights, investment arbitration and international commercial arbitration. Section 3.03 showed that the well-accepted notions of *audiatur et altera pars* – due notice, equality of arms, right to be heard and impartiality and independence of arbitrators – developed in international arbitration and other international regimes can concretise the normative content of the due process defence under the New York Convention.

Most international lawyers with experience in litigation or arbitration find it relatively easy to agree with the basic elements of due process as elaborated in §3.03. The principled nature of due process has been generally accepted by the community of nations, even if not by all nations.[204] However, the same body of lawyers may find it more difficult to agree on a specific set of rules or standards to implement the concept of due process. In practice, it is left to national courts to determine, on a case-by-case basis, exactly what constitutes a 'fair hearing' in a manner consistent with transnational due process. Chapter 4 examines the sources of transnational due process rules in international arbitration on which enforcing courts may rely, while Chapters 5, 6 and 7 discuss the subsequent practice of State Parties with respect to due process in concrete scenarios and assess the predictability of the due process rule, its degree of compatibility with legal expectations, and its degree of balance with efficiency in a concrete case where divergence occurs.

204. Some national systems of law have little or no conception of due process in arbitration, such as the case in China discussed in Chapter 2.

CHAPTER 4

Sources of Transnational Due Process in International Commercial Arbitration

§4.01 INTRODUCTION

Chapter 3 argued that the due process requirement under the New York Convention should be interpreted in the light of the general principle of law – *audiatur et altera pars* – within the wider interpretative framework established by the VCLT. Therefore, the due process defence under the New York Convention can be interpreted as part of a transnational due process protection derived from the consensus of State Parties, drawing on the shared features of the major domestic systems, and transposed to the international level. Accordingly, Chapter 3 explored the core elements of *audiatur et altera pars* developed in international legal regimes and argued that such core elements could concretise the normative content of the due process defence under the New York Convention.

While the general principle of law – *audiatur et altera pars* – in international legal regimes provides the basic normative content of the principle of due process in international judicial proceedings, it is its specific application to arbitral proceedings that precisely delineates the contours of the due process defence under the New York Convention in concrete cases. What is missing from Chapter 3 are the sources of procedural rules on which enforcing courts can rely to give specific content to the due process defence in individual cases. This question is now addressed in Chapter 4.

In this chapter, I argue that the normative framework of arbitral procedure is built on international conventions, modern arbitration law, established arbitration rules, soft law[1] and the practice of international commercial arbitration. These are sources of

1. In the context of international commercial arbitration, the 'soft law' to which international commercial arbitration law scholars refer is instruments with normative power to some extent but without either formal legal sources or binding legal force as opposed to 'hard law' that is imposed by arbitration statutes and treaties. For more details, *see* §4.03[D].

procedural rules that implement the abstract core elements of *audiatur et altera pars* in concrete cases. Chapter 3 examined how the relevant provisions of the New York Convention and national arbitration laws in the major legal systems of the world contribute to the distillation and generalisation of the general principle of due process and its core elements in international commercial arbitration. With respect to arbitral procedure, Article V(1)(d) of the New York Convention gives preference to the will of the parties, with the law of the seat being applied only in the absence of agreement. The principle that states shall recognise and give effect to an arbitration agreement is confirmed in Article II(3) of the New York Convention. The VCLT's context and purpose interpretation requires enforcing courts to coordinate Article V(1)(b) with the purposes of other articles of the New York Convention.[2] This context and purpose interpretation allows enforcing courts to take into account some of the more 'transnational' materials, such as institutional arbitration rules, well-established arbitration practice, and soft law, by virtue of reference to them and/or endorsement of them by the parties' agreement. These transnational materials better reflect the nature of international arbitral proceedings and promote due process under the New York Convention as a genuinely transnational standard, distinct from any national legal system.

Accordingly, this chapter is structured as follows. Section 4.02 discusses the structure of international arbitration procedure and its implications for the sources of procedural rules relating to due process. Section 4.03 examines the sources of procedural rules in international commercial arbitration to which enforcing courts may refer when implementing the general principle of due process under the New York Convention. Section 4.04 concludes the chapter.

§4.02 THE STRUCTURE OF INTERNATIONAL ARBITRAL PROCEEDINGS

'[T]here are no fixed, detailed rules of procedure governing an international arbitration: each case is different; each tribunal is different; and each dispute deserves to be treated differently.'[3] The lack of a universal arbitration procedure provides flexibility and the opportunity to tailor procedures that promote the efficient resolution of particular issues in dispute, thereby meeting the needs of the parties. This flexibility is one of the reasons why parties choose international commercial arbitration over other forms of dispute resolution.[4]

The flexibility of international commercial arbitration does not mean that there are no procedural safeguards for certain fundamental procedural rights, such as proper

2. For more details, *see* §2.06[A][2].
3. Nigel Blackaby et al., *Redfern and Hunter on International Arbitration* (Oxford University Press, 6th ed., 2015) 64.
4. *See* School of International Arbitration at Queen Mary University of London and White & Case, '2015 International Arbitration Survey: Improvements and Innovations in International Arbitration' (Queen Mary University of London and White & Case, 2015) 6, which suggests that 65% of the respondents regard 'enforceability of awards' as the most valuable characteristic of arbitration compared with 'avoiding specific legal systems' (64%), 'flexibility' (38%) and other characteristics.

notice, equality of arms, the right to be heard, and an independent and impartial tribunal in international arbitration. As William W Park notes, procedural formality is often another term for due process.[5] For the purpose of guaranteeing due process, the international arbitration procedure has a basic structure based on three essential systems: first, the international conventions and the UNCITRAL Model Law, which have, to a large extent, helped states to shape modern arbitration law; second, the established arbitration rules; and, third, the practice of international arbitration.[6]

As discussed in more detail in §4.03, national arbitration laws and international conventions establish general principles designed to ensure a fair procedure and an award that is enforceable both domestically and internationally. As discussed in Chapter 3, national arbitration laws and international conventions generally provide that parties should be treated equally and that each party should be given an opportunity to present its case. However, national arbitration laws do not attempt to prescribe in detail how an international arbitration should be conducted. As shown in Chapters 5–7, the rules of due process and their application vary from state to state. Instead, national arbitration laws focus primarily on defining the relationship between national courts and arbitral tribunals, including but not limited to the role of courts in assisting arbitral proceedings by challenging arbitrators, setting aside awards or enforcing awards.[7]

The more specific rules of arbitral procedure that guarantee due process are generally set out in the rules of international arbitral institutions or are administered by the parties and tribunals.[8] However, standard institutional or ad hoc arbitration rules[9] do not, and do not attempt to, prescribe in detail the manner in which an arbitration should be conducted, such as the production of documents and the examination of witnesses. Instead, such rules are intended to set out the general framework or outline of the arbitral proceedings, from the constitution of the arbitral tribunal to the making of the award. It is more common for experienced counsel or arbitrators to address more specific practical issues. In the exercise of the parties' agreement and the arbitrators' discretion, they may adopt or take into account the well-accepted international commercial arbitration practice. In addition to codified guidelines, arbitration practice includes the practice of experienced arbitrators and counsel. While there are obvious challenges in identifying 'well-accepted practice' in the absence of an instrument or guideline that certifies that a practice is 'well accepted', there are some practices that

5. Willian W Park, 'The Procedural Soft Law of International Arbitration: Non-Governmental Instruments' in Loukas A Mistelis and Julian D M Lew QC (eds), *Pervasive Problems in International Arbitration* (Kluwer Law International, 2006) 144.
6. Blackaby et al. (n. 3) 358.
7. Nevertheless, the case law, as one of the sources of national laws in common law systems, provides more detailed rules governing the application of due process, which I explain in more detail in §4.03[A] and the following Chapters 5–7.
8. School of International Arbitration at Queen Mary University of London and White & Case (n. 4) 17 (showing that around eighty percent of all international commercial arbitrations are administered by an arbitral institution).
9. *See, e.g.*, the UNCITRAL Arbitration Rules, which are specifically designed for procedural management in ad hoc arbitrations.

are recognised as such – for example, in reference works on arbitration. One example is the use of the 'Redfern Schedule'.

§4.03 SOURCES OF DUE PROCESS IN INTERNATIONAL ARBITRATION

As discussed above, international conventions, modern arbitration laws, established arbitration rules, and the practice of international arbitration together provide the normative framework for arbitral proceedings. As detailed in Chapters 5–7, transnational arbitration-specific instruments (formal, soft law or contractual), as well as domestic statutes and case law, shed light on the interpretation and application of the due process principle in specific cases. Enforcing courts usually consult these sources when deciding specific cases. In particular, 'private' sources of law,[10] which include institutional arbitral rules and soft law issued by transnational organisations, are also useful and indispensable sources of due process in international commercial arbitration. Through endorsement or reference by the parties, these 'private' sources provide enforcing courts with material beyond their own national rules and a perspective from the community of international arbitration in which actors include, but are not limited to, parties, arbitrators, arbitral institutions, and transnational professional organisations.

[A] National Law

As discussed in Chapter 3, the due process defence under the New York Convention can be seen as an expression of the general principle of *audiatur et altera pars* in international commercial arbitration, which is transnational in nature. The general principle of *audiatur et altera pars* and its core elements are derived from the consensus of the principal national legal systems of the world, which is also reflected in international treaties. The sources of national law for the determination of this transnational due process in the New York Convention are not limited to a particular jurisdiction, be it the law of the seat of the arbitration or the law of the forum of enforcement.

These sources of national law include the arbitration statutes and case law of all the State Parties to the New York Convention. As shown in §3.02[B][1] and §3.03, comparative methods are used to determine the consensus of national arbitration rules on due process in the major national legal systems. According to these national arbitration laws, the core elements of due process are proper notice, equality of the parties, a reasonable opportunity to be heard, and impartial and independent arbitrators. The following Chapters 5–7 provide a comparative analysis of the New York Convention's due process defence cases among State Parties. They examine more specific standards of due process, such as the content and form of due notice, the

10. S I Strong, 'Research in International Commercial Arbitration: Special Skills, Special Sources' (2009) 20(2) *American Review of International Arbitration* 119, 130 DOI: 10.1093/law/9780199238309.003.0002.

proper address and addressee of the notice, the language and timing of due notice, the right to make submissions and present evidence (admissibility of submissions and time limits), oral hearings, the right to comment on the submissions of the opposing party and the arbitrators, the right to have submissions considered, and equality of arms.

With regard to case law, Chapters 5–7 of this book deal with the interpretation and application of the due process defence in the recognition and enforcement proceedings by the courts of the State Parties to the New York Convention. As explained in §1.04[B], a comparative approach is used to examine the judicial decisions of the State Parties on the due process defence under the New York Convention. In addition, as explained in Chapter 2, several national courts interpret the due process defence under the New York Convention in the light of certain requirements of due process for setting-aside proceedings. Accordingly, this book will analyse their case law on these due process requirements in setting-aside proceedings as a complement to their interpretation of the due process defence under the New York Convention.

In common law jurisdictions, a number of important rules relating to the due process defence are not set out in statute but in case law. It is therefore both permissible and appropriate to refer to case law which is binding on common law courts. Even some civil law jurisdictions recognise the persuasive authority of case law. France, for example, recognises that the 'liberal Code of Civil Procedure' and 'well-established case law' together constitute the sources of French international commercial arbitration.[11]

[B] International Conventions

As discussed in Chapter 2, the New York Convention itself does not provide more specific guidance on the concretisation of the due process defence, although it is an authoritative source. In contrast, other international treaties, particularly those relating to human rights, contribute to the core elements of the general principle of due process, including due notice, equality of the parties, the right to be heard, and impartial and independent arbitrators, which may be referred to by enforcing courts through 'relevant rules of international law' under Article 31(3)(c) of the VCLT.

International conventions, such as the New York Convention and the European Convention on International Commercial Arbitration (hereinafter the 'European Arbitration Convention'),[12] are a compelling force for the unification of national laws governing the conduct of international arbitration and the recognition and enforcement of international arbitral awards. International conventions have helped to link national legal systems into a network of laws which, while differing in wording, have as their common objective the international enforcement of arbitration agreements and arbitral awards. Because of its broad acceptance, the New York Convention is the most

11. Emmanuel Gaillard and John Savage (eds), *Fouchard Gaillard Goldman on International Commercial Arbitration* (Kluwer Law International, 1999) 69.
12. *European Convention on International Commercial Arbitration*, opened for signature 21 April 1961, 484 UNTS 349 (entered into force 18 October 1965).

important international convention in promoting the uniform recognition and enforcement of foreign and non-domestic arbitral awards. Although the New York Convention deals with the recognition and enforcement procedure and the European Convention on Arbitration deals mainly with the setting aside of awards, both endorse and promote the concept of transnational due process in international commercial arbitration at the international level.[13]

As shown in more detail in Chapter 3, due process is identifiable by its systematic presence not only in the major national legal systems but also in the public international legal order itself and in other sub-fields of international law, such as international human rights law and international investment law. Through the interpretative rule 'relevant rules of international law' under Article 31(3)(c) of the VCLT, enforcing courts may refer to relevant provisions on due process in human rights law to concretise the core concepts of due process under the New York Convention, such as the ECHR,[14] the Universal Declaration of Human Rights,[15] the ICCPR,[16] and the EUCFR.[17]

[C] Established Rules of International Arbitration

Once the parties have referred to specific arbitration rules in their arbitration agreement, those rules become part of their contract and thus legally binding. Regarding the status of guidelines and notes of arbitral institutions (binding or non-binding), the ICC, the HKIAC and the SIAC articulate the significance of notes in supplementing, regulating and implementing institutional arbitration rules.[18] Although the LCIA does not specify the status of its Notes, Article 1(4) of its Notes for Arbitrators provides that the Notes are intended to guide the arbitrators in conducting the arbitration in accordance with the LCIA Rules. Where the parties have agreed to have an arbitration administered by an arbitral institution, it is usual for that institution to use its guidelines and notes in administering the arbitration. Therefore, such guidelines and notes may also be considered to be part of the parties' agreement. According to Article V(1)(d) of the New York Convention, enforcing courts should respect the institutional

13. Article V(1)(b) of the New York Convention provides the due process defence as one of the grounds for refusing recognition and enforcement of foreign arbitral awards, while Art. IX(1)(b) of the European Convention on arbitration regards the due process defence as one of the grounds for setting aside awards.
14. *Convention for the Protection of Human Rights and Fundamental Freedoms*, opened for signature 4 November 1950, 213 UNTS 221 (entered into force 3 September 1953) Art. 6(1).
15. *Universal Declaration of Human Rights*, adopted 10 December 1948, UNGA Res 217 A (III), Art. 10.
16. *International Covenant on Civil and Political Rights*, opened for signature 19 December 1966, 999 UNTS 171 (entered into force 23 March 1976) Art. 14.
17. Charter of Fundamental Rights of the European Union (entered into force 1 December 2009), Art. 47.
18. International Chamber of Commerce, *Arbitration Rules* (adopted 1 January 2021) ('*ICC Arbitration Rules*') Appendix II, Art. 5(2); Hong Kong International Arbitration Centre, *Administered Arbitration Rules* (adopted 1 November 2018) ('*HKIAC Arbitration Rules*') Schedule 3, Art. 1(4); Singapore International Arbitration Centre, *SIAC Arbitration Rules* (adopted 1 August 2016) ('*SIAC Arbitration Rules*') Art. 9(6).

arbitration rules, guidelines and notes agreed by the parties. As mentioned in Chapter 2, the interpretation of purpose and context under the VCLT also requires enforcing courts to take into account these institutional arbitration rules, guidelines and notes chosen by the parties when determining the issues of due process.

Although rules, guidelines and notes of arbitral institutions become 'hard law' and binding rules of law once they are incorporated into a contract, these institutional arbitration rules, guidelines and notes exist and express the choices made by an arbitral institution, irrespective of whether or not they are incorporated into an arbitration agreement. As Gabrielle Kaufmann-Kohler stated, institutional arbitration rules convey the views and choices of the arbitral institution on matters of arbitral procedure and are a perfect illustration of the impact of non-state actors on the development of arbitration law.[19] An experienced arbitrator usually has in mind the principles and provisions of these increasingly convergent rules of arbitral institutions and tends to apply them to ensure orderly and fair proceedings leading to a well-considered award. Accordingly, as shown in Chapters 5–7, subsequent judicial practice among the State Parties has shown that most enforcing courts generally consider these arbitration rules when determining the application of the due process defence under the New York Convention where the parties have chosen an arbitral institution.

In the interests of efficiency and economy, the arbitration rules of international institutions need to be adapted to the changes in the market and trends in practice. In particular, there is a growing convergence of institutional arbitration rules between the leading international arbitration institutions, such as the ICC, LCIA, SIAC, SCC and HKIAC.[20] It is common to see that, as soon as one arbitral institution changes its arbitration rules, other institutions begin to shorten their timelines for the appointment of arbitrators, arbitral proceedings and the like in their new arbitration rules in order to keep up with the trends in international arbitration.

Ad hoc arbitration is conducted without the administration of an arbitral institution. However, the parties sometimes will refer to the UNCITRAL Arbitration Rules for the conduct of the arbitration. The UNCITRAL published its Model Arbitration Rules in 1976, which are widely used in ad hoc arbitration and were amended in 2010. Compared to the UNCITRAL Model Law, the UNCITRAL Arbitration Rules provide more specific procedural rules for arbitration, which better ensure fair proceedings in ad hoc arbitration.

As discussed above, national law and international conventions prioritise proper notice, equality of arms, the right to be heard, and impartial and independent arbitrators as key elements of due process. Institutional or ad hoc arbitration rules add more specific requirements to these elements. With respect to 'proper notice', institutional or ad hoc arbitration rules, such as those of the ICC, LCIA, SCC, and SIAC, all provide that the tribunal shall give the parties '*reasonable*' notice of the date, time and

19. Gabrielle Kaufmann-Kohler, 'Soft Law in International Arbitration: Codification and Normativity' (2010) 1(2) *Journal of International Dispute Settlement* 283, 293–294.
20. Gordon Smith, 'Comparative Analysis of Joinder and Consolidation Provisions under Leading Arbitral Rules' (2018) 35(2) *Journal of International Arbitration* 173.

place of any meeting or hearing.[21] Although the HKIAC Arbitration Rules and the UNCITRAL Arbitration Rules provide that the tribunal shall give the parties '*adequate*' advance notice of the date, time and place of the hearing, it is appropriate to interpret this as reasonable notice.[22] Under the heading 'Conduct of Arbitration', institutional arbitration rules usually establish the principle that the tribunal shall give each party an equal and reasonable opportunity to present its case during the arbitration.[23] Institutional arbitration rules usually provide for instruments to safeguard impartiality and independence, as discussed in §3.03[D].

Nevertheless, the institutional or ad hoc arbitration rules are not intended to provide the details of how an international arbitration should be conducted. For instance, most institutional rules are sparse on evidentiary matters, except to the extent that they empower the tribunal to rule on questions of admissibility.[24] Instead, these rules merely outline the various steps to be taken. A more detailed regulation of the procedure to be followed will be established either by agreement of the parties or by direction of the arbitral tribunal, or a combination of the two. This is a deliberate policy, as the institutional or ad hoc arbitration rules are designed to be flexible enough to accommodate a wide range of disputes in different countries around the world with many different systems of trial proceedings. In practice, commercial parties rarely pay much attention to the arbitration clause at the drafting stage of negotiations. All too often, arbitration clauses are not so much the product of thoughtful negotiation and drafting as a gap-filler inserted at the eleventh hour with little or no discussion. Some consideration may be given to the choice of the institution, the arbitral seat and the procedure for appointing arbitrators, but more practical issues such as the taking of evidence are unlikely to feature in these discussions. It is therefore common for arbitrators to deal with the specific procedural issues of the arbitration, apart from challenges to arbitrators for conflicts of interest.

[D] International Arbitration Practice and Soft Law

With respect to the discretion of arbitrators in arbitral proceedings, the leading institutional arbitration rules and the UNCITRAL Arbitration Rules provide that arbitrators may establish the facts by 'all appropriate means'[25] and have the 'widest

21. *ICC Arbitration Rules* (n. 18) Art. 26(1); London Court of International Arbitration, *LCIA Arbitration Rules* (adopted 1 October 2014) ('*LCIA Arbitration Rules*') Art. 19(3); Arbitration Institute of the Stockholm Chamber of Commerce, *SCC Arbitration Rules* (adopted 1 January 2017) ('*SCC Arbitration Rules*') Art. 32(2); *SIAC Arbitration Rules* (n. 18) Art. 24(2) (emphasis added).
22. *HKIAC Arbitration Rules* (n. 18) Art. 22(4) (emphasis added); United Nations Committee on International Trade Law, *UNCITRAL Arbitration Rules* (2nd ed., 2010), GA Res 65/22, 6th Comm A/65/465, 66th sess., Agenda Item 77, UN Doc. A/RES/65/22 (6 December 2010) ('*UNCITRAL Arbitration Rules*') Art. 28(1).
23. ICC Arbitration Rules (n. 18) Art. 22(4); LCIA Arbitration Rules (n. 21) Art. 14(4)(i); SCC Arbitration Rules (n. 21) Art. 23(2); HKIAC Arbitration Rules (n. 18) Art. 13(1).
24. *LCIA Arbitration Rules* (n. 21) Art. 22(1)(vi); *SIAC Arbitration Rules* (n. 18) Art. 19 (2); *UNCITRAL Arbitration Rules*, UN Doc. A/RES/65/22 (n. 22) Art. 27 (4).
25. ICC Arbitration Rules (n. 18) Art. 25(1).

discretion to discharge duties'[26] in 'such manner as they consider appropriate'.[27] While this lack of guidance may not matter when all arbitrators, counsel and parties are from the same jurisdiction, inconsistencies in matters such as the examination of witnesses and the production of documents may cause confusion when arbitrators or parties are from different jurisdictions.[28] The significant differences in approaches to procedure and evidence in different legal systems create a risk of unfairness if one of the parties is forced to proceed according to rules with which it is unfamiliar. In this context, the field of international arbitration has seen the emergence of soft law instruments promulgated by international professional organisations, which offer a wide range of practical and workable guidelines and recommendations for arbitral proceedings.[29] These guidelines and rules are intended to codify the internationally accepted practice of the international arbitral community and to provide the parties with a degree of consistency and predictability in the arbitral process. The practice of experienced arbitrators and counsel, which is well accepted by the community of arbitration but not in the form of codified guidelines with a complex mechanism for regulating the activities or ethics of international arbitration, such as the 'Redfern Schedule', may also be referred to by arbitrators in the administration of arbitral proceedings.

Many sets of 'rules' and 'guidelines' have been developed by international organisations or established professional bodies, some of which have gained wide recognition and acceptance by the international arbitration community. Among them, the IBA Rules on the Taking of Evidence in International Arbitration (hereinafter 'IBA Rules'),[30] the IBA Guidelines on Conflicts of Interest in International Arbitration (hereinafter 'IBA Guidelines'),[31] the IBA Rules' competitor – the Prague Rules,[32] and the UNCITRAL documents have had a widespread impact on arbitral practice. The practice of experienced arbitrators and counsel, which is well accepted by the community of arbitration but not as complicated as soft law, such as the 'Redfern Schedule', will also be examined in this section. For enforcing courts, these rules, guidelines and practices are merely persuasive and not binding unless the parties have agreed to them or have given the tribunal the discretion to follow these documents or practices. Nevertheless, this section examines these soft law and the well-accepted international arbitral practice that contribute to procedural fairness, as they are widely relied upon by the parties.

26. LCIA Arbitration Rules (n. 21) Art. 14(5).
27. *UNCITRAL Arbitration Rules*, UN Doc. A/RES/65/22 (n. 22) Art. 17.
28. Park (n. 5) 148.
29. Joshua Karton, 'International Arbitration as Comparative Law in Action' (2020) 2020(2) *Journal of Dispute Resolution* 293, 308–309.
30. International Bar Association, IBA Rules on the Taking of Evidence in International Arbitration (adopted 29 May 2010).
31. International Bar Association, IBA Guidelines on Conflicts of Interest in International Arbitration (adopted 23 October 2014).
32. Rules on the Efficient Conduct of Proceedings in International Arbitration (Prague Rules, adopted 14 December 2018).

[1] Soft Law in International Commercial Arbitration

The concept of soft law originated in public international law. It has been difficult to establish a clear and unified definition of soft law ever since Lord McNair introduced the idea into legal discourse.[33] Nevertheless, scholars generally use the term to describe two situations in international law. Some define it as the norms with some normative element but without the formal legal sources recognised by international law, while others see it as norms that have hard legal elements but do not specify the precise obligations undertaken or rights granted and are therefore unenforceable (e.g., most Resolutions and Declarations of the UN General Assembly).[34] In the first category, the lack of formal legal sources means that they lack the binding force and coercive power of states. Consequently, the first category cannot be enforced by public authority. Although the latter category has formal legal authority, it is still unenforceable due to the absence of identifiable rights and obligations.

In the context of international commercial arbitration, 'soft law', as scholars generally refer to it, comprises instruments that have some normative power but neither formal legal sources nor binding legal force, as opposed to 'hard law', which is imposed by arbitration statutes and treaties.[35] First, soft law in international commercial arbitration has some normative power. Compared to public international law, which includes soft law with a hortatory character and general guidance or policy,[36] soft law in international arbitration usually contains normative rules of conduct with specific rights and obligations and even a complex mechanism for regulating the activities or ethics of international arbitration. Second, soft law in international arbitration is usually non-binding and cannot be coercively enforced, in contrast to hard law, which is binding and can be enforced by public authority. As Gabrielle Kaufmann-Kohler has noted, '"soft law" norms are generally understood to be those that cannot be enforced through public force'.[37] Unlike institutional arbitration rules, which are part of the parties' agreement and thus binding on the parties, soft law

---

33. László Blutman, 'In the Trap of a Legal Metaphor: International Soft Law' (2010) 59 *International and Comparative Law Quarterly* 605, 606 DOI: 10.1017/s0020589310000242.
34. *Ibid.*; Christine Mary Chinkin, 'The Challenge of Soft Law: Development and Change in International Law' (1989) 38 *International and Comparative Law Quarterly* 850, 851 DOI: 10.1093/iclqaj/38.4.850; Henry Deeb Gabriel, 'The Advantages of Soft Law in International Commercial Law: The Role of UNIDROIT, UNCITRAL, and the Hague Conference' (2009) 34 *Brooklyn Journal of International Law* 655, 658; Andrew T Guzman and Timothy L Meyer, 'International Soft Law' (2010) 2(1) *Journal of Legal Analysis* 171, 174–175. For the Resolutions and Declarations of the UN General Assembly, *see, e.g., Universal Declaration of Human Rights*, adopted 10 December 1948, UNGA Res 217 A (III); *United Nations Declaration on the Rights of Indigenous People*, GA Res 61/295, UN GAOR, 61st sess., 107th plen mtg, Supp No. 49, UN Doc. A/RES/61/295 (13 September 2007).
35. Park (n. 5) 141; Kaufmann-Kohler (n. 19) 284; The IBA Arbitration Guidelines and Rules Subcommittee, 'The Report on the Reception of the IBA Arbitration Soft Law Products' (International Bar Association, September 2016) ('*IBA Report*' or '*Report*').
36. *See, e.g., Universal Declaration on Human Rights*, GA Res 217 A (III), UN GAOR, 3rd sess., 183rd plen mtg, UN Doc. A/810 (10 December 1948); *United Nations Declaration on the Rights of Indigenous People*, GA Res 61/295, UN GAOR, 61st sess., 107th plen mtg, Supp No. 49, UN Doc. A/RES/61/295 (13 September 2007).
37. Kaufmann-Kohler (n. 19) 284.

guidelines and rules are not directly binding on the parties until they or their tribunals adopt such soft rules or guidelines. Although soft law is not formally binding, it is persuasive, especially since it has been widely adopted. Third, soft law in international arbitration is usually issued by private noncoercive actors, such as transnational professional organisations – the International Bar Association (IBA), and noncoercive intergovernmental organisations, such as the United Nations Commission on International Trade Law (UNCITRAL).

Soft law in international arbitration can be either substantive or procedural. This book focuses on procedural soft law relevant to arbitration as a dispute resolution mechanism, particularly in relation to due process. Accordingly, this chapter will not deal with the substantive soft law, such as the UNIDROIT Principles of International Commercial Contracts, applied by arbitrators to the merits of the dispute.

[2] IBA Rules, IBA Guidelines and Prague Rules

It would be remiss to discuss soft law without reference to the International Bar Association. The Arbitration Committee of the IBA's Business Law Section seeks to standardise practice in a manner that is acceptable to different jurisdictions and legal cultures. It is perhaps the most prominent of the bodies in the field of international arbitration to recognise the need to develop rules and guidelines to help parties, counsel and arbitrators alike establish a level playing field on certain key procedural issues. It has published a set of guidelines and rules on the impartiality and independence of arbitrators, the taking of evidence, and the conduct of counsel. The work of the IBA Arbitration Committee includes three widely used guides: the IBA Rules on the Taking of Evidence in International Arbitration,[38] the IBA Guidelines on Conflicts of Interest in International Arbitration,[39] and the IBA Guidelines on Party Representation in International Arbitration.[40] The IBA Rules on Evidence and the IBA Guidelines on Conflicts of Interest are relevant to the study of due process. Therefore, this subsection focuses on these two documents and the IBA Rules on Evidence's competitor – the Prague Rules. Where the parties have agreed to adopt them or have given the tribunal discretion to follow them, enforcing courts should consult them when interpreting the due process defence.

(a) IBA Rules on the Taking of Evidence and Prague Rules

An area of international arbitration that is critical but least addressed by institutional arbitration rules is the submission of documents and the presentation of evidence. Institutional rules typically leave the taking of evidence to the parties and arbitrators to allow for flexibility in the arbitral process, provided that the parties are treated equally and fairly and that each party has a reasonable opportunity to present its case. However, misunderstandings and disputes may arise between parties, particularly

38. International Bar Association, *IBA Rules on Evidence* (n. 30).
39. International Bar Association, *IBA Guidelines on Conflicts of Interest* (n. 31).
40. International Bar Association, IBA Guidelines on Party Representation in International Arbitration (adopted 25 May 2013).

those from different jurisdictions, over matters such as expert testimony, witness examination, cross-examination, and the production of documents by the other party. The IBA Rules on Taking of Evidence seek to provide guidance to arbitrators on how to deal with these issues, which has been recognised by several national courts.[41] For example, the Singapore High Court held that the IBA Rules on Evidence provided more comprehensive guidance on the issue of disclosure of documents than the SIAC Arbitration Rules.[42]

The essential principle of the IBA Rules is that 'each party shall act in good faith and be entitled to know, reasonably in advance of any evidentiary hearing or any fact or merits determination, the evidence on which the other parties rely'.[43] This requires that neither party should take the other by surprise when presenting evidence to the tribunal. The IBA Rules therefore seek to allow the parties to present evidence in an orderly fashion and to give the other party an opportunity to respond.

In 2016, the IBA Subcommittee published the Report on the Reception of the IBA Arbitration Soft Law Products (hereinafter 'IBA Report').[44] According to the IBA Report, Article 3 on the production of documents and Article 9 on the admissibility of evidence were the most frequently cited provisions of the IBA Rules on the Taking of Evidence.[45] Importantly, these two provisions are the main areas in which due process issues would arise. Article 3 deals with the content of a Request to Produce, the form of submission or production of documents and confidentiality, while Article 9 addresses issues such as legal privilege, commercial or technical confidentiality, political or institutional sensitivity and the equality of parties when deciding the admissibility, relevance, materiality, and weight of evidence.

The IBA Rules on the Taking of Evidence were drafted by the Arbitration Committee, which consists of experienced arbitration lawyers from a number of jurisdictions. They have sought to provide a balanced approach to the production of documents between different jurisdictions, including, but not limited to, the differences between civil law and common law proceedings.[46] These differences between jurisdictions can lead to bias. For instance, what criteria will arbitrators use to

41. The IBA Arbitration Guidelines and Rules Subcommittee (n. 35) 21–22.
42. *Dongwoo Mann + Hummel Co Ltd v. Mann + Hummel GmbH* [2008] 3 SLR (R) 871.
43. International Bar Association, *IBA Rules on Evidence* (n. 30) Preamble, para. 3.
44. The IBA Arbitration Guidelines and Rules Subcommittee (n. 35). In 2015, the IBA Arbitration Committee set up the IBA Arbitration Guidelines and Rules Subcommittee to conduct a global survey on the reception of the three IBA Guidelines and Rules. The Subcommittee conducted a survey by means of a questionnaire consisting of thirty-five questions and received 811 valid responses (Europe 323, Latin America 199, Asia Pacific 136, North America 78, the Middle East 42 and Africa 33). Additionally, the IBA Subcommittee also received 57 Country Reports (Europe 23, Latin America 13, Asia Pacific 9, North America 2, the Middle East 8 and Africa 2), each of which discussed the survey responses collected within a country and the use of the IBA Rules and Guidelines as reflected in arbitral jurisprudence and doctrine. To some extent, the survey process and the scale of the data collected statistically provide an adequate sample for the analysis of the status and utility of the IBA Rules and Guidelines.
45. *Ibid.*, 16.
46. International Bar Association, *IBA Rules on Evidence* (n. 30) Art. 3(2) (allowing the production of documents, as is the case in common law jurisdictions, but prescribing a much more limited scope than is permitted in US civil procedure). *See also* 1999 IBA Working Party and 2010 IBA Rules of Evidence Review Subcommittee, 'Commentary on the Revised Text of the 2010 IBA

determine whether a particular document should be produced? Should the tribunal adopt an American-style discovery procedure, or should it require the production of only those specific documents that can be shown to be relevant to the issues? The losing party could raise the due process defence before the enforcing court, arguing that it could have proven the other party's meritless claims if the tribunal had not rejected its request to produce documents. Article 3 of the IBA Rules on production of documents can address these issues and thus ensure equal treatment of the parties and their right to be heard.

In common law systems, the rationale for discovery suggests that justice can be established only if both sides have access, as far as possible, to the same materials. Discovery is seen as an important tool in the fact-finding process. Accordingly, a party may produce not only the documents on which it intends to rely but also those which may be prejudicial to its case. In civil law jurisdictions, however, judges investigate the facts with the assistance of the parties. The parties can only produce the documents they wish to rely on, but certainly not anything that would damage their own case.[47] In contrast to the civil law systems where the parties are not obliged to produce documents they do not wish to provide, the IBA Rules on Evidence allow each party to submit to the tribunal a request for production requiring the counterparty to produce certain documents within a narrow and specific category of requested documents, provided that the requested documents are 'relevant to the case and material to its outcome'.[48] This shows that the IBA Rules on Evidence do not adopt the expansive American or English approach to discovery. Instead, they require that requests for documents be limited to matters that are relevant and material to the determination of the case. Meanwhile, a party may raise any of the objections set out in Article 9(2) of the IBA Rules on Evidence or prove that the requested documents are irrelevant to the case or immaterial to its outcome. From the perspective of users of international commercial arbitration, the IBA Rules attempt to strike a compromise between civil law and common law systems in different approaches to the taking of evidence.[49] Also, the IBA Rules on Evidence provide certainty in the production of documents, preventing one party from surprising the other and thus ensuring procedural fairness.

Nevertheless, the IBA Rules on Evidence have been criticised for being 'too American'. According to the IBA Report, this criticism arose in civil law jurisdictions such as Germany, Italy, Switzerland, Finland, Japan and Brazil, as well as in some common law jurisdictions such as England, Canada, New Zealand, Singapore and Ireland.[50] For example, some critics of the IBA Report, based in both civil and common law jurisdictions, called for a revision of Article 3 (Production of Documents) to limit

---

Rules on the Taking of Evidence in International Arbitration' (2011) 5(1) *Dispute Resolution International* 45, 53 DOI: 10.1017/cbo9781139424714.004.

47. Judd Epstein, 'Use of Comparative Law in Commercial International Arbitration and Commercial Mediation' (2001) 75(4) *Tulane Law Review* 913, 917.
48. International Bar Association, *IBA Rules on Evidence* (n. 30) Art. 3(3).
49. Amanda Lees et al., 'Report on the Breakout Sessions on Arbitral Legitimacy: The Users' and Judges' Perspectives' in Albert Jan van den Berg (ed.), *Legitimacy: Myths, Realities, Challenges*, ICCA Congress Series 18 (Kluwer Law International, 2015) 901, 905.
50. The IBA Arbitration Guidelines and Rules Subcommittee (n. 35) 27.

the number and scope of documents to be disclosed in order to achieve a better balance between the American-style approach and that of other jurisdictions.[51] In competition with the IBA Rules, the Rules on the Efficient Conduct of Proceedings in International Arbitration ('Prague Rules' 2018) adopt a more continental European approach to the taking of evidence,[52] providing parties and tribunals with another choice regarding the taking of evidence. The Prague Rules emphasise the inquisitorial approach to the taking of evidence and encourage a more active role for arbitral tribunals in the management of arbitral proceedings.[53] For example, the Prague Rules limit extensive document production[54] and encourage the tribunal to examine witnesses and manage the examination of witnesses by counsel.[55]

In addition, the IBA Rules on Evidence represent a concession by civil lawyers to common law practice in relation to witnesses. In contrast to civil law practice, where neither the parties nor their representatives may act as witnesses, the IBA Rules on Evidence make it clear that the parties, their officers, employees, legal advisers and other representatives may present testimony.[56] The IBA Rules on Evidence also clarify that it is not inappropriate for parties to interview witnesses or potential witnesses and discuss their prospective testimony with them,[57] which is not permitted in many civil law jurisdictions.

(b) IBA Guidelines on Conflicts of Interest

Another IBA document – the IBA Guidelines on Conflicts of Interest – sets out general standards for disclosure and challenge of arbitrators, including lists of specific circumstances in which issues of impartiality and independence may arise.[58] They also provide three non-exhaustive lists of specific situations that commonly arise in practice and assign each situation to one of the three colour-coded lists – Green, Orange, and Red Lists – in descending order of gravity.

Under the general standards of impartiality, independence and disclosure, the IBA Guidelines on Conflicts of Interest set out the continuing duty of impartiality and independence, the subjective test for disclosure ('in the eyes of the parties') and the objective test for challenge ('justifiable doubt').[59] Typically, national arbitration laws and institutional arbitration rules that provide for the 'justifiable doubt' standard for challenge do not specifically define this standard. The IBA Guidelines provide some

51. *Ibid.*
52. The Prague Rules comprise twelve articles, which can be divided into the following aspects of procedural handling: case management (section 2.1); the taking of evidence (section 2.2); and decision (section 2.3).
53. Gonzalo Stampa, 'The Prague Rules' (2019) 35(2) *Arbitration International* 221, 224 DOI: 10.1093/arbint/aiz010.
54. Rules on the Efficient Conduct of Proceedings in International Arbitration (Prague Rules, adopted 14 December 2018) Art. 4.2.
55. *Ibid.*, Art. 5.9. Under the Prague Rules, the tribunal has the final say regarding the number of witnesses to be heard, but the tribunal has no ultimate control of this matter under the IBA Rules on Taking of Evidence.
56. International Bar Association, *IBA Rules on Evidence* (n. 30) Art. 4(2).
57. *Ibid.*, Art. 4(3).
58. International Bar Association, *IBA Guidelines on Conflicts of Interest* (n. 31).
59. *Ibid.*, General Standard 3(a).

concrete context for this decision: a justifiable doubt exists if a reasonable third person, having knowledge of the relevant facts and circumstances, would conclude that there is a likelihood that the arbitrator may be influenced by factors other than the merits of the case.[60]

Another innovation of the IBA Guidelines is that they assign different colours to lists of practical situations in relation to the standards of disclosure and challenge. While admittedly not exhaustive, the Application Lists have been developed to provide an objective basis for assessing arbitrator integrity. Specifically, the Green List identifies situations where disclosure is not required, and these situations are considered not to meet the test for disqualification. The Orange List identifies situations which may give rise to justifiable doubts as to the arbitrator's impartiality and independence in the eyes of the parties. The Red List describes the situations which give rise to justifiable doubts as to the arbitrator's independence and impartiality. The Red List is divided into two categories: the 'waivable' Red List and the 'non-waivable' Red List. The 'waivable' Red List contains matters which must be disclosed to the parties but which may be waived by the parties together with the arbitrator in deciding whether to accept the appointment, while the 'non-waivable' Red List contains conflicts which are sufficient to justify an arbitrator's refusal to be appointed, regardless of the parties' views on the conflict. The specific rules of the colour lists are set out in Table 4.1.

Table 4.1 Colour Lists of IBA Guidelines on Conflicts of Interest

Test	*Disclosure (Subjective)*	*Waiver by Parties*	*Disqualification (Objective)*
Colour List			
Green List	No	Yes	No
Orange List	Yes	Yes	Case by Case
Waivable Red List	Yes	Yes	Case by Case
Non-waivable Red List	Yes	No	Yes

In addition, the IBA Guidelines are more adaptable to new circumstances in international arbitration than are arbitration statutes. This is well illustrated by the provisions of the IBA Guidelines on third-party funding. Third-party funding is a procedural facilitation mechanism that allows a party to the arbitration to finance the costs of the arbitration through the funding of a third party. In the event of a favourable award, the third-party funder is usually remunerated according to a pre-agreed percentage of the amount of the award; otherwise, the funder's investment is lost.[61] The presence of a third party with a financial interest in the award may create new

60. *Ibid.*, Part I (2)(c).
61. Burcu Osmanoglu, 'Third-Party Funding in International Commercial Arbitration and Arbitrator Conflict of Interest' (2015) 32(3) *Journal of International Arbitration* 325, 325–326 DOI: 10.54648/joia2015013.

conflicts of interest that may lead to unfair treatment of the parties. To address the potential conflicts of interest between the third-party funder and the arbitrators, the IBA Guidelines provide that any party with third-party funding in arbitration must disclose any direct or indirect relationship between any of the arbitrators and the third-party funder.[62]

(c) Influence of IBA Documents and the Prague Rules

In principle, the IBA has no power to regulate the conduct of arbitrators, counsel and parties in arbitration, and its documents do not apply as binding rules of law to any of the above. The IBA Documents and the Prague Rules should only apply to them if the parties agree to them or have given the tribunal discretion to follow them. Although for most courts the IBA Rules and Guidelines are merely persuasive and non-binding, as shown below, they generally represent the high level of self-regulation by the international arbitration community and are frequently relied upon by parties and tribunals.

According to the IBA Report, the IBA Rules and Guidelines have been widely accepted by the international arbitration community. Half of the arbitrations of which the respondents were aware referred to the IBA Guidelines on Conflicts of Interest and the IBA Rules on the Taking of Evidence (57% and 48%, respectively).[63] The Conflicts of Interest Guidelines were frequently consulted by counsel (67%) and arbitrators (61%) when deciding whether to accept an appointment and when making a disclosure (56%).[64] Another survey conducted by the IBA Conflicts of Interest Subcommittee found that most international arbitrators consult the IBA Guidelines on Conflicts of Interest when deciding whether a conflict situation arises.[65] As Gabrielle Kaufman-Kohler noted, 'Practitioners know equally well that no reasonable arbitrator would make a decision on a non-obvious disclosure issue without consulting the IBA Guidelines on Conflicts of Interest.'[66]

Several arbitral institutions recognise the persuasive effect of the IBA Guidelines on the Conflicts of Interest when deciding whether to appoint or challenge an arbitrator. A good example of such persuasive effect on arbitral institutions is the SCC. During the course of the arbitration, the SCC Board normally considers applicable law, jurisprudence, and best practice in international arbitration.[67] It routinely consults the Guidelines on Conflicts of Interest for their persuasive, but not conclusive, value in deciding whether to challenge arbitrators under the SCC Rules.[68] Similarly, the LCIA Court digests of challenge cases show that the LCIA Court has on occasions referred to

62. International Bar Association, *IBA Guidelines on Conflicts of Interest* (n. 31) General Standard 7(a) & Explanation to General Standard 7(a).
63. The IBA Arbitration Guidelines and Rules Subcommittee (n. 35) 10, 32.
64. *Ibid.*, 34–35.
65. The IBA Conflicts of Interest Subcommittee, 'The IBA Guidelines on Conflicts of Interest in International Arbitration: The First Five Years, 2004-2009' (2010) 4(1) *Dispute Resolution International* 5, 6.
66. Kaufmann-Kohler (n. 19) 296.
67. Anja Havedal and Elena Burova, 'SCC Practice Note-SCC Board Decisions on Challenges to Arbitrators 2013-1015' (23 January 2016), http://www.sccinstitute.com/media/176447/scc-decisions-on-challenges-to-arbitrators-2013-2015.pdf.
68. *Ibid.*, 4, 10.

the IBA Guidelines on Conflicts for guidance in deciding the parameters of arbitrator independence and impartiality, as the IBA Guidelines 'reflect actual practice in significant parts of the arbitration community'.[69] Other arbitral institutions, such as the Centro de Arbitragem Comercial da Câmara de Comércio e Indústria Portuguesa (Portugal's most active arbitration centre), the Arbitration Centre of the Lima Chamber of Commerce (La Cámara de Comercio de Lima), the American Chamber of Commerce (AmCham), most of the active arbitral institutions in Brazil, and the Court of Arbitration for Sport in Switzerland consider the Conflicts of Interest Guidelines to be persuasive guidance when deciding on the appointment or challenge of an arbitrator.[70]

In contrast, the ICC explicitly states that it applies its own test for determining the impartiality and independence of arbitrators (subjective test for disclosure of independence and objective test for disclosure of impartiality).[71] The ICC has not adopted the IBA Guidelines due to concerns that their objective nature of disclosure conflicts with the ICC's subjective independence disclosure requirement. While the ICC Court may consider the IBA Guidelines on Conflicts of Interest if the parties rely on them, its decision on the challenge will be based primarily on an assessment of all the facts of the case and not solely on the IBA Guidelines.

In the absence of an agreement between the parties, most courts consider the IBA Guidelines on Conflicts of Interest to be a persuasive and useful, albeit non-binding, tool for assessing an arbitrator's independence or impartiality.[72] The IBA Report shows that reference to the IBA Guidelines on Conflicts of Interest by courts is much lower than by practitioners and arbitral institutions.[73] Nevertheless, some courts recognise the model role of the IBA Guidelines on Conflicts of Interest in arbitral practice and refer to them when determining the impartiality and independence of arbitrators. For instance, a Canadian court held that the IBA Guidelines on Conflicts of Interest were 'widely recognised as an *authoritative* source of information as to how the international arbitration community may regard particular fact situations in reasonable apprehension of bias cases'.[74] Likewise, the Swedish Court of Appeal held that, while its decisions were based on the provisions of the Swedish Arbitration Act, it may also consider the IBA Guidelines on Conflicts of Interest, particularly in cases involving non-Swedish parties.[75] The Swedish Supreme Court has also found the IBA Guidelines to be a critical supporting document when considering situations of bias.[76] Swiss courts

69. Thomas W Walsh and Ruth Teitelbaum, 'The LCIA Court Decisions on Challenges to Arbitrators: An Introduction' (2011) 27(3) *Arbitration International* 283, 288 DOI: 10.1093/arbitration/27.3.283.
70. The IBA Arbitration Guidelines and Rules Subcommittee (n. 35) 38, 40, 43.
71. ICC Arbitration Rules (n. 18) Art. 11(2).
72. The IBA Arbitration Guidelines and Rules Subcommittee (n. 35) 57–61.
73. *Ibid.*, 32.
74. *Jacob Securities Inc v. Typhoon Capital BV* [2016] ONSC 604, [41] (emphasis added).
75. *China State Construction Engineering Co v. CJSC INTEKO*, Svea Court of Appeal, Case No. T2484-11, 10 April 2013 reported in Swedish Arbitration Portal by Arbitration Institute of the Stockholm Chamber of Commerce, 22, https://www.arbitration.sccinstitute.com/Swedish-Arbitration-Portal/Court-of-Appeal/Court-of-Appeal/Court-of-Appeal/d_1973471-judgment-of-the-svea-court-of-appeal-10-april-2013-case-no.-t-2484-11.
76. Svea Court of Supreme, Case No. T 2448-06, 19 November 2007 reported in Swedish Arbitration Portal by Arbitration Institute of the Stockholm Chamber of Commerce, 6 https://www.

show a similar attitude towards the persuasive authority of the IBA Guidelines. In a Swiss case in which the parties had not referred to the IBA Guidelines on Conflicts of Interest, the Swiss Federal Tribunal stated that although the Guidelines did not have the force of law, they were a valuable working tool that contributed to the uniformisation of standards in international arbitration in the area of conflicts of interest and would undoubtedly influence the practice of arbitral institutions and courts.[77]

Regarding the taking of evidence, the IBA Report found that in 79% of arbitrations, the arbitral tribunals consulted the IBA Rules on Evidence as non-binding guidance, while in the remaining 21% of cases, the tribunals considered the IBA Rules on Evidence to be binding.[78] However, the IBA Rules on Evidence were followed in most (93%) of the cases in which the tribunal consulted the IBA Rules on Evidence for guidance.[79] Some practitioners even argue that even if the parties do not refer to them, the IBA Rules on the Taking of Evidence have become standard practice, and arbitrators routinely seek guidance from them, whether they so state or not.[80] For enforcing courts, however, the IBA Rules on the Taking of Evidence are not binding unless the parties have explicitly chosen them.

[3] The Practice of Arbitrators and Counsel

The practice of experienced arbitrators and counsel also plays an important role in addressing specific procedural issues in arbitration. Where document requests are disputed, they are usually dealt with using the 'Redfern Schedule' as the medium of exchange for document production. This device, devised by Alan Redfern, is designed to filter out genuine requests for document production in order to prevent 'fishing expeditions' and to limit the documents exchanged to those pertinent to the issues in the parties' pleadings. Where the parties have agreed to adopt the 'Redfern Schedule' or have given the tribunal discretion to follow it, enforcing courts should consult it when interpreting the due process defence.

The usual way to apply the 'Redfern Schedule' is by express agreement of the parties in the first procedural order identifying the 'Redfern Schedule' as the medium of engagement on document production issues. The typical form of a 'Redfern Schedule' will include: (a) the documents requested; (b) the relevance and materiality of the documents requested to the outcome of the dispute; (c) the opposing party's reasons for its opposition to production (if any); (d) and the decision of the arbitral tribunal.[81]

---

arbitration.sccinstitute.com/Swedish-Arbitration-Portal/Supreme-Court/The-Supreme-Court2/The-Supreme-Court/d_1083436-judgment-of-the-supreme-court-of-sweden-19-november-2007-case-no.-t-2448-06nja-2007-s.-481.

77. Swiss Federal Supreme Court, No. 4A 506/2007, 20 March 2008 reported in (2008) 26 *ASA Bulletin* 565, 565–579.
78. The IBA Arbitration Guidelines and Rules Subcommittee (n. 35) 17.
79. *Ibid.*, 20.
80. Kaufmann-Kohler (n. 19) 296.
81. Blackaby et al. (n. 3) 68.

The 'Redfern Schedule' has been translated into an arbitration-specific procedural tool as a well-established arbitration practice. The 'Redfern Schedule' helps to ensure equal treatment of the parties in terms of document production and, together with the IBA Rules on Evidence, has been widely used in the document production process. In Brazil, for example, it is common practice to use a 'Redfern Schedule' for the production of documents and written witness statements, which then form the basis for the cross-examination in the hearing.[82] The ICC Report also considered the 'Redfern Schedule' to be a useful tool for the efficient management of production requests.[83] In practice, some practitioners have improved the 'Redfern Schedule', suggesting the addition of a column – 'Estimated Cost of Compliance' – to help the tribunal strike a balance between due process and procedural economy. It is also suggested that a narrowed down cost of production figure helps the arbitral tribunal filter out unreasonable requests for documents from the initial requests.[84]

[4] UNCITRAL Documents

In addition to the UNCITRAL Model Law and the UNCITRAL Arbitration Rules, certain case management techniques have been developed by UNCITRAL. UNCITRAL has involved all major arbitral institutions and organisations in the drafting process as observers, such as the ICC, IBA, American Arbitration Association, and LCIA, in order to reflect the diverse interests and perspectives of the international arbitration community.[85] To a certain extent, UNCITRAL documents reflect the latest issues and their resolutions and provide models for the conduct of arbitral proceedings.

The UNCITRAL Notes on Organising Arbitral Proceedings (hereinafter 'UNCITRAL Notes') were designed to provide a comprehensive checklist for arbitral tribunals to consult when preparing for arbitration.[86] The UNCITRAL Notes are not legally binding until the parties or the tribunal decide to apply them. They cover issues ranging from the identification of the applicable arbitration proceedings to the parameters of the award in ad hoc or institutional arbitrations. They assist arbitral tribunals by providing an annotated list of issues on which a tribunal may wish to formulate decisions, such as advice on the organisation of the arbitration, procedural meetings, the language of the arbitration, confidentiality and transparency, the conduct of hearings and the taking of evidence (documents, fact witnesses, experts, inspection).

82. Rafael Francisco Alves, 'Chapter 3: Country Report: Brazil' in Friedrich Rosenfeld, Dietmar Czernich and Franco Ferrari (eds), *Due Process as a Limit to Discretion in International Commercial Arbitration* (Kluwer Law International, 2020) 55, 59.
83. ICC Commission, 'ICC Commission Report: Controlling Time and Costs in Arbitration' (International Chamber of Commerce, 2018)12.
84. Sam Luttrell and Peter Harris, 'Reinventing the Redfern' (2016) 33(4) *Journal of International Arbitration* 353, 355–358 DOI: 10.54648/joia2016021.
85. United Nations Commission on International Trade Law, *Report of the Working Group on Arbitration and Conciliation on the Work of its Forty-Fourth Session*, 39th sess., UN Doc. A/CN.9/592 (19 June–7 July 2006) 4.
86. United Nations Committee on International Trade Law, *UNCITRAL Notes on Organizing Arbitral Proceeding* (2nd ed., 2016), UN GAOR, 71st sess., Supp No. 17, UN Doc. A/71/17.

It is worth noting that the UNCITRAL Notes are similar to the IBA Rules on the Taking of Evidence in several respects. According to the UNCITRAL Notes, the request for disclosure of documents typically contains the same four elements as the IBA Rules on Evidence: the documents requested; the reasons for the request; a statement as to why the requested documents are believed to be in the possession of the other party and are not otherwise available to the requesting party.[87] Also, both the IBA Rules on Evidence and the UNCITRAL Notes confirm the widespread acceptance of witness pre-testimony and questioning but fail to specify the extent to which a party (or its representative) may assist witnesses in preparing for the hearing.[88] In addition, both the UNCITRAL Notes and the IBA Rules allow both party-appointed and tribunal-appointed experts to clarify issues of fact or law.[89]

In addition, in order to promote universal adherence to the New York Convention and its uniform interpretation and effective implementation, the UNCITRAL Secretariat in 2016 issued the *UNCITRAL Secretariat Guide on the Convention on the Recognition and Enforcement of Foreign Arbitral Awards* (hereinafter 'UNCITRAL Guidelines').[90] The UNCITRAL Guidelines contribute significantly to the comparative case studies on the application of the due process defence among State Parties. In addition to the UNCITRAL Guidelines, the ICCA has also issued the *ICCA Guide to the Interpretation of the 1958 New York Convention* to provide guidance to enforcing courts on the application and interpretation of the Convention in cases where confusion and some uncertainties arise, including but not limited to the due process defence.[91]

§4.04 CONCLUSION

This chapter argued that international conventions, modern arbitration laws, established arbitration rules, soft law, and the practice of international arbitration together provide the procedural rules that guarantee the principle of due process. Chapter 3 showed that international conventions and national arbitration laws have established the general principle of due process and its core elements, which enforcing courts should refer to when interpreting and applying the due process defence under the New York Convention. These international conventions and national arbitration laws are designed to support the idea of a common international due process obligation and have established a consensus on the principled nature of due process in both public international law and international commercial arbitration.

87. United Nations Committee on International Trade Law, *UNCITRAL Notes* (n. 86) Art. 13(b). *See also* International Bar Association, *IBA Rules on Evidence* (n. 30) Art. 3.
88. United Nations Committee on International Trade Law, *UNCITRAL Notes* (n. 86) Art. 14(a)(iii). *See also* International Bar Association, *IBA Rules on Evidence* (n. 30) Art. 4(3).
89. United Nations Committee on International Trade Law, *UNCITRAL Notes* (n. 86) Art. 15. *See also* International Bar Association, *IBA Rules on Evidence* (n. 30) Arts 5, 6.
90. Emmanuel Gaillard and George A Bermann (eds), *The UNCITRAL Secretariat Guide on the New York Convention* (Brill, 2017).
91. ICCA, *ICCA's Guide to the Interpretation of the 1958 New York Convention: A Handbook for Judges* (International Council for Commercial Arbitration, 2011).

This chapter has focused on the role of 'private' sources of law, which include institutional arbitration rules, well-accepted arbitral practice and soft law, in ensuring due process in international commercial arbitration. The contextual and purposive interpretation of the VCLT allows enforcing courts to take these sources into account by virtue of reference to them and/or endorsement of them by the parties' agreement. These 'private' sources provide enforcing courts with transnational materials beyond their own national rules and with a perspective of the international arbitration community in which actors include, but are not limited to, parties, arbitrators, arbitral institutions, and transnational professional organisations. These transnational materials better reflect the nature of international arbitral proceedings and promote due process under the New York Convention as a genuinely transnational standard, distinct from any particular national legal system.

The following Chapters 5–7 will examine the application of another source of due process rules – the domestic judicial decisions of State Parties' courts in specific cases. As discussed in more detail in Chapters 5–7, national legal systems have less-evidently uniform rules for the application of due process in more specific cases. The narrower the rules, the greater the likelihood of divergence in the interpretation of due process. It is in this context – the tension between universal aspiration and local application – that this book argues that enforcing courts should use comparative law methods to explore the subsequent practice of State Parties in order to construe the due process rule that should be applied in a particular case.[92]

92. For the way that comparative methods are used in the case studies, *see* §1.04[B].

CHAPTER 5

Policy Considerations of and Relevant Limits to the Interpretation and Application of the Due Process Defence

§5.01 INTRODUCTION

Chapter 3 has illustrated that the due process defence of the New York Convention mirrors the general principle of *audiatur et altera pars* and that its core elements encompass: (a) due notice of the appointment of arbitrators and proceedings; (b) equality of arms; (c) the right to be heard; and (d) impartiality and independence of arbitrators. Chapter 4 showed that in concrete cases, implementing these abstract elements typically involves an enforcing court consulting due process rules taken from international conventions, modern arbitration laws (arbitration statutes and case law), established arbitration rules, soft law, and the practices of international commercial arbitration.

Chapters 3 and 4 do not feature a thorough examination of legal precedent on which enforcing courts may rely to provide precise parameters for the due process defence in individual cases. In Chapters 5–7, however, this issue is given priority. In any given scenario, however, court decisions may diverge across jurisdictions. It is in this context – the tensions between universal aspiration and local application – that the author contends an enforcing court should employ comparative legal methods to explore the subsequent judicial practices of State Parties to construe the due process that should be applied in a particular case.[1] Beginning with this chapter, a comparative analysis of national judicial decisions made by State Parties is conducted to identify similarities and differences in the interpretation and application of the due process defence and relevant issues.

1. Regarding the way that comparative methods are used in such case studies, *see* §1.04[B].

This chapter explores the policies and potential limitations concerning the interpretation and application of Article V(1)(b) of the New York Convention. The chapter begins by conducting a comparative analysis of State Parties' case law, examining the policies governing the interpretation and application of the grounds for refusal, including the due process defence. It shows that courts have generally confirmed the following policies: pro-enforcement policy, non-review of merits, judicial deference to arbitrators' procedural discretion and adherence to institutional arbitration rules, as well as due consideration of the international nature of the arbitration. Judicial recognition of these policies indicates agreements by State Parties and constitutes subsequent practice within the meaning of Article 31(3)(b) of the VCLT and thus should be considered by enforcing courts.[2] Additionally, according to the 'object and purpose' interpretation of the VCLT, enforcing courts should give weight to a pro-enforcement policy, which aligns with one of the objects and purposes of the New York Convention. Further, arbitral tribunals' procedural discretion and the authority of institutional arbitration rules stem from parties' agreement, which the New York Convention's Article V(1)(d) obliges enforcing courts to respect. The VCLT's 'context, object and purpose' interpretation mandates enforcing courts to defer to parties' authorised tribunal discretion and arbitration rules. Since these policies or principles will impact the decisions of an enforcing court when determining due process issues, they will be examined here before analysing more specific scenarios concerning proper notice, equality between parties and the right to be heard, which will be done in Chapters 6 and 7.

Other issues such as threshold, party waiver, and the deference given by enforcing courts at the recognition and enforcement stage to the decisions of courts at the seat of arbitration may influence the interpretation of specific scenarios involving proper notice, right to be heard, and equality between parties. These issues and their corresponding policies are discussed here before turning to the more precise scenarios of the due process defence, which are covered in Chapters 6 and 7. Enforcing courts display substantial divergences when evaluating these matters. To determine the most suitable approaches, this chapter applies normative criteria, including predictability, compatibility with legal expectations, and balance with efficiency. According to the VCLT, these criteria are relevant to the New York Convention interpretation as they are fundamental to the 'object and purpose' of the New York Convention.[3] Additionally, decisions made by courts in multiple jurisdictions have clarified these criteria and their interrelatedness and may constitute subsequent practice within the meaning of Article 32 of the VCLT, thus possessing persuasive authority for enforcing courts.[4]

2. The VCLT sets forth two categories of subsequent practice: (1) different conducts between a limited number of State Parties that, taken together, establish an agreement between all State Parties (Article 31(3)(b) VCLT); (2) conducts by one or more (but not all) parties that *do not* presuppose an agreement of all parties, but which may nevertheless be relevant as a subsidiary means of interpretation (Article 32 VCLT). For more about the first category in detail, *see* §2.06[B][1].
3. *See* §2.06[A][2].
4. For more about subsequent practice under Article 32 VCLT, *see* §2.06[C][2].

Accordingly, this chapter is structured as follows. Section 5.02 examines the principles for interpreting the grounds for refusal contained in the New York Convention, including the due process defence. Section 5.03 assesses types of waivers by parties that can be recognised by enforcing courts. Section 5.04 reviews the threshold requirements for the due process defence. Section 5.05 explores how decisions made by the court at the seat of arbitration regarding due process impact enforcing courts. Section 5.06 concludes the chapter.

§5.02 POLICY CONSIDERATIONS FOR INTERPRETING THE DUE PROCESS DEFENCE

The case law of State Parties to the New York Convention reveals considerable agreement in the principles that guide the interpretation and application of the due process defence.[5] These include a pro-enforcement policy, non-review of merits, judicial deference to arbitration rules and tribunal discretion, and the necessity to acknowledge the unique characteristics of international arbitration. Judicial recognition of these policies indicates agreements among State Parties and constitutes subsequent practice within the meaning of Article 31(3)(b) of the VCLT. Therefore, enforcing courts should consider this when interpreting the due process defence under the New York Convention. This section outlines the guiding principles before examining the interpretation and application of the due process defence, with specific focus on factual scenarios related to proper notice, right to be heard, and equality between parties, which are discussed in Chapters 6 and 7.

[A] Pro-enforcement Policy and Court Discretion under Article V of the New York Convention

The majority of courts adopt a pro-enforcement policy and tend to interpret the due process defence narrowly. The New York Convention aims to encourage the recognition and enforcement of international arbitral awards through minimal conditions.[6] Article III of the Convention affirms this position:

5. Friedrich Rosenfeld, Dietmar Czernich and Franco Ferrari, 'General Report' in Friedrich Rosenfeld, Dietmar Czernich and Franco Ferrari (eds), *Due Process as a Limit to Discretion in International Commercial Arbitration* (Kluwer Law International, 2020) 7–8; Albert Jan van den Berg, *The New York Arbitration Convention of 1958: Towards a Uniform Judicial Interpretation* (Kluwer Law and Taxation Publishers, 1981) 264–274; Patricia Nacimiento, 'Article V(1)(a)' in Herbert Kronke et al. (eds), *Recognition and Enforcement of Foreign Arbitral Awards: A Global Commentary on the New York Convention* (Kluwer Law International, 2010) 206, 206–216; Herman Verbist, 'Challenges on Grounds of Due Process Pursuant to Article V(1)(B) of the New York Convention' in Emmanuel Gaillard and Domenico Di Pietro (eds), *Enforcement of Arbitration Agreements and International Arbitral Awards: The New York Convention in Practice* (Cameron May, 2008) 679, 687–689.
6. President of the District Court of Amsterdam, 12 July 1984 reported in (1985) X *Yearbook Commercial Arbitration* 487, 489.

> Each Contracting State shall recognise arbitral awards as binding and enforce them in accordance with the rules of procedure of the territory where the award is relied upon, under the conditions laid down in the following articles. There shall not be imposed substantially more onerous conditions or higher fees or charges on the recognition or enforcement of arbitral awards to which this Convention applies than are imposed on the recognition or enforcement of domestic arbitral awards.[7]

Article III highlights the pro-enforcement stance of arbitral awards.[8] In accordance with Article 31(1) of the VCLT, a contextual and purposive interpretation of Article V(1)(b) of the New York Convention necessitates alignment with other articles of the Convention. As established by a Singaporean ruling, 'there is the principle of international comity enshrined in the Convention that strongly inclines the courts to give effect to foreign arbitration awards'.[9] The pro-enforcement policy mandates that national courts recognise awards as enforceable prima facie,[10] except when they fall under the exhaustive grounds for refusal in Article V of the New York Convention.

This pro-enforcement approach has been upheld by various courts in their interpretation and application of Article V of the New York Convention, including the due process defence. For instance, US courts take a 'general pro-enforcement bias' towards the New York Convention[11] and hold 'strong public policy favouring confirmation of foreign arbitration awards'.[12] Also, they have confirmed that the purpose of the New York Convention is to 'encourage the recognition and enforcement of commercial arbitration agreements in international contracts and to unify the standards by which agreements to arbitrate are observed, and arbitral awards are enforced in signatory countries'.[13] Swedish courts also adhere to a pro-enforcement policy. In a particular Swedish case concerning 'proper notice', the Swedish Supreme Court determined that the due process defence should be interpreted considering the Convention's general objective of facilitating the enforcement of arbitral awards, despite the lack of specification in both the Swedish Act and the New York Convention as to what constitutes proper notice.[14]

---

7. *Convention on the Recognition and Enforcement of Foreign Arbitral Awards*, open for signature 10 June 1958, 330 UNTS 3 (entered into force 7 June 1959) Art. III.
8. van den Berg (n. 5) 243–245; Andreas Börner, 'Article III' in Herbert Kronke et al. (eds), *Recognition and Enforcement of Foreign Arbitral Awards: A Global Commentary on the New York Convention* (Kluwer Law International, 2010) 115, 116; Christoph Liebscher, 'Preliminary Remarks' in Reinmar Wolff (ed.), *New York Convention: Convention on the Recognition and Enforcement of Foreign Arbitral Awards of 10 June 1958 Commentary* (C.H. Beck, 2012) 21.
9. *Aloe Vera of Am Inc v. Asianic Food (S) Pte Ltd* [2006] SGHC 78, [40].
10. United Nations Commission on International Trade Law, Secretariat Guide on the Convention on the Recognition and Enforcement of Foreign Arbitral Awards (2016) 77.
11. *Parsons & Whittemore Overseas Co v. Société Générale De L'Industrie Du Papier (RAKTA)*, 508 F 2d 969, 973 (2nd Cir, 1974).
12. *Ministry of Defense and Support for the Armed Forces of the Islamic Republic of Iran v. Cubic Defense Systems Inc*, 665 F 3d 1091, 1098 (9th Cir, 2011).
13. *Scherk v. Alberto-Culver Co*, 417 US 506, 520 (1974).
14. *Lenmorniiproekt OAO v. Arne Larsson & Partner Leasing Aktiebolag, Högsta Domstolens* [Supreme Court], Ö 13-09, 16 April 2010 reported in (2010) XXXV Yearbook Commercial Arbitration 456, 457; *Belaya Ptitsa – Kursk v. Robot Grader AB, Högsta Domstolens* [Supreme Court], Ö 3626-17, 04 May 2018 reported in the Arbitration Institute of the Stockholm Chamber of Commerce, 5 [13], https://www.arbitration.sccinstitute.com/Swedish-Arbitration-Portal/

It is reasonable to deduce from the pro-enforcement policy that the grounds for refusing recognition and enforcement of arbitral awards should be applied restrictively.[15] With respect to the due process defence, courts have interpreted narrowly the notion of being 'unable to present his case' when the complaining party has been unable to attend proceedings or hearings.[16] Furthermore, a further indication of a pro-enforcement stance lies in the courts' ability to exercise discretion when it comes to recognising or enforcing awards, even if a ground for refusal has been established.[17] It is noteworthy that, apart from the French version, the official wording of Article V stipulates that enforcement 'may' be refused rather than 'must' be refused when one of the grounds for refusal listed in Article V is proved. The wording is permissive rather than mandatory. Additionally, French case law indicates that the French approach is permissive rather than compulsory, as it pertains to the more-favourable-right provision set out in Article VII(1) of the New York Convention.[18]

This discretion of courts has been generally accepted by both academics and courts.[19] UK courts, for instance, confirm a tendency to favour enforcing New York Convention awards. Even if one of the grounds for resisting enforcement is established, UK courts still retain the discretion to enforce the award.[20] This is because the comparable phrasing in the English Arbitration Act 1996, which implements the New York Convention, states that recognition and enforcement 'may be refused' if any of the grounds for refusal under Article V are established.[21] When determining whether the procedural irregularity in the case of *Minmetals* violated public policy, the court found that an investigation of all surrounding circumstances material to the US court's decision on whether to refuse enforcement, as a matter of policy, was necessary. The court emphasised that public policy considerations entail an examination of not only the core procedural defect but also all other relevant factors. In certain cases, policy considerations may strongly support enforcement, outweighing opposing considerations.[22] This applies also to the Hong Kong courts. The Supreme Court of Hong Kong heard a case where Article V(1)(d) was proven but the judge exercised discretion to enforce the award:

> [E]ven if a ground for opposition is proved, there is still a residual discretion left in the enforcing court to enforce nonetheless. This shows that the grounds of

---

Supreme-Court/The-Supreme-Court2/The-Supreme-Court/d_3259325-judgment-in-the-swedish-supreme-court-4-may-2018.-case-no.-o-3626-17.

15. van den Berg (n. 5) 267–268.
16. United Nations Commission on International Trade Law (n. 10) 166.
17. *Ibid.*, 125.
18. Jan Paulsson, 'May or Must under the New York Convention: An Exercise in Syntax and Linguistics' (1998) 14 *Journal of International Arbitration* 227 DOI: 10.1093/arbitration/14.2.227.
19. van den Berg (n. 5) 265.
20. *IPCO (Nigeria) Ltd v. Nigerian National Petroleum Corp* [2005] EWHC 726 (Comm) (27 April 2005) [11].
21. *Arbitration Act 1996* (UK) c 23, s. 103(2).
22. *Minmetals Germany GmbH v. Ferco Steel Ltd* [1999] CLC 647, 660 ('Minmetals').

> opposition are not to be inflexibly applied. The residual discretion enables the enforcing court to achieve a just result in all the circumstances...[23]

Regarding the due process defence, the High Court of Hong Kong ruled that the court may exercise its discretion to enforce an award even if due process has been violated, provided it is beyond doubt that the tribunal's decision would have been the same even if due process were not seriously violated.[24]

[B] Non-review of the Merits

Most courts have cautioned against misusing the post-award procedure for reviewing the merits. The New York Convention prohibits any review of the merits of an award to which the Convention applies.[25] As an Indian court once held, 'the scope of enquiry before the court in which the award is sought to be enforced is limited and does not enable a party to the said proceedings to impeach the award on merits'.[26] Most experienced jurisdictions in modern arbitration, including France,[27] Germany,[28] the Netherlands,[29] the US,[30] and the UK,[31] have established the principle that the enforcing court is not permitted to review the merits of the award. As detailed in §7.04, enforcing courts generally respect tribunals' discretion on the admission or exclusion of evidence to prevent reviewing the merits of an award. Even if a party argues that the tribunal breached their right to be heard by refusing their evidence, this discretion is maintained.

For example, US courts have established that they cannot address factual or legal errors as a court of second jurisdiction.[32] US courts have stated that they are not permitted to review the merits of an arbitral award, even if there are allegations of factual errors or misinterpretation of the contract.[33] Furthermore, US courts have ruled that an arbitrator's erroneous interpretations or applications of law cannot be challenged.[34] Similarly, UK courts have clarified that it is not the role of the enforcing court to evaluate the decision's correctness in terms of law or fact.[35]

---

23. Supreme Court of Hong Kong, High Court, No MP 24118, 13 July 1994 reported in (1995) XX *Yearbook Commercial Arbitration* 671, 677.
24. *Paklito Investment Ltd v. Klockner East Asia Ltd* [1993] 2 HKLR 39, 49.
25. Nigel Blackaby et al., *Redfern and Hunter on International Arbitration* (Oxford University Press, 6th ed., 2015) 622.
26. *Renusagar Power Co Ltd v. General Electric Co*, Supreme Court of India, 7 October 1993 reported in (1995) XX *Yearbook Commercial Arbitration* 681, 691.
27. Cour d'appel de Paris [Paris Court of Appeal], 2003/09894, 10 June 2004 reported in 2005 (XXX) *Yearbook Commercial Arbitration* 499, [18].
28. *See* below nn. 36–38.
29. District Court of Arnhem, 221871 I KV RK 11-999, 27 September 2012 reported in (2013) XXXVIII *Yearbook Commercial Arbitration* 431, [17].
30. *See* below nn. 32–34.
31. *See* below n. 35.
32. *Karaha Bodas Co v. Perusahaan Pertambangan Minyak Dan Gas Bumi Negara*, 364 F 3d 274, 288 (5th Cir, 2004); *OJSC Ukrnafta v. Carpatsky Petroleum Corp, et al.* (SD Tex, Civ No H-09-891, 2 October 2017) slip op 29.
33. *United Paperworkers Int'l Union, AFLCIO v. Misco Inc*, 484 US 29, 38 (1987).
34. *ARW Exploration Corp v. Aguirre*, 45 F 3d 1455, 1463 (10th Cir, 1995).
35. *Cukurova Holding AS v. Sonera Holding BV* [2014] UKPC 15 (13 May 2014) [53] ('Cukurova').

German courts have emphasised that the assessment of the award's merits during enforcement proceedings is not permitted under the Convention.[36] Hence, German courts would not review legal or factual issues previously affirmed by the tribunal. As a result, German courts have held that 'a defective evaluation of the submitted facts by the arbitral tribunal does not lead per se to a violation of due process, for instance, for the failure to take into account requests for evidence'.[37] In other words, German courts do not scrutinise the accuracy of evidence used by the arbitral tribunal in great detail. A failure to give reasons for refusing a request for evidence, where the tribunal does not wholly disregard the request for evidence but deals with it at least briefly, may not be considered a violation of due process by German courts.[38]

[C] Judicial Deference to the Discretion of Arbitrators' Procedural Decisions and Institutional Arbitration Rules

As detailed in §4.03[C], institutional arbitration rules, especially those of leading international institutions such as the ICC, LCIA, SCC and SIAC, provide a transnational and overall framework for international arbitration within which to proceed, as do the UNCITRAL Rules for ad hoc arbitration. Nevertheless, it is crucial for the parties or the arbitral tribunal to supplement these institutional arbitral rules with more specific propositions. It is well accepted that the tribunal 'is the master of its own procedure'[39] and has the power to fill any gaps in the institutional arbitral rules by giving procedural directions. While fairness is important, other factors like proportionality, procedural economy, and party autonomy should also be taken into account while making procedural decisions. The tribunal is better placed than the enforcing court to balance these various concerns.[40]

The authority of institutional arbitration rules and the broad discretion of arbitrators in procedural issues are derived from party autonomy. Such party agreement on procedural issues has been recognised by Article V(1)(d) of the New York Convention. The interpretation under Article 31(1) of the VCLT, regarding 'context, object and purpose', necessitates that the interpretation of the due process defence under Article V(1)(b) of the New York Convention aligns with other grounds for refusal. This includes recognising institutional arbitration rules and the tribunal's

---

36. Oberlandesgericht Munich [High Regional Court of Munich], 34 Sch 21/11, 11 April 2012 reported in (2014) XXXIX *Yearbook Commercial Arbitration* 389, [13]; Oberlandesgericht Naumburg [Higher Regional Court of Naumburg], 10 Sch 04/10, 4 March 2011 reported in (2012) XXXVII *Yearbook Commercial Arbitration* 226, [21].
37. Oberlandesgericht Munich [High Regional Court of Munich], 34 Sch 21/11, 11 April 2012 reported in (2014) XXXIX *Yearbook Commercial Arbitration* 389, [8].
38. Oberlandesgericht Munich [Higher Regional Court of Munich], 34 Sch 10/11, 14 November 2011 reported in (2012) XXXVII *Yearbook Commercial Arbitration* 231, [11].
39. *See*, e.g., International Chamber of Commerce, *Arbitration Rules* (adopted 1 January 2021) ('*ICC Arbitration Rules*') Art. 22. *See also Triulzi Cesare SRL v. Xinyi Group (Glass) Co Ltd* [2015] 1 SLR 114, [128].
40. *Tronic International Pte Ltd v. Topco Scientific Co Ltd* [2016] HKEC 1780, [13].

discretion, which parties have conferred. Enforcing courts generally show considerable deference to institutional arbitration rules and the broad discretion of arbitrators in managing cases and conducting independent assessments of facts when determining the due process defence under the Convention.

For example, UK courts held that it was necessary to have regard for the public policy of discouraging the re-litigation of issues already determined by the arbitrators by presenting evidence not shown to have been unavailable before the tribunal.[41] In the case of *Zavod Ekran Oao*, where the standard of proper notice was in question, the English High Court of Justice took the institutional arbitral rules into account and held that:

> There is little English authority as to the meaning of 'proper notice', but in context, it is an aspect of the wider notion that the party contesting enforcement was unable to present its case, so that lack of proper notice suggests some unfairness. In the context of s 103(2)(c) Arbitration Act 1996, 'proper notice' is such as is likely to bring the relevant information to the attention of the person notified, taking account of the parties' contractual dispute resolution mechanism, including any applicable *institutional arbitration rules*.[42]

Moreover, the Dutch courts exhibit deference towards the rules of arbitral institutions that have been agreed upon by the parties. For example, the opposing party alleged that the award before the Dutch court should not be enforced due to the lack of explanation by the arbitrators regarding the rejection of its defences. However, the Dutch judge determined that according to the chosen American Arbitration Association, the arbitrators were not obliged to provide a detailed explanation for their decision unless specifically requested by the parties or deemed necessary by the arbitrators themselves, which was not applicable in this case.[43]

It is important to note that the Convention does not grant the losing party the right to challenge procedural decisions made by the arbitration tribunal. The due process defence under Article V(1)(b) is not intended to refuse recognition or enforcement of an award solely based on a court's differing legal interpretation regarding due process matters. These issues may include, for example, the hearing of witness statements or the number of permitted written submissions. Instead, Article V(1)(b) addresses more fundamental deviations from the due process principle. This deferential approach shows 'respect for the capacities of foreign and transnational tribunals and sensitivity to the need of the international commercial system for predictability in the resolution of disputes',[44] thus avoiding overly intrusive court reviews at the post-award stage.[45]

41. *Minmetals Germany GmbH v. Ferco Steel Ltd* [1999] CLC 647, 660.
42. *Zavod Ekran Oao v. Magneco Metrel UK Ltd* [2017] EWHC 2208 (Comm) (1 September 2017) ('*Zavod Ekran Oao*') [12] (emphasis added).
43. Rechtbank [Court of First Instance] of Amsterdam, 411230/KG RK 08-3652, 18 June 2009 reported in (2009) XXXIV *Yearbook Commercial Arbitration* 715, [12].
44. *Grow Biz International Inc v. DLT Holdings Inc, Debbie Tanton*, Supreme Court, Province of Prince Edward Island, Trial Division, Docket No GSC-17431, 23 March 2001 reported in (2005) XXX *Yearbook Commercial Arbitration* 450.
45. Rosenfeld, Czernich and Ferrari (n. 5) 18.

[D] Due Consideration of the Specificities of Arbitration and Its International Nature

Many courts have duly considered the specificities of arbitration and its international nature when determining the due process defence. Accordingly, they have endorsed the proposition that the standard of the due process defence under the New York Convention differs from that applied in domestic arbitration or court proceedings. As shown in Chapter 2, even courts that prefer to apply their own domestic standards for the due process defence under the New York Convention take into account the unique aspects of arbitration and its international character.[46]

The courts acknowledge that arbitral tribunals are not obligated to follow all procedural safeguards that would be applicable in court proceedings. As explained by US courts, parties opt for arbitration due to its convenience or other benefits, but in doing so they relinquish their right to seek recourse from the domestic court for all but the most exceptional errors at arbitration.[47] The South District Court of New York has stated that:

> Arbitration by its nature does not have all of the procedural niceties of litigation. It is the parties' choice to arbitrate their disputes and once they have made that choice, they must be content with its informalities; they may not hedge it about with those procedural limitations which is precisely its purpose to avoid.[48]

This view is also prevalent in Germany. German procedural law's requirements for judicial due process, such as clarification and indication, do not extend to international arbitration. In contrast to civil procedural laws, German courts do not mandate the arbitral tribunal to provide references or specific reasons for its decision based on each party's argument, nor does it need to discuss the law with the parties concerned.[49]

Some courts have indicated that the circumstances leading to the annulment of domestic awards may not necessarily amount to a breach of due process under the New York Convention. This is particularly applicable to Swiss courts. The Swiss Federal Supreme Court has ruled that not all breaches in procedure will automatically result in the refusal of enforcing a foreign award, even if such an irregularity would lead to the annulment of an award made in Switzerland. Instead, refusal of enforcement should only occur in cases where there has been a clear violation of fundamental principles of the Swiss legal order, resulting in significant harm to the concept of justice.[50]

46. *See* §2.03[B][2].
47. *Consorcio Rive, SA De CV v. Briggs of Cancun*, 134 F Supp 2d 789, 796 (ED La, 2001).
48. *Caja Nacional de Ahorro y Seguros in Liquidation, Argentine National Treasury and others v. Deutsche Ruckversicherung AG* (SDNY, Civ No. 06-5826-PKL, 1 August 2007).
49. Oberlandesgericht Munich [Higher Regional Court of Munich], 34 Sch 10/11, 14 November 2011 reported in (2012) XXXVII *Yearbook Commercial Arbitration* 231, [9]; Oberlandesgericht Düsseldorf [Court of Appeal Düsseldorf], I-4 Sch 10/09, 15 December 2009 reported in (2010) XXXV *Yearbook Commercial Arbitration* 386, [16].
50. Tribunal Fédéral [Federal Supreme Court of Switzerland], 8 February 1978 reported in (1986) XI *Yearbook Commercial Arbitration* 538, 540.

§5.03 WAIVER

The principles of good faith and the prohibition of abuse of rights have gained wide acceptance as general principles of law.[51] Enforcing courts should consider these principles when determining the due process defence under the VCLT's interpretative framework.[52] If parties fail to raise objections in a timely and active manner regarding procedural irregularities in prior proceedings, they may be deemed to have waived their right to make such objections during later enforcement proceedings. A party may fail to raise objection on a breach of due process during arbitration proceedings or to apply for setting aside the award based on procedural irregularities before the court at the arbitral seat. The question that arises pertains to whether these two circumstances result in a waiver of the due process defence by the opposing party before the enforcing court. In addition to the *ex post* waiver regarding the opposing party's passive conduct, it is also necessary to examine the *ex ante* waiver of fundamental procedural rights that parties expressly renounce before any breach occurs.

Subsequent judicial practice of State Parties recognises a waiver when a party fails to raise a due process violation that could have been presented to an arbitral panel. However, enforcing courts are divided on the matter of *ex ante* waivers and whether a failure to raise setting-aside proceedings based on a due process breach constitutes a waiver of the due process defence in subsequent recognition and enforcement proceedings. Interpretative rules of 'ordinary meaning', 'purpose' and 'preparatory works' based on the VCLT approach can help to resolve questions regarding the latter two circumstances.

[A] Failure to Raise a Due Process Objection in Arbitration

Even though the text of the New York Convention does not mention estoppel, some national arbitration laws, court decisions, and leading institutional arbitration rules provide that parties to arbitration may be deemed to have waived their right to object to procedural irregularities in the setting-aside or recognition and enforcement proceedings if they did not raise their objections during the arbitral proceedings. For instance, the ICC, LCIA, HKIAC, SCC, SIAC, and UNCITRAL Arbitration Rules provide that if a party fails to object promptly to any failure to comply with the arbitration agreement, arbitral rules, or other rules applicable to the proceedings during the arbitral proceedings, they will be deemed to have waived their right to raise such an objection.[53]

---

51. *Mobil Corporation, Venezuela Holding et al. v. Bolivarian Republic of Venezuela* (Jurisdiction) (ICSID Arbitral Tribunal, Case No. ARB/07/27, 19 June 2010) [169]–[185].
52. *Vienna Convention on the Law of Treaties*, opened for signature 23 May 1969, 1155 UNTS 331 (entered into force 27 January 1980) Arts 31(1), 31(3)(c).
53. United Nations Committee on International Trade Law, *UNCITRAL Arbitration Rules* (2nd ed., 2010), GA Res 65/22, 6th Comm A/65/465, 66th sess., Agenda Item 77, UN Doc. A/RES/65/22 (6 December 2010) ('*UNCITRAL Arbitration Rules*') Art. 32; Arbitration Institute of the Stockholm Chamber of Commerce, *SCC Arbitration Rules* (adopted 1 January 2017) ('*SCC Arbitration Rules*') Art. 36; Singapore International Arbitration Centre, *SIAC Arbitration Rules* (adopted 1

Also, Article 4 of the UNCITRAL Model Law confirms this waiver:

> A party who knows that any provision of this Law from which the parties may derogate or any requirement under the arbitration agreement has not been complied with and yet proceeds with the arbitration without stating his objection to such non-compliance without undue delay or, if a time-limit is provided therefor, within such period of time, shall be deemed to have waived his right to object.[54]

For jurisdictions that have not adopted the UNCITRAL Model Law, the English Arbitration Act and the French Code of Civil Procedure contain provisions similar to Article 4 of the UNCITRAL Model Law. As discussed in §5.02[A], English courts have interpreted the phrase 'may be refused' in Article V as indicative of a limited discretion, meaning that the court is unlikely to exercise its discretion to enforce an award that presents a fundamental or structural defect.[55] If one of the grounds stipulated in section 103(2) or (3) of the English Arbitration Act (corresponding to Articles V(1) and V(2) of the New York Convention) has been satisfied, then the court would normally enforce the award only if the right to rely upon one of the stated grounds had been lost, such as by another agreement or estoppel.[56] When applying estoppel to enforcement proceedings, English courts prefer the section 73 standard of the English Arbitration Act (1996) entitled 'Loss of Right to Object',[57] which states that:

> If a party to arbitral proceedings takes part, or continues to take part, in the proceedings without making, either forthwith or within such time as is allowed by the arbitration agreement or the tribunal or by any provision of this Part, any objection –
>
> (a) that the tribunal lacks substantive jurisdiction,
> (b) *that the proceedings have been improperly conducted,*
> (c) that there has been a failure to comply with the arbitration agreement or with any provision of this Part, or
> (d) *that there has been any other irregularity affecting the tribunal or the proceedings,*
> he may not raise that objection later, before the tribunal or the court, unless he shows that, at the time he took part or continued to take part in the

August 2016) Art. 20(9); *ICC Arbitration Rules* (n. 39) Art. 40; Hong Kong International Arbitration Centre, *Administered Arbitration Rules* (adopted 1 November 2018) ('*HKIAC Arbitration Rules*') Art. 32; London Court of International Arbitration, *LCIA Arbitration Rules* (adopted 1 October 2014) ('*LCIA Arbitration Rules*') Art. 2(4).

54. *UNCITRAL Model Law on International Commercial Arbitration*, UN GAOR, 40th sess., Supp No. 17, UN Doc. A/40/17 (adopted 21 June 1985) annex I, as amended by UN GAOR, 61st sess., Supp No. 17, UN Doc. A/61/17 (7 July 2006), annex I ('*UNCITRAL Model Law*') Art. 4.
55. *Honeywell International Middle East Ltd v. Meydan Group LLC* [2014] EWHC 1344 (TCC) (30 April 2014) [66].
56. *Dardana Ltd v. Yukos Oil Co* [2002] EWCA Civ 543 (18 April 2002) [8]; *Ajay Kanoria, Esols Worldwide Ltd & Indekka Software PVT Ltd v. Tony Francis Guinness* [2006] EWCA Civ 222 (21 February 2006) [25]–[26]; *Honeywell International Middle East Ltd v. Meydan Group LLC* [2014] EWHC 1344 (TCC) (30 April 2014) [66]; *Tesco Ltd v. William Moffett, Richard Mclaughlin, James Mclaughlin & Anson Logue* [2015] NIQB 68 (1 July 2015)[21]; *Dallah Real Estate and Tourism Holding Co v. Ministry of Religious Affairs* [2010] UKSC 46 (3 November 2010).
57. *Tesco Ltd v. William Moffett, Richard Mclaughlin, James Mclaughlin & Anson Logue* [2015] NIQB 68 (1 July 2015) [22].

> proceedings, he did not know and could not with reasonable diligence have discovered the grounds for the objection.[58]

Moreover, the reformed French Code of Civil Procedure (2011) has clearly been inspired by previous French case law as well as the common law notion of estoppel.[59] Article 1466 of the French Code of Civil Procedure provides that:

> A party which, knowingly and without a legitimate reason, fails to object to an irregularity before the arbitral tribunal promptly shall be deemed to have waived its right to avail itself of such irregularity.[60]

Judicial decisions in both common law jurisdictions, including the UK,[61] Hong Kong,[62] and the US,[63] and civil law jurisdictions such as Germany,[64] France,[65] Switzerland,[66] the Netherlands,[67] Spain,[68] China,[69] and Brazil[70] usually recognise the waiver of due process rights in cases where there is a failure to object to a breach of due process in arbitral proceedings. In *Minmetals*, another English case, the losing party opposed the enforcement of an award on the grounds that the award was made based on facts discovered through the tribunal's own investigations. The English High Court rejected this challenge on the grounds that the opposing party had been given an opportunity to ask for the disclosure of relevant evidence and to comment on it but had failed to do so.[71] The opposing party proceeded with the arbitration without explicitly contesting the procedural irregularity with the arbitrators. Therefore, it was deemed that the losing party had waived its right to rely on the violation of due process before the enforcing court.[72] The English High Court held that, in order to rely on the due process defence, parties must demonstrate that their inability to present their case resulted from factors beyond their control rather than their own failure to make use of an opportunity.[73] Likewise, in the case of *Tesco*, the court decided that the defendants' failure to object to procedural irregularities during the arbitral proceedings constituted

58. *Arbitration Act 1996* (UK) c 23, s. 73(1) (emphasis added).
59. Maxi Scherer, 'Long-Awaited New French Arbitration Law Revealed' on Kluwer Arbitration Blog (15 January 2011), http://arbitrationblog.kluwerarbitration.com/2011/01/15/long-awaited-new-french-arbitration-law-revealed (accessed on 25 May 2022).
60. *Code de procédure civile* [Code of Civil Procedure] (France), Art. 1466 [Emmanuel Gaillard et al., *Code of Civil Procedure*, https://sccinstitute.com/media/37105/french_law_on_arbitration.pdf].
61. *See* below nn. 71, 74.
62. *See* below n. 79.
63. *See* below nn. 75–78.
64. *See* below n. 80.
65. *See* below n. 84.
66. *See* below nn. 81–82.
67. *See* below n. 80.
68. *See* below n. 80.
69. *See* below n. 86.
70. *See* below n. 85.
71. *Minmetals Germany GmbH v. Ferco Steel Ltd* [1999] CLC 647, 657–8.
72. *Ibid.*, 659.
73. *Ibid.*, 647.

a waiver and that they could not raise such objections at a later stage before the enforcing court.[74]

In the US, when a party fails to raise a defence that could have been presented to an arbitral panel, it may be precluded from raising such arguments at a later stage of proceedings to resist enforcement of the award. This criterion of waiver is generally applicable to both domestic and international arbitration awards.[75] The US courts determined that a party 'cannot remain silent, raising no objection during the course of the arbitration proceeding, and when an award adverse to him has been handed down complain of a situation of which he had knowledge from the first'.[76] Furthermore, it was also established that if the party was given a fair and equal opportunity to present their case during the arbitral proceedings, they must accept the consequences if they failed to do so.[77] Further, the court considered that permitting parties to remain silent during arbitration and raise objections during enforcement proceedings could compromise the very objective of arbitration, which is to offer a quick and cost-effective dispute resolution mechanism.[78]

A similar ruling was handed down by Hong Kong courts. In the case of *Hebei Import & Export Corp v. Polytek Engineering Co Ltd*, a dispute arose regarding the quality of equipment sold by Polytek Engineering to Hebei Import & Export which was subsequently installed at the end-user's factory. Polytek sought to challenge enforcement, arguing that the tribunal violated the notion of natural justice and displayed bias through communication between the chief arbitrator and the end-user's technicians via tribunal-appointed experts conducting investigations of the equipment at the factory. The Hong Kong Court of Final Appeal determined that Polytek should have raised its objections before the tribunal during arbitral proceedings when it became aware of the chief arbitrator's communications with technicians. Its failure to do so deprived the tribunal of an opportunity to remedy any alleged procedural irregularity.[79] Therefore, the court dismissed the objection and enforced the award.

Although the notion of estoppel is typically associated with common law jurisdictions, civil law jurisdictions such as Germany, France, Switzerland, the Netherlands, and Spain also recognise the use of estoppel based on the principle of good faith.[80] The Swiss Supreme Court upheld this principle in a case, ruling that:

74. *Tesco Ltd v. William Moffett, Richard Mclaughlin, James Mclaughlin & Anson Logue* [2015] NIQB 68 (1 July 2015) [23].
75. *Research and Development Center 'Teploenergetika' LLC v. EP International LLC & Worldwide Vision LLC* (ED Va, Civ No. 2:15-CV-362) slip op 16–17.
76. *Cook Industries Inc v. C Itoh & Co (America) Inc*, 449 F 2d 106, 107-08 (2nd Cir, 1971).
77. *Jorf Lasfar Energy Company v. AMCI Export Corporation* (WD Pa, Civ No. 05-0423, 22 Dec 2005) slip op 6–7.
78. *Research and Development Center 'Teploenergetika' LLC v. EP International LLC & Worldwide Vision LLC* (ED Va, Civ No. 2:15-CV-362) slip op 19.
79. *Hebei Import & Export Corp v. Polytek Engineering Co Ltd* [1999] 2 HKLRD 665, [89]–[94].
80. *See, e.g.*, Germany: Oberlandesgericht Hamm [Hamm Court of Appeal], 2 November 1983 reported in (1989) XIV *Yearbook Commercial Arbitration* 629, 632–633; Netherlands: Zutphen Arrondissementsrechtbank [District Court of Zutphen], 11 November 1998 reported in (1999) XXIV *Yearbook Commercial Arbitration* 724; Zutphen Arrondissementsrechtbank [District Court of Zutphen], 11 November 1998 reported in (1999) XXIV *Yearbook Commercial Arbitration* 724, 725–726 (the appointment of co-arbitrator for award-debtor by chairman of arbitral tribunal,

> All participants to a proceeding must abide by the rules of good faith. The principle of good faith, as set out by ordinary civil procedure, is of general application, so that it also applies to arbitration, both domestic and international. According to this principle, *complaints concerning procedural defects that could have been set straight immediately may not be kept in reserve in order to be raised only if the arbitration results in an unfavourable outcome.* This principle also prevents Convention grounds for refusing recognition of the foreign award based on such defects from being validly invoked unless they have been *invoked timeously* while the arbitration was pending.[81]

In another Swiss case, the opposing party raised an objection against the enforcement of an award before the Supreme Court of Switzerland based on the fact that the tribunal had heard an expert on practices concerning the vital issue of the case in the absence of the parties.[82] Nonetheless, the Supreme Court found that the opposing party had been informed of the questions which had been put to the expert, but it had not responded to these questions. Accordingly, the Supreme Court determined that the opposing party acted in bad faith through its conduct, thus constituting an abuse of rights.[83] The French Supreme Court echoed this finding by confirming that the scope of application of estoppel and waiver could be identical in certain cases, and a party that failed to bring up any potential procedural irregularities during arbitration may be subject to estoppel.[84]

Similarly, the Brazilian Superior Court of Justice dismissed the opposing party's claim of violating due process, given that they and their counsel were present at all hearings and did not raise any objections. It was determined that, in accordance with the applicable arbitration rules, parties must raise any due process violations at the earliest opportunity before the arbitral tribunal. However, in this case, the opposing party failed to do so. Thus, the court determined that the opposing party's conduct constituted a tacit waiver under the applicable rules.[85]

Chinese courts recognise the waiver of due process rights if the breach of procedural irregularities during arbitral proceedings is not objected to and such waiver is allowed by the governing law of the arbitral proceedings. For instance, in the case of *CHENCO Chemical Engineering and Consulting GMBH*, the applicable arbitration rules, which were the ICC Rules, required parties to raise objections to non-compliance with

---

pursuant to CIETAC Rules, did not constitute grounds for non-recognition where award-debtor could have made own nomination and did not object); Spain: Tribunal Supremo [Supreme Court], Civil Chamber, 3536 of 1998, 11 April 2000 reported in (2007) XXXII *Yearbook Commercial Arbitration* 525, 530.

81. Tribunal Fédéral [Federal Supreme Court of Switzerland, First Civil Law Chamber], No. 4A 374/2014, 26 February 2015 reported in (2016) XLI *Yearbook Commercial Arbitration* 567, [9], [10] (emphasis added).
82. Tribunal Fédéral [Federal Supreme Court of Switzerland], 8 February 1978 reported in (1986) XI *Yearbook Commercial Arbitration* 538.
83. *Ibid.*, 541–542.
84. Cour de Cassation [Supreme Court], First Civil Chamber, No. 509, 6 May 2009 reported in (2010) XXXV *Yearbook Commercial Arbitration* 353, 355 [2]–[3].
85. STJ SEC 3709, Reporting Justice Teori Albino Zavascki, 29 June 2012. For detailed discussion, *see* Rafael Francisco Alves, 'Chapter 3: Country Report: Brazil' in Friedrich Rosenfeld, Dietmar Czernich and Franco Ferrari (eds), *Due Process as a Limit to Discretion in International Commercial Arbitration* (Kluwer Law International, 2020) 55, 72–74.

the arbitration rules related to proceedings' conduction. Failure to do so would waive their right to object. During the arbitral proceedings, the German party presented significant evidence in a language not previously agreed upon by the parties. The court found that the Chinese party did not raise any objections to the language and instead cross-examined this evidence before the tribunal. Based on these findings, the court held that the Chinese party had waived its right to rely on a breach of due process during the post-award proceedings.[86]

The aforementioned cases show that most courts consider that parties should promptly challenge any procedural irregularities during the arbitration proceedings instead of waiting until the enforcement stage to raise the objection for the first time.[87] First, parties who had the opportunity to correct a procedural irregularity but failed to do so during arbitral proceedings should not invoke the protection of the due process defence under Article V(1)(b) of the New York Convention. No person ought to benefit from his own negligence or wrongdoing. What is specified as the 'inability to present its case before the tribunal' should apply to situations where the opposing party has been prevented from presenting its case due to circumstances beyond its control. In other words, if the opposing party has been responsible for not taking advantage of the opportunity given to it to present its case, this situation does not qualify for the due process exception to enforcement under the Convention.[88] Also, parties could reasonably have foreseen what the consequences of their conduct would be.[89] By failing to raise an objection promptly during arbitral proceedings, it is deemed that the party has accepted and endorsed the violation and thus is estopped from objecting to it at a later stage either during the setting-aside or recognition and enforcement proceedings.[90]

Further, it is useful to recall '*Vigilantibus Et Non Dormientibus Jura Subveniunt*' (equity aids the vigilant, not the indolent) and 'long-dormant claims often have more of cruelty than justice in them'[91] when examining a party's failure to raise objection of procedural irregularities in arbitral proceedings. The strong rationale for the admissibility of this waiver is that the arbitral tribunal should be put into the position to redress a procedural error once it has occurred. If a party makes a procedural objection during

86. 《成可化学工程和咨询公司(CHENCOChemicalEngineeringandConsultingGMBH)与多氟多化工股份有限公司仲裁裁决承认执行案》[*CHENCO Chemical Engineering and Consulting GMBH v. Do-Fluoride Chemicals Co Ltd – Recognition and Enforcement of a Foreign Arbitral Award rendered by the ICC*], 河南省新乡市中级人民法院[Xinxiang Intermediate People's Court of Henan Province] (2015) 新中民三初字第53号 [Xin Zhong Min San Chu Zi No. 53], 5 May 2017.
87. *United Nations Commission on International Trade Law* (n. 10) 165, 169–170.
88. *Minmetals Germany GmbH v. Ferco Steel Ltd* [1999] CLC 647, 658.
89. *See, e.g.*, *Sejdovic v. Italy*, Application No. 56581/00, ECtHR, 1 March 2006, para. 87; *Panovits v. Cyprus*, Application No. 4268/04, ECtHR, 11 December 2008, para. 68; *Lopata v. Russia*, Application No. 72250/01, ECtHR, 13 July 2010; *Yerokhina v. Ukraine*, Application No. 12167/04, ECtHR, 15 November 2012; para. 65; *Vanfuli v. Russia*, Application No. 24885/05, ECtHR, 3 November 2011, para. 96.
90. Massimo V Benedettelli, 'Human Rights as A Litigation Tool in International Arbitration: Reflecting on the ECHR Experience' (2015) 31(4) *Arbitration International* 631, 646 DOI: 10.1093/arbint/aiv036.
91. Samuel Comyn, *The Law of Contracts and Promises Upon Various Subjects and with Particular Persons: As Settled in the Action of Assumpsit* (Gould, Banks, & Co, 1835) 85.

arbitral proceedings, it is very likely for an arbitral tribunal to redress such procedural deficiencies in arbitration.

Last, as discussed in Chapter 2,[92] Article V(1)(b) has the purpose of protecting parties' due process rights as well as ensuring efficiency. There is always an attempt to balance due process and efficiency in arranging arbitral proceedings. The value of efficiency outweighs the protection of due process where parties failed to avail themselves of the means at their disposal to object to procedural deficiencies during arbitral proceedings, unless they prove that they were unaware of the grounds for objection or could not have discovered them with reasonable diligence at the time of their participation or continued involvement in the arbitral proceedings.

[B] A Failure to Raise Procedural Irregularities in the Setting-Aside Proceedings

As discussed above, most courts in State Parties confirm that a party is estopped from raising the due process defence under the Convention that could have been raised in the arbitration proceedings. What if a party raised the due process objection before the tribunal unsuccessfully but did not challenge the award before the court at the seat of arbitration? Put simply, the issue is whether the party's failure to seek to set aside an award resulted in the forfeiture of its right to raise a procedural challenge at the recognition and enforcement phase. Despite varying views among the courts of State Parties, the interpretation that the failure to pursue the annulment of an award based on a breach of due process does not constitute a waiver in the subsequent enforcement proceedings is in line with the interpretative rules under the VCLT.

UK Courts[93] and their German counterparts[94] have held that a party's failure to challenge arbitration awards on the grounds of procedural deficiencies at the seat of arbitration would result in a waiver of procedural objections in the subsequent enforcement procedure. Additionally, these courts have held that the New York Convention does not leave the parties free to choose between setting-aside and enforcement proceedings on the same grounds. The English High Court of Justice determined that a party who alleged a defective award or defective conduct during arbitration must in the first place invoke the supervisory jurisdiction at the seat of arbitration.[95] Procedural issues not raised in a setting-aside action may only be raised during recognition and enforcement proceedings in '[e]xceptional cases [which] are those cases in which the powers of the supervisory court are so limited that the

92. *See* §2.06[A][2].
93. *Minmetals Germany GmbH v. Ferco Steel Ltd* [1999] CLC 647, 661.
94. Hamm Oberlandesgericht [Hamm Court of Appeal], 27 September 2005 reported in (2006) XXXI *Yearbook Commercial Arbitration* 685, 686; Karlsruhe Oberlandesgericht [Karlsruhe Court of Appeal], 9 Sch 02/05, 26 March 2006 reported in (2007) XXXII *Yearbook Commercial Arbitration* 342, 344; Berlin Kammergericht [Berlin Court of Appeal], 20 Sch 02/08, 17 April 2008 reported in (2009) XXXIV *Yearbook Commercial Arbitration* 510, 510–14; Hamm Oberlandesgericht [Hamm Court of Appeal], 25 Sch 09/08, 28 November 2008 reported in (2009) XXXIV *Yearbook Commercial Arbitration* 536, 539.
95. *Minmetals Germany GmbH v. Ferco Steel Ltd* [1999] CLC 647, 661.

supervisory court cannot intervene even where there has been serious disregard for basic principles of justice by the arbitrators or where for unjust reasons, such as corruption, they disregard such principles'.[96]

However, certain courts have held that the award-debtor may raise the due process defence as grounds to decline enforcing the award, even if they have not pursued setting-aside proceedings based on the procedural deficiencies in the country where the award was rendered. This holds true in Switzerland, Singapore, and Hong Kong, for example. The Swiss Supreme Court opted to examine the estoppel matter in a pragmatic manner rather than in an abstract way and thus would consider the conduct of the parties in accordance with the principles of good faith.[97] The court acknowledged that it was strongly disputed whether the failure to make use of an available means of recourse at the seat of arbitration may lead to the estoppel of the due process defence. This is because the opposing party and the enforcement court can initiate the due process defence, which falls under procedural public policy under Article V(2)(b).[98] The court held that the New York Convention does not mandate that in recognition and enforcement proceedings, a party who has unsuccessfully objected to a procedural defect in arbitration must challenge the award in the courts of the seat of arbitration as a precondition for resisting enforcement of the award on the same basis.[99]

Similarly, in Hong Kong, it is not necessary for the opposing party to seek the setting aside of awards based on the due process objection before resisting enforcement on the same basis, provided that the opposing party has raised the procedural irregularity during arbitration. The High Court of Hong Kong held that the New York Convention does not require the opposing party to apply for the award to be set aside in the country where it was made in order to resist its enforcement elsewhere.[100] Further, the court ruled that if a party received an unfavourable award, they could seek to have the award set aside by the courts in the country where the award was made, or they could await enforcement and then seek to establish grounds for refusing enforcement under the New York Convention.[101]

In Singapore, courts also consider that a failure to challenge an award in setting-aside proceedings does not prevent a party from bringing up the same ground for refusal in enforcement proceedings. The Court of Appeal in Singapore held that the UNCITRAL Model Law provides a system of 'choice of remedies' which is applicable to foreign awards; thus, a failure to challenge an award in setting-aside proceedings

96. *IPOC International Growth Fund Limited v. LV Finance Group Limited* (Unreported, British Virgin Islands Court of Appeal, 18 June 2007) [34].
97. Tribunal Fédéral [Federal Supreme Court of Switzerland, First Civil Law Chamber], No. 4A 374/2014, 26 February 2015 reported in (2016) XLI *Yearbook Commercial Arbitration* 567, [12]–[13].
98. *Ibid.*, [11], [42].
99. *Ibid.*, [10]; Bundesgerichtshof [Federal Supreme Court of Switzerland, First Civil Law Chamber], No. 4A 124/2010, 4 October 2010 reported in (2011) XXXVI *Yearbook Commercial Arbitration* 340, [52].
100. *Paklito Investment Ltd v. Klockner East Asia Ltd* [1993] 2 HKLR 39, 48.
101. *Ibid.*, 48–49.

would not constitute a waiver of the right to depend on the 'passive' remedy of raising defences to enforcement.[102]

This issue has shown considerable differences in German courts' approaches. Some German courts hold the view that the opposing party should be precluded from relying on the grounds for refusal under Article V(1) of the New York Convention if the party had failed to mention these grounds at the appropriate time in the annulment action before the court at the arbitral seat.[103] Although the New York Convention does not contain a provision on estoppel, these German courts hold the view that the Convention does not forbid a practice that is more favourable to recognition and enforcement according to Article VII(1) of the New York Convention.[104] Further, these courts have ruled that, according to section 1059(3) of the German Code of Civil Procedure,[105] the estoppel shall be applied to domestic arbitral awards when the losing party has not filed timely setting-aside proceedings on the same grounds, and it was reasonable to apply the same estoppel rule to foreign awards under the New York Convention to safeguard legal certainty and the finality of the arbitral awards.[106]

In contrast, some other German courts adopt a different approach on this matter. The German Supreme Court held that the failure to seek annulment of an award based on a breach of due process did not preclude a party from raising the same grounds in the subsequent enforcement procedure.[107] In another German case, the Court of Appeal of Bavaria held that although the defendant had not sought the annulment of the award based on a due process violation, they were not precluded from relying on the same grounds for refusal of an award in recognition and enforcement proceedings.[108] This approach is consistent with the thread of the doctrine of estoppel in German Arbitration Law. It is worth recalling the development of the estoppel in terms of the validity of arbitration agreement prescribed in Article V(1)(a) of the New York Convention in Germany. Before the 1998 reform, German courts had consistently

102. *PT First Media TBK (formerly known as PT Broadband Multimedia TBK) v. Astro Nusantara International BV and others and another appeal* [2014] 1 SLR 372, [26], [71].
103. Oberlandesgericht Hamm [Court of Appeal Hamm], 25 Sch 09/08, 28 November 2008 reported in (2009) XXXIV *Yearbook Commercial Arbitration* 536, [5]; Berlin Kammergericht [Berlin Court of Appeal], 20 Sch 02/08, 17 April 2008 reported in (2009) XXXIV *Yearbook Commercial Arbitration* 510, [7].
104. Oberlandesgericht Karlsruhe [Karlsruhe Court of Appeal], 9 Sch 02/05, 26 March 2006 reported in (2007) XXXII *Yearbook Commercial Arbitration* 342, [2]–[3].
105. *Zivilprozessordnung* [Code of Civil Procedure] (Germany), s. 1059(3).
106. Oberlandesgericht Karlsruhe [Karlsruhe Court of Appeal], 9 Sch 02/05, 26 March 2006 reported in (2007) XXXII *Yearbook Commercial Arbitration* 342, [4].
107. Bundesgerichtshof [Supreme Court], 26 April 1990 reported in (1996) XXI *Yearbook Commercial Arbitration* 532, 533–534 [4].
108. Bayern Oberlandesgericht [Court of Appeal of Bavaria], 4Z Sch 50/99, 16 March 2000 reported in (2002) XXVII *Yearbook Commercial Arbitration* 445, 449–450 [14]–[16]. *See also* Schleswig Oberlandesgericht [Higher Regional Court of Schleswig-Holstein], 85, 30 March 2000 reported in (2006) XXXI *Yearbook Commercial Arbitration* 652, 658–659 [14]–[16]; Munich Oberlandesgericht [Munich Court of Appeal], 23 November 2009 (upheld by Bundesgerichtshof [Federal Supreme Court of Germany], 16 December 2010) reported in (2011) XXXVI *Yearbook Commercial Arbitration* 273, 276 [25] (these two cases involve grounds for refusal based on an invalid arbitration agreement, which the opposing party did not invoke to set aside the award. However, the German courts ruled that the opposing party could raise such an objection before the recognition and enforcement courts).

considered that under the German Arbitration Law, the defendant would have been estopped from raising an objection to the validity of arbitration agreement in recognition and enforcement proceedings if it failed to challenge the award on the same grounds in the country of the arbitral seat. However, the current German Arbitration Law stipulates that foreign arbitral awards should be recognised and enforced in accordance with the New York Convention. Thus, the defendant in enforcement proceedings is granted the right to challenge the validity of arbitration agreement, as explicitly permitted by Article V(1)(a) of the Convention.[109] A more recent case from the German Supreme Court has confirmed that, with the entry into force of the 1998 German Arbitration Law Reform, the parties' failure to challenge the award within the given time limit at the seat of arbitration does not prevent them from opposing enforcement based on the invalidity of the arbitration agreement.[110] The same reasoning should apply to Article V(1)(b) of the New York Convention. There is no reasonable basis for the application of different criteria in this regard, considering that both grounds are raised by the parties, which is distinct from the grounds under Article V(2) of the Convention.

If a party raises procedural deficiencies during arbitration, as the Hong Kong High Court held, it may seek to set aside the award at the seat of arbitration or object to the recognition or enforcement of the award based on the due process defence.[111] First, according to the 'ordinary meaning' under Article 31(1) of the VCLT, the wording of the New York Convention does not require the party to challenge the award in the courts of the seat of arbitration as a precondition for opposing the enforcement of the award on the same basis.

According to the 'object and purpose' interpretation under Article 31(1) of the VCLT, the due process defence aims to safeguard the fundamental procedural rights of parties in arbitral proceedings. As opposed to objecting to procedural deficiencies before the arbitral tribunal, seeking to set aside the award based on a breach of due process may not effectively redress the procedural deficiencies in arbitral proceedings, nor is it conducive to the efficient and cost-effective settlement of the dispute. Requiring the initiation of setting-aside proceedings as a condition for opposing enforcement elsewhere would result in parallel proceedings, which would significantly undermine the efficiency of international arbitration and the objective of the New York Convention, which is to facilitate the recognition or enforcement of arbitral awards. The New York Convention has expressly abandoned the doctrine of double exequatur prescribed by the 1927 Geneva Convention that required the award-creditor to first obtain the final confirmation of an award in the arbitral seat before seeking the recognition and enforcement of the award.[112]

109. Schleswig Oberlandesgericht [Higher Regional Court of Schleswig-Holstein], 85, 30 March 2000 reported in (2006) XXXI *Yearbook Commercial Arbitration* 652, 658-659 [14]-[16].
110. Munich Oberlandesgericht [Munich Court of Appeal], 23 November 2009 (upheld by Bundesgerichtshof [Federal Supreme Court of Germany], 16 December 2010 reported in (2011) XXXVI *Yearbook Commercial Arbitration* 273, 276.
111. *Paklito Investment Ltd v. Klockner East Asia Ltd* [1993] 2 HKLR 39, 48-49.
112. *Convention on the Execution of Foreign Arbitral Awards*, open for signature 26 September 1927, 92 LNTS 301 (entered into force 25 July 1929) Art. I (d). *See also* Christoph Liebscher,

Further, as explained in §5.05, the court's decision in the arbitral seat concerning the validity of an award based on the due process objection should not eliminate or exclude the independent assessment of the award's validity by the enforcing court. Therefore, a party should not be precluded from raising the due process defence in the recognition and enforcement proceedings, even if it had not sought to set aside an award based on a breach of due process or had been denied the setting-aside procedure in the country where the award was rendered.

[C] Waiver of Due Process Rights *Ex Ante*

Party autonomy is the principle guiding the entire arbitral process in international arbitration.[113] However, the exercise of party autonomy is subject to the mandatory rules concerning due process to ensure that arbitral proceedings are conducted fairly. The requirements that the parties must have equal treatment and that each be given the same opportunity to present its case place limitations on party autonomy, as discussed in §2.02[C].

The case law of the State Parties to the New York Convention shows that *ex ante* waivers of due process rights are viewed more critically and are, therefore, unenforceable in some jurisdictions,[114] such as Germany and the UK. Courts in Germany[115] and the UK,[116] either in setting-aside or in recognition and enforcement proceedings, consider that advance waiver agreements concerning due process rights are unenforceable. As discussed in §2.03[C], German courts treat serious procedural irregularities as violations of public policy, which is deemed to be in the public interest and thus cannot be waived by the parties under any circumstance.[117]

The advance waiver of due process rights by parties' agreement is unenforceable in these jurisdictions for several reasons. First, it is necessary to ensure that the fundamental interests of the parties are protected. The purpose of Article V(1)(b) is to guarantee parties' fundamental procedural rights. An advance waiver of due process rights would be contrary to basic protections of procedural fairness for parties. As previously mentioned, one of the main rationales for supporting the waiver of due process rights where parties failed to raise due process objection during arbitral

---

'Non-binding Award, Article V (1) (e)' in Reinmar Wolff (ed.), *New York Convention: Convention on the Recognition and Enforcement of Foreign Arbitral Awards of 10 June 1958: Commentary* (C.H. Beck • Hart • Nomos, 2012) 357–358.

113. Blackaby et al. (n. 25) 355; Gary B Born, *International Commercial Arbitration* (Kluwer Law International, 2nd ed., 2014) 3442.
114. Rosenfeld, Czernich and Ferrari (n. 5) 15.
115. Hans-Joachim Musielak and Wolfgang Voit (eds), *Code of Civil Procedure: ZPO* (Vahlen, 16th ed., 2019) s. 1059 [27]; Stefan Michael Kröll and Peter Kraft, 'Recourse Against the Award, § 1059 – Application for Setting Aside' in Karl-Heinz Böckstiegel, Stefan Michael Kröll and Patricia Nacimiento (eds), *Arbitration in Germany: The Model Law in Practice* (Kluwer Law International, 2nd ed., 2015) 383, 387.
116. *Arbitration Act 1996* (UK) c 23, Schedule 1 (expressly providing that requirements for due process prescribed in section 68 are mandatory rules and thus cannot be opted out of by parties' agreement).
117. Kröll and Kraft (n. 115) 383, 387.

proceedings is to motivate the parties to raise procedural defects and redress them as early as possible and not to 'hold back' until after the award is rendered. It is important to note that the same justification does not apply to cases where the parties waived their fundamental procedural rights in advance. Giving effect to such waiver by enforcing courts will not encourage parties to actively and promptly exercise their due process rights.

Second, parties should only be able to waive their due process rights if they fully understand the implications of doing so. Conversely, they cannot exclude due process rights in advance without knowing the exact consequences of such a waiver. German law allows parties to waive the due process defence *ex post* but not *ex ante* due to this concern.[118] As Benedettelli explains:

> Rights cannot be waived in advance, i.e., at the time of execution of an arbitration agreement, but only after their beneficiary has become aware that a breach of them has been committed to his/her damage and is therefore best positioned to appreciate the impact of his/her decision [...] This applies to the right to a fair hearing, to the right to be heard and to the right of equality of arms, as well as to the consequent rights to be judged by an independent and impartial tribunal.[119]

§5.04 THE THRESHOLD

Enforcing courts of State Parties have reached consensus on the consideration of policy when interpreting the due process defence. However, they have opposing views on the thresholds for breaches of due process, whether it is a qualified impact upon the arbitral award or a qualified breach. As discussed in §5.02, subsequent judicial practice of State Parties shows agreement on 'non-review of merits', which can be used to establish the threshold. Despite the differences in the applicable thresholds among State Parties, there is a considerable degree of convergence in that not every minor procedural defect may justify the refusal of recognition and enforcement. This is in line with the pro-enforcement policy and the pursuit of efficiency.

Some national courts require that procedural defects have a material impact on the outcome of the award and cause substantial prejudice to the party seeking non-enforcement. This means that the impact on the arbitral award and prejudice to the opposing party must be qualified. For instance, German courts have held that although Article V(1)(b) of the New York Convention does not explicitly require that a procedural defect must have affected the award, there must still be a causal link between any procedural defect and the arbitral award in order to satisfy the due process defence.[120] When assessing the existence of a causal link, German courts examine

118. *Ibid.*, 383, 387.
119. Benedettelli (n. 90) 646.
120. Oberlandesgericht Düsseldorf [Court of Appeal Düsseldorf], I-4 Sch 10/09, 15 December 2009 reported in (2010) XXXV *Yearbook Commercial Arbitration* 386, [13].

whether the arbitral tribunal could have arrived at a different conclusion if it had respected the right to be heard and ensured equality between the parties.[121]

Courts in Singapore also require an 'appreciable impact' on an arbitral award and a showing of prejudice.[122] These requirements are based on Article 24(b) of the Singapore IAA, which provides that a breach of the rules of natural justice must have occurred in connection with the making of the award and that the rights of any party must be prejudiced.[123] These two requirements are not provided for under Article 34(2)(a)(ii) of the UNCITRAL Model Law. Nevertheless, Singaporean courts have applied the requirement of 'appreciable impact' and 'prejudice' to both grounds. This is because they consider the natural justice ground in section 24(b) of the IAA to be the same as the ground in Article 34(2)(b)(ii) of the Model Law.[124] 'Appreciable impact' involves a threshold enquiry into whether a breach influenced or affected the ultimate decision of arbitrators.[125] The Singapore Court of Appeal ruled that the opposing party is not required to prove with certainty that a different outcome would have resulted if due process had not been violated. Instead, they only need to demonstrate that the issue '*could reasonably* have made a difference to the arbitrator' in terms of showing prejudice.[126]

Similarly, Hong Kong courts consider it sufficient to demonstrate that the outcome could or might have been different.[127] In most cases, however, Hong Kong courts exercise their discretion to enforce an arbitral award after finding a serious breach of due process when the arbitral tribunal would have reached the same decision had there been no due process violation. In this case, 'qualified impact' is not a factor that affects the threshold. Instead, the Hong Kong courts take into account the impact when exercising their discretion to enforce an award, even if the award satisfies the due process defence.[128] However, the courts' discretion is restrained and must be exercised

121. Oberlandesgericht Frankfurt [Court of Appeal Frankfurt], 26 SchH 03/09, 12 October 2009 reported in (2010) XXXV *Yearbook Commercial Arbitration* 377 (the court held that tribunal's refusal of an oral hearing does not necessarily violate due process if the defendant has had the opportunity to fully present its case in writing and failed to argue or prove how arguments presented at the oral hearing could have resulted in a different decision); Oberlandesgericht Hamm [Court of Appeal Hamm], 25 Sch 09/08, 28 November 2008 reported in (2009) XXXIV *Yearbook Commercial Arbitration* 536, [17] (the defendant alleged that the arbitrator was biased, but the German court held that the violation of the impartial arbitral justice must have a concrete impact on the award, which means that the defendant must prove that the arbitrator was biased and his or her decision was influenced by this prejudice).
122. *Soh Beng Tee & Co Pte Ltd v. Fairmount Development Pte Ltd* [2007] SGCA 28, [77], [81], [86], [91]; *Triulzi Cesare SRL v. Xinyi Group (Glass) Co Ltd* [2015] 1 SLR 114, [126]; *John Lolland Pty Ltd v. Toyo Engineering Corp (Japan)* [2001] 1 SLR 443, [18].
123. *International Arbitration Act* (Singapore, cap 143 A, 2002 rev ed) s. 24(b).
124. *Government of the Republic of the Philippines v. Philippine International Air Terminals Co Inc* [2007] 1 SLR (R) 278, [18].
125. *Soh Beng Tee & Co Pte Ltd v. Fairmount Development Pte Ltd* [2007] SGCA 28, [77], [81].
126. *L W Infrastructure Pte Ltd v. Lim Chin San Contractors Pte Ltd* [2013] 1 SLR 125, [51]–[54] (emphasis added).
127. *Pang Wai Hak v. Hua Yunjian* [2012] 4 HKLRD 113, [29].
128. *Paklito Investment Ltd v. Klockner East Asia Ltd* [1993] 2 HKLR 39, 49 (the High Court of Hong Kong held that the court might exercise its discretion to enforce the award falling within the due process defence if it was *beyond any doubt* that the decision of the tribunal could have been the same even if there was no severe violation of due process).

with caution. In the case of *Apex Tech Investment Ltd v. Chuang's Development (China) Ltd*, the Court of Appeal of the High Court of Hong Kong overturned the lower court's decision to enforce an award under the New York Convention despite the opposing party being unable to present its case in the arbitral proceedings. The Hong Kong High Court considered whether the lower court erred in deciding that the arbitral tribunal's decision would have been the same even if the opportunity to present its case had been given.[129] The High Court of Hong Kong refused to exercise its discretion to enforce the award, stating that it could not be certain that the defendant's further representations to the arbitral tribunal would not have affected the outcome of the award.[130] The doctrine of avoiding a review of the merits of the award also limits the exercise of this discretion.[131]

However, some courts hold that recognition and enforcement can only be refused in cases of serious breach of due process without reviewing the impact of procedural defects on the award. For instance, courts in Quebec and Brazil have held that recognition and enforcement can only be refused in cases where there has been a 'significant' breach of procedural fairness.[132] Several commentators, including Redfern and Hunter, Born, and van den Berg, support the view that only a 'serious' and 'material' procedural defect can be sufficient for the court to determine a denial of due process.[133] Gaillard and Savage argued that '[i]n itself, a breach of due process is considered to be sufficiently important to justify such redress without the need for the party involving it to establish actual damage'.[134]

When determining the threshold, subsequent judicial practice of State Parties shows that judges usually consider the procedural value vis-à-vis efficiency and the award-debtor's right to due process vis-à-vis the award-creditor's right to enforcement. Refusing enforcement would be inappropriate and inconsistent with judicial efficiency and the award-creditor's right to enforcement if the arbitral award had been the same even if the violation of due process was removed. Based on this reasoning, some enforcing courts require an examination of the impact of breach on the arbitral award to satisfy the due process defence.

However, the ordinary meaning interpretation of Article 31(1) of the VCLT suggests that Article V(1)(b) does not require procedural irregularities to have a substantial impact on the outcome of the award. Besides, determining the impact of such irregularities on the outcome of an award can be challenging.[135] Enforcing courts

129. *Apex Tech Investment Ltd v. Chuang's Development (China) Ltd* [1996] 2 HKLR 155, 157–158.
130. *Ibid.*, 159.
131. *Ibid.*, 158 ('it is important that the court should meticulously avoid any consideration of the merits of the award').
132. *Hachette Distribution Services (Canada) inc v. 2295822 Canada inc* [2018] QCCS 1213, [41]; Alves (n. 85) 55, 60.
133. Blackaby et al. (n. 25) 628; Born (n. 113) 3532–3537; van den Berg (n. 5) 297.
134. Emmanuel Gaillard and John Savage (eds), *Fouchard Gaillard Goldman on International Commercial Arbitration* (Kluwer Law International, 1999) 987.
135. Born (n. 113) 3535; Maxi Scherer, 'New York Convention: Violation of Due Process, Article V(1)(b)' in Reinmar Wolff (ed.), *New York Convention: Convention on the Recognition and Enforcement of Foreign Arbitral Awards of 10 June 1958: Commentary* (C.H. Beck • Hart • Nomos, 2012) 279, 287.

hold differing views on when a procedural irregularity has a substantial impact on an arbitral award. Some require the applicant to prove that the award would certainly have been different without the procedural irregularity, while others only require a reasonable probability or likelihood of a different outcome. It is important to note that precise definitions of 'substantial impact' may vary between jurisdictions.

Also, the requirement of qualified impact places the enforcing courts at risk of having to review the merits of disputes and how an arbitrator would have decided if the violation had not occurred. For instance, it can be challenging to apply the criteria for qualified impact in a case where the opposing party was prevented from commenting on evidence that was decisive for the outcome of the award. It would be challenging for a judge to determine whether the evidence not presented during arbitral proceedings was a decisive factor in the outcome without reviewing the merits.

As shown in §5.02[B], the subsequent judicial practice of State Parties has indicated agreement on the doctrine of non-review of the merits of disputes when applying and interpreting the New York Convention. Accordingly, some courts have expressly refused the requirement of qualified impact on the arbitral award on the grounds of prohibiting a review of merits. For instance, in a Dutch case, the opposing party contested that the enforcing court should consider whether the arbitral tribunal would have made a different decision if due process had not been violated. However, the Court of Appeal of Hague rejected this argument and held that:

> Answering the question raised in this ground for appeal would require an examination of the merits of the disputes between the parties which were submitted to the arbitral tribunal. There is no place for [such an examination] in the present proceedings for obtaining enforcement of an arbitral award.[136]

Due to the prohibition on reviewing merits, it can be argued that courts should apply the qualified breach test. This test requires that only obvious breaches of a fundamental procedural principle could result in a refusal of enforcement rather than the qualified impact on the outcome of the award. Chapters 6 and 7 will examine situations where the failure to provide notice or a reasonable opportunity to present a case is a violation of form, which is not considered fundamental or essential enough to constitute a material violation of the right to be heard. It will also explore scenarios where this failure constitutes a material violation that denies the right to be heard. Meanwhile, based on a pro-enforcement policy, the court may exercise its discretion to enforce the award under the due process defence with caution if it was beyond any doubt that the tribunal's decision could have been the same even if there was no severe violation of due process.[137]

136. Arrondissementsrechtbank Rotterdam [District Court of Rotterdam], 2 October 1997 reported in (1998) XXIII *Yearbook Commercial Arbitration* 731, 734 [11]–[12] (upheld by Gerechtshof the Hague [Court of Appeal of the Hague], 28 April 1998 reported in (1998) XXIII *Yearbook Commercial Arbitration* 731).

137. *Paklito Investment Ltd v. Klockner East Asia Ltd* [1993] 2 HKLR 39, 49. *See also* van den Berg (n. 5) 302.

§5.05 DECISIONS MADE BY THE COURT AT THE ARBITRAL SEAT ON THE DUE PROCESS OBJECTION

When the court at the seat of arbitration is called upon to decide on the validity of an arbitral award based on due process grounds, the situation can become complicated. This decision, which will be referred to as an 'award decision' for the purposes of this book, includes the court's determination of whether to uphold or set aside the award. Enforcing courts hold varying views on the significance of this award decision made by the courts at the arbitral seat. This section employs interpretative rules under the VCLT to resolve discrepancies in award decisions.

Many enforcing courts apply the judgment route – the principles for recognition and enforcement of foreign judgments – to award decisions.[138] This approach is taken by courts in the UK,[139] Germany,[140] and the Netherlands.[141] Accordingly, if an award decision satisfies the enforcing forum's requirements for recognising a foreign judgment (e.g., if it has been rendered by a competent court, in fair proceedings, and does not violate the forum's public policy), enforcing courts would grant preclusive effects to such decisions determined by the courts of the supervisory jurisdiction on the due process grounds and refuse to re-investigate procedural defects in the conduct of arbitration under the doctrines of res judicata or claim estoppel.[142] If an award decision fails to meet the foreign judgment requirements of the enforcing forum, the enforcing court can choose whether or not to recognise or enforce the award according to the New York Convention.

However, some courts, including those in France, Sweden,[143] and Spain, focus on whether to recognise or enforce the arbitral award rather than the award decision made by the court at the arbitral seat.[144] As stated by the Spanish Supreme Court, 'the claim's

138. For more in detail, *see* Maxi Scherer, 'Effects of Foreign Judgments Relating to International Arbitral Awards: Is the "Judgment Route" the Wrong Road?' (2013) 4(3) *Journal of International Dispute Settlement* 587 DOI: 10.1093/jnlids/idt013.
139. *Malicorp Ltd v. Government of the Arab Republic of Egypt, Egyptian Holding Co for Aviation & Egyptian Airports Co* [2015] EWHC 361 (Comm) (19 February 2015) [21]; *Yukos Capital SARL v. OJSC Rosneft Oil Company* [2014] EWHC 2188 (Comm) (03 July 2014) [19]–[20]; *Minmetals Germany GmbH v. Ferco Steel Ltd* [1999] CLC 647, 661; *IPOC International Growth Fund Limited v. LV Finance Group Limited* (Unreported, British Virgin Islands Court of Appeal, 18 June 2007) [34].
140. Oberlandesgericht Munich [Court of Appeal Munich], 34 Sch 26/08, 22 June 2009 reported in (2010) XXXV *Yearbook Commercial Arbitration* 371, 373 [9].
141. Gerechtshof [Court of Appeal] of Amsterdam, 200,005,269, 28 April 2009 reported in (2009) XXXIV *Yearbook Commercial Arbitration* 703, [4]–[6].
142. Jonathan Hill, 'The Significance of Foreign Judgments Relating to an Arbitral Award in the Context of an Application to Enforce the Award in England' (2012) 8(2) *Journal of Private International Law* 159, 179 DOI: 10.5235/jprivintl.8.2.159; Roy Goode, 'The Role of the *Lex Loci Arbitri* in International Commercial Arbitration' (2001) 17(1) *Arbitration International* 19, 34 DOI: 10.1023/a:1008973626914.
143. *Belaya Ptitsa* (n. 14) 8 [23].
144. For commentaries in support of this position, *see* Jan Paulsson, 'Arbitration Unbound: Award Detached from the Law of Its Country of Origin' (1981) 30(2) *International and Comparative Law Quarterly* 358 DOI: 10.1093/iclqaj/30.2.358; Jan Paulsson, 'Delocalisation of International Commercial Arbitration: When and Why it Matters' (1983) 32(1) *International and Comparative Law Quarterly* 53 DOI: 10.1093/iclqaj/32.1.53; Emmanuel Gaillard, 'Enforcement of

real aim is to enforce the arbitral award, [not the judgment on the validity of the award determined by the court at the arbitral seat]'.[145] Accordingly, these courts hold that the decision made by the court of the supervisory jurisdiction, whether upholding or setting aside, should not bind enforcing courts. Instead, enforcing courts should be free to decide whether to recognise or enforce an arbitral award in accordance with the New York Convention. In a case before the Paris Court of Appeal, the court refused to defer to a decision made by a Swiss court regarding the validity of an arbitral award on the grounds of due process. The Paris Court of Appeal held that the decision made by the Swiss court did not eliminate or exclude the French judge's control over the validity of the award, which is necessary for the award to be inserted into the French legal order.[146] French courts consider that a foreign award concerning 'international commercial interests' is not integrated into the legal system of the arbitral seat.[147]

The interpretative rules of the VCLT require a court enforcing the New York Convention to treat Article V(1)(b) as an independent basis for non-enforcement. It is inappropriate to draw an analogy to the principles that apply to the recognition of foreign judgments. The New York Convention aims to establish a uniform set of international standards that facilitate the recognition and enforcement of foreign arbitral awards. Its purpose is to prevent the application of parochial rules that could hinder the arbitral process.[148] The New York Convention expressly restricts the grounds for refusing recognition and enforcement to the seven grounds specified in Article V, according to the 'ordinary meaning and purpose' interpretation under Article 31(1) of the VCLT. Therefore, when enforcing courts determine the recognition and enforcement of arbitral awards, they must consider whether the grounds for refusal under Article V are satisfied rather than the principles applicable to foreign judgments.

Granting extraterritorial effects to award decisions will lead to the application of a different control standard for the due process defence under the New York Convention. This is inconsistent with the purpose of the New York Convention, which is to unify the grounds for refusal. The review standards for the recognition and enforcement of foreign awards differ significantly from those for enforcing award decisions. Article V of the New York Convention regulates the former, which focuses on a valid arbitral agreement, fair procedure, the constitution and jurisdiction of arbitrators based on the arbitral agreement, no violation of public policy, and arbitrability. The latter enforces the court's domestic principles for recognition and enforcement of foreign

Awards Set Aside in the Country of Origin: The French Experience' in Albert Jan van den Berg (ed.), *Improving the Efficiency of Arbitration Agreements and Awards: 40 Years of Application of the New York Convention* (Kluwer Law International, 1999) 505.

145. *Union Naval de Levante SA v. Bisba Comercial Inc*, 9 October 2003 reported in (2005) XXX Yearbook Commercial Arbitration 623, 625 [4].

146. *Société Unichips Finanziaria SpA S A, Unichips International BV and others v. François Gesnouin, Michèle Gesnouin*, Paris Cour d'appel [Court of Appeal of Paris], 12 February 1993 reported in (1994) XIX *Yearbook Commercial Arbitration* 658, 660 [5].

147. Cour d'appel de Paris [Paris Court of Appeal], 2003/09894, 10 June 2004 reported in 2005 (XXX) *Yearbook Commercial Arbitration* 499, [1]–[2]; Cour d'appel de Paris [Paris Court of Appeal], 23 October 1997 reported in (1998) XXIII *Yearbook Commercial Arbitration* 644, [25].

148. *See* UNCITRAL's website, https://uncitral.un.org/en/texts/arbitration/conventions/foreign_arbitral_awards (accessed on 25 January 2024).

judgments. For example, it must have been rendered by a competent court, in fair proceedings, and not violate the forum's public policy. Article V of the New York Convention specifies that enforcing courts examine a foreign arbitral award per se rather than an award decision. However, if enforcing courts follow the principles that govern foreign judgments to determine whether to enforce award decisions, the focus of review by enforcing courts would shift from an arbitral award and arbitral proceedings to a foreign judgment and adjudication proceedings.

Article V(1)(e) of the New York Convention allows the enforcing court to refuse to recognise or enforce an award that has been set aside by the court at the arbitral seat on the grounds of due process. Nevertheless, as explained in §5.02[A], courts responsible for enforcement can independently decide on the due process defence under Article V(1)(b) and have the discretion to recognise or enforce an award that has been set aside due to a breach of due process. This is permitted by the wording 'may' in Article V, the pro-enforcement policy of Article III, and the more-favourable-right of Article VII of the New York Convention.

The application of principles for recognising and enforcing foreign judgments in award decisions often overlooks the distinct ancillary nature of award decisions compared to pure foreign judgments. The fact that these award decisions are ancillary to arbitration awards means that they depend on the previous adjudication. The main subject of an award decision is a prior adjudication, namely the arbitral award. However, it is important to note that an award decision does not re-litigate the merits of the underlying dispute that was decided by arbitrators. Instead, award decisions decide the validity of the award and its effect in the territory of the arbitral seat.[149] Due to the ancillary nature of such award decisions, it is not advisable for the enforcing forum to automatically apply the requirements for the recognition and enforcement of foreign judgments to award decisions.

Accordingly, the underlying policies supporting the recognition and enforcement of foreign judgments do not apply to award decisions.[150] Comity, fairness, efficiency, harmony, and predictability are generally regarded as the policies for granting extraterritorial effect to foreign judgments. The dispute is resolved solely through arbitration rather than the award decision made by the court at the arbitral seat. Therefore, it is the arbitration award, not the award decision, that should be subject to comity.[151] To ensure fairness and efficiency, it would be unfair and inefficient for the enforcing court to disregard the fact that a foreign court has reviewed the evidence and made a decision. However, the award decision does not review the merits of the dispute and therefore has no reason to apply the fairness and efficiency policy.[152] Additionally, the parties have an interest in the predictability that the original final adjudication in arbitration will stand and that the same dispute cannot be relitigated. It is important to

149. Scherer, 'Effects of Foreign Judgments Relating to International Arbitral Awards' (n. 138) 606.
150. *Ibid.*, 610–611.
151. *Ibid.*
152. *Ibid.*, 611.

note that the decision pertained to the original award, not the award decision made by the supervisory court. Therefore, the original award should stand.[153]

In principle, an award decision should not be open to enforcement or given extraterritorial effects in enforcing courts due to the sovereign nature of court judgments. The court at the arbitral seat can only decide on the effects of the validity of an award on due process grounds within its territory. Hence, award decisions made by the court at the arbitral seat have a limited territorial effect, only applying within the state in which they are rendered and cannot have any extraterritorial effects in other jurisdictions. As stated by the Court of Appeal of Paris: '[j]udgments delivered pursuant to an annulment proceeding, like execution orders, do not have an international effect because they apply only to defined territorial sovereignty, and no consideration can be given to these judgments by a foreign judge in an indirect proceeding'.[154]

One reason why some courts, including English courts, give extraterritorial effect to award decisions is that the foreign court applied the same standard as the enforcing court would apply in its determination.[155] However, the court of the arbitral seat decides whether to set aside an award according to its national notions of due process. This means that national standards may well be different from transnational due process standards under the New York Convention based on subsequent practice and the general principles of law under the interpretative framework of the VCLT.[156]

Moreover, giving effect to award decisions carries a significant risk of parallel proceedings being conducted elsewhere during recognition and enforcement proceedings. To avoid wasting judicial resources and undermining the efficiency and economy of international arbitration, it is not advisable to impose a stay on the recognition and enforcement proceedings while the setting-aside proceedings are ongoing at the arbitral seat. The preferable approach is to grant the enforcing court the ultimate authority on the due process defence under the New York Convention. This is supported by the New York Convention, which explicitly rejected the double-exequatur doctrine that mandated the award-creditor to initially obtain confirmation of the finality of an award at the arbitral seat before seeking recognition and enforcement.[157]

§5.06 CONCLUSION

The courts of State Parties have widely accepted the principles of pro-enforcement, non-review of the merits, and judicial deference to arbitration rules and the discretion of arbitrators' procedural decisions. This chapter suggested that, based on the policy of non-review of the merits, courts should focus on the qualified breach rather than the qualified impacts in terms of the threshold of the due process defence. Nevertheless,

153. *Ibid.*
154. Cour d'appel de Paris [Paris Court of Appeal], 29 September 2005 reported in (2006) XXXI *Yearbook Commercial Arbitration* 629, 633 [5].
155. Scherer, 'Effects of Foreign Judgments Relating to International Arbitral Awards' (n. 138) 594.
156. As discussed in Chapters 2 and 3, the enforcing court should apply transnational due process derived from the general principle of *audiatur et altera pars* and subsequent practice of State Parties.
157. Liebscher (n. 112) 357–358.

the court may exercise its discretion to enforce an award falling within the due process defence if it was beyond any doubt that the decision of the tribunal would have been the same even if there had been no severe violation of due process. This is in line with the pro-enforcement policy.

This chapter showed that in most jurisdictions, failing to raise a due process objection during arbitration constitutes a waiver of due process rights in later recognition and enforcement proceedings. This is based on the principles of good faith or estoppel. In contrast, an *ex ante* waiver and a failure to raise setting-aside proceedings based on breaches of due process do not deprive the opposing party of raising the due process defence before enforcing courts. Also, this chapter argued that the decision made by the court of the arbitral seat on the validity of an arbitral award concerning the due process objection should not have extraterritorial effects on enforcing courts.

Most international lawyers experienced in arbitration should find it relatively easy to agree with the basic elements of due process as elaborated in §3.03. However, while the principled nature of due process has been generally accepted by the community of nations, even if not by all nations, the same group of lawyers may find it more difficult to agree with a specific set of rules or standards designed to implement the concept of due process. In practice, it is left to national courts to determine, case by case, exactly what constitutes a 'fair hearing'. The following two chapters will explore how the due process defence can be applied in concrete cases in a manner most consistent with the notion of transnational due process under the interpretative framework of the VCLT by examining subsequent judicial practices by State Parties.

CHAPTER 6

The Proper Notice of the Appointment of the Arbitrator or of the Arbitration Proceedings

§6.01 INTRODUCTION

Chapter 2 argued that general principles of law and subsequent practice provide important guidance for the interpretation and application of Article V(1)(b) of the New York Convention within the interpretative framework established by the VCLT. Chapter 3 linked Article V(1)(b) with the general principle of *audiatur et altera pars*, clarifying the normative content of Article V(1)(b) and concretising it into core elements - proper notice, equality between parties, the right to be heard, and impartial and independent arbitrators. The subsequent practice of State Parties concerning the interpretation and application of the due process defence, in particular domestic court decisions among State Parties, can also help to concretise the meaning and operation of due process in more specific contexts. Accordingly, Chapters 5-7 conduct a comparative analysis of domestic judicial decisions across State Parties in order to determine the similarities and differences in the interpretation and application of the due process defence under the New York Convention. The similarities of domestic court decisions, such as the policies for the interpretation of the due process defence discussed in Chapter 5, may constitute subsequent practice establishing agreements within the meaning of Article 31(3)(b) of the VCLT, which should be considered by enforcing courts.[1]

Recourse to subsequent practice requires enforcing courts to consider how the same or similar facts have been assessed by various State Parties when determining

1. *See* §2.06[B][1], §5.02.

whether a specific tribunal's conduct constitutes a breach of due process. Article V(1)(b) establishes two categories of due process violations. The first category concerns cases in which the party 'was not given proper notice of the appointment of the arbitrator or of the arbitration proceedings', while the second concerns cases in which the party was 'otherwise unable to present his case'. This chapter discusses the similarities and differences in the application and interpretation of the first category ('proper notice') by State Parties. The commonly adopted interpretations of proper notice by enforcing courts may constitute subsequent practice establishing agreements among State Parties under Article 31(3)(b) of the VCLT and thus should be considered by enforcing courts. When dealing with differences, enforcing courts should strive for predictability and compatibility of decisions with the legal expectations of parties and tribunals while also balancing due process and efficiency. These goals are considered to be some of the purposes of Article V.[2] An examination of the ways that other State Parties have developed trade-offs and a critical evaluation of each model can provide a useful guide for policy development regarding the interpretation of proper notice. Those that are more predictable, more compatible with the legal expectations of parties or maintain a good balance with efficiency may constitute subsequent practice within the meaning of Article 32 of the VCLT and thus have persuasive authority for enforcing courts.[3]

Accordingly, §6.02 analyses the standard for proper notice and relevant considerations such as efficiency and burden of proof. Section 6.03 discusses the content and form of proper notice. Section 6.04 examines the way to ascertain the proper addressee, while §6.05 explores the language of communications. Additionally, §6.06 covers the reasonable timing of notifications. Finally, §6.07 concludes the chapter.

§6.02 THE STANDARD FOR PROPER NOTICE AND BURDEN OF PROOF

This section discusses several criteria and considerations on which there is a general consensus in determining when a notice constitutes a violation of proper notice. 'Proper notice' in arbitral proceedings requires that all essential steps and information affecting each party's opportunity to present their case be communicated to them. Also, enforcing courts should give due consideration to certain values such as efficiency, predictability, and the legal expectations of parties, as discussed in Chapter 2.[4] The burden of proving a failure to give 'proper notice' lies with the opposing party, according to the New York Convention. Nevertheless, in circumstances where it is difficult for the opposing party to prove negative facts of not providing proper notice, enforcing courts may allow the applicant seeking recognition and enforcement to prove that they have provided the opposing party with proper notice.

2. For 'context, object and purpose' interpretation under the VCLT, *see* §2.06[A].
3. *See* §2.06[C][2].
4. These values constitute some of the purposes of Article V under the New York Convention: *see* §2.06[A].

[A] The Standard of Proper Notice

Regarding the standard of proper notice, the New York Convention and the implementing national arbitration laws merely express the requirements as a broad standard of 'proper', without specifying the extent of notice required. The case law in this chapter indicates that enforcing courts generally accept that 'proper notice' is such as is likely to bring all essential steps in the arbitral proceedings until the final award is rendered – the pendency of the arbitration and the information influencing a party's opportunity to present its case – to the attention of the person notified, which largely depends on the facts.[5] In practice, a notice would be proper when it is: (a) in an adequate language; (b) with necessary content; (c) in a proper form; (d) delivered in a timely way; and (e) sent to the correct addressee(s).

It appears that Article V(1)(b) deals with issues of form related to the proper notification of the appointment of arbitrators and the arbitration proceedings. However, the main purpose of Article V(1)(b) is to guarantee that each party has a reasonable opportunity to present its case. The wording of Article V(1)(b) 'was otherwise unable to present his case' clearly indicates that 'proper notice' is closely connected with the right to be heard. This is because parties cannot defend themselves or respond to the counterparty's arguments and evidence unless they are duly notified of the arbitral proceedings.[6] In general, inadequate notice that merely breaches the form of notice but does not substantially affect parties' right to be heard does not violate Article V(1)(b) due to the pro-enforcement policy of the New York Convention.

Additionally, in determining whether there has been a breach of due process concerning proper notice, enforcing courts must give efficiency, legal expectations of parties and tribunals, and predictability due consideration. Although the New York Convention is primarily for national judges in State Parties, the implementers of due process in arbitral proceedings are the arbitrators and the parties. Article V(1)(d) of the New York Convention confirms that enforcing courts should respect and honour parties' agreement on procedural issues, including their conferred institutional arbitration rules and the tribunal's discretion. Efficiency is an important objective of parties' agreement.[7] The achievement of efficiency is one of the responsibilities of the arbitrators and is confirmed by all leading arbitration rules.[8] As shown in Chapter 2, a

5. Albert Jan van den Berg, *The New York Arbitration Convention of 1958: Towards a Uniform Judicial Interpretation* (Kluwer Law and Taxation Publishers, 1981) 303.
6. Some situations violate 'proper notice' and 'equality between parties': *see* §7.05.
7. Veijo Heiskanen, 'Key to Efficiency in International Arbitration' (2015) 30(3) *ICSID Review* 481, 481–485 DOI: 10.1093/icsidreview/siv026; Fabricio Fortese and Lotta Hemmi, 'Procedural Fairness and Efficiency in International Arbitration' (2015) 3(1) *Groningen Journal of International Law* 110, 110–124 DOI: 10.21827/5a86a89d8e651; Nana Japaridze, 'Fair Enough? Reconciling the Pursuit of Fairness and Justice with Preserving the Nature of International Commercial Arbitration' (2008) 36(4) *Hofstra Law Review* 1415, 1415–1446.
8. International Chamber of Commerce, *Arbitration Rules* (adopted 1 January 2021) ('*ICC Arbitration Rules*') Art. 22(1); London Court of International Arbitration, *LCIA Arbitration Rules* (adopted 1 October 2014) ('*LCIA Arbitration Rules*') Art. 14.4; Arbitration Institute of the Stockholm Chamber of Commerce, *SCC Arbitration Rules* (adopted 1 January 2017) ('*SCC Arbitration Rules*') Art. 23(2); Hong Kong International Arbitration Centre, *Administered Arbitration Rules* (adopted 1 November 2018) ('*HKIAC Arbitration Rules*') Art. 13.1; Singapore

balance between due process and efficiency is understood as being one of the purposes of Article V(1)(b).[9] The 'context, object and purpose' interpretation of the VCLT requires enforcing courts to consider efficiency and parties' agreement when determining whether proper notice was violated.[10] Accordingly, enforcing courts should defer to parties' agreement on how notice would be conveyed, including their chosen arbitration rules and the tribunal's discretion, provided that each party's right to be heard is guaranteed. This deference to parties' autonomy should be considered as part of the broader principle that what due process demands in each case turns on a proper construction of the agreement to arbitrate.[11]

When dealing with complex notice issues that have multiple options, it is important to consider due process and other criteria such as efficiency and predictability. However, these considerations may not always point in the same direction; thus, trade-offs may need to be made. One of the most controversial issues is that of proportionality. Nevertheless, the subsequent practice of domestic courts discussed in this chapter shows that they now accept this expressly or by implication. 'A notion of proportionality lies at the heart of intelligent truth-seeking in arbitration, accommodating the interconnected pillars of due process and efficiency.'[12] When determining the adequacy of a notice, enforcing courts should consider proportionality. This means that the amount of time and attention given to the notice should be proportionate to the risk of it affecting the parties' right to be heard.

[B] The Burden of Proof

It is evident that the introductory sentence of Article V(1) of the New York Convention stipulates that the party refusing recognition and enforcement should provide grounds for refusal. According to the wording of the New York Convention, the national courts of State Parties generally recognise that the burden of proving a failure to give 'proper notice' lies with the party making the allegation.[13]

However, proving the negative fact of not having received any documents can be challenging for the opposing party. To address this difficulty, some enforcing courts

International Arbitration Centre, *SIAC Arbitration Rules* (adopted 1 August 2016) ('*SIAC Arbitration Rules*') Art. 19.1; United Nations Committee on International Trade Law, *UNCITRAL Arbitration Rules* (2nd ed., 2010), GA Res 65/22, 6th Comm A/65/465, 66th sess., Agenda Item 77, UN Doc. A/RES/65/22 (6 December 2010) ('*UNCITRAL Arbitration Rules*') Art. 17(1).

9. *See* §2.06[A].
10. *Triulzi Cesare SRL v. Xinyi Group (Glass) Co Ltd* [2015] 1 SLR 114, [131].
11. *China Machine New Energy Corp v. Jaguar Energy Guatemala LLC and another* [2018] SGHC 101, [118].
12. William W Park, 'Arbitrators and Accuracy' (2010) 1(1) *Journal of International Dispute Settlement* 25, 52 DOI: 10.1093/jnlids/idp004.
13. *See, e.g.*, France: Court of Cassation of France, First Civil Law Chamber, Arrêt no 1281 FS-P + B, Pourvoi no K 13-11.745, 5 November 2014 reported in (2015) XL *Yearbook Commercial Arbitration* 413, [6]; the UK: *Zavod Ekran Oao v. Magneco Metrel UK Ltd* [2017] EWHC 2208 (Comm) (1 September 2017) [12]; Sweden: *Lenmorniiproekt OAO v. Arne Larsson & Partner Leasing Aktiebolag*, Högsta Domstolens [Swedish Supreme Court], Ö 13-09, 16 April 2010 reported in (2010) XXXV *Yearbook Commercial Arbitration* 456, 457 [4]; Australia: *Uganda Telecom Limited v. Hi-Tech Telecom Pty Ltd* [2011] FCA 131 (22 February 2011) [92]–[118].

allow the applicant seeking recognition and enforcement to demonstrate that they have provided the opposing party with proper notice.[14] In this case, if the opposing party cannot provide contrary evidence, the enforcing court will reject its claim of breaches of proper notice. For instance, Dutch courts may permit the applicant seeking enforcement to submit documents that provide a practical reason to support the argument that the opposing party was informed of the arbitration.[15] Chinese courts have explicitly placed the burden of proof regarding proper notice on the applicant seeking recognition and enforcement.[16]

Another reason for reversing the burden of proof is that certain institutional arbitration rules require the claimant to deliver the notice of Request for Arbitration before the constitution of the arbitral tribunal.[17] This is the case with the LCIA Arbitration Rules, SIAC Arbitration Rules, UNCITRAL Arbitration Rules, and HKIAC Arbitration Rules, which stipulate that the claimant must send the Request for Arbitration and its annexed documents to the respondent.[18]

In terms of emails, as explained in §6.03, enforcing courts often place the burden of proof on the applicant seeking recognition and enforcement due to the difficulty of proving receipt. The applicant must demonstrate that the email was delivered to the respondent's mailbox. Failure to do so may have negative consequences for the applicant.

§6.03 THE CONTENT AND FORM OF PROPER NOTICE

This subsection discusses the content and format of a notice, including when an electronic notice is considered effective. 'Proper notice' requires that the party is informed of the appointment of arbitrators. The parties must be notified of the request for the appointment of an arbitrator, as well as the appointment of an arbitrator by the other party and confirmation of the appointment of an arbitrator. In particular, the parties must be informed of the names of the arbitrators to ensure their right to

14. Nevertheless, several courts, such as Swiss courts, held that there would be no reason to reverse the burden of proof based on the rule *negativa non sunt probanda* (negative facts are not to be proven): *see* Bezirksgericht, Zurich, 14 February 2003 and Obergericht, Zurich, 17 July 2003 reported in (2004) XXIX *Yearbook Commercial Arbitration* 819, 819–833.
15. District Court of Arnhem, 221871 I KV RK 11-999, 27 September 2012 reported in (2013) XXXVIII *Yearbook Commercial Arbitration* 431, [9].
16. 《最高人民法院关于裁定不予承认和执行社团法人日本商事仲裁协会东京05-03号仲裁裁决的报告的答复（2008）民四他字第18号》[Reply of the SPC to the Request for Instructions on non-Recognition of No. 05-03 Tokyo Arbitration Award of the Japan Commercial Arbitration Association], 最高人民法院 [Supreme People's Court] (2008) 民四他字第18号 [Min Si Ta Zi No. 18], 10 September 2008 (the Chinese Supreme People's Court held that the applicant did not prove that the arbitration tribunal had mailed the change of claims to the respondent, and the absence of proper notice violated Article V(1)(b)).
17. Once the arbitral tribunal is established, the tribunal and/or Secretariat has the obligation to notify the parties.
18. *LCIA Arbitration Rules* (n. 8) Art. 1(1)(vii); *SIAC Arbitration Rules* (n. 8) Art. 3(4); *UNCITRAL Arbitration Rules*, UN Doc. A/RES/65/22 (n. 8) Art. 3(1); *HKIAC Arbitration Rules* (n. 8) Art. 4(1). In contrast, the ICC Arbitration Rules and SCC Arbitration Rules set out that the Secretariat shall send a copy of the Request for Arbitration to the respondent.

determine any potential conflicts of interest and challenge the appointment of a biased arbitrator.[19] Also, 'proper notice' requires keeping the parties informed of all essential steps of the arbitral proceedings until the final award is rendered. Thus, it is essential to provide notification of the commencement of arbitration, including the Request for Arbitration or any equivalent documents; the disputed issues, the arguments and evidence of both parties; the date, time, and location of hearings; arbitrator-appointed expert reports; procedural orders; directions given by the arbitral tribunal; and the final award.[20]

Parties should be informed of any changes or corrections to the previous notification, especially those related to claims or submissions. If one party modifies its claims, the other party must be promptly notified so that it can respond and present its case. Otherwise, failing to inform a party of changes or corrections to the other side's submissions may deprive them of the opportunity to comment on the altered claims, which would violate the due process defence.[21]

Subsequent judicial practice of State Parties has established two principles for determining the content and form of proper notice. First, in institutional arbitration, arbitral tribunals and arbitral institutions typically conduct arbitration and communicate in accordance with the arbitration rules and the parties' agreement. Therefore, enforcing courts usually defer to the relevant provisions of the arbitration rules and the parties' agreement to determine the content and format of proper notice.[22]

---

19. van den Berg (n. 5) 305–306; *Triulzi Cesare SRL v. Xinyi Group (Glass) Co Ltd* [2015] 1 SLR 114, 136–141.
20. ICC Arbitration Rules (n. 8) Art. 4; LCIA Arbitration Rules (n. 8) Art. 19(3); SCC Arbitration Rules (n. 8) Art. 32(2); SIAC Arbitration Rules (n. 8) Art. 15(1); UNCITRAL Arbitration Rules, UN Doc. A/RES/65/22 (n. 8) Arts 2, 13.
21. 《最高人民法院关于裁定不予承认和执行社团法人日本商事仲裁协会东京05-03号仲裁裁决的报告的答复（2008）民四他字第18号》[Reply of the SPC to the Request for Instructions on non-Recognition of No. 05-03 Tokyo Arbitration Award of the Japan Commercial Arbitration Association], 最高人民法院 [Supreme People's Court] (2008) 民四他字第18号 [Min Si Ta Zi No. 18], 10 September 2008; 《最高人民法院关于不予承认日本商事仲裁协会东京07-11号仲裁裁决一案的请示的复函（2010）民四他字第32号》[Reply of the SPC to the Request for Instructions on non-Recognition of No. 07-11 Tokyo Arbitration Award of the Japan Commercial Arbitration Association], 最高人民法院 [Supreme People's Court] (2010) 民四他字第32号 [Min Si Ta Zi No. 32], 29 June 2010.
22. *See, e.g.*, China: 《昂佛化品合资有限责任公司申请承认白俄罗斯工商会国际仲裁院仲裁裁决民事裁定书》[*Angfohuapin Co Ltd v. Henan Harvest Chemical Co – Enforcement of A Foreign Arbitral Award*], 郑州市中级人民法院 [Intermediate People's Court of Zhengzhou] (2013) 郑民三初字第37号 [Zheng Min San Chu Zi No. 37], 26 June 2013, English translation available at, http://cicc.court.gov.cn/html/1/219/199/204/665.html; 《来宝资源有限公司申请承认执行外国仲裁裁决民事裁定书》[*Noble Resources Pte Ltd v. Xiongsheng Co Ltd – Enforcement of A Foreign Arbitral Award by International Cotton Association*], 绍兴市中级人民法院 [Intermediate People's Court of Shaoxing] (2014) 浙绍仲确字第1号 [Zhe Shao Zhong Que Zi No. 1], 12 June 2016 (holding that notice should accord to the Rules of International Cotton Association chosen by parties); 《嘉能可国际股份有限公司申请承认和执行外国仲裁裁决民事裁定书》[*Glencore International AG v. Qiying Energy Chemical Engineering Co Ltd – Enforcement of A Foreign Arbitral Award by London Court of International Arbitration*], 宁波市中级人民法院 [Intermediate People's Court of Ningbo] (2014) 浙甬仲确字第1号 [Zhe Yong Zhong Que Zi No. 1], 24 June 2016 (holding that 'proper notice' should be determined by parties' agreement and LCIA Arbitration Rules).

Second, most enforcing courts have confirmed that the formal requirements of domestic judicial proceedings regarding service of notice do not necessarily apply to international arbitration. This is because parties have tacitly waived their judicial formality requirements by resorting to arbitration.[23] Thus, enforcing courts have confirmed that the formality required by the Hague Convention on the Service Abroad of Judicial and Extrajudicial Documents in Civil or Commercial Matters does not apply to the notifications of international arbitration proceedings under the New York Convention.[24]

As far as the proper methods of delivering notice, arbitration rules typically permit communication via hand delivery, registered post, courier service, or other appropriate means that can provide a record of delivery.[25] These forms of notice have been deemed adequate by enforcing courts.[26] Additionally, any proof of actual receipt of the notice, including parties' conduct, is also sufficient. However, not all arbitration rules allow communication delivery to facsimile numbers or email addresses due to the absence of a generally recognised record of delivery. The ICC, SCC, HKIAC and SIAC Rules permit electronic delivery, while the UNCITRAL and LCIA Rules allow electronic delivery only when the address is designated or authorised by the receiving party.[27]

§6.04 PROPER ADDRESS AND ADDRESSEE OF NOTICE

Subsequent judicial practice of State Parties indicates that enforcing courts typically apply the applicable arbitration rules or the arbitration law at the seat of the arbitration to decide the proper address and addressee of the notice. The person who has the authority to accept the service of proceedings is considered the appropriate addressee.

23. Mexico Superior Court of Justice of the Federal District, 1 August 1977 reported in (1979) IV *Yearbook Commercial Arbitration* 302, 303; van den Berg (n. 5) 303; Maxi Scherer, 'New York Convention: Violation of Due Process, Article V (1)(b)' in Reinmar Wolff (ed.), *New York Convention: Convention on the Recognition and Enforcement of Foreign Arbitral Awards of 10 June 1958: Commentary* (C.H. Beck • Hart • Nomos, 2012) 279, 294.
24. *See, e.g.*, Switzerland: Bezirksgericht, Zurich, 14 February 2003 and Obergericht, Zurich, 17 July 2003 reported in (2004) XXIX *Yearbook Commercial Arbitration* 819, 819–33; China: 《昂佛化品合资有限责任公司申请承认白俄罗斯工商会国际仲裁院仲裁裁决民事裁定书》 [*Angfohuapin Co Ltd v. Henan Harvest Chemical Co – Enforcement of A Foreign Arbitral Award*], 郑州市中级人民法院 [Intermediate People's Court of Zhengzhou] (2013) 郑民三初字第37号 [Zheng Min San Chu Zi No. 37], 26 June 2013, English translation available at http://cicc.court.gov.cn/html/1/219/199/204/665.html.
25. ICC Arbitration Rules (n. 8) Art. 3(2); LCIA Arbitration Rules (n. 8) Art. 4(1); SCC Arbitration Rules (n. 8) Art. 5(2); SIAC Arbitration Rules (n. 8) Art. 2(1); UNCITRAL Arbitration Rules, UN Doc. A/RES/65/22 (n. 8) Art. 2(1); HKIAC Arbitration Rules (n. 8) Arts 3(1)–(2).
26. For simple mail, *see* Tribunal Fédéral, Second Civil Chamber [Federal Supreme Court of Switzerland, Second Civil Law Chamber], 5P.353/2004, 21 February 2005 reported in (2007) XXXII *Yearbook Commercial Arbitration* 619, 625–626. For registered mail, *see* Tribunal Supremo [Supreme Court], Civil Chamber, 3536 of 1998, 11 April 2000 reported in (2007) XXXII *Yearbook Commercial Arbitration* 525, 530 [13]. For fax, *see* Oberlandesgericht Celle [Court of Appeal Celle], 8 Sch 14/05, 14 December 2006 reported in (2007) XXXII *Yearbook Commercial Arbitration* 372, 381–382.
27. ICC Arbitration Rules (n. 8) Art. 3(2); LCIA Arbitration Rules (n. 8) Art. 4(3); SCC Arbitration Rules (n. 8) Art. 5(2); SIAC Arbitration Rules (n. 8) Art. 2(1); UNCITRAL Arbitration Rules, UN Doc. A/RES/65/22 (n. 8) Art. 2(2); HKIAC Arbitration Rules (n. 8) Arts 3(1)–(2).

In the case of *Tesco*, two respondents had previously left the partnership and were not informed of the commencement of arbitration concerning their partnership. These two respondents only received notice of arbitration after a liability hearing. They were then represented at a quantum hearing by solicitors who were not designated by them. The court rejected the claim of two respondents that their right to be heard was violated due to not receiving the notice of arbitration. The court held that as long as the solicitor had the authority to accept the service of proceedings and to represent all respondents in those proceedings, there was no impediment preventing the respondents from presenting their case.[28]

The UNCITRAL Model Law and modern arbitration rules, such as the ICC, HKIAC, LCIA and UNCITRAL Rules, generally require written notifications or communications to be sent to the address agreed or designated by a party or its representative.[29] It is important to send all notifications to the agreed or designated address to prevent parties from impeding effective notice by changing their address. In a case before the Chinese SPC, it was found that the opposing party had changed their address after the conclusion of the arbitration agreement without informing the other party, which made him unable to receive arbitral notifications. The court held that the delivery to the previous address provided by the opposing party did not violate the 'proper notice' requirements, as the opposing party's lack of awareness was due to circumstances within their control.[30] In the absence of such agreement or designation, communications shall be sent to an address regularly used in the parties' previous dealings according to the HKIAC Rules and LCIA Rules.[31] Alternatively, communications are *deemed* to have been received if they are delivered to the addressee's place of business, habitual residence, or mailing address according to the UNCITRAL Rules.[32] In practice, even though there is no such explicit agreement or designation by parties, where a party indicates its address in communications with the arbitral institution, enforcing courts may hold that the party thereby accepts the risk of receiving relevant notifications at the address provided.[33]

If the address cannot be located after reasonable efforts, some applicable arbitration rules (e.g., UNCITRAL Rules, ICC Rules, SIAC Rules, SCC Rules, HKIAC

28. *Tesco Ltd v. William Moffett, Richard Mclaughlin, James Mclaughlin & Anson Logue* [2015] NIQB 68 (1 July 2015) [16].
29. *UNCITRAL Model Law on International Commercial Arbitration*, UN GAOR, 40th sess., Supp No. 17, UN Doc. A/40/17 (adopted 21 June 1985) annex I, as amended by UN GAOR, 61st sess., Supp No. 17, UN Doc. A/61/17 (7 July 2006), annex I ('*UNCITRAL Model Law*') Art. 3(1)(a); *ICC Arbitration Rules* (n. 8) Art. 3(2); *HKIAC Arbitration Rules* (n. 8) Art. 3(1)(a); *LCIA Arbitration Rules* (n. 8) Art. 4.2; *UNCITRAL Arbitration Rules*, UN Doc. A/RES/65/22 (n. 8) Art. 2(2).
30. 《最高人民法院关于博而通株式会社申请承认外国仲裁裁决一案的请示的复函》 [Letter of Reply of the SPC on Request for Instructions Re Application of Boertong Corp For Recognition of a Foreign Award Against Beijing Liantaichang Trade Co Ltd], 最高人民法院 [Supreme People's Court] (2006) 民四他字第36号 [Min Si Ta Zi No. 36], 14 December 2006.
31. HKIAC Arbitration Rules (n. 8) Art. 3(1)(b); LCIA Arbitration Rules (n. 8) Art. 4.2.
32. *UNCITRAL Arbitration Rules*, UN Doc. A/RES/65/22 (n. 8) Art. 2(3).
33. *Autorobot-Strefa Sp Zoo v. Sollers Elabuga Limited Liability Company*, Supreme Arbitrazh Court of the Russian Federation, 21 April 2014, and Presidium of the Supreme Arbitrazh Court of the Russian Federation, 24 June 2014 reported in (2014) XXXIX *Yearbook Commercial Arbitration*, 483–485.

Rules) or the arbitration law of the arbitral seat (e.g., the UNCITRAL Model Law) rely on 'deemed service' – a legal fiction whereby communications would be deemed to be received by a party if they are sent to the addressee's last-known address by a means that provides a record of attempted communication.[34] In cases of deemed service, it is not evident whether the actual receipt of communications has occurred. To support the presumption that the notifications were delivered, parties should keep proper records and receipts as sufficient evidence of the attempted notification.[35] Such evidentiary records of the notification attempts can be produced at the later enforcement stage to demonstrate that the defaulting party was 'given every opportunity to attend and present its case, was adequately notified of the timeframe, and was continually invited to take part and offer its own views as to a fair and reasonable process',[36] unless the opposing party can rebut that presumption with evidence.

For example, German courts do not require actual receipt of communications and accept 'deemed service' when applicable arbitration rules or the arbitration law at the arbitral seat allow it. In a specific case, the Berlin Court of Appeal found that registered letters notifying the commencement of arbitration and hearings were returned to the file of the arbitration with the postal note 'not collected' and the stamp of the German Mail Service. The respondent in the recognition and enforcement proceedings argued that it was not aware of these notifications. The court applied the law at the arbitral seat – Ukrainian Law on International Commercial Arbitration – to determine whether proper notice had been given. According to Article 3(1) of the Ukrainian Law on International Commercial Arbitration, the court held that assumptions of communication suffice for proper summons, and the registered letter was deemed to have been delivered to the respondent.[37]

However, when neither the applicable arbitration rules nor the arbitration statute at the arbitral seat set forth 'deemed service', it is very controversial whether this legal fiction automatically applies to arbitration-related communications. The reason for this is that 'deemed service' does not require actual receipt of notice, which may prevent the recipient from presenting its case in arbitration. Accordingly, the use of 'deemed notice' as provided by the applicable arbitration rules or the arbitration law at the seat of arbitration requires the tribunal and the claimant to make genuine and reasonable efforts to find the correct address and use an appropriate method to deliver to this address in good faith. This requirement was demonstrated in the case of *Yancheng v. Joctextile* before the Beijing Fourth Intermediate People's Court. Although *Yancheng v.*

34. *UNCITRAL Model Law*, UN Docs A/40/17 and A/61/17 (n. 29) Art. 3(1)(a); *ICC Arbitration Rules* (n. 8) Art. 3(2); *SCC Arbitration Rules* (n. 8) Art. 5(1); *SIAC Arbitration Rules* (n. 8) Art. 2(1); *UNCITRAL Arbitration Rules*, UN Doc. A/RES/65/22 (n. 8) Arts 2(4); *HKIAC Arbitration Rules* (n. 8) Arts 3(2).
35. Wolfgang Kühn, 'Defaulting Parties and Default Awards in International Arbitration' in Arthur W Rovine (ed.), *Contemporary Issues in International Arbitration and Mediation: The Fordham Papers 2014* (Brill, 2014) 408.
36. Jeff Waincymer, *Procedure and Evidence in International Arbitration* (Kluwer Law International, 2012) 486–487.
37. Kammergericht Berlin [Court of Appeal Berlin], 20 Sch 02/08, 17 April 2008 reported in (2009) XXXIV *Yearbook Commercial Arbitration* 510, [10]–[11].

Joctextile is a foreign-related arbitration,[38] Chinese courts typically apply the same standards of due process when setting aside foreign-related awards rendered in Mainland China as those for refusing recognition or enforcement of foreign awards under the New York Convention.[39] Thus, this case is analysed here for reference.

The case of *Yancheng v. Joctextile*[40] involves an arbitration in which the China International Economic and Trade Arbitration Commission (CIETAC) delivered the notice of arbitration via Express Mail Service (EMS). However, the EMS was returned to the CIETAC. As a result, the CIETAC used a public notary service to deliver all communications. Unfortunately, the respondent did not receive these communications until the eve of the award rendered, which made it unable to present its case. As discussed in §2.02[A], Chinese courts interpret proper notice by following the parties' agreement or the applicable arbitration rules chosen by the parties. In the absence of any indication thereon, the courts will follow the law of the country where the award was made. In this case, the Beijing Fourth Intermediate People's Court relied on the applicable arbitration rules – the CIETAC Arbitration Rules – and considered that Article 8(3) provides three modes of service: direct service ('to the recipient in person'); postal service ('sent to the recipient's business place, registered place, domicile, habitual residence or mailing address', where 'sent to' should be interpreted as recipient's actual receipt); and deemed delivery.[41] The court explained that the three

38. Chinese arbitration framework distinguishes domestic, foreign-related and foreign arbitration and applies different regimes, respectively. 'Domestic arbitration' refers to purely domestic arbitration proceedings administered by a Chinese arbitration commission. 'Foreign-related arbitration' refers to arbitration with 'foreign-related factors' administered by specific authorised foreign-related arbitration commission in China (i.e., China International Economic and Trade Arbitration Commission (CIETAC), the China Maritime Arbitration Commission (CMAC), the Shanghai International Economic and Trade Arbitration Commission, and the South China International Economic and Trade Arbitration Commission). 'Foreign-related factors' refer to circumstances where there is a non-Chinese party, any party has its habitual residence outside China, the subject matter pertains to issues outside China, or the relevant legal facts occur outside China. 'Foreign arbitration' refers to arbitration administered by an arbitral institution outside the territory of China. As discussed in Chapter 2, Chinese courts apply the 'prior-reporting mechanism' requiring higher level courts' review of court decisions involving foreign-related and foreign arbitral awards before a negative decision can be made by a lower court to ensure the uniform application and interpretation.

39. In China, courts distinguish awards into pure domestic awards without foreign-related factors, foreign-related awards and New York Convention awards and apply same jurisprudence of foreign-related awards in setting-aside proceedings as that of the New York Convention awards in recognition and enforcement proceedings: *see*《中华人民共和国民事诉讼法》[Civil Procedure Law of the People's Republic of China] Standing Committee of the National People's Congress, Order of the President of the People's Republic of China No. 71, promulgated on 27 June 2017, effective on 1 July 2017, Art. 274.

40. 《盐城市宏铭达纺织有限公司等申请撤销仲裁裁决民事裁定书》[*Yancheng Hongmingda Textile Co Ltd and others v. Joctextile Co Ltd (Tanzania)* – Annulment of Arbitral Award], 北京市第四中级人民法院 [Beijing Fourth Intermediate People's Court] (2017)京04民特30号 [(2017) Jing 04 Min Te No. 30], 16 May 2019.

41. CIETAC Arbitration Rules, Art. 8(3) providing that:

> Any arbitration correspondence to a party or its representative(s) shall be deemed to have been properly served on the party if delivered to the recipient in person or sent to the recipient's place of business, place of registration, domicile, habitual residence or mailing address, or where, after reasonable enquiries by the other party, none of the

modes of service should be applied sequentially. Only when direct service or actual delivery is difficult, and after reasonable enquiries by the other party, none of the aforementioned addresses can be found, can 'deemed delivery' be used to presume service as a supplement. In this case, the court found that the Post Office had informed the CIETAC that the recipient's address was a post office box that could not receive mail by EMS but could receive airmail. However, the CIETAC did not attempt to inform the respondent via airmail. After using EMS for delivery, the CIETAC concluded that the recipient's address made the notice 'undeliverable' and thus adopted 'deemed service' - a public notary service for all communications. The court found that the tribunal did not comply with the relevant provisions of the CIETAC Arbitration Rules on notifications, which require reasonable efforts to deliver notice in good faith.

In another case before the Swedish Supreme Court concerning 'deemed service', the respondent did not receive any communication from the claimant or the arbitral institution because it changed its address before the arbitral proceedings commenced and failed to inform the claimant of the change despite being contractually required to do so. The applicable arbitration rules merely provided that documents be sent to the respondent's 'last-known address' against receipt for delivery to be deemed as having occurred. However, the Swedish Supreme Court ruled that 'proper notice' was not given because the notice sent to the respondent's last-known address was returned with a note stating that the addressee was not at the stated address. The court concluded that 'it is not acceptable that an arbitral award be recognised and enforced against a party who has not been informed of the arbitration proceedings or even had no possibility to gain knowledge of the fact that proceedings are ongoing'.[42] Further, the court found that the respondent's failure to inform the claimant of its new address, as contractually required, did not affect the fact that it did not receive 'proper notice' of the proceedings.[43] This case indicates that in situations where there is evidence that the address provided by the recipient is incorrect, 'proper notice' may necessitate that the tribunal or participating party undertake *reasonable efforts* to investigate the defaulting party's current address and contact information rather than solely relying on the 'last-known address' provided by the recipient. Meanwhile, to achieve a better balance between due process and efficiency, enforcing courts should recognise that 'deemed service' under applicable arbitration rules or arbitration statutes at the seat of arbitration will be satisfied when the participating party and the arbitral tribunal have made reasonable efforts to search for the current address of the defaulting party.

---

aforesaid addresses can be found, the arbitration correspondence is sent by the Arbitration Court to the recipient's last known place of business, place of registration, domicile, habitual residence or mailing address by registered or express mail, or by any other means that can provide a record of the attempt at delivery, including but not limited to service by public notary, entrustment or retention.

42. *Lenmorniiproekt OAO v. Arne Larsson & Partner Leasing Aktiebolag*, Högsta Domstolens [Supreme Court], Ö 13-09, 16 April 2010 reported in (2010) XXXV *Yearbook Commercial Arbitration* 456, 457.
43. *Ibid.*

§6.05 THE LANGUAGE OF THE NOTICE

Proper notice can be an issue when arbitral communications are drafted in a language that the recipient does not understand, even though the relevant communications are received. There is no issue if the language of the notice is the one chosen and agreed upon by the parties. However, enforcing courts have conflicting views on whether the language of communications provided by the applicable arbitration rules should be respected. Most enforcing courts defer to the language provision of applicable arbitration rules, while a few courts rely on the criteria of the forum where enforcement is sought.

As explained in §5.02[C], the interpretation of 'context, object and purpose' grounded in the VCLT requires an enforcing court to defer to the applicable arbitration rules agreed to by the parties, which is confirmed by Article V(1)(b) of the New York Convention, when interpreting the due process defence. As shown in §6.02[A], such deference can also help enforcing courts to maintain a balance between due process, efficiency, and predictability when determining proper notice.

Subsequent judicial practice of State Parties indicates that, in the absence of parties' agreement, most enforcing courts, such as those in the UK,[44] Germany,[45] Austria,[46] Japan,[47] China,[48] and Brazil,[49] defer to applicable arbitration rules and the tribunal's decision on communication language. This judicial practice does not establish an agreement among State Parties but can constitute subsequent practice under Article 32 of the VCLT and has persuasive authority for other enforcing courts. By agreeing to arbitration under certain arbitration rules, parties may anticipate receiving

44. *Zavod Ekran Oao v. Magneco Metrel UK Ltd* [2017] EWHC 2208 (Comm) (1 September 2017) [24]–[26].
45. Oberlandesgericht Munich [Court of Appeal Munich], 34 Sch 26/08, 22 June 2009 reported in (2010) XXXV *Yearbook Commercial Arbitration* 371, 373[12]–[13]; Oberlandesgericht Hamm [Higher Regional Court of Hamm], 25 Sch 09/08, 28 November 2008 reported in (2009) XXXIV *Yearbook Commercial Arbitration* 536, 541[12]; Oberlandesgericht Celle [Higher Regional Court of Celle], 8 Sch 03/01, 2 October 2001 reported in (2007) XXXII *Yearbook Commercial Arbitration* 303, 307 [7].
46. Oberster Gerichtshof [Supreme Court], 3Ob141/07t, 23 October 2007 reported in (2008) XXXIII *Yearbook Commercial Arbitration* 354.
47. District Court of Yokohama, Case No. Heisei 10 (wa) 3851, 25 August 1999, reported in (2002) XXVII *Yearbook Commercial Arbitration* 515, 515–518 (the opposing party argued that due process was violated because notifications had been made in Chinese without translation into Japanese, which the enforcing court dismissed on the findings that the applicable arbitration rules provide for Chinese as the default language in the absence of parties' agreement or of the determination by the tribunal).
48. 《最高人民法院关于是否承认与执行大韩商事仲裁院仲裁裁决的请示的复函》 [Reply of the SPC to the Request for Instructions about Whether or Not to Recognise and Enforce an Award rendered the Korean Commercial Arbitration Board] 最高人民法院 [Supreme People's Court] (2005) 民四他字第46号 [Min Si Ta Zi No. 46], 3 March 2006 (the opposing party argued that the award breached due process because notifications had been made in Korean without Chinese translation, which Chinese Supreme People's Court dismissed on the findings that delivery without Chinese translation was consistent with the applicable arbitration rules).
49. Rafael Francisco Alves, 'Chapter 3: Country Report: Brazil' in Friedrich Rosenfeld, Dietmar Czernich and Franco Ferrari (eds), *Due Process as a Limit to Discretion in International Commercial Arbitration* (Kluwer Law International, 2020) 55, 63.

documents in a language according to the applicable arbitration rules and thus accept the risk that the language may be foreign to them. Accordingly, a tribunal's decision regarding a language that the recipient does not understand does not necessarily violate the due process defence under Article V(1)(b), which applies not only to English, but also to other languages.[50] The responsibility of finding an interpreter or translator to present the party's case lies with the party when the language designated by the applicable arbitration rules or determined by the tribunal is foreign to them.[51] As explained in §6.02[A], enforcing courts do not necessarily apply the requirements for the language of judicial services to arbitration.[52]

In the case of *Zavod Ekran Oao*, the English defendant received the arbitration statement of claim and annexed documents in Russian, accompanied by a covering letter from the International Commercial Arbitration Court (ICAC). Although the body of the letter was in Russian, the letterhead displayed ICAC Moscow's name in English. The High Court of Justice in England found that the parties had agreed to conduct arbitration through the ICAC in Moscow under Russian law, with the arbitration language being Russian, as stated in their contract.[53] Also, the court considered that the notice requirements were met by the English letterhead indicating ICAC, and the defendant could not argue that due process was violated on the grounds of not understanding Russian.[54] The court emphasised that a notice of arbitration received in England, but not drafted in English, does not, in principle, affect the validity of the notice. It may do so in certain circumstances, which did not pertain to this case.[55]

German courts also show deference to applicable arbitration rules and do not require that the language of communications be that of the serving country. In addition, German courts typically assess whether the party who is not proficient in the language used in communications was given reasonable time to prepare their case with the assistance of an interpreter or translator. In a case before the Higher Regional Court of Hamm, one party sought to enforce a Russian award in which the arbitration language was Russian under the ICAC Arbitration Rules, while the opposing party argued that there was a violation of due process since it was unaware that Russian would be the language of the arbitral proceedings.[56] The court dismissed the claim of a due process violation and ruled that, unless the parties agreed otherwise, Russian would be the language of the arbitration under the ICAC Arbitration Rules. Further, the court argued that the defendant's opportunity to be heard had been ensured, even if the defendant did not have to be aware of the provision of ICAC Arbitration Rules regarding the language of proceedings. This was because the date of the hearing had

50. Oberlandesgericht Celle [Higher Regional Court of Celle], 8 Sch 03/01, 2 October 2001 reported in (2007) XXXII *Yearbook Commercial Arbitration* 303.
51. *Ibid.*, 307 [7].
52. *Ibid.*
53. *Zavod Ekran Oao v. Magneco Metrel UK Ltd* [2017] EWHC 2208 (Comm) (1 September 2017) [25].
54. *Ibid.*
55. *Ibid.*, [24]–[25].
56. Oberlandesgericht Hamm [Higher Regional Court of Hamm], 25 Sch 09/08, 28 November 2008 reported in (2009) XXXIV *Yearbook Commercial Arbitration* 536.

been postponed at the defendant's request on the grounds that it was not familiar with Russian. Additionally, the tribunal had considered the defendant's statement in Russian.[57] In another case, the Munich Court of Appeal held that the opposing party had presented its case before the tribunal despite the inconsistency between the language of communication regulated by the applicable arbitration rules (Spanish) and the parties' agreement in the arbitration clause (English). This was due to the opposing party being represented by a Spanish-speaking counsel throughout the entire arbitral proceedings.[58]

In contrast to the aforementioned cases, American courts have issued conflicting decisions regarding *CEEG v. LUMOS* and *CEEG v. Sunvalley*. In these cases, the notifications were written in Chinese, in accordance with the applicable arbitration rules but were sent to American recipients who could not understand the language.[59] The American parties in both cases argued that the proper notice standard had not been met because the communications were in Chinese instead of English. However, the US District Court for the Central District of California granted the enforcement of the award in the *CEEG v. Sunvalley* case, as the notice was prepared according to the applicable arbitration rules, which stated that the arbitration would be conducted in Chinese.[60] Also, the court considered that the opposing party was aware of the arbitration proceedings as it did not contest receiving the notice of arbitration and was in communication with the arbitral tribunal during that period.[61]

However, with the exception of *CEEG v. Sunvalley*, American courts have consistently endorsed the opposite position. They have held that a party's right to be heard was violated when the notice language did not reasonably apprise the parties of the pending arbitration, even if the language was consistent with the applicable arbitration rules.[62] For instance, in *CEEG v. LUMOS*, the District Court of Colorado found that the notice of arbitration in Chinese prevented LUMOS from realising that the arbitration had begun, which resulted in LUMOS being unable to participate in the

57. *Ibid.*, 541 [12].
58. Oberlandesgericht Munich [Court of Appeal Munich], 34 Sch 26/08, 22 June 2009 reported in (2010) XXXV *Yearbook Commercial Arbitration* 371, 373 [12]–[13].
59. *CEEG (Shanghai) Solar Science & Technology Co Ltd v. LUMOS LLC, n/k/a LUMOS Solar LLC* (10th Cir, No. 15-1256, 19 July 2016) ('*CEEG v. LUMOS*'); *CEEG (Shanghai) Solar Science & Technology Co, Ltd v. Sunvalley Solar, Inc* http://www.newyorkconvention.org/news/us+district+court+for+the+central+district+of+california+confirms+new+york+convention+award+rendered+by+shiac ('CEEG v. Sunvalley').
60. *CEEG (Shanghai) Solar Science & Technology Co, Ltd v. Sunvalley Solar, Inc* http://www.newyorkconvention.org/news/us+district+court+for+the+central+district+of+california+confirms+new+york+convention+award+rendered+by+shiac.
61. *Ibid.*
62. *Qingdao Free Trade Zone Genius International Trading Co v. P & S International Inc* (D Or, No. 08-1292-HU, 16 September 2009) ('Qingdao v. P & S') slip op 9–10; *CEEG (Shanghai) Solar Science & Technology Co Ltd v. LUMOS LLC, n/k/a LUMOS Solar LLC* (10th Cir, No. 15-1256, 19 July 2016) slip op 10. In both cases, Chinese claimants provided American respondents with the notice of arbitration in Chinese according to the applicable arbitration rules. Both the District Court of Oregon and the Tenth Circuit Court of Appeals held that the documents and circumstances of these two cases did not demonstrate that the respondents received notice reasonably calculated to apprise them of the pending arbitration and afford them an opportunity to be heard.

selection of arbitrators.[63] The Tenth Circuit Court of Appeals upheld the District Court of Colorado's decision and emphasised that the failure to provide the right to participate in the tribunal-selection process was not a minor procedural error, given that the tribunal had the power to determine the parties' rights with virtually no possibility of appeal or review.[64]

However, the decisions of the District Court of Colorado and the Tenth Circuit Court of Appeals in *CEEG v. LUMOS* disregarded the applicable arbitration rules regarding the language of the arbitration. They chose to use substantive criteria to determine whether the language was sufficient to inform the party of the pendency of arbitration.[65] As discussed in §6.02[A], when determining proper notice, enforcing courts should strike a balance between due process, efficiency, and predictability. It is important to consider all of these factors rather than solely focusing on the substantive criteria. This is because doing so could negatively impact the efficiency of arbitration and the predictability of the other party. It is worth noting that by agreeing to arbitration under the CIETAC Rules, parties are deemed to have accepted the risk of receiving communications in Chinese unless the parties have agreed otherwise. Also, LUMOS was unable to prove that it could not defend itself due to the use of Chinese in arbitration, considering that the tribunal granted a two-month extension of time for the first hearing so that LUMOS could present its case. Although LUMOS missed the deadline for the appointment of the chief arbitrator, who ultimately handed down the arbitration award, LUMOS challenged the tribunal's jurisdiction. However, the challenge was rejected by the tribunal.[66] Enforcing courts should not review a tribunal's decision on its jurisdiction or the challenge of arbitrators. Instead, they should show deference to the tribunal's decision.

In accordance with the provisions of applicable arbitration rules on communication language, leading arbitration rules, such as the ICC, LCIA, SIAC, HKIAC, SCC and UNCITRAL, generally state that the arbitral tribunal shall determine the language of the arbitration, subject to all relevant circumstances and parties' agreement.[67] Prior to the constitution of the arbitral tribunal, certain arbitration rules include provisions regarding the initial language of the arbitration. Typically, this grants authority to the arbitral institution (e.g., LCIA Court) or the Registrar to determine the language of communications. For instance, the LCIA Arbitration Rules explicitly provide that the initial language of the arbitration shall be the language or prevailing language of the

63. *CEEG (Shanghai) Solar Science & Technology Co Ltd v. LUMOS LLC, n/k/a LUMOS Solar LLC* (10th Cir, No. 15-1256, 19 July 2016) slip op 11.
64. *Ibid.*, slip op 12–13.
65. *See also Crooks v. Mabus*, 845 F 3d 412, 423 (DC Cir, 2016); *Reeve Aleutian Airways Inc v. United States*, 982 F 2d 594, 599 (DC Cir, 1993) ('[d]ue process requires notice reasonably calculated, under all the circumstances, to apprise interested parties of the pendency of the action and afford them an opportunity to present their objections').
66. *CEEG (Shanghai) Solar Science & Technology Co Ltd v. LUMOS LLC, n/k/a LUMOS Solar LLC* (D Colo, Civ No. 14-CV-03118, 29 May 2015) slip op 6.
67. ICC Arbitration Rules (n. 8) Art. 20; HKIAC Arbitration Rules (n. 8) Art. 15(2); LCIA Arbitration Rules (n. 8) Art. 17(4); SCC Arbitration Rules (n. 8) Art. 26(1); SIAC Arbitration Rules (n. 8) Art. 22(1); UNCITRAL Arbitration Rules, UN Doc. A/RES/65/22 (n. 8) Art. 19.

arbitration agreement.[68] Where the arbitration agreement is written in multiple languages of equal standing, the LCIA Court may determine which language to use.[69] Similarly, the SIAC Arbitration Rules state that the Registrar shall decide on the language of the arbitration before the tribunal is formed.[70] In contrast, the ICC uses its own languages and requires the Secretariat to draft correspondence to parties in either the language of the contract when it is one of the languages used by the Secretariat (English, French, Spanish, Portuguese, German) or in one of the official languages of the ICC Court (English or French).[71]

Certain arbitration rules permit the use of the language of the arbitral seat for communications prior to the establishment of the arbitral tribunal. The LCIA Arbitration Rules, for instance, explicitly provide that 'a non-participating or defaulting party shall have no cause for complaint if communications to and from the LCIA Court and Registrar are conducted in the initial language of the arbitration or *of the arbitral seat* [until the formation of the Arbitral Tribunal]'.[72] The HKIAC Rules also consider the language used at the seat of the arbitration and provide that where the parties have not agreed on the language of the arbitration beforehand, any party shall communicate in either English or Chinese until the arbitral tribunal makes a determination.[73]

§6.06 THE REASONABLE TIMING OF NOTIFICATIONS

'Proper notice' also requires that each party is notified within a reasonable time so that it has sufficient time to appoint the arbitrator, challenge the arbitrator, and prepare its case. However, when the parties have agreed to expedite the process, they will not be granted the same reasonable time for issuing notice in a full-length arbitration.[74]

The breach of the right to be heard can be a significant criterion for determining whether the timeline is sufficient. Proper notice is only violated if the late notification prevents the party from presenting its case.[75] In other words, if the timing of notice only inconvenienced the party or made it difficult, but not impossible, to participate in the arbitral proceedings meaningfully, this does not constitute a violation of proper notice.[76]

68. LCIA Arbitration Rules (n. 8) Art. 17(1).
69. *Ibid.*, Art. 17(4).
70. SIAC Arbitration Rules (n. 8) Art. 22(2).
71. Jason Fry, Simon Greenberg and Francesca Mazza, *The Secretariat's Guide to ICC Arbitration* (2012) § 3-739.
72. *LCIA Arbitration Rules* (n. 8) Art. 17(3) (emphasis added).
73. HKIAC Arbitration Rules (n. 8) Art. 15(1).
74. *China Machine New Energy Corp v. Jaguar Energy Guatemala LLC and another* [2018] SGHC 101, [125]–[127]. The court noted that having agreed to expedition 'the tribunal had to [ensure due process] within the strictures that the parties had placed it in, principally the constraint of time'.
75. Supreme Court of Cassation of Italy, No. 3221, 3 April 1987 reported in (1992) XVII *Yearbook Commercial Arbitration* 529, 676; Supreme Court of Spain, First Civil Law Chamber, No. 332 of 2000, 31 July 2000 reported in (2007) XXXII *Yearbook Commercial Arbitration* 532, 538 [18]–[19].
76. Supreme Court of Cassation of Italy, No. 671, 21 January 2000 reported in (2002) XXVII *Yearbook Commercial Arbitration* 492, 496 [9].

The sufficiency of the notice timing mainly depends on the evaluation of the facts.[77] Some courts have even considered exceptional situations, such as earthquakes[78] and 'thinning out of juridical activities',[79] which could make a sufficient period longer than usual, as mail and courier services routinely refuse delivery. In those cases, the period specified by the applicable arbitration rules may not be sufficient to guarantee the recipient's fundamental right to a fair arbitration.

The tribunal's decision on interpretation or translation may necessitate prior notification to allow the parties to locate appropriate interpreters to prepare their cases. Failure to do so may result in a violation of due process. For instance, Chinese courts have ruled that the tribunal's decision not to provide interpretation and translation services during hearings must be communicated to the parties in advance, allowing them sufficient time to prepare for the hearings and present their cases. In the case of *Shin-Etsu Chemical Co Ltd v. Jiangsu Zhongtian Technology Co*, the Japan Commercial Arbitration Association's secretary consulted the parties regarding the management of simultaneous translators for the hearings. The Chinese party responded in writing, expressing their preference to use Chinese during the hearings. On 4 April 2008, just five days before the first hearing, the tribunal recommended that the parties use English if possible. The parties were also informed by post that any submissions prepared in a language other than English should be translated into English. The Chinese SPC ruled that due to the public holiday in China from 4 April to 6 April, the notice of 4 April was deemed received by the Chinese party on 7 April. As a result, the Chinese party had only three days to prepare its case before the first hearing. This insufficient notice deprived the Chinese party of a reasonable opportunity to appoint suitable alternative legal representatives with qualified knowledge of the case and fluency in English. The court found that the Chinese party was disadvantaged by the tribunal's denial to provide simultaneous English-Chinese interpretation during hearings requested by the Chinese party and late notice of this decision, which together deprived the Chinese party of the right to present its case.[80]

§6.07 CONCLUSION

This chapter examined subsequent judicial practice of State Parties regarding proper notice under Article V(1)(b) of the New York Convention. The case law indicates that enforcing courts generally consider that proper notice should convey the relevant

77. Supreme Court of Cassation of Italy, No. 3221, 3 April 1987 reported in (1992) XVII *Yearbook Commercial Arbitration* 529, 676 [1].
78. Corte Di Appello Di Napoli [Court of Appeal of Naples], 18 May 1982 reported in (1985) X *Yearbook Commercial Arbitration* 461, 461.
79. Supreme Court of Cassation of Italy, No. 3221, 3 April 1987 reported in (1992) XVII *Yearbook Commercial Arbitration* 529, 533.
80. 《最高人民法院关于不予承认日本商事仲裁协会东京07-11号仲裁裁决一案的请示的复函(2010)民四他字第32号》 [Reply of the SPC to the Request for Instructions on non-Recognition of No. 07-11 Tokyo Arbitration Award of the Japan Commercial Arbitration Association], 最高人民法院 [Supreme People's Court] (2010) 民四他字第32号 [Min Si Ta Zi No. 32], 29 June 2010.

information to the intended recipient, including the pendency of the arbitration and any information that may affect a party's opportunity to present its case. In practice, the effectiveness of a notice may be influenced by its content, form, addressee, language, and timing. Enforcing courts usually consider the parties' agreement on how the notice will be conveyed and defer to applicable arbitration rules to balance due process, efficiency, and predictability. This respect for party autonomy and the deference to applicable arbitration rules on notice, which is required by Article V(1)(d) of the New York Convention, are consistent with the 'context, object and purpose' interpretation under Article 31(1) of the VCLT. In the absence of relevant provisions in the applicable arbitration rules, the notice shall be communicated in good faith and with reasonable attempts to ensure the parties' right to be heard.

This chapter demonstrated that the subsequent practice of states is largely consistent in its approach to the interpretation and application of 'proper notice' under Article V(1)(b) of the New York Convention. Under the interpretative framework of the VCLT, this practice of multiple State Parties establishes a transnational standard of due process that domestic courts of State Parties should adopt in enforcement proceedings. The following chapter will examine the subsequent judicial practice of State Parties with regard to two other significant attributes of due process: the right to be heard and the equality of parties.

CHAPTER 7

The Opportunity to Present Its Case and Equal Treatment

§7.01 INTRODUCTION

The book argues that the due process defence can be concretised by the general principle of due process and subsequent practice of State Parties concerning Article V(1)(b). Chapter 3 has shown that the general principle of *audiatur et altera pars* includes the notions of proper notice, the right to be heard, equality between parties, and the impartiality and independence of arbitrators. Chapter 6 examined the subsequent judicial practice of State Parties regarding proper notice under Article V(1)(b). This chapter focuses on the subsequent judicial practice of State Parties regarding the right to be heard and equal treatment. Accordingly, this chapter helps to elucidate the subsequent practice of State Parties regarding the right to make submissions and evidence, the right to comment on submissions and evidence, the right to have submissions considered, and equality between parties.

During the twenty-third meeting of the United Nations Conference on International Commercial Arbitration, the Netherlands representative's proposal to replace the phrase 'in sufficient time to enable him to present his case' with 'was otherwise unable to present his case' was successful, as evidenced by the *travaux préparatoires* of the New York Convention.[1] It is evident that Article V(1)(b) is intended to cover a broader range of situations where parties have been deprived of their right to be heard, in addition to inadequate notice.[2]

1. United Nations Conference on International Commercial Arbitration: Summary Record of the Twenty-Third Meeting, UN Doc. E/CONF.26/SR.23 (12 September 1958) 15.
2. Albert Jan van den Berg, *The New York Arbitration Convention of 1958: Towards a Uniform Judicial Interpretation* (Kluwer Law and Taxation Publishers, 1981) 306; Maxi Scherer, 'New York Convention: Violation of Due Process, Article V(1)(b)' in Reinmar Wolff (ed.), *New York Convention: Convention on the Recognition and Enforcement of Foreign Arbitral Awards of 10 June 1958: Commentary* (C.H. Beck • Hart • Nomos, 2012) 279, 298.

Unlike the UNCITRAL Model Law, which expressly requires equal treatment,[3] the New York Convention does not explicitly refer to the principle of equality of arms. However, it is generally accepted that Article V(1)(b) also lays down the principle of equal treatment concerning the right to be heard.[4] Equality of arms guarantees that a party is not treated less favourably than its counterparty when informed of arbitral proceedings and given the opportunity to present its case.

As explained in Chapter 3, the independence and impartiality of arbitrators are essential requirements of due process. On the one hand, arbitrators' partiality and dependence are often cited as evidence of violations of Article V(1)(d) ('the composition of the arbitral authority or the arbitral procedure was not in accordance with the agreement of the parties, or, failing such agreement, was not in accordance with the law of the country where the arbitration took place'). On the other hand, Article V(1)(b) would be violated only when the arbitrator's partiality or dependence prevents the parties from presenting their cases.

The right to present one's case has multiple facets and governs all steps of arbitral proceedings, including the right to make submissions, comment on submissions, and have submissions considered. Accordingly, §7.02 discusses the right to make submissions and present evidence, including the administration of submissions and time limits, oral hearings, and the right to have an interpreter. Section 7.03 explores a party's right to comment on submissions and evidence provided by the opposing party and on findings of the tribunal. It explores whether the tribunal has the power to investigate facts or laws ex officio and whether *iura novit curia* applies to international arbitration. Section 7.04 covers the party's right to have submissions considered, circumstances of exclusion or admission of evidence, and the absence of reasons in awards. Section 7.05 examines the equality of arms. Section 7.06 concludes the chapter.

§7.02 THE RIGHT TO MAKE SUBMISSIONS AND PRODUCE EVIDENCE

First, the right to present one's case requires that each party has a reasonable opportunity to make written or oral submissions and to put forward factual and legal evidence supporting its position. National arbitration statutes and leading arbitration rules usually require that the tribunal allow the parties to submit written submissions that set out and explain their positions.[5] The tribunal should allow a party to amend or supplement its claim or defence, unless it considers such amendment inappropriate due to resulting delay, prejudice to the other party, or other relevant circumstances.[6] As

3. *UNCITRAL Model Law on International Commercial Arbitration*, UN GAOR, 40th sess., Supp No. 17, UN Doc. A/40/17 (adopted 21 June 1985) annex I, as amended by UN GAOR, 61st sess., Supp No. 17, UN Doc. A/61/17 (7 July 2006), annex I ('*UNCITRAL Model Law*') Art. 18.
4. van den Berg (n. 2) 306.
5. *See, e.g.*, Wetboek van Burgerlijke Rechtsvordering [Dutch Code of Civil Procedure] (Netherlands) Art. 1036 (2); Arbitration Institute of the Stockholm Chamber of Commerce, *SCC Arbitration Rules* (adopted 1 January 2017) ('*SCC Arbitration Rules*') Art. 29; Hong Kong International Arbitration Centre, *Administered Arbitration Rules* (adopted 1 November 2018) ('*HKIAC Arbitration Rules*') Arts 16, 17.
6. SCC Arbitration Rules (n. 5) Art. 30; HKIAC Arbitration Rules (n. 5) Art. 18.

stated in §5.02[C], the subsequent judicial practice of State Parties indicates that enforcing courts generally defer to arbitrators' procedural decisions, which is in line with the interpretation of the 'context, object and purpose' under the VCLT through its alignment with Article V(1)(b) and Article V(1)(d) of the New York Convention. Accordingly, enforcing courts usually respect arbitral tribunals' assessment of whether submissions on particular substantive issues were necessary, unless the tribunals prohibited parties from making submissions on issues central to the tribunal's decision-making.[7]

As discussed in Chapter 6, parties must be given reasonable time to prepare their case, including proper notice and the ability to present their case as stated in Article V(1)(b). However, arbitral tribunals are not required to grant parties multiple rounds of written submissions due to policy objectives of ensuring efficiency and minimising costs, as discussed in §6.02[A]. A party's right to submit evidence is also restricted by the other party's right to be heard, which includes the right to comment on further submissions within a reasonable time. Thus, enforcing courts have consistently affirmed that tribunals possess broad case management powers to set time limits for submitting documents to ensure that justice is done expeditiously and efficiently.[8] Also, courts generally defer to tribunals' decisions on the length of such deadlines and the need for further submissions or additional evidence.[9] If a submission is not filed before the established deadline, the tribunal may reject it without breaching due process.

Another important aspect of parties' right to make submissions is the right to be heard by the arbitral tribunal in an oral hearing when requested. This type of hearing offers the benefit of a live, adversarial exchange between parties and the tribunal. It also provides the opportunity to cross-examine witnesses and experts. Some arbitration statutes, such as those in Germany and the Netherlands, and institutional arbitration rules provide that the tribunal shall hold oral hearings for parties to present evidence or oral arguments when requested by either party.[10] If parties do not make such a request, the tribunal may exercise its discretion to conduct the arbitration based solely on documents and other materials.[11] Courts may reject a party's objection that it

7. *CRW Joint Operation v. PT Perusahan Gas Negara (Persero) TBK* [2011] 4 SLR 305, [94]–[96].
8. Friedrich Jakob Rosenfeld, 'Chapter 8: Country Report: Germany' in Friedrich Rosenfeld, Dietmar Czernich and Franco Ferrari (eds), *Due Process as a Limit to Discretion in International Commercial Arbitration* (Kluwer Law International, 2020) 177, 182–183.
9. *Triulzi Cesare SRL v. Xinyi Group (Glass) Co Ltd* [2015] 1 SLR 114, 136–141; *ADG and another v. ADI and another matter* [2014] 3 SLR 481, 121.
10. *See, e.g.*, Germany: *Zivilprozessordnung* [Code of Civil Procedure](Germany) § 1047; the Netherlands: Wetboek van Burgerlijke Rechtsvordering [Dutch Code of Civil Procedure] (Netherlands) Art. 1038 (b); London Court of International Arbitration, *LCIA Arbitration Rules* (adopted 1 October 2014) ('*LCIA Arbitration Rules*') Art. 19(1); Singapore International Arbitration Centre, *SIAC Arbitration Rules* (adopted 1 August 2016) ('*SIAC Arbitration Rules*') Art. 24(1); United Nations Committee on International Trade Law, *UNCITRAL Arbitration Rules* (2nd ed., 2010), GA Res 65/22, 6th Comm A/65/465, 66th sess., Agenda Item 77, UN Doc. A/RES/65/22 (6 December 2010) ('*UNCITRAL Arbitration Rules*') Art. 17(3); *HKIAC Arbitration Rules* (n. 5) Art. 22(4).
11. *UNCITRAL Model Law*, UN Docs A/40/17 and A/61/17 (n. 3) Art. 24 (1); *Swedish Arbitration Act* (Sweden) SFS No. 1996:116, s. 24 [Joel Dahlquist Cullborg trans, *The Swedish Arbitration*

was denied the opportunity to make oral submissions when there was no indication that the parties had requested an oral hearing during the arbitral proceedings.[12] Although parties did not request oral hearings, if the tribunal gave parties the impression that there would be an oral hearing to examine certain issues but failed to conduct one without prior notification, it would violate a party's right to present its case.[13]

The arbitral tribunal should inform the parties of the hearing time and provide them with reasonable time to prepare. The amount of time allocated for preparation depends primarily on the specific circumstances of the case. As previously mentioned, enforcing courts generally defer to tribunals' decisions on timelines, except in cases where the time allotted is insufficient for parties to prepare their case. For example, an Italian court ruled that twenty days to participate in a hearing was inadequate, given that the party had been affected by an earthquake.[14]

A tribunal's refusal to postpone a hearing does not necessarily infringe upon the right to be heard as long as there is a balance between due process and efficiency. As stated by the Singapore High Court, 'the right of each party to be heard does not mean that the Tribunal must "sacrifice all efficiency in order to accommodate unreasonable procedural demands by a party"'.[15] However, if the tribunal refused the party's request to postpone the hearing, which resulted in the party's inability to present its main arguments, this may violate the party's right to be heard. This was illustrated in a case before the Swedish Supreme Court, where the parties initiated the settlement after the arbitration had commenced. During the main hearing on 5 February 2016, the parties notified the tribunal that they had failed to reach an amicable settlement and requested the tribunal to resolve the dispute. Simultaneously, the respondent requested the tribunal to postpone the main hearing to prepare its position on the merits and submit a Statement of Defence. However, the tribunal rejected the request. The Swedish court found that the parties had negotiated a settlement, but the tribunal had not provided the respondent with instructions on how to manage the dispute before the main hearing on 5 February 2016. It was only on the last scheduled date of the main hearing that it became apparent that the parties had failed to reach an amicable settlement. Until that point, the respondent was justified in assuming that the dispute would not be reviewed on its merits at the hearing. Based on these findings, the court held that the respondent had justifiable reasons for not submitting a Statement of Defence and not being prepared to argue the case at the main hearing. It also found that the tribunal

---

Act (2019), https://sccinstitute.com/media/408924/the-swedish-arbitration-act_1march2019_eng.pdf]; *Arbitration Act 1996* (UK) c 23, s. 34(2)(h); *UNCITRAL Arbitration Rules*, UN Doc. A/RES/65/22 (n. 10) Art. 17(3); *SIAC Arbitration Rules* (n. 10) Art. 24(1); *SCC Arbitration Rules* (n. 5) Art. 32(1); *LCIA Arbitration Rules* (n. 10) Art. 19(1); International Chamber of Commerce, *Arbitration Rules* (adopted 1 January 2021) ('*ICC Arbitration Rules*') Art. 25(6); *HKIAC Arbitration Rules* (n. 5) Art. 22(4).

12. *Government of the Republic of the Philippines v. Philippine International Air Terminals Co Inc* [2007] 1 SLR (R) 278.
13. *Guangdong Overseas Shenzhen Co Ltd v. Yao Shun Group International Ltd* [1998] 1 HKC 451.
14. Corte Di Appello Di Napoli [Court of Appeal of Naples], 18 May 1982 reported in (1985) X *Yearbook Commercial Arbitration* 461.
15. *Triulzi Cesare SRL v. Xinyi Group (Glass) Co Ltd* [2015] 1 SLR 114, 151.

should have given the respondent a reasonable opportunity to prepare its case on the merits and invoke evidence at the main hearing but failed to do so.[16]

When allocating time for oral arguments at a hearing, tribunals should ensure the equality of arms and grant each party a reasonable time to comment on the other's submissions. Section 7.05 will discuss equal treatment in terms of allocated time in more detail.

§7.03 THE RIGHT TO COMMENT ON SUBMISSIONS AND EVIDENCE BY THE COUNTERPARTY AND FINDINGS OF THE TRIBUNAL

Another important aspect of the right to present one's case is the ability to comment on evidence and arguments presented by the counterparty or on certain findings of the tribunal.[17] The arbitral tribunal shall not base its decision, which may be unfavourable to one party, on documents or other information on which that party has not had sufficient opportunity to comment. The tribunal must provide both parties with the chance to comment on the factual and legal arguments presented by the other side. Failure to do so may result in the award being denied recognition and enforcement due to a violation of due process.

[A] The Right to Comment on Submissions Presented by the Counterparty

The right to comment on evidence and arguments submitted by the other side is a fundamental element of adversarial proceedings.[18] The right to comment requires that written pleadings, documents, and other communications submitted by one party are made available to the other party. This is confirmed by national arbitration statutes, such as the German Code of Civil Procedure[19] and the Dutch Arbitration Act.[20]

16. *Belaya Ptitsa – Kursk v. Robot Grader AB*, Högsta Domstolens [Supreme Court], Ö 3626-17, 04 May 2018 reported in the Arbitration Institute of the Stockholm Chamber of Commerce, 4[10], https://www.arbitration.sccinstitute.com/Swedish-Arbitration-Portal/Supreme-Court/The-Supreme-Court2/The-Supreme-Court/d_3259325-judgment-in-the-swedish-supreme-court-4-may-2018.-case-no.-o-3626-17.
17. Gary B Born, *International Commercial Arbitration* (Kluwer Law International, 2nd ed., 2014) 3515–3516; Scherer (n. 2) 306. *See also* Wetboek van Burgerlijke Rechtsvordering [Dutch Code of Civil Procedure] (Netherlands) Art. 1036 (2); Oberlandesgericht Celle [Court of Appeal Celle], 8 Sch 06/06, 31 May 2007 reported in (2008) XXXIII *Yearbook Commercial Arbitration* 524.
18. Arrondissementsrechtbank Rotterdam [District Court of Rotterdam], 2 October 1997 reported in (1998) XXIII *Yearbook Commercial Arbitration* 731, 732 [5] (upheld by Gerechtshof the Hague [Court of Appeal of the Hague], 28 April 1998 reported in (1998) XXIII *Yearbook Commercial Arbitration* 731).
19. *Zivilprozessordnung* [Code of Civil Procedure] (Germany) s. 1047(3) ('the respective other party is to be made aware of any written pleadings, documents, and other communications that a party may submit to the arbitral tribunal, while expert reports and other written evidence on which the arbitral tribunal may base its decision are to be sent to both parties for their information').
20. Wetboek van Burgerlijke Rechtsvordering [Dutch Code of Civil Procedure] (Netherlands) Art. 1036 (2) ('the arbitral tribunal shall give the parties the opportunity to set out and explain their

Subsequent judicial practice of State Parties shows that a tribunal's denial of one party's opportunity to comment on the counterparty's submissions, either orally or in writing, may constitute a violation of due process.[21] For instance, the District Court of Bremen refused to enforce an award because the respondent had not been informed of the claimant's arguments. The court held that it was not sufficient for due process to have the mere possibility of submitting documents on a disputed contract or giving an opinion without knowing the opponent's arguments.[22] In recent cases, it is uncommon for a tribunal to fail to give a party any opportunity to comment on submissions by the counterparty. Instead, it is more frequent to see cases where one party was not granted an opportunity to respond to a particular factual or legal submission. For instance, the Court of Appeal in Hague upheld the decision of the District Court in Rotterdam to refuse the enforcement of an award. This was due to the claimant being permitted to submit new documents before the hearing without giving the defendant an opportunity to comment on them. The court considered that the tribunal's denial of the defendant's chance to respond to the newly submitted documents by the counterparty violated the fundamental right to adversarial proceedings and constituted a breach of due process.[23]

However, the denial of the opportunity to comment on a particular legal argument or evidence does not necessarily breach one party's right to comment if the counterparty did not raise any new factual or legal arguments in their submission or if the tribunal clearly did not rely on such evidence or legal arguments to make the decision. For example, in a case before the English High Court, the opposing party claimed the due process defence on the grounds that it was not given an oral reply to the counterparty's oral submission. However, the court rejected this claim, stating that the counterparty had not raised any new points that had not already been covered in the hearing and therefore had not been addressed on behalf of the opposing party either orally or in writing.[24] In another case before the Hamm Court of Appeal, the opposing party argued that the applicant had submitted a document to the tribunal only three days before the oral hearing, which was so close to the hearing that it did not have enough time to prepare its rebuttal. However, the German court rejected the due process argument on the grounds that the arbitral award did not indicate that the tribunal had considered the document, and the opposing party did not prove that the

---

positions and to comment on each other's positions and all documents and other information brought to the attention of the arbitral tribunal during the proceedings. The arbitral tribunal shall not base its decision, where it is unfavourable for one party, upon documents and other information on which that party was not sufficiently able to comment').

21. Arrondissementsrechtbank Rotterdam [District Court of Rotterdam], 2 October 1997 reported in (1998) XXIII *Yearbook Commercial Arbitration* 731, 732 [5] (upheld by Gerechtshof the Hague [Court of Appeal of the Hague], 28 April 1998 reported in (1998) XXIII *Yearbook Commercial Arbitration* 731); Landgericht [Court of First Instance] of Bremen, 20 January 1983 reported in (1987) XII *Yearbook Commercial Arbitration* 486, 486.
22. Landgericht [Court of First Instance] of Bremen, 20 January 1983 reported in (1987) XII *Yearbook Commercial Arbitration* 486, 486 [2].
23. Arrondissementsrechtbank Rotterdam [District Court of Rotterdam], 2 October 1997 reported in (1998) XXIII *Yearbook Commercial Arbitration* 731, 732 [5] (upheld by Gerechtshof the Hague [Court of Appeal of the Hague], 28 April 1998 reported in (1998) XXIII *Yearbook Commercial Arbitration* 731).
24. *Margulead Ltd v. Exide Tech* [2004] EWHC 1019 (6 May 2004) [26]–[29].

document contained any new factual arguments.[25] However, in some cases, proving that new factual or legal arguments have influenced the tribunal's decision can be challenging since the tribunal is not obligated to provide reasons for an award.[26] Additionally, as discussed in §5.04, it is not recommended to assess whether the exclusion of comments on the counterparty's factual or legal arguments has affected the award, as evaluating the merits of the award is prohibited. Nevertheless, under the pro-enforcement policy, enforcing courts may enforce an award when there is evident contrary evidence in the award showing that the tribunal did not consider such new documents without the risk of reviewing the merits.

[B] The Right to Comment on Findings of the Tribunal

In practice, there is a risk of violating parties' right to be heard when arbitrators take initiatives to investigate facts or the content of applicable law without giving parties the opportunity to comment on this independent research. Also, arbitrators' factual or legal investigations may violate the principles of equality of arms and impartiality. If an arbitrator takes the initiative to obtain evidence of facts or law, there is every prospect that the new facts or legal arguments will have a bearing on the substantive outcome, potentially benefiting one party and disadvantaging the other. This could raise concerns about the arbitrator's impartiality and the parties' equality of arms.[27]

A tribunal's ex officio factual investigations can include publicly available information, an arbitrator's specific knowledge or expertise, and individual research, such as the consultation of an expert without the parties' knowledge. In terms of laws, in certain civil law courts, the principle of *iura novit curia* (judges know the law) is often followed. According to this principle, the judge can apply the law ex officio without being bound by the legal arguments raised by the parties. To a certain extent, this principle may influence arbitral practices, particularly when arbitrators, counsel and parties are from different jurisdictions. In the context of international arbitration, the question arises as to whether the tribunal can rely on its own research or knowledge of the applicable law beyond the legal arguments or reasoning pleaded by the parties without giving the parties the opportunity to comment.

Article V(1)(d) of the New York Convention requires arbitral procedures to follow the agreement of the parties or, failing such agreement, follow the law of the country where the arbitration takes place. VCLT's 'context, object and purpose' interpretation requires enforcing courts to consider parties' agreement, including their agreed arbitration rules and the discretion of the tribunal, as well as the *lex arbitri* regarding arbitrators' independent legal investigations when determining the due process defence under the New York Convention. Accordingly, this section examines

25. Hamm Oberlandesgericht [Hamm Court of Appeal], 25 Sch 09/08, 28 November 2008 reported in (2009) XXXIV *Yearbook Commercial Arbitration* 536, 541 [13].
26. *See* §7.04[B].
27. Gisela Knuts, 'Jura Novit Curia and the Right to Be Heard – An Analysis of Recent Case Law' (2012) 28(4) *Arbitration International* 669, 674 DOI: 10.1093/arbitration/28.4.669.

these sources, along with subsequent judicial practices of State Parties when dealing with the due process defence. The aim is to address the issues of arbitrators' ex officio factual and legal investigations and their implications for due process.

[1] Arbitrators' Independent Investigations of Facts and Parties' Right to Be Heard

This subsection first discusses the powers of arbitrators to investigate facts under *lex arbitri* and applicable arbitration rules and how this relates to the scope of Article V(1)(b) of the New York Convention under the interpretative approach required by the VCLT. Arbitration statutes in various countries, including Switzerland,[28] Germany,[29] China,[30] and the UK,[31] grant arbitrators the authority to initiate fact-finding. However, in some jurisdictions, such as the Netherlands, a tribunal's independent investigations are only lawful with the parties' explicit prior authorisation.[32]

Arbitration rules, such as the UNCITRAL Rules,[33] HKIAC Rules,[34] ICC Rules,[35] SCC Rules,[36] and SIAC Rules,[37] generally empower an arbitral tribunal to take initiatives to obtain facts from the parties. However, there are some exceptions, such as the LCIA Rules[38] and the CIETAC Arbitration Rules,[39] where unequivocal statements give arbitrators the power to take initiatives to obtain factual evidence independently of the parties, provided that the parties are given a reasonable opportunity to state their views. When national arbitration statutes and applicable arbitration rules permit the tribunal to appoint one or more experts to report on specific factual issues after consulting the parties,[40] at the request of any party, the tribunal-appointed expert shall

---

28. *Federal Act on Private International Law* (Switzerland) 18 December 1987, Art. 184 [Andreas Bucher trans, The English translations of Federal Act on Private International Law, http://www.andreasbucher-law.ch/images/stories/pil_act_1987_as_amended_until_1_7_2014.pdf] ('[t]he arbitral tribunal shall itself take the evidence').
29. *Zivilprozessordnung* [Code of Civil Procedure] (Germany) § 1042(4).
30. 《中华人民共和国仲裁法》 [Arbitration Law of the People's Republic of China] Standing Committee of the National People's Congress, Order of the President of the People's Republic of China [2017] No. 76, promulgated on 1 September 2017, effective on 1 January 2018, Art. 43 ('an arbitral tribunal may collect evidence on its own if it considers necessary').
31. *Arbitration Act* 1996 (UK) c 23, s. 34.
32. District Court of Rotterdam (Rechtbank Rotterdam), ECLI:NL:RBROT:2005:AU7659, 21 April 2005.
33. *UNCITRAL Arbitration Rules*, UN Doc. A/RES/65/22 (n. 10) Art. 27(3).
34. *HKIAC Arbitration Rules* (n. 5) Art. 22(3).
35. *ICC Arbitration Rules* (n. 11) Art. 25(5).
36. *SCC Arbitration Rules* (n. 5) Art. 31(3).
37. *SIAC Arbitration Rules* (n. 10) Art. 20(6).
38. *LCIA Arbitration Rules* (n. 10) Art. 22(1)(iii).
39. China International Economic and Trade Arbitration Commission, Arbitration Rules (effective on 1 January 2015) Art. 43.
40. *UNCITRAL Model Law*, UN Docs A/40/17 and A/61/17 (n. 3) Art. 26; *UNCITRAL Arbitration Rules*, UN Doc. A/RES/65/22 (n. 10) Art. 29; *ICC Arbitration Rules* (n. 11) Art. 25(4); *LCIA Arbitration Rules* (n. 10) Art. 21(1); *SCC Arbitration Rules* (n. 5) Art. 34(1); *HKIAC Arbitration Rules* (n. 5) Art. 25(1); *SIAC Arbitration Rules* (n. 10) Art. 26(1)(a).

participate in a hearing to be examined by the parties so that parties can comment on the expert's findings.[41]

Enforcing courts have confirmed that a violation of due process occurs when the tribunal concludes the award based on its own investigations into the facts without giving parties the opportunity to comment on its findings.[42] In a case before the Supreme Court of Hong Kong, the tribunal issued the final award based on factual findings from expert reports appointed by the tribunal, which the opposing party had asked for but had not been given the opportunity to comment thereon. The judge considered that the right of the defendants to comment on these reports was such a fundamental right that he could not conceive that the position would be otherwise.[43] The judge ruled that a party was entitled to adduce evidence to rebut the view of the tribunal-appointed expert, and the fact that the defendants were prevented from presenting their case constituted a violation of their right to a fair and equal opportunity to be heard.[44]

Parties' right to be heard may be violated when the tribunal bases its decision, fully or in part, on its own independent factual investigations without giving parties the opportunity to comment. This can be illustrated by a case before the Hong Kong Court of Appeal. The court found that the tribunal had conducted its own investigations into the Guangdong Province State-Owned Land Office to establish facts and based its award on the findings without informing the parties or inviting their submissions.[45] Therefore, the court concluded that there was a procedural irregularity and refused to enforce the award.

With respect to a tribunal's inquisitorial powers, courts have made a distinction between evidence and inferences that can be drawn from it. For the former, courts have held that the tribunal must provide each party with a reasonable opportunity to present its position on the evidence. In contrast, for the latter, tribunals 'have autonomy in drawing inferences as they deem fit' and 'are entitled to depart from the positions advanced by the parties'.[46] For instance, where the parties had been given a reasonable opportunity to present their factual evidence, but the tribunal applied a method of calculating damages that neither party had raised or argued during the arbitration, this would not be considered a violation of the right to be heard.[47] For instance, in the case of *Brunswick Bowling*, the respondents claimed that the tribunal had violated due

41. *UNCITRAL Arbitration Rules*, UN Doc. A/RES/65/22 (n. 10) Art. 29; *UNCITRAL Model Law*, UN Docs A/40/17 and A/61/17 (n. 3) Art. 26; *SIAC Arbitration Rules* (n. 10) Art. 26; *SCC Arbitration Rules* (n. 5) Art. 34; *LCIA Arbitration Rules* (n. 10) Art. 21(4); *ICC Arbitration Rules* (n. 11) Art. 25(4); *HKIAC Arbitration Rules* (n. 5) Art. 25; *Arbitration Act 1996* (UK) c 23, s. 37; *Swedish Arbitration Act* (Sweden) SFS No. 1996:116, s. 25 [Joel Dahlquist Cullborg trans, *The Swedish Arbitration Act* (2019), https://sccinstitute.com/media/408924/the-swedish-arbitration-act_1march2019_eng.pdf].
42. *Minmetals Germany GmbH v. Ferco Steel Ltd* [1999] CLC 647, 656.
43. *Paklito Investment Ltd v. Klockner East Asia Ltd* [1993] 2 HKLR 39, 46.
44. *Ibid.*, 47.
45. *Apex Tech Investment Ltd v. Chuang's Development (China) Ltd* [1996] 2 HKLR 155, 157.
46. *Brunswick Bowling & Billiards Corp v. Shanghai Zhonglu Industrial Co Ltd* [2011] 1 HKLRD 707, [26].
47. *X Chartering v. Y* [2014] HKCFI 494, [13].

process by awarding damages based on loss of revenue, while the claimant had formulated its claim based on loss of profits. The argument was rejected by the Hong Kong court because the award of damages was not based on any findings of primary facts that were not discussed in the evidence. Instead, it was based on the evidence or facts disclosed to the parties, and the arbitrators' opinion differed from that of the parties regarding the quantum of damages.[48]

[2] Arbitrators' Independent Investigations of Law and Parties' Right to Be Heard

First, this section examines the extent to which arbitrators are empowered to investigate the law under *lex arbitri* and applicable arbitration rules. It then shows how this is relevant to the scope of Article V(1)(b) of the New York Convention under the interpretative approach required by the VCLT. The tribunal's power to investigate the law in arbitral proceedings raises the question of the applicability of *iura novit curia* to arbitration. The *iura novit curia* principle is a component of civil procedure that governs the behaviour of judges in state courts.[49] This principle is based on the premise that the court knows the law and will therefore apply it *sua sponte*, beyond the parties' submissions of legal arguments and reasoning.[50] However, in international arbitration, *iura novit curia* does not apply to arbitrators automatically. Arbitrators do not have the *lex fori* granted to judges. Unless an arbitrator is an expert in certain national laws, arbitrators cannot be assumed to have knowledge of the applicable laws in international commercial arbitration, especially in transnational disputes where parties come from different jurisdictions. Often, arbitrators are called upon to decide matters of law under legal systems in which they have little or no experience or training. Most importantly, arbitrators derive their authority to resolve disputes from the parties, making them non-national and neutral. This distinguishes them from national courts, which possess the *jure imperii* of the state.[51]

As shown in Article V(1)(d) of the New York Convention, party autonomy is the guiding principle in determining the arbitral proceedings.[52] The parties may confer upon the arbitral tribunal the power to raise legal arguments not pleaded by the parties

48. *Brunswick Bowling & Billiards Corp v. Shanghai Zhonglu Industrial Co Ltd* [2011] 1 HKLRD 707, [50]–[52].
49. Phillip Landolt, 'Arbitrators' Initiatives to Obtain Factual and Legal Evidence' (2012) 28(2) *Arbitration International* 173, 184 DOI: 10.1093/arbitration/28.2.173.
50. Filip JM De Ly, Mark Friedman and Luca Radicati di Brozolo, 'International Law Association International Commercial Arbitration Committee's Report and Recommendations on "Ascertaining the Contents of the Applicable Law in International Commercial Arbitration"*Report for the Biennial Conference in Rio de Janeiro, August 2008' (2010) 26(2) *Arbitration International* 193, 193–220 DOI: 10.1093/arbitration/26.2.191.
51. Teresa Giovannini, 'Ex Officio Powers to Investigate: When Do Arbitrators Cross the Line?' in Bernd Ehle and Domitille Baizeau (eds), *Stories from the Hearing Room: Experience from Arbitral Practice (Essays in Honour of Michael E Schneider)* (Kluwer Law International, 2015) 63.
52. It is a principle that is endorsed not only in national laws but also by leading arbitral institutions, as well as by international instruments such as the New York Convention. *See*, *UNCITRAL Model Law*, UN Docs A/40/17 and A/61/17 (n. 3) Art. 19(1); *ICC Arbitration Rules* (n. 11) Art. 19; *LCIA*

as they consider appropriate to the specific case. In the absence of parties' explicit authorisation, the arbitral tribunal resorts to the *lex arbitri* and applicable arbitral rules to determine whether it has the power. As shown below, *iura novit curia* is generally not a part of the *lex arbitri* in most jurisdictions, except for Switzerland, Finland, and Sweden.

Most national arbitration statutes and applicable arbitration rules rarely regulate whether the tribunal should plead and prove the content of law ex officio. Instead, they usually provide the tribunal with broad discretion regarding the conduct of arbitral proceedings, subject to ensuring the parties have the opportunity to present their case.[53] Even though some arbitration statutes and applicable arbitration rules, such as the English Arbitration Act, Hong Kong Arbitration Ordinance and LCIA Rules, explicitly empower arbitrators to decide whether and to what extent they should take the initiative in ascertaining the content of applicable law,[54] arbitrators are still obliged to ensure that the hearing is conducted fairly and that parties are given reasonable opportunities to present their case.[55]

Switzerland, Sweden, and Finland are exceptions to the rule. Although their national arbitration statutes do not expressly empower the tribunal to apply ex officio legal arguments or legal reasoning that are not invoked in parties' submissions, their case law has confirmed the applicability of *iura novit curia* in arbitration concerning domestic disputes without giving parties an opportunity to comment. For instance, the Swiss Supreme Court has consistently held that arbitrators may apply legal arguments ex officio without violating the right to be heard, as long as the legal argument or authority relied upon in the award would not surprise the parties.[56] However, Swiss court decisions on the 'surprise application of the law' and the judgment of foreseeability create uncertainty in the criteria.[57] Determining the extent to which a legal argument or provision would surprise the parties is not always straightforward. It is important to note that examining courts in terms of the 'surprise application of the law' may result in a review of merits, which is prohibited by most national arbitration statutes. Although the Swedish Arbitration Act does not explicitly address the applicability of *iura novit curia*, the *travaux préparatoires* of the Act stated that, at least in domestic disputes, the principle of *iura novit curia* should be assumed to apply to

Arbitration Rules (n. 10) Art. 14(2); *Convention on the Recognition and Enforcement of Foreign Arbitral Awards*, open for signature 10 June 1958, 330 UNTS 3 (entered into force 7 June 1959) Art. V(1)(d).

53. *UNCITRAL Model Law*, UN Docs A/40/17 and A/61/17 (n. 3) Arts 18, 19; *UNCITRAL Arbitration Rules*, UN Doc. A/RES/65/22 (n .10) Art. 17(1); *ICC Arbitration Rules* (n. 11) Art. 22(4); *LCIA Arbitration Rules* (n. 10) Art. 14(4)(i); *SCC Arbitration Rules* (n. 5) Art. 23(2); *HKIAC Arbitration Rules* (n. 5) Art. 13(1).
54. *Arbitration Ordinance* (Hong Kong) cap 609, s. 56(7); *Arbitration Act 1996* (UK) c 23, s. 34; *LCIA Arbitration Rules* (n. 10) Art. 22(1)(c).
55. For the right to be heard, *see Arbitration Ordinance* (Hong Kong) cap 60, s. 46; *Arbitration Act 1996* (UK) c 23, s. 33; *LCIA Arbitration Rules* (n. 10) Art. 14(4).
56. Swiss Federal Tribunal Decision, No. 4P.100/2003, 30 September 2003 reported in (2004) 22 *ASA Bulletin* 574; Manuel Arroyo, 'Chapter 2, Part II: Commentary on Chapter 12 PILS, Article 190 [Finality, Challenge: Principle]' in Manuel Arroyo (ed.), *Arbitration in Switzerland: The Practitioner's Guide* (Kluwer Law International, 2nd ed., 2018) 315–316; Knuts (n. 27) 675–676.
57. Knuts (n. 27) 682–686.

arbitral proceedings for the time being.[58] Similarly, the Finnish Supreme Court held that arbitrators were not limited to the point of law pleaded by the parties and thus refused to set aside an award governed by Finnish law, even though the tribunal did not bring it to the parties' attention.[59]

However, it appears that even courts in Switzerland, Sweden, and Finland do not apply *iura novit curia* to the recognition and enforcement of awards under the New York Convention.[60] Also, for enforcement in other states, awards made in Switzerland, Sweden, and Finland should respect parties' right to be heard when the tribunal is entitled to conduct independent legal research that is not advanced by the parties.

As shown in §3.03, national arbitration statutes typically mandate that the arbitral tribunal guarantees the parties' right to be heard, which has been well accepted as one of the attributes of the general principle of due process. Thus, for the recognition and enforcement of the New York Convention, even if the *lex arbitri* or applicable arbitration rules may entitle a tribunal to rely on legal grounds that are not submitted by the parties, the tribunal shall seek the parties' views on these legal grounds.[61] Subsequent judicial practice of State Parties, both in common law (e.g., UK and Hong Kong) and civil law jurisdictions (e.g., France and Quebec), shows that the right to be

58. Christer Danielsson, 'Chapter 8: Applicable Law' in Anneette Magnusson and Jakob Rognwaldh (eds), *International Arbitration in Sweden: A Practitioner's Guide* (Kluwer Law International, 2nd ed., 2021) 210; Jakob Ragnwaldh, Fredrik Andersson and Celeste E Salinas Quero, *A Guide to the SCC Arbitration Rules* (Wolters Kluwer, 2019) 86 (the commentary to the 2017 SCC Rules considers that *iura novit curia* applies in domestic arbitration in Sweden, while 'this practice is not widely accepted in international arbitration'). Regarding opposite views, *see* Kaj Hobér, *International Commercial Arbitration in Sweden* (Oxford University Press, 2011) 317 (arguing that even in domestic arbitration, arbitrators should ensure that the parties are properly informed of how and which laws and legal principles might be applied by the arbitrators to avoid surprises to the parties once the award is rendered).
59. *Werfen Austria GmbH v. Polar Electro Europé BV, Zug branch*, Case No. S2006/716, decision by the Finnish Supreme Court of 2 July 2008, reported in 2008(3) Stockholm International Arbitration Review 259 (in this case, both parties were non-Finnish).
60. For Switzerland, *see* Gabrielle Kaufmann-Kohler, 'The Governing Law: Fact or Law? – A Transnational Rule on Establishing Its Contents' (2006) 26 *ASA Special Series* 79, 84. For Sweden, *see* above n. 58; Hobér (n. 58) 257, 317.
61. For commentaries, *see* Knuts (n. 27) 673, 680; Ieva Kalnina, 'Iura Novit Curia: Scylla and Charybdis of International Arbitration?' (2008) 8(1) *Baltic Yearbook of International Law* 89, 101; Scherer (n. 2) 307; Claus Werner Von Wobeser Hoepfner, 'The Effective Use of Legal Sources: How Much Is Too Much and What Is the Role for Iura Novit Curia?' in Albert Jan van den Berg (ed.), *Arbitration Advocacy in Changing Times* (Kluwer Law International, 2011) 207, 213–214; Kaufmann-Kohler, 'The Governing Law: Fact or Law?'(n. 60) 84; Emmanuel Gaillard and John Savage (eds), *Fouchard Gaillard Goldman on International Commercial Arbitration* (Kluwer Law International, 1999) 692. For arbitration rules and arbitration practice, *see also* Polish Chamber of Commerce, *Arbitration Rules* (adopted on 1 January 2015) Art. 6(2) ('an award may not be based on legal grounds different from those relied on by either of the parties unless the Arbitral Tribunal notifies the parties in advance and gives them an opportunity to be heard concerning such legal grounds'); *Rules on the Efficient Conduct of Proceedings in International Arbitration* (Prague Rules, adopted 14 December 2018) Art. 7.2 ('the arbitral tribunal may apply legal provisions not pleaded by the parties if it finds it necessary, including, but not limited to, public policy rules. In such cases, the arbitral tribunal shall *seek* the parties' views on the legal provisions it intends to apply. The arbitral tribunal may also rely on legal authorities even if not submitted by the parties if they relate to legal provisions pleaded by the parties and provided that the parties have been given an opportunity to express their views in relation to such legal authorities').

heard should prevail regardless of whether the *iura novit curia* principle applies when determining the due process defence under the New York Convention.

English courts have consistently demonstrated a rigorous concern for protecting the right to be heard properly, undistorted by any effects of the *iura novit curia* principle. In *Malicorp*, for instance, the English High Court refused to enforce an award because the remedies granted were based on arguments that were not presented by the parties.[62] The tribunal did not rule on the respondent's claim of entitlement to avoid the concession contract for fraud. Instead, the tribunal ruled that there had been an 'essential mistake' under Article 142 of the Egyptian Civil Code that the parties had not argued. The tribunal then granted damages to the claimant, Malicorp, based on this 'essential mistake'.[63] The English High Court noted that granting remedies on a basis that was neither pleaded nor argued could be capable of falling within 'unable to present its case'.[64] The English High Court argued that the award of damages under Article 142 of the Egyptian Civil Code came as a complete surprise to the respondent (Egypt), and it was necessary to inform the respondent of the basis on which the tribunal would grant any remedy and decide the amount of any monetary award.[65] Although the English High Court had the discretion to enforce the award despite due process violations, it declined to do so. This was because the tribunal failed to ensure that parties were informed of the basis on which damages would be calculated, which constituted a serious breach of natural justice under English law.[66]

The French courts take the same approach as the English courts. Malicorp also applied for the enforcement of the award in France. The French Court of Cassation rejected Malicorp's request for enforcement because the tribunal's decision violated due process by relying on legal provisions of the Egyptian Civil Code that were not argued by the parties.[67] Similarly, in a case before the Court of Appeal of Paris, the tribunal's decision was based on a legal principle of Austrian law that neither party had presented.[68] The Court of Appeal of Paris held that the tribunal had not respected the due process principle since it had based its decision on a legal principle on its own motion without giving the parties an opportunity to comment on its application. This approach is also followed in Quebec. In the case of *Dreyfus v. Tusculum*,[69] the tribunal issued a partial award terminating the joint venture agreement based on the doctrine of frustration under New York law, even though neither party had pleaded this doctrine

---

62. *Malicorp Ltd v. Government of the Arab Republic of Egypt, Egyptian Holding Co for Aviation & Egyptian Airports Co* [2015] EWHC 361 (Comm) (19 February 2015) ('Malicorp').
63. *Ibid.*, [35].
64. *Ibid.*, [31].
65. *Ibid.*, [32], [41].
66. *Ibid.*, [42].
67. Cour de Cassation [French Court of Cassation], 23 June 2010 reported in (2011) *Revue de l'Arbitrage* 446, 448.
68. Case Reference CA Paris, Pôle 1, 1 Re Ch, 3 Dec 2009, No RG:08/13618, Cour d'appel de Paris [Paris Court of Appeal]. *See also* Case Reference CA Paris, Pôle 1-Chambree1, 15 March 2016, Cour d'appel de Paris [Paris Court of Appeal], https://www.italaw.com/sites/default/files/case-documents/italaw7208.pdf; Court of Cassation, First Civil Chamber, 29 June 2011, No. 10-23. 321, https://www.courdecassation.fr/jurisprudence_2/premiere_chambre_civile_568/785_29_20477.html.
69. *Louis Dreyfus SAS v. Holding Tusculum BV* [2008] QCCS 5903.

as grounds for termination. The Quebec Supreme Court held that the tribunal had violated due process by applying a remedy that neither party had requested.

Hong Kong courts have consistently held that the tribunal should provide parties with the opportunity to address any new issues raised by the tribunal on its own motion.[70] For instance, in the case of *Brunswick Bowling*, the tribunal made its own assessment of contractual requirements under Chinese law without taking into account the evidence adduced by the parties on Chinese law and other applicable laws. The tribunal awarded damages to the claimant for conversion under Chinese law despite both parties arguing that Illinois law applied to the conversion. The Hong Kong court ruled that due process had been breached as the parties were not given an opportunity to present their case on the tribunal's views regarding the validity of the contract and its conversion under Chinese law.[71]

[3] Expert Arbitrators

The use of 'expert arbitrators' who are chosen for their expertise in a particular field raises questions about whether they can apply their expertise to factual or legal issues without allowing parties to make submissions on the matter. In the case of *Grand Pacific Holdings*, the Hong Kong Court of First Instance held, which was confirmed by the Court of Appeal, that the award based on New York law authorities that had not been disclosed to the parties for further submission thereon was not such a serious matter as to constitute a violation of the parties' right to present their case. The court came to this decision because the tribunal members all had legal education or were licensed to practise law in New York. Therefore, they were capable of dealing with a New York law issue without relying on the parties or evidence related to the matter at hand.[72]

When parties choose their own expert arbitrators, they may agree that expert arbitrators can use their specialised knowledge to decide their disputes by raising new arguments or issues that have not been considered by the parties. Nevertheless, this does not mean that the parties intended to allow expert arbitrators to resolve the dispute based on their privately discussed arguments and issues without inviting parties to make submissions on them. The parties only imply that they desire the appointed arbitrators to be more capable of addressing the dispute due to their knowledge and experience.

In some cases, the parties may not have agreed to appoint an expert arbitrator. Instead, it may be that one party manifestly nominated an arbitrator due to their particular skill and experience in certain factual or legal matters. The tribunal must balance one party's desire for a more active tribunal with the other party's request for

70. *Tronic International Pte Ltd v. Topco Scientific Co Ltd* [2016] HKEC 1780, [20]-[21]. *See also Paklito Investment Ltd v. Klockner East Asia Ltd* [1993] 2 HKLR 39.
71. *Brunswick Bowling & Billiards Corp v. Shanghai Zhonglu Industrial Co Ltd* [2011] 1 HKLRD 707, [67].
72. *Pacific China Holdings Ltd (in liq) v. Grand Pacific Holdings Ltd* [2011] 4 HKLRD 188, [142]-[145].

the tribunal's autonomy. The impartiality of arbitrators may be called into question if they are required to act as both arbitrators and experts. This is because arbitrators may give more weight to their own assessment than to that of other experts involved, which would violate the principle of equality of arms and impartiality if the expert arbitrator distinguishes between the parties in taking initiatives. Arbitrators must remain independent and impartial and give equal treatment to both parties throughout the whole arbitral proceedings. This requires an expert arbitrator who is nominated by one party to seek the views of both parties on its mandate to take factual or legal initiatives to guarantee the parties' right to be heard.

Some cases confirm that when a tribunal relies on its own knowledge to decide factual or legal issues, the failure to provide parties with an opportunity to comment on the result of the tribunal's investigations breaches the right to be heard. This is illustrated by a set-aside decision of the Paris Court of Appeal. In this case, the presiding arbitrator partially translated and *proprio motu* extracted parts of an expertise report from German to French, which was the language of the arbitral proceedings. However, the parties were not given the opportunity to comment on the translated material. The tribunal then issued its award based on the French version of the report.[73] The Paris Court of Appeal held that this derogation from the language of the arbitration constituted a breach of due process and thus set aside the award. Since the grounds for setting aside international arbitral awards in France are directly referred to in the context of recognition and enforcement of foreign arbitral awards under the New York Convention,[74] and the due process ground is applied by French case law in the same manner to setting-aside and enforcement proceedings,[75] the relevant setting-aside French decisions concerning due process have the value of reference as well.

The Dutch courts adopt the same stance as the Paris Court of Appeal when an arbitrator conducts their own research or assessment using their knowledge. The Dutch courts have held that not allowing parties to comment on an arbitrator's independent research may infringe on the parties' right to be heard and raise concerns about the arbitrator's impartiality. In a case before the Rotterdam District Court, the claimant challenged the impartiality of arbitrators in a medical arbitration on the basis that they had acted as both arbitrators and medical experts.[76] The court held that the arbitrators' medical expertise enabled them to better evaluate the medical evidence before them. However, the arbitrators were not appointed to conduct their own examination of the claimant (patient).[77] The court held that acting as both arbitrators and experts may raise questions about the impartiality of arbitrators since they might

73. Cour de Cassation, First Civil Chamber, 18 March 2015, No. 13-22.391.
74. *Code de procédure civile* [Code of Civil Procedure] (France) 13 January 2011, Art. 1525 [Emmanuel Gaillard et al., Code of Civil Procedure, https://sccinstitute.com/media/37105/french_law_on_arbitration.pdf].
75. Caroline Kleiner, 'Chapter 7: Country Report: France' in Friedrich Rosenfeld, Dietmar Czernich and Franco Ferrari (eds), *Due Process as a Limit to Discretion in International Commercial Arbitration* (Kluwer Law International, 2020) 171.
76. District Court of Rotterdam (Rechtbank Rotterdam), ECLI:NL:RBROT:2005:AU7659, 21 April 2005.
77. *Ibid.*, [3.5].

place more weight on their own assessment than that of other experts involved.[78] On appeal, the Dutch Supreme Court confirmed the decision of the District Court and emphasised that arbitrators appointed for their expertise were not entitled to conduct independent expert assessments unless parties expressly allowed them to consider the research outcome as evidence and use it in their decision. Even though the parties permit arbitrators to conduct independent research, arbitrators still need to ensure the parties' right to be heard and grant them opportunities to comment on the methodology and results of the arbitrators' research.[79]

To conclude, the tribunal may conduct its own research on points of fact and law not argued by the parties, as permitted by some arbitration statutes or applicable arbitration rules. However, most arbitration statutes and leading arbitration rules still oblige arbitrators to ensure the parties' right to be heard, as confirmed by the judicial practice of State Parties when interpreting and applying the due process defence.

§7.04 THE RIGHT TO HAVE SUBMISSIONS CONSIDERED

The right to present one's case would be undermined if the tribunal could disregard parties' submissions at will. As a corollary of the right to be heard, the arbitral tribunal must guarantee the parties' right to have their submissions considered.[80] This requires the tribunal to listen to and assess parties' submissions and give them due consideration when deciding the award. Enforcing courts usually respect the tribunal's discretion regarding the admissibility, relevance, materiality, and weight of evidence, as demonstrated in this section. While tribunals are not required to discuss all parties' submissions in detail in the award's reasoning, the right to present one's case may be breached if it is evident that the tribunal did not acknowledge or consider the parties' core submissions.[81]

[A] The Exclusion and Admission of Evidence

National arbitration statutes[82] and leading institutional arbitration rules[83] generally grant tribunals broad discretion regarding the admissibility, relevance, materiality, and weight of evidence. Article V(1)(d) of the New York Convention requires enforcing courts to respect parties' agreed arbitration rules on proceedings and failing such agreement to follow the law of the country where the award was made. VCLT's contextual interpretation requires enforcing courts to consider the requirements of

78. *Ibid.*
79. Supreme Court (Hoge Raad), ECLI:NL:HR:2007:AV7405, 29 June 2007 [3.3.4].
80. Oberlandesgericht Celle [Court of Appeal Celle], 8 Sch 06/06, 31 May 2007 reported in (2008) XXXIII *Yearbook Commercial Arbitration* 524.
81. *A v. B* [2015] 3 HKLRD 586, [33].
82. *UNCITRAL Model Law*, UN Docs A/40/17 and A/61/17 (n. 3) Art. 19(2); *Arbitration Act 1996* (UK) c 23, s. 34(2)(f).
83. *SCC Arbitration Rules* (n. 5) Art. 31(1); *UNCITRAL Arbitration Rules*, UN Doc. A/RES/65/22 (n. 10) Art. 27(4); *SIAC Arbitration Rules* (n. 10) Art. 19(2); *LCIA Arbitration Rules* (n. 10) Art. 22(1)(vi); *HKIAC Arbitration Rules* (n. 5) Art. 22(2).

Article V(1)(d) when interpreting and applying Article V(1)(b). Accordingly, enforcing courts generally defer to tribunals' broad discretion when dealing with evidence and are inclined to reject the opposing party's due process defence based solely on the tribunal's evidentiary rulings regarding the exclusion or admission of specific evidence unless such exclusion or admission of relevant evidence deprives a party of a fair hearing.[84] Additionally, enforcing courts generally consider the tribunal's conduct as a whole when deciding whether the exclusion or admission of certain evidence deprived parties of their right to be heard.

For instance, in a case before the Brazilian Superior Court of Justice, the award-debtor alleged that due process had been violated since the arbitral tribunal rejected the evidence presented by the award-debtor and the examination of witnesses via videoconference. The court ruled that the rejection of evidence did not violate due process as the tribunal had given the opposing party an opportunity to defend itself and present its case.[85]

As another example, US courts also held that arbitrators have 'wide discretion to require the exchange of evidence, and to admit or exclude evidence, how and when they see fit',[86] unless 'the arbitrators were guilty of misconduct in refusing to hear evidence pertinent and material to the controversy'.[87] Accordingly, '[a]n arbitrator is not bound to hear all of the evidence tendered by the parties...[H]e must [merely] give each of the parties to the dispute an adequate opportunity to present its evidence and arguments'.[88] In the *Parsons* case, the opposing party requested due process relief from the New York Convention due to the tribunal's refusal to postpone proceedings to accommodate the schedule of one of its witnesses. The US Court of Appeals for the Second Circuit held that the arbitral tribunal was not obligated to hear all the evidence presented by the parties. The court held that the inability to produce witnesses before an arbitral tribunal is a risk that is inherent in an agreement to submit to arbitration. By agreeing to submit disputes to arbitration, a party relinquishes their courtroom rights, including the right to subpoena witnesses.[89] In US case law, a tribunal's refusal to hear evidence can only be justified if it demonstrates bad faith or amounts to misconduct,[90] including refusing to accept or give weight to crucial and otherwise acceptable

84. *Generica Ltd v. Pharmaceutical Basics, Inc*, 125 F 3d 1123, 1130 (7th Cir, 1997).
85. STJ SEC 611, Reporting Justice João Otávio de Noronha, 11 December 2006. For a detailed discussion, *see* Rafael Francisco Alves, 'Chapter 3: Country Report: Brazil' in Friedrich Rosenfeld, Dietmar Czernich and Franco Ferrari (eds), *Due Process as a Limit to Discretion in International Commercial Arbitration* (Kluwer Law International, 2020) 55, 72.
86. *Indus Risk Insurers v. MAN Gutenhoffnungshutte GmbH*, 141 F 3d 1434, 1444 (11th Cir, 1998); *US Life Ins Co v. Superior Nat'l Ins Co*, 591 F 3d 1167, 1175 (9th Cir, 2010).
87. 9 USC § 10(a)(3) (2012). US courts have consistently held that tribunals should take evidence on disputed facts that are *relevant* and *material*: *see Hoteles Condado Beach, La Concha & Convention Center v. Union De Tronquistas Local 901*, 763 F 2d 34, 39–40 (1st Cir, 1985); *Tempo Shain Corp v. Bertek Inc*, 120 F 3d 16, 19–21 (2nd Cir, 1997).
88. *Generica Ltd v. Pharm Basics Inc*, 125 F 3d 1123, 1130 (7th Cir, 1997).
89. *Parsons & Whittemore Overseas Co v. Société Générale De L'Industrie Du Papier (RAKTA)*, 508 F 2d 969, 975 (2nd Cir, 1974).
90. *United Paperworkers Int'l Union, AFLCIO v. Misco Inc*, 484 US 29, 38 (1987); *Immersion Corp v. Sony Computer Enter Am LLC*, 188 F Supp 3d 960, 974 (ND Cal, 2016).

evidence.[91] In the *Dastime* case, the District Court in California held that the party arguing for non-enforcement must establish that the arbitrator's evidentiary determinations were made in bad faith or resulted in a denial of a meaningful opportunity to present its case.[92]

The examination of the tribunal's decisions regarding evidence by enforcing courts may risk reviewing merits, which the New York Convention does not allow, as discussed in §5.02[B]. Not reviewing merits has been well accepted by enforcing courts when they determine the due process defence in relation to a tribunal's decisions on evidence.[93] This approach reinforces the courts' deference to the tribunal's decisions on evidence.

For instance, US courts have held that enforcing courts should not second-guess the tribunal's evaluation of evidence and that retrying the merits of arbitration would undermine the purpose of the New York Convention.[94] Federal courts do not oversee arbitral proceedings but only review whether the procedure was fundamentally unfair.[95] Chinese courts have consistently been reluctant to review tribunals' decisions on the admission and assessment of evidence through the prism of due process guarantees. This is because they hold that the admission and assessment of evidence are substantive rather than procedural issues and thus do not fall within the scope of due process defence under the New York Convention. For instance, in a case where the tribunal did not accept an audio recording of an important witness as evidence and did not grant the other party's request for cross-examination, the court held that the evidence matters, including the admission of evidence, were classified as substantive matters instead of procedural issues, and thus would not trigger the due process defence.[96]

In summary, enforcing courts generally show deference to the tribunal's broad discretion regarding the admissibility, relevance, materiality, and weight of evidence unless the tribunal refuses to hear crucial evidence such that the exclusion of the evidence deprives a party of the opportunity to present its case.

---

91. *Research and Development Center 'Teploenergetika' LLC v. EP International LLC & Worldwide Vision LLC* (ED Va, Civ No. 2:15-CV-362) slip op 14; *Tempo Shain Corp v. Bertek Inc*, 120 F 3d 16, 21 (2nd Cir, 1997); *Hoteles Condado Beach, La Concha & Convention Center v. Union De Tronquistas Local 901*, 763 F 2d 34, 42 (1st Cir, 1985).
92. *Dastime Group Ltd, et al., v. Moonvale Investments Ltd, et al.* (ND Cal, No. 17-CV-01859-JSW, 11 October 2017) slip op 13.
93. STJ SEC 611, Reporting Justice João Otávio de Noronha, 11 December 2006. For a detailed discussion, *see* Alves (n. 85) 72.
94. *Anatolie Stati, Gabriel Stati, Ascom Group SA, Terra Raf Trans Traiding Ltd v. Republic of Kazakhstan* (DC, Civ No. 14-1638-ABJ, 23 March 2018) slip op 30; *Bosack v. Soward*, 586 F 3d 1096, 1105 (9th Cir, 2009).
95. *Tempo Shain Corp v. Bertek Inc*, 120 F 3d 16, 20 (2nd Cir, 1997); *Hispasat SA v. Bantel Telecom LLC* (SD Fla, No. 17-20534-CV, 2 August 2017) slip op 9.
96. 《最高人民法院关于申请人DMT有限公司（法国）与被申请人潮州市华业包装材料有限公司、被申请人潮安县华业包装材料有限公司申请承认和执行外国仲裁裁决一案请示的复函 (2010) 民四他字第48号》 [Reply of the SPC to the Request for Instructions on Recognition and Enforcement of A Foreign Arbitral Award Between DMT Co Ltd (France, Applicant) and Chaozhou City Huaye Packing Materials Co Ltd and Chao'An County Huaye Packing Materials Co Ltd (China, Respondents)], 最高人民法院 [Supreme People's Court] (2010) 民四他字第48号 [Min Si Ta Zi No. 48], 12 October 2010.

[B] The Absence of Reasons in an Award

The parties' right to present their case before the arbitral tribunal implies that the tribunal must consider the parties' arguments. Meanwhile, by signing an arbitration agreement, parties are deemed to have waived their right to obtain a reasoned decision guaranteed by the court. As shown in this section, most enforcing courts recognise that due process does not require arbitral tribunals to address each party's submission in detail in the reasoning of an award.

For instance, the Court of Appeal of the British Virgin Islands held that while arbitrators were duty-bound to give reasons for their decisions, the New York Convention did not include a free-standing rule to the effect that a court must refuse to enforce an award due to the absence of reasons.[97] The English High Court emphasised that 'no arbitration tribunal should be criticised for succinctness; nor is any tribunal required to set out every point raised before it, still less at length'.[98] An arbitral tribunal is not obligated to address every point in a case.[99] In Germany, courts have consistently held that an arbitral tribunal is under no general obligation to give references and explicit reasons for decisions regarding each party's arguments.[100]

Silence in respect of one argument does not necessarily mean that it has been ignored unless that argument is essential for rendering the award.[101] For instance, in a case before the Frankfurt Court of Appeal, the challenging party had submitted to the tribunal that the tribunal-appointed expert had used outdated figures. However, the final award stated only that the tribunal-appointed expert had 'proceeded from correct facts' without any justification for this finding. The court considered that the challenging party's objections to the expert report were the 'essential core' of its factual submissions and should have been addressed in the award, and such failure to sufficiently address this submission violated the right to be heard.[102]

Also, subsequent judicial practices of State Parties indicate that some enforcing courts show due deference to the parties' agreement or to the law of the country where the award was made regarding the requirements of awards, which Article V(1)(d) of the New York Convention requires. For example, a Dutch court enforced an unreasoned award because the arbitration agreement provided that the arbitrators were not

97. *Cukurova Holding AS v. Sonera Holding BV* [2014] UKPC 15 (13 May 2014) [35].
98. *IPCO (Nigeria) Ltd v. Nigerian National Petroleum Corp* [2005] EWHC 726 (Comm) (27 April 2005) [49].
99. *Ibid.*
100. Oberlandesgericht Frankfurt [Court of Appeal Frankfurt], 26 SchH 03/09, 12 October 2009 reported in (2010) XXXV *Yearbook Commercial Arbitration* 377, [20]; Oberlandesgericht Munich [Higher Regional Court of Munich], 34 Sch 10/11, 14 November 2011 reported in (2012) XXXVII *Yearbook Commercial Arbitration* 231, [9]; Oberlandesgericht Düsseldorf [Court of Appeal Düsseldorf], I-4 Sch 10/09, 15 December 2009 reported in (2010) XXXV *Yearbook Commercial Arbitration* 386, [16].
101. Oberlandesgericht Frankfurt [Court of Appeal Frankfurt], 26 SchH 03/09, 12 October 2009 reported in (2010) XXXV *Yearbook Commercial Arbitration* 377, [20].
102. Court of Appeals Frankfurt, No. 26 Sch 14/18, BeckRS 2020, 4606. Although it is a judgment in setting-aside proceedings, it is analysed here for enlightening the assessment of the right to be heard since German courts apply its domestic standards to the due process defence under the New York Convention as discussed in Chapter 2.

bound to give reasons for their decision. The court ruled that an unreasoned foreign arbitral award can be enforced in the Netherlands if the arbitral seat does not require reasons to be given.[103] Similarly, Brazilian courts refer to the law of the country where the award was made when determining whether the award requires reasoning. In a case before the Brazilian Superior Court of Justice, the award-debtor alleged a violation of due process due to a lack of reasoning in the arbitral award. The Superior Court of Justice determined that the appropriate standards to be considered when evaluating whether the arbitrators had properly reasoned the award and observed the formal requirements for the award were those of the country where the award was made.[104]

§7.05 EQUALITY OF ARMS

The right to equal treatment is inextricable from the right to be heard, which has been confirmed by provisions such as Article 18 of the UNCITRAL Model Law and leading arbitration rules.[105] As discussed in Chapter 3, the equality of arms requires that 'the same procedural rights are to be provided to all the parties unless distinctions are based on law and can be justified on objective and reasonable grounds, not entailing actual disadvantage or other unfairness to the defendant'.[106] This requires enforcing courts to examine: (a) whether the same procedural rights are granted to each party; (b) whether distinctions between parties are based on law or reasonable grounds; (c) whether such distinctions create a substantial disadvantage to any party, ensuring a fair balance between parties.

To achieve equality of arms, the tribunal must afford parties equal opportunities to make submissions and comments. For instance, if one party is given the opportunity to produce evidence while the other is denied this chance, it may be considered a breach of equal treatment. This was demonstrated in a case heard by the Hamburg Court of Appeals. During the hearing, the tribunal examined a witness for one party but rejected the other party's request for examination, which the court held violated the right to be heard and equal treatment.[107]

Additionally, it is important to note that equal treatment is a substantive form of equality rather than a purely formalistic notion. Aristotle argued that treating unequal

103. Provisions Judge of the District Court of Rotterdam, 24 November 1994 reported in (1996) XXI *Yearbook Commercial Arbitration* 635, 640 [16]–[17].

104. STJ SEC 5692, Reporting Justice Ari Pargendler, 1 September 2014. For detailed discussion, *see* Alves (n. 85) 75.

105. *See UNCITRAL Arbitration Rules*, UN Doc. A/RES/65/22 (n. 10) Art. 17(1); *ICC Arbitration Rules* (n. 11) Art. 22(4); *SIAC Arbitration Rules* (n. 10) Art. 17(1); *LCIA Arbitration Rules* (n. 10) Art. 14(4)(i); *HKIAC Arbitration Rules* (n. 5) Art. 13(1); *SCC Arbitration Rules* (n. 5) Art. 23(2).

106. United Nations Human Rights Council, *General Comment No 32, Article 14: Right to Equality Before Courts and Tribunals and to a Fair Trial*, CCPR/C/GC/32, 19th session, 23 August 2007, [13]. *See also Dombo Beheer BV v. the Netherlands* (European Court of Human Rights, Application No. 14448/88, 27 October 1993) [33]; Kleiner (n. 75) 166.

107. Court of Appeals Hamburg, 6 Sch 01/04, 16 September 2004. Although it is a judgment in setting-aside proceedings, it is analysed here for enlightening the assessment of equal treatment between parties since German courts apply its domestic standards to the due process defence under the New York Convention as discussed in chapter 2.

persons identically is not true equality.[108] Instead, it involves treating comparable situations equally while also addressing any relevant differences.[109] To achieve substantive equality, enforcing courts should consider parties' claims, evidence and the arbitral process as a whole to decide what constitutes equal treatment in each individual case.[110] For instance, the tribunal's allocation of different hearing times based on the number of witnesses provided by the parties or the burden of proof does not necessarily violate the principle of equal treatment.[111] In another case before the Singapore High Court, the opposing party claimed that the tribunal treated it unequally by excluding its expert report. The opposing party argued that the tribunal did not provide a reasonable opportunity to present its case by rejecting its requests for extensions of time and granting much shorter extensions than requested.[112] The Singapore High Court held that equality of treatment did not require identical treatment and that the situations surrounding the reports were not comparable. The excluded report was submitted very late, barely one week before the main hearing, while the report of the other party was submitted and accepted three weeks earlier without objection.[113] Based on these findings, the court dismissed the objection of inequality.

In determining whether different time limits given to parties violate equality of arms, some courts not only examine whether they formally differ but also assess whether one party is actually disadvantaged by the different time limits.[114] A failure of equal mathematical timekeeping does not necessarily violate due process. Instead, a violation of due process would only be upheld where the difference in the period of time allocated to a party would give it a real or 'decisive' advantage. One situation where equal time may be considered unfair is when the parties have significantly different abilities to present their arguments. In a case concerning a chess-clock method of allocating time at the oral hearing, the tribunal decided to add three days to the hearing time and to allocate more of the additional time to the claimant since the respondents' witnesses required an interpreter. The Hong Kong court dismissed the respondents' claims that the tribunal had violated the agreed arbitration procedure and the principle of equality between parties on the basis that the parties' agreement was subject to the 'overriding objective' prescribed in Article 18 of the UNCITRAL Model

108. Aristotle, *Nichomachean Ethics* (Martin Ostwald trans, Upper Saddle River: Prentice Hall, 1999) 1131a22–1131a25.
109. Gabrielle Kaufmann-Kohler and Antonio Rigozzi, *International Arbitration: Law and Practice in Switzerland* (Oxford University Press, 2015) 279; Elliott Geisinger and Pierre Ducret, 'The Arbitral Procedure' in Elliott Geisinger, Nathalie Voser and Angelina M Petti (eds), *International Arbitration in Switzerland: A Handbook for Practitioners* (Kluwer Law & Business, 2nd ed., 2013) 90.
110. *Triulzi Cesare SRL v. Xinyi Group (Glass) Co Ltd* [2015] 1 SLR 114, [112]; Born (n. 17) 2174.
111. Geisinger and Ducret (n. 109) 89.
112. *China Machine New Energy Corp v. Jaguar Energy Guatemala LLC and another* [2018] SGHC 101, [184], [189].
113. *Ibid.*, [189].
114. Cour d'appel de Paris [Paris Court of Appeal], 22 January 2004, reported in (2004) *Revue de l'Arbitrage* 647; Cour d'appel de Paris [Paris Court of Appeal], 15 June 2006, reported in (2006) *Revue de l'Arbitrage* 1002.

Law.[115] The court ruled that strictly adhering to the chess-clock arrangement would violate the parties' right to present their cases fairly, and the tribunal was obliged to take action to address the issue instead of being bound by an unworkable agreement between the parties.[116]

Differences in procedural rights between parties do not necessarily constitute a breach of equality if they are based on law or reasonable grounds. For instance, one party may claim a breach of equality or violation of the right to be heard when the other party argues that certain information is commercially or technically sensitive and should not be disclosed to that party or its counsel, which may result in that party being at an unequal position or unable to present its case regarding the information disclosure. In a case before the Singapore High Court, the tribunal established an 'attorneys' eyes only' document production regime (AEO) following the disclosing party's statement that the requested documents contained sensitive information. The requested documents would be disclosed first only to external counsel and then to specified employees of the other side upon application to the tribunal. The opposing party claimed that the AEO did not treat the parties equally because it was an asymmetrical regime that allowed only the disclosing party to withhold or redact large volumes of documents while placing a disproportionate burden on the opposing party.[117] The court considered that such an AEO regime had to operate asymmetrically to ensure that the opposing party could not misuse the disclosure documents and to safeguard the interests of both parties in making the production order.[118]

In *Dongwoo Mann + Hummel Co Ltd v. Mann + Hummel GmbH* ('M + H'), the tribunal issued a ruling ordering M + H to produce certain technical documents, but M + H refused to do so, citing confidentiality and the proprietary nature of the information.[119] Dongwoo claimed that it was unable to present its case regarding the technical issue due to M + H's failure to produce documents. The Singapore High Court found that the tribunal had warned M + H that failing to comply with the production ruling may result in an adverse inference being drawn against it, and both parties were given sufficient opportunity to submit their positions on whether an adverse inference should be drawn against M + H.[120] The Singapore High Court held that the failure to produce documents does not necessarily mean that a party is unable to present its case. In this context, Dongwoo's inability to explain why an adverse inference should be drawn against M + H for not producing the documents is crucial.[121] The court concluded that there was no breach of the parties' right to be heard because both parties

115. *Brunswick Bowling & Billiards Corp v. Shanghai Zhonglu Industrial Co Ltd* [2011] 1 HKLRD 707, [88].
116. *Ibid.*, [84]-[89].
117. *China Machine New Energy Corp v. Jaguar Energy Guatemala LLC and another* [2018] SGHC 101, [183].
118. *Ibid.*, [187]-[188].
119. *Dongwoo Mann + Hummel Co Ltd v. Mann + Hummel GmbH* [2008] 3 SLR (R) 871.
120. *Ibid.*, [65].
121. *Ibid.*, [66].

were given an opportunity to fully present their case regarding the adverse inference question.[122]

§7.06 CONCLUSION

It is required by Article V(1)(d) of the New York Convention that the arbitral procedure follows the agreement of the parties or, in the absence of such agreement, the law of the country where the arbitration took place. VCLT's interpretation of 'context, object and purpose' requires enforcing courts to coordinate Article V(1)(b) and Article V(1)(d) of the New York Convention. Enforcing courts generally consider the applicable arbitration rules and the national arbitration statutes of the arbitral seat regarding the form of an arbitral award when determining whether to enforce an award without reasoning. Arbitration rules agreed to by parties and national arbitration statutes generally grant tribunals broad discretion in case management and procedural decisions. Subsequent judicial practice of State Parties indicates that enforcing courts generally show deference to arbitrators' procedural decisions on the admissibility, relevance, materiality, and weight of evidence and setting time limits for filing.

Subsequent judicial practices falling within Article 32 of the VCLT provide a more specific interpretation and application of the due process defence. Certain enforcing courts have confirmed that a tribunal's failure to ensure that each party has the opportunity to comment on the factual and legal arguments introduced by the counterparty may constitute a violation of due process, unless there is obvious evidence to the contrary in the award showing that the tribunal did not consider such new documents.

If the parties' agreement, the *lex arbitri* or applicable arbitration rules authorise an arbitral tribunal the power to investigate fact or law ex officio, the subsequent judicial practice has shown that the application of this power must be subject to due process. Enforcing courts have held that parties must be provided with the arbitrators' independent factual and legal investigations and given a reasonable opportunity to comment on them, including the opportunity to submit further factual or legal evidence in response. Failure to grant parties this opportunity to comment on a tribunal's independent findings may violate due process.

Enforcing courts generally defer to the tribunal's discretion regarding the admissibility, relevance, materiality, and weight of evidence. However, arbitrators' refusal to hear crucial evidence, which deprives a party of the opportunity to present its case, can constitute a breach of due process. Further, enforcing courts have held that arbitrators do not need to discuss all parties' submissions in the award's reasoning as long as they have reviewed and considered the main arguments and evidence before making their decision.

Last, enforcing courts have recognised that equality of arms requires the tribunal to provide equal opportunities for parties to make submissions and comments. Equal treatment is a form of substantive equality rather than a purely formalistic concept.

122. *Ibid.*, [72].

Therefore, distinctions in procedural rights between parties do not necessarily violate the principle of equality if they are based on law or reasonable grounds or do not create a substantial disadvantage for any party.

Chapters 3 to 7 use the VCLT's rules to interpret and apply the due process defence under the New York Convention. Chapter 3 demonstrated that the due process defence of the New York Convention reflects the general principle of *audiatur et altera pars*. Its core elements include: (a) due notice of the appointment of arbitrators and proceedings; (b) equality of arms; (c) the right to be heard; and (d) the impartiality and independence of arbitrators. Chapter 4 showed that when implementing abstract elements in concrete cases, enforcing courts generally refer to due process rules derived from international conventions, modern arbitration laws, established arbitration rules, soft law, and the practice of international commercial arbitration. However, the application of these due process rules may vary from one jurisdiction to another, resulting in different court decisions in specific cases. when applying these concrete due process rules in a specific case. Starting from Chapter 5, this book used a comparative method to explore the subsequent judicial practice of State Parties in construing due process in specific cases. Chapters 5 to 7 present a comparative analysis of domestic judicial decisions made in the courts of State Parties. The aim is to identify similarities and differences in the interpretation and application of proper notice, right to be heard, equality between parties, and relevant issues such as policy considerations, waiver, threshold, and implications of decisions made by the court of the arbitral seat. The following chapter will conclude this book and discuss the implications of transnational due process, which is based on the general principle of due process and subsequent practice, on the stakeholders of arbitration.

Chapter 8

Conclusion

The book argues that the due process defence under the New York Convention should be interpreted consistently with the interpretative framework set out in the VCLT and, more specifically, by recourse to the general principle of *audiatur et altera pars* and the subsequent practice of State Parties to the New York Convention.[1] This interpretative approach ensures that due process under the New York Convention is a genuinely transnational standard that is distinct from any particular national legal system.

By drawing on the general principle of *audiatur et altera pars*, it is submitted that enforcing courts can achieve agreement on the core concepts of due process under the New York Convention - due notice of the appointment of arbitrators and of the proceedings themselves, equality of arms, the right to be heard, and the impartiality and independence of arbitrators.[2] In implementing these core concepts, the subsequent practice of State Parties can further refine and concretise the application of the due process defence under the New York Convention in specific factual cases. Through a comparative analysis of the case law of State Parties, Chapter 5 showed that courts have generally confirmed the following policies for the interpretation and application of the due process defence: pro-enforcement policy, no review of merits, judicial deference to arbitrators' procedural discretion and institutional arbitration rules, and due consideration of the international character of international arbitration. The judicial recognition of these policies indicates agreements among State Parties. This constitutes subsequent practice referred to in Article 31(3)(b) of the VCLT, which should be considered by the enforcing court.

Despite the widespread international agreement on these core concepts and policies, court decisions may differ from one jurisdiction to another in terms of their application of more concrete due process rules in specific cases. These cases may concern the content, form, address, addressee, language and timing of proper notice;[3]

1. *See* Chapter 2.
2. *See* Chapter 3.
3. *See* Chapter 6.

the right to make submissions;[4] the right to comment on the submissions;[5] the right to have the submissions considered;[6] and equality of arms.[7] Chapters 6 and 7 present comparative case studies of decisions made by domestic courts to identify differences and similarities among State Parties in their application of due process rules. The studies also evaluate different solutions to specific cases based on the criteria of predictability, compatibility with the parties' legal expectations, and balance with efficiency, as these criteria serve the purposes of Article V.[8] When State Parties have differing opinions on the specific standards of due process in concrete cases, these purposes are integrated into a wider interpretative exercise outlined in Chapters 6 and 7. This exercise evaluates the weight that should be given to the judicial practices that are more predictable and compatible with the legal expectations of the parties or that achieve a good balance with efficiency. Judicial practices by one or more State Parties that do not establish agreement of *all* State Parties but that do accord with the purposes of Article V may be relevant as a supplementary means of interpretation according to Article 32 of the VCLT. Enforcing courts can contribute to the uniform interpretation and application of the due process defence in concrete cases by referring to subsequent practice established by domestic judicial decisions of State Parties under Articles 31(3)(b) and 32 of the VCLT.

In contrast to the *lex arbitri* and *lex fori* approaches, a transnational approach to due process grounded in the VCLT's interpretative framework can effectively safeguard and harmonise the interests of various stakeholders, including parties, arbitrators, enforcing states, and the state of the arbitral seat. First, in contrast to the *lex fori* approach, the transnational due process approach can contribute to legal certainty and protect the legal expectations of parties and arbitrators. Although the primary addressees of the New York Convention are national judges of the enforcing forums, the arbitrators and parties are the implementers of due process in arbitral proceedings. As provided in Article 19 of the UNCITRAL Model Law, parties have the freedom to set forth arbitral proceedings by agreement; failing such agreement, the arbitral tribunal may conduct the arbitral procedure in a manner it deems appropriate.[9] Applying the law of the enforcing forum to determine whether minimum due process standards were met in arbitration undermines predictability and legal certainty for arbitrators and parties. The selection of the forum for recognition and enforcement is often influenced by the location of the losing party's assets. In most arbitrations, however, parties and arbitrators cannot always anticipate all future enforcing forums and thus abide by their due process requirements during arbitral proceedings. Applying the law of the enforcing forum to the due process defence under the New York Convention may impose

4. *See* §7.02.
5. *See* §7.03.
6. *See* §7.04.
7. *See* §7.05.
8. For more in detail about the contextual and purposive interpretation applied in Article V, *see* §2.06[A][2].
9. *UNCITRAL Model Law on International Commercial Arbitration*, UN GAOR, 40th sess., Supp No. 17, UN Doc. A/40/17 (adopted 21 June 1985) annex I, as amended by UN GAOR, 61st sess., Supp No. 17, UN Doc. A/61/17 (7 July 2006), annex I ('*UNCITRAL Model Law*') Art. 19.

impractical and burdensome obligations on arbitral tribunals to ascertain and comply with the due process standards of each potential recognition or enforcement forum.

In contrast, in theory, transnational due process based on the principle of *audiatur et altera pars*, which is common to the principal legal systems in the world, can provide the parties with some needed certainty and predictability. At the practical level, 'subsequent practice' exemplified by national court decisions of State Parties identifies an agreement of all or some State Parties regarding the interpretation of Article V(1)(b), which provides parties with a certain level of predictability about what due process should entail in concrete cases. In these ways, transnational due process contributes to the uniform interpretation and application of Article V(1)(b), thereby creating a level playing field for parties from different legal cultures. This relatively uniform interpretation enables arbitral awards to apply wherever the property of the award-debtor is located and obtain similar results of recognition and enforcement.

Second, in comparison to the other two approaches, namely the *lex fori* or the *lex arbitri*, the transnational due process approach based on the general principle of *audiatur et altera pars* and subsequent practice of State Parties can be largely aligned with the core concepts of normatively appropriate levels of procedural fairness that the state of the arbitral seat and the enforcing state aim to protect and can resolve discrepancies between the two. When interpreting Article V(1)(b), the context interpretation requires enforcing courts to consider the explicit protection of the arbitral seat's interests in Articles V(1)(a), V(1)(d), and V(1)(e), as well as the enforcing state's interests in Articles V(2)(a) and V(2)(b). As shown in Chapter 2, both the state of the arbitral seat and the enforcing state uphold their own standards of normatively appropriate procedural fairness and have interests in ensuring that their mandatory rules concerning due process are adhered to. Whether the *lex arbitri* or *lex fori* applies, the other may indirectly affect the standards of due process under the New York Convention, potentially creating conflicts.[10] If enforcing courts apply their own laws to the due process defence, the *lex arbitri* can still protect its mandatory laws concerning due process in two ways. Enforcing courts may refuse to enforce an award that has been set aside for violating the arbitral seat's mandatory procedural laws based on Articles V(1)(d) and V(1)(e) of the New York Convention.[11] Additionally, the arbitral tribunal must comply with the mandatory procedural laws of the arbitral seat to prevent the award from being set aside. Enforcing courts usually defer to the procedural decisions of arbitral tribunals,[12] and in so doing, these courts indirectly respect and protect the mandatory procedural laws of the arbitral seat. Similarly, if enforcing courts apply the *lex arbitri* to the due process defence, as demonstrated in Chapter 2, several enforcing states consider procedural fairness as a requirement of procedural public policy, and they may still apply their own standards of procedural public policy under Article V(2)(b) to decide procedural irregularities.[13]

10. There are possible conflicts between the *lex arbitri* and the *lex fori* over the same issue, *see* §6.05.
11. Regarding the effects of set-aside decisions by courts at the arbitral seat upon enforcing courts, *see* §5.05.
12. Regarding the judicial deference to arbitrators' procedural discretion, *see* §5.02[C].
13. *See* §2.03[C].

In any case, privileging the supposed interests of either state in relation to due process standards can lead to the sorts of practical problems as identified above. In this context, Article V(1)(b) is better understood as primarily safeguarding the interests of the parties in a fair process and the wider integrity of international arbitration as a means of resolving disputes. Since *audiatur et altera pars* is derived from the fundamental procedural principles common to the major national legal systems worldwide, it is widely accepted as a general principle of law. Therefore, transnational due process grounded in *audiatur et altera pars* can be more easily accepted and applied by State Parties, whether at the arbitral seat or the enforcing forum.[14] Regarding specific standards of due process in concrete cases, the transnational due process established on the subsequent practice of State Parties can improve certainty, predictability, and uniformity in the interpretation and application of the due process defence, especially when there are differences among State Parties.

Lastly, recourse to the *lex arbitri* or the *lex fori* may result in the application of an unfair or idiosyncratic national law. The law of the arbitral seat or the law of the enforcing forum regarding due process may be unfair, underdeveloped, or silent on the interpretation and application of due process in international arbitral proceedings. In contrast, the transnational due process is a truly international standard based not on parochial views in a particular legal system but on the universal views taken by the principal legal systems. This transnational approach to due process can prevent the application of unfair and idiosyncratic national standards of due process and address gaps in some national legal systems that have little or no legislation on due process.

The book presents a particular understanding of the transnational approach to the due process defence under the New York Convention grounded in the interpretative framework set out in the VCLT and, more specifically, by recourse to the general principle of *audiatur et altera pars* and the subsequent practice of State Parties to the New York Convention. Accordingly, the book makes three major contributions to the theorisation and development of the transnational approach. First, although arbitration scholars have discussed the importance of an autonomous approach to ensure predictability, previous work has not put this on a stable or principled footing. This book shows how an interpretative approach grounded in the VCLT can achieve this goal while also proposing a structured way for courts to consider and assess legal materials from beyond their own jurisdiction (Chapters 2–7). It specifies a transnational-informed approach to considering the general principle of *audiatur et altera pars* (Chapter 3) and the subsequent state practice in international law of interpreting and applying Article V(1)(b) of the New York Convention (Chapters 4–7).

Second, the book shows how much of the arbitration scholarship on transnationalism can be reshaped within the framework of public international law, thereby contributing to debates within international law scholarship about the decentralised interpretation of international law by domestic courts (Chapters 3–7). The grounding of the interpretation of the New York Convention in international law contrasts with the autonomous validity of arbitration, which imagines arbitration as a process established

14. *See* Chapter 3.

by parties' consent that is not grounded in any legal order.[15] According to the argument developed in the book, the interpretation of the New York Convention might still be described as autonomous in a distinct sense, in that it should be interpreted in a way that is distinct from any particular system of domestic law. However, the interpretation of the New York Convention is not autonomous in the sense the term was used in the autonomous validity of arbitration. Under the approach advocated in the book, the principles of due process contained in states' domestic laws and their practice remain relevant to interpreting the New York Convention, but only to the extent they enter through the interpretative 'gateways' specified in the VCLT – for example, to the extent they constitute relevant subsequent practice of State Parties to the New York Convention. This contrasts with the autonomous validity of arbitration which takes states out of the equation as much as possible.

In the decentralised international legal system, the primary interpreter of the law is the state, as the law's main addressee. However, as organs of the state, domestic judges are called upon to interpret and apply international law in cases brought before them.[16] This book argues that the New York Convention requires domestic judges to engage in 'judicial dialogue' of sorts,[17] namely to consider domestic court decisions of other State Parties, to the extent that such foreign judicial decisions on the due process defence may constitute subsequent practice with respect to the New York Convention, thus impacting on its proper interpretation. Thus, the book contributes to the discussions about whether judicial dialogue can be qualified as a means for the interpretation of international law. The answer is a qualified yes, especially if this judicial dialogue is framed as part of public international law exercise rather than an ad hoc recourse to foreign material.

Third, this book demonstrates how the transnational approach, based on the framework of public international law for treaty interpretation, can address a range of

15. Regarding the proponents of the autonomous international arbitration legal order, *see* Emmanuel Gaillard, 'Sociology of International Arbitration' (2015) 31(1) *Arbitration International* 1; Julian D M Lew, 'Is There a Global Free-Standing Body of Substantive Arbitration Law?' in Albert Jan van den Berg (ed.), *International Arbitration: The Coming of a New Age*, ICCA Congress 17 (Kluwer Law International, 2013) 53; Emmanuel Gaillard, 'The Emerging System of International Arbitration: Defining System' (2012) 106(1) *American Society of International Law Proceedings of Annual Meetings* 287; Emmanuel Gaillard, *Legal Theory of International Arbitration* (Martinus Nijhoff Publishers, 2010); Gabrielle Kaufmann-Kohler, 'Soft Law in International Arbitration: Codification and Normativity' (2010) 1(2) *Journal of International Dispute Settlement* 283; Julian D M Lew, 'Achieving the Dream: Autonomous Arbitration' (2006) 22 *Arbitration International* 179.
16. Anne-Marie Slaughter, *A New World Order* (Princeton University Press, 2004) 268.
17. For transnational judicial dialogue in general and its role in the development of international law, *see* Antonios Tzanakopoulos, 'Judicial Dialogue as a Means of Interpretation' in Helmut Philipp Aust and Georg Nolte (eds), *The Interpretation of International Law by Domestic Courts* (Oxford University Press, 2016) 72; Antonios Tzanakopoulos, 'Domestic Courts in International Law: The International Judicial Function of National Courts' (2011) 34(1) *Loyola of Los Angeles International & Comparative Law Review* 133; Slaughter (n. 16); Anne-Marie Slaughter, 'A Global Community of Courts' (2003) 44(1) *Harvard International Law Journal* 191; Anne-Marie Slaughter, 'Judicial Globalization' (2000) 40 *Virginia Journal of International Law* 1103; Anne-Marie Slaughter, 'A Typology of Transjudicial Communication' (1994) 29 *University of Richmond Law Review* 99.

practical questions raised in enforcing courts about the precise content of the due process defence (Chapters 5–7). This transnational approach to due process defence can enhance judicial capacity in states where national law does not offer a solution to the case at hand. This may be due to unclear applicable rules regarding due process or the absence of any rule available at all, as is the case in China, as discussed in Chapter 2. Also, this transnational approach can build on citation to familiar jurisdictions, such as Commonwealth jurisdictions where citational practices are already common,[18] and encourage their development in states where they are not.

18. Jan M Smits, 'Comparative Law and Its Influence on National Legal Systems' in Mathias Reimann and Reinhard Zimmeremann (eds), *The Oxford Handbook of Comparative Law* (Oxford University Press, 2nd ed., 2019) 503, 519–520; Mads Andenas and Duncan Fairgrieve, 'Courts and Comparative Law: In Search of a Common Language for Open Legal Systems' in Mads Andenas and Duncan Fairgrieve (eds), *Courts and Comparative Law* (Oxford University Press, 2015) 5.

Bibliography

A. Articles/Books/Reports

Alstine, Michael P Van, 'Dynamic Treaty Interpretation' (1998) 146(3) *University of Pennsylvania Journal Law Review* 687

Alves, Rafael Francisco, 'Chapter 3: Country Report: Brazil' in Friedrich Rosenfeld, Dietmar Czernich and Franco Ferrari (eds), *Due Process as a Limit to Discretion in International Commercial Arbitration* (Kluwer Law International, 2020)

Andenas, Mads and Duncan Fairgrieve, 'Courts and Comparative Law: In Search of a Common Language for Open Legal Systems' in Mads Andenas and Duncan Fairgrieve (eds), *Courts and Comparative Law* (Oxford University Press, 2015)

Aristotle, *Nichomachean Ethics* (Martin Ostwald trans, Upper Saddle River: Prentice Hall, 1999)

Arroyo, Manuel, 'Chapter 2, Part II: Commentary on Chapter 12 PILS, Article 190 [Finality, Challenge: Principle]' in Manuel Arroyo (ed.), *Arbitration in Switzerland: The Practitioner's Guide* (Kluwer Law International, 2nd ed., 2018)

Aust, Anthony, *Modern Treaty Law and Practice* (Cambridge University Press, 3rd ed., 2013)

Aust, Helmut Philipp, 'Between Universal Aspiration and Local Application' in Helmut Philipp Aust and Georg Nolte (eds), *The Interpretation of International Law by Domestic Courts* (Oxford University Press, 2016)

Bachand, Frederic, 'Court Intervention in International Arbitration: The Case for Compulsory Judicial Internationalism Symposium' (2012) 2012(1) *Journal of Dispute Resolution* 83

Bantekas, Ilias, 'Equal Treatment of Parties in International Commercial Arbitration' (2020) 69(4) *The International and Comparative Law Quarterly* 991

Benedettelli, Massimo V, 'Human Rights as a Litigation Tool in International Arbitration: Reflecting on the ECHR Experience' (2015) 31(4) *Arbitration International* 631

Berg, Albert Jan van den, *The New York Arbitration Convention of 1958: Towards a Uniform Judicial Interpretation* (Kluwer Law and Taxation Publishers, 1981)

Berger, Klaus Peter and J Ole Jensen, 'Due Process Paranoia and the Procedural Judgment Rule: A Safe Harbour for Procedural Management Decisions by International Arbitrators' (2016) 32(3) *Arbitration International* 415

Bermann, George A, *International Arbitration and Private International Law* (Hague Academy of International Law, 2017)

Bermann, George A, 'Recognition and Enforcement of Foreign Arbitral Awards: The Interpretation and Application of the New York Convention by National Courts' in George A Bermann (ed.), *Recognition and Enforcement of Foreign Arbitral Awards – The Interpretation and Application of the New York Convention by National Courts* (Springer, 2017)

Besson, Samantha, 'General Principles in International Law – Whose Principles?' in Samantha Besson and Pascal Pichonnaz (eds), *Les principes en droit européen–Principles in European Law* (Schulthess, 2011)

Binder, Peter, *International Commercial Arbitration and Mediation in UNCITRAL Model Law Jurisdictions* (Kluwer Law International, 4th ed., 2019)

Bingham, Peregrine, *Reports of Cases Argued and Determined in the Court of Common Pleas, and Other Courts: With Tables of the Cases and Principal Matters* (J Butterworth, 1825)

Bjorge, Eirik, 'Public Law Sources and Analogies of International Law' (2018) 49(4) *Victoria University of Wellington Law Review* 533

Blackaby, Nigel, et al., *Redfern and Hunter on International Arbitration* (Oxford University Press, 6th ed., 2015)

Blutman, László, 'In the Trap of a Legal Metaphor: International Soft Law' (2010) 59 *International and Comparative Law Quarterly* 605

Böckstiegel, Karl-Heinz, Stefan Michael Kröll and Patricia Nacimiento (eds), *Arbitration in Germany: The Model Law in Practice* (Kluwer Law International, 2nd ed., 2015)

Bonomi, Andrea, 'Chapter 13: The Concept of Public Policy under the 1958 New York Convention: An Autonomous Interpretation?' in Franco Ferrari and Friedrich Jakob Rosenfeld (eds), *Autonomous Versus Domestic Concepts under the New York Convention* (Kluwer Law International, 2021)

Bonomi, Andrea and Elza Reymond-Eniaeva, 'Interpretation and Application of the New York Convention in Switzerland' in George A Bermann (ed.), *Recognition and Enforcement of Foreign Arbitral Awards – The Interpretation and Application of the New York Convention by National Courts* (Springer, 2017)

Born, Gary B, *International Commercial Arbitration* (Kluwer Law International, 2nd ed., 2014)

Börner, Andreas, 'Article III' in Herbert Kronke et al. (eds), *Recognition and Enforcement of Foreign Arbitral Awards: A Global Commentary on the New York Convention* (Kluwer Law International, 2010)

Bouthillier, Yves le, 'Commentary on Article 32 of the Vienna Convention' in Olivier Corten and Pierre Klein (eds), *The Vienna Conventions on the Law of Treaties: A Commentary* (Oxford University Press, 2011)

Cananea, Giacinto della, *Due Process of Law Beyond the State: Requirements of Administrative Procedure* (Oxford University Press, 2016)

Cassese, Antonio, *International Law* (Oxford University Press, 2nd ed., 2005)

Cheng, Bin, *General Principles of Law as Applied by International Courts and Tribunals* (Cambridge University Press, 2nd ed., 2006)

Chinkin, Christine Mary, 'The Challenge of Soft Law: Development and Change in International Law' (1989) 38 *International and Comparative Law Quarterly* 850

Comair-Obeid, Nayla and Zeina Obeid, 'Chapter 13: Country Report: Middle East' in Friedrich Rosenfeld, Dietmar Czernich and Franco Ferrari (eds), *Due Process as a Limit to Discretion in International Commercial Arbitration* (Kluwer Law International, 2020)

Comyn, Samuel, *The Law of Contracts and Promises Upon Various Subjects and with Particular Persons: As Settled in the Action of Assumpsit* (Gould, Banks, & Co, 1835)

Costelloe, Daniel, 'The Role of Domestic Law in the Identification of General Principles of Law under Article 38(1)(c) of the Statute of the International Court of Justice' in Mads Andenas et al. (eds), *General Principles and the Coherence of International Law* (Brill, 2019)

Crawford, James (ed.), *Brownlie's Principles of Public International Law* (Oxford University Press, 8th ed., 2012)

Croft, Clyde, 'Recent Developments in Arbitration in Australia' (2011) 28(6) *Journal of International Arbitration* 599

Danielsson, Christer, 'Chapter 8: Applicable Law' in Anneette Magnusson and Jakob Rognwaldh (eds), *International Arbitration in Sweden: A Practitioner's Guide* (Kluwer Law International, 2nd ed., 2021)

Dannemann, Gerhard, 'Comparative Law: Study of Similarities or Differences?' in Mathias Reimann and Reinhard Zimmermann (eds), *The Oxford Handbook of Comparative Law* (Oxford University Press, 2nd ed., 2019)

De Ly, Filip JM, 'Chapter 2: Uniform Interpretation: What Is Being Done?' in Franco Ferrari and Friedrich Jakob Rosenfeld (eds), *Autonomous Versus Domestic Concepts under the New York Convention* (Kluwer Law International, 2021)

De Ly, Filip JM, Mark Friedman and Luca Radicati di Brozolo, 'International Law Association International Commercial Arbitration Committee's Report and Recommendations on "Ascertaining the Contents of the Applicable Law in International Commercial Arbitration"*Report for the Biennial Conference in Rio de Janeiro, August 2008' (2010) 26(2) *Arbitration International* 193

Degan, Vladimir-Djuro, 'General Principles of Law' (1992) 3 *Finnish Yearbook of International Law* 1

Diehl, Alexandra, *The Core Standard of International Investment Protection* (Wolters Kluwer, 2012)

Dizgovin, Farshad Rahimi, 'Enforcement of International Treaties by Domestic Courts of Iran: New Developments' (2018) 58(1) *Virginia Journal of International Law* 227

'Draft Conclusion on Subsequent Agreements and Subsequent Practice in Relation to the Interpretation of Treaties' (2018) 2 *Yearbook of the International Law Commission*, Part Two

Duca, Louis Del and Nancy A Welsh, 'Interpretation and Application of the New York Convention in the United States' in George A Bermann (ed.), *Recognition and Enforcement of Foreign Arbitral Awards – The Interpretation and Application of the New York Convention by National Courts* (Springer, 2017)

Dumberry, Patrick, *A Guide to General Principles of Law in International Investment Arbitration* (Oxford University Press, 2020)

Ellis, Jaye, 'General Principles and Comparative Law' (2011) 22 *European Journal of International Law* 949

Epstein, Judd, 'Use of Comparative Law in Commercial International Arbitration and Commercial Mediation' (2001) 75(4) *Tulane Law Review* 913

Fatima QC, Shaheed, *Using International Law in Domestic Courts* (Hart Publishing, 2005)

Fellmeth, Aaron X and Maurice Horwitz, *Guide to Latin in International Law* (Oxford University Press, 2009)

Fitzmaurice, Malgosia, 'The History of Article 38 of the Statute of the International Court of Justice: The Journey from the Past to the Present' in Samantha Besson and Jean d'Aspremont (eds), *The Oxford Handbook of the Sources of International Law* (Oxford University Press, 2017)

Forteau, Mathias, 'The Role of the International Rules of Interpretation for the Determination of Direct Effect of International Agreements' in Helmut Philipp Aust and Georg Nolte (eds), *The Interpretation of International Law by Domestic Courts* (Oxford University Press, 2016)

Friedmann, Wolfgang, 'The Uses of "General Principles" in the Development of International Law' (1963) 57(2) *American Journal of International Law* 279

Fry, Jason, Simon Greenberg and Francesca Mazza, *The Secretariat's Guide to ICC Arbitration* (ICC Publishing, 2012)

Gabriel, Henry Deeb, 'The Advantages of Soft Law in International Commercial Law: The Role of UNIDROIT, UNCITRAL, and the Hague Conference' (2009) 34 *Brooklyn Journal of International Law* 655

Gaillard, Emmanuel, 'The Emerging System of International Arbitration: Defining System' (2012) 106(1) *American Society of International Law Proceedings of Annual Meetings* 287

Gaillard, Emmanuel, 'Enforcement of Awards Set Aside in the Country of Origin: The French Experience' in Albert Jan van den Berg (ed.), *Improving the Efficiency of Arbitration Agreements and Awards: 40 Years of Application of the New York Convention* (Kluwer Law International, 1999)

Gaillard, Emmanuel, *Legal Theory of International Arbitration* (Martinus Nijhoff Publishers, 2010)

Gaillard, Emmanuel, 'Sociology of International Arbitration' (2015) 31(1) *Arbitration International* 1

Gaillard, Emmanuel and George A Bermann (eds), *The UNCITRAL Secretariat Guide on the New York Convention* (Brill, 2017)

Gaillard, Emmanuel and John Savage (eds), *Fouchard Gaillard Goldman on International Commercial Arbitration* (Kluwer Law International, 1999)

Gaja, Giorgio, 'General Principles in the Jurisprudence of the ICJ' in Mads Andenas et al. (eds), *General Principles and the Coherence of International Law* (Brill, 2019)

Gaja, Giorgio, 'General Principles of Law' in Rüdiger Wolfrum (ed.), *The Max Planck Encyclopedia of Public International Law* (Oxford University Press, 2013)

Gardiner, Richard, *Treaty Interpretation* (Oxford University Press, 2nd ed., 2015)

Gardiner, Richard, 'The Vienna Convention Rules on Treaty Interpretation' in Duncan B Hollis (ed.), *The Oxford Guide to Treaties* (Oxford University Press, 2nd ed., 2020)

Geisinger, Elliott, 'Implementing the New York Convention in Switzerland' (2008) 25(6) *Journal of International Arbitration* 691

Geisinger, Elliott and Pierre Ducret, 'The Arbitral Procedure' in Elliott Geisinger, Nathalie Voser and Angelina M Petti (eds), *International Arbitration in Switzerland: A Handbook for Practitioners* (Kluwer Law & Business, 2nd ed., 2013)

Giovannini, Teresa, 'Ex Officio Powers to Investigate: When Do Arbitrators Cross the Line?' in Bernd Ehle and Domitille Baizeau (eds), *Stories from the Hearing Room: Experience from Arbitral Practice (Essays in Honour of Michael E Schneider)* (Kluwer Law International, 2015)

Glenn, H Patrick, 'Comparative Legal Families and Comparative Legal Traditions' in Mathias Reimann and Reinhard Zimmermann (eds), *The Oxford Handbook of Comparative Law* (Oxford University Press, 2nd ed., 2019)

Glenn, H Patrick, *Legal Traditions of the World: Sustainable Diversity in Law* (Oxford University Press, 2nd ed., 2004)

Glenn, H Patrick, 'Persuasive Authority' (1987) 32(2) *McGill Law Journal* 261

Goode, Roy, 'The Role of the *Lex Loci Arbitri* in International Commercial Arbitration' (2001) 17(1) *Arbitration International* 19

Gorence, Brianna, 'The Constructive Role of General Principles in International Arbitration' (2018) 17(3) *The Law and Practice of International Courts and Tribunals* 455

Gu, Weixia, 'When Local Meets International: Mediation Combined with Arbitration in China and Its Prospective Reform in a Comparative Context' (2015) 10(2) *Journal of Comparative Law* 84

Guzman, Andrew T and Timothy L Meyer, 'International Soft Law' (2010) 2(1) *Journal of Legal Analysis* 171

Havedal, Anja and Elena Burova, 'SCC Practice Note-SCC Board Decisions on Challenges to Arbitrators 2013-1015' (23 January 2016), http://www.sccinstitute.com/media/176447/scc-decisions-on-challenges-to-arbitrators-2013-2015.pdf

Hazelhorst, Monique, *Free Movement of Civil Judgments in the European Union and the Right to a Fair Trial* (Springer, 2017)

Heidemann, Maren and Andreas Knebel, 'Double Taxation Treaties: The Autonomous Interpretation Method in German and English Law; as Demonstrated by the Case of the Silent Partnership' (2010) 38(3) *Intertax* 136

Heiskanen, Veijo, 'Key to Efficiency in International Arbitration' (2015) 30(3) *ICSID Review* 481

Hemmi, Lotta and Fabricio Fortese, 'Procedural Fairness and Efficiency in International Arbitration' (2015) 3(1) *Groningen Journal of International Law* 110

Herczegh, Géza, *General Principles of Law and the International Legal Order* (International Publications Service, 1969)

Hill, Jonathan, 'The Significance of Foreign Judgments Relating to an Arbitral Award in the Context of an Application to Enforce the Award in England' (2012) 8(2) *Journal of Private International Law* 159

Hobér, Kaj, *International Commercial Arbitration in Sweden* (Oxford University Press, 2011)

Hoepfner, Claus Werner Von Wobeser, 'The Effective Use of Legal Sources: How Much Is Too Much and What Is the Role for Iura Novit Curia?' in Albert Jan van den Berg (ed.), *Arbitration Advocacy in Changing Times* (Kluwer Law International, 2011)

Holtzmann, Howard M and Joseph E Neuhaus, *A Guide to the UNCITRAL Model Law on International Commercial Arbitration: Legislative History and Commentary* (Kluwer Law International, 2015)

Holtzmann, Howard M, et al. (eds), *A Guide to the 2006 Amendments to the UNCITRAL Model Law on International Commercial Arbitration: Legislative History and Commentary* (Kluwer Law International, 2015)

Horvath, Günther J, 'The Duty of the Tribunal to Render an Enforceable Award' (2001) 18(2) *Journal of International Arbitration* 135

ICC Commission, 'ICC Commission Report: Controlling Time and Costs in Arbitration' (International Chamber of Commerce, 2018)

ICCA, 'ICCA's Guide to the Interpretation of the 1958 New York Convention: A Handbook for Judges' (International Council for Commercial Arbitration, 2011)

Inoue, Osamu, 'The Due Process Defense to Recognition and Enforcement of Foreign Arbitral Awards in United States Federal Courts: A Proposal for a Standard' (2000) 11 *The American Review of International Arbitration* 247

International Law Commission, 'Draft Conclusion on Subsequent Agreements and Subsequent Practice in Relation to the Interpretation of Treaties with Commentaries' (2018), https://legal.un.org/ilc/texts/instruments/english/commentaries/1_11_2018.pdf

Jacobs, Francis Geoffrey, 'Introduction' in Francis Geoffrey Jacobs and Shelley Roberts (eds), *The Effects of Treaties in Domestic Law* (Sweet & Maxwell, 1987)

Jaksic, Aleksandar, *Arbitration and Human Rights* (Peter Lang, 2002)

Jaksic, Aleksandar, 'Procedural Guarantees of Human Rights in Arbitration Proceedings: A Still Unsettled Problem?' (2007) 24(2) *Journal of International Arbitration* 159

Jana, Andrés, Angie Armer and Johanna Klein Kranenberg, 'Article V (1)(b)' in Herbert Kronke et al. (eds), *Recognition and Enforcement of Foreign Arbitral Awards: A Global Commentary on the New York Convention* (Kluwer Law International, 2010)

Japaridze, Nana, 'Fair Enough? Reconciling the Pursuit of Fairness and Justice with Preserving the Nature of International Commercial Arbitration' (2008) 36(4) *Hofstra Law Review* 1415

Jurists, Advisory Committee of, *Procès-verbaux of the Proceedings of the Advisory Committee of Jurists, June 16th–July 24th 1920, with Annexes* (Van Langenhuysen Brothers, 1920)

Kalnina, Ieva, 'Iura Novit Curia: Scylla and Charybdis of International Arbitration?' (2008) 8(1) *Baltic Yearbook of International Law* 89

Karton, Joshua, 'International Arbitration as Comparative Law in Action' (2020) 2020(2) *Journal of Dispute Resolution* 293

Kaufmann-Kohler, Gabrielle, 'Globalization of Arbitral Procedure' (2003) 36 *Vanderbilt Journal of Transnational Law* 1313

Kaufmann-Kohler, Gabrielle, 'The Governing Law: Fact or Law? – A Transnational Rule on Establishing Its Contents' (2006) 26 *ASA Special Series* 79

Kaufmann-Kohler, Gabrielle, 'Identifying and Applying the Law Governing the Arbitration Procedure – The Role of the Law of the Place of Arbitration' in Albert Jan van den Berg (ed.), *Improving the Efficiency of Arbitration Agreements and Awards: 40 Years of Application of the New York Convention* (Kluwer Law International, 1999)

Kaufmann-Kohler, Gabrielle and Antonio Rigozzi, *International Arbitration: Law and Practice in Switzerland* (Oxford University Press, 2015)

Kessedjian, Catherine, 'Transnational Public Policy' in Albert Jan van den Berg (ed.), *International Arbitration 2006: Back to Basics?* (Kluwer Law International, 2007)

Kleiner, Caroline, 'Chapter 7: Country Report: France' in Friedrich Rosenfeld, Dietmar Czernich and Franco Ferrari (eds), *Due Process as a Limit to Discretion in International Commercial Arbitration* (Kluwer Law International, 2020)

Knuts, Gisela, 'Jura Novit Curia and the Right to Be Heard – An Analysis of Recent Case Law' (2012) 28(4) *Arbitration International* 669

Kaufmann-Kohler, Gabrielle, 'Soft Law in International Arbitration: Codification and Normativity' (2010) 1(2) *Journal of International Dispute Settlement* 283

Kolb, Robert, 'General Principles of Procedural Law' in Andreas Zimmermann et al. (eds), *The Statute of the International Court of Justice: A Commentary* (Oxford University Press, 3rd ed., 2019)

Kolb, Robert, 'Principles as Sources of International Law (With Special Reference to Good Faith)' (2006) 53(1) *Netherland International Law Review* 1

Kotuby, Charles T, 'General Principles of Law, International Due Process, and the Modern Role of Private International Law' (2013) 23(3) *Duke Journal of Comparative & International Law* 411

Kotuby, Charles T and Luke A Sobota, *General Principles of Law and International Due Process: Principles and Norms Applicable in Transnational Disputes* (Oxford University Press, 2017)

Kröll, Stefan Michael and Peter Kraft, 'Recourse Against the Award, § 1059 – Application for Setting Aside' in Karl-Heinz Böckstiegel, Stefan Michael Kröll and Patricia Nacimiento (eds), *Arbitration in Germany: The Model Law in Practice* (Kluwer Law International, 2nd ed., 2015) 383

Krūmiņš, Toms, *Arbitration and Human Rights: Approaches to Excluding the Annulment of Arbitral Awards and Their Compatibility with the ECHR* (Springer, 2020)

Kühn, Wolfgang, 'Defaulting Parties and Default Awards in International Arbitration' in Arthur W Rovine (ed.), *Contemporary Issues in International Arbitration and Mediation: The Fordham Papers 2014* (Brill, 2014)

Lalive, Pierre, 'Transnational (or Truly International) Public Policy and International Arbitration' in Pieter Sanders (ed.), *Comparative Arbitration Practice and Public Policy in Arbitration: ICCA International Arbitration Congress*, ICCA Congress Series 3 (Kluwer Law International, 1986)

Lammers, Johan G, 'General Principles of Law Recognized by Civilized Nations' in Frits Kalshoven, Pieter Jan Kuyper and Johan G Lammers (eds), *Essays in the Development of the International Legal Order: In Memory of Haro F Van Panhuys* (Springer, 1980)

Landolt, Phillip, 'Arbitrators' Initiatives to Obtain Factual and Legal Evidence' (2012) 28(2) *Arbitration International* 173

Lauterpacht, Hersch, 'Decisions of Municipal Courts as a Source of International Law' (1929) 10 *British Yearbook of International Law* 65

Lees, Amanda et al., 'Report on the Breakout Sessions on Arbitral Legitimacy: The Users' and Judges' Perspectives' in Albert Jan van den Berg (ed.), *Legitimacy: Myths, Realities, Challenges*, ICCA Congress Series 18 (Kluwer Law International, 2015)

Leiss, Johann R, 'The Juridical Nature of General Principles' in Mads Andenas et al. (eds), *General Principles and the Coherence of International Law* (Brill, 2019)

Lenaerts, Koen and Kathleen Gutman, 'The Comparative Law Method and the Court of Justice of the EU Courts and Comparative Law' in Mads Andenas and Duncan Fairgrieve (eds), *Courts and Comparative Law* (Oxford University Press, 2008)

Leurent, Bruno, 'Reflections on the International Effectiveness of Arbitration Awards' (1996) 12(3) *Arbitration International* 269

Lew, Julian D M, 'Achieving the Dream: Autonomous Arbitration' (2006) 22 *Arbitration International* 179

Lew, Julian D M, 'Is There a Global Free-standing Body of Substantive Arbitration Law' in Albert Jan van den Berg (ed), *International Arbitration: The Coming of a New Age*, ICCA Congress 17 (Kluwer Law International, 2013)

Lew, Julian D M, Loukas A Mistelis and Stefan M Kröll, *Comparative International Commercial Arbitration* (Kluwer Law International, 2003)

Leyda, José Alejandro Carballo, 'A Uniform, Internationally Oriented Legal Framework for the Recognition and Enforcement of Foreign Arbitral Awards in Mainland China, Hong Kong and Taiwan?' (2007) 6(2) *Chinese Journal of International law* 345

Liebscher, Christoph, 'Non-binding Award, Article V (1) (e)' in Reinmar Wolff (ed.), *New York Convention: Convention on the Recognition and Enforcement of Foreign Arbitral Awards of 10 June 1958: Commentary* (C.H. Beck • Hart • Nomos, 2012)

Liebscher, Christoph, 'Preliminary Remarks' in Reinmar Wolff (ed.), *New York Convention: Convention on the Recognition and Enforcement of Foreign Arbitral Awards of 10 June 1958 Commentary* (C.H. Beck, 2012)

Lo, Chang-fa, *Treaty Interpretation under the Vienna Convention on the Law of Treaties: A New Round of Codification* (Springer, 2017)

Luttrell, Sam and Peter Harris, 'Reinventing the Redfern' (2016) 33(4) *Journal of International Arbitration* 353

MacCormick, Neil, *Legal Reasoning and Legal Theory* (Clarendon, 1978)

Mann, FA, 'Reflections on a Commercial Law of Nations' (1957) 20 *British Yearbook of International Law* 33

Mann, Francis, 'The UNCITRAL Model Law-Lex Facit Arbitrum' (1986) 2(3) *Arbitration International* 241

Mapesbury, Lord Collins of and Jonathan Harris (eds), *Dicey, Morris and Collins on the Conflict of Laws* (Sweet & Maxwell, 15th ed., 2012)

Marcoux, Jean-Michel, 'Transnational Public Policy as an International Practice in Investment Arbitration' (2019) 10(3) *Journal of International Dispute Settlement* 496

Maurer, Anton G, *The Public Policy Exception under the New York Convention: History, Interpretation, and Application* (JurisNet, 2013)

Mclachlan, Campbell, 'The Principle of Systemic Integration and Article 31(3)(c) of the Vienna Convention' (2005) 54(2) *International and Comparative Law Quarterly* 279

McNair, Arnold, 'The General Principles of Law Recognized by Civilized Nations' (1957) 33 *British Yearbook of International Law* 1

Mcnair, Arnold, *The Law of Treaties* (Oxford University Press, 1961)

Mehren, Arthur von, *Limitations on Party Choice of the Governing Law: Do They Exist for International Commercial Arbitration* (Tel Aviv University, 1986)

Merryman, John Henry, 'On the Convergence (and Divergence) of the Civil Law and the Common Law' (1981) 17 *Stanford Journal of International Law* 357

Michaels, Ralf, 'The Functional Method of Comparative Law' in Mathias Reimann and Reinhard Zimmermann (eds), *The Oxford Handbook of Comparative Law* (Oxford University Press, 2nd ed., 2019)

Mills, Alex, *The Confluence of Public and Private International Law: Justice, Pluralism and Subsidiarity in the International Constitutional Ordering of Private Law* (Cambridge University Press, 2009)

Mistelis, Loukas, 'Delocalization and Its Relevance in Post-Award Review' in Fabien Gelinas and Frederic Bachand (eds), *25 Years of the UNCITRAL Model Law* (Juris, 2013)

Mistelis, Loukas, 'Setting Aside of Arbitral Awards and Forum Shopping in International Arbitration: Delocalization, Party Autonomy and National Courts in Post-Award Review' in Franco Ferrari (ed.), *Forum Shopping in the International Commercial Arbitration Context* (Sellier, 2013)

Mo, Shijian, 'Interpretation and Application of the New York Convention in China' in George A Bermann (ed.), *Recognition and Enforcement of Foreign Arbitral Awards – The Interpretation and Application of the New York Convention by National Courts* (Springer, 2017)

Mortenson, Julian Davis, 'Is the Vienna Convention Hostile to Drafting History' (2013) 107(4) *American Journal of Comparative Law* 780

Moses, Margaret L, 'Chapter 11: Public Policy under the New York Convention: National, International, and Transnational' in Katia Fach Gomez and Ana M Lopez-Rodriguez (eds), *60 Years of the New York Convention: Key Issues and Future Challenges* (Kluwer Law International, 2019)

Musielak, Hans-Joachim and Wolfgang Voit (eds), *Code of Civil Procedure: ZPO* (Vahlen, 16th ed., 2019)

Nacimiento, Patricia, 'Article V (1)(a)' in Herbert Kronke et al. (eds), *Recognition and Enforcement of Foreign Arbitral Awards: A Global Commentary on the New York Convention* (Kluwer Law International, 2010)

Nollkaemper, André, 'Grounds for the Application of International Rules of Interpretation in National Courts' in Helmut Philipp Aust and Georg Nolte (eds), *The Interpretation of International Law by Domestic Courts* (Oxford University Press, 2016)

Osmanoglu, Burcu, 'Third-Party Funding in International Commercial Arbitration and Arbitrator Conflict of Interest' (2015) 32(3) *Journal of International Arbitration* 325

Palombino, Fulvio Maria, *Fair and Equitable Treatment and the Fabric of General Principles* (TMC Asser, 2018)

Pargendler, Mariana, 'The Rise and Decline of Legal Families' (2012) 60(4) *The American Journal of Comparative Law* 1043

Park, William W, 'Arbitration in Autumn' (2011) 2(2) *Journal of International Dispute Settlement* 287

Park, William W, 'Arbitrators and Accuracy' (2010) 1(1) *Journal of International Dispute Settlement* 25

Park, William W, 'The Lex Loci Arbitri and International Commercial Arbitration' (1983) 32(1) *The International and Comparative Law Quarterly* 21

Park, Willian W, 'The Procedural Soft Law of International Arbitration: Non-governmental Instruments' in Loukas A Mistelis and Julian D M Lew QC (eds), *Pervasive Problems in International Arbitration* (Kluwer Law International, 2006)

Paulsson, Jan, 'Arbitration in Three Dimensions' (2011) 60(2) *International and Comparative Law Quarterly* 291

Paulsson, Jan, 'Arbitration Unbound: Award Detached from the Law of Its Country of Origin' (1981) 30(2) *International and Comparative Law Quarterly* 358

Paulsson, Jan, 'Delocalisation of International Commercial Arbitration: When and Why It Matters' (1983) 32 *International and Comparative Law Quarterly* 53

Paulsson, Jan, *Denial of Justice in International Law* (Cambridge University Press, 2005)

Paulsson, Jan, *The Idea of Arbitration* (Oxford University Press, 2013)

Paulsson, Jan, 'May or Must under the New York Convention: An Exercise in Syntax and Linguistics' (1998) 14 *Journal of International Arbitration*

Paulsson, Marike RP, *The 1958 New York Convention in Action* (Kluwer Law International, 2016)

Peerenboom, Randall, 'The Evolving Regulatory Framework For Enforcement of Arbitral Awards in the People's Republic of China' (2011) 1(2) *Asian-Pacific Law and Policy Journal* 1

Pellet, Alain and Daniel Müller, 'Article 38' in Andreas Zimmermann (ed.), *The Statute of the International Court of Justice: A Commentary* (Oxford University Press, 3rd ed, 2019)

Petrochilos, Georgios, *Procedural Law in International Arbitration* (Oxford University Press, 2004)

Polkinghorne, Michael and Benjamin Ainsley Gill, 'Due Process Paranoia: Need We Be Cruel to Be Kind' (2017) 34(6) *Journal of International Arbitration* 935

Popova, Ina C and Duncan Pickard, 'Chapter 20: Country Report: The United States of America' in Friedrich Rosenfeld, Dietmar Czernich and Franco Ferrari (eds), *Due Process as a Limit to Discretion in International Commercial Arbitration* (Kluwer Law International, 2020)

Poudret, Jean-François and Sébastien Besson, *Comparative Law of International Arbitration* (Sweet & Maxwell, 2nd ed., 2007)

Pryles, Michael, 'Reflections on Transnational Public Policy' (2007) 24(1) *Journal of International Arbitration* 1

Ragnwaldh, Jakob, Fredrik Andersson and Celeste E Salinas Quero, *A Guide to the SCC Arbitration Rules* (Wolters Kluwer, 2019)

Raimondo, Fabián O, *General Principles of Law in the Decisions of International Criminal Courts and Tribunals* (Martinus Nijhoff, 2008)

Rainey, Bernadette, Elizabeth Wicks and Clare Ovey, *Jacobs, White and Ovey: The European Convention on Human Rights* (Oxford University Press, 2014)

Reed, Lucy, 'Ab(use) of Due Process: Sword vs Shield' (2017) 33 *Arbitration International* 361

Reisman, Michael, *Systems of Control in International Adjudication and Arbitration* (Duke University Press, 1992)

Reitz, John C, 'How to Do Comparative Law' (1998) 46(4) *American Journal of Comparative Law* 617

Roberts, Anthea, 'Comparative International Law? The Role of National Courts in Creating and Enforcing International Law' (2011) 60(1) *International and Comparative Law Quarterly* 57

Roberts, Anthea, et al., 'Conceptualizing Comparative International Law' in Anthea Roberts et al. (eds), *Comparative International Law* (Oxford University Press, 2018)

Rosenfeld, Friedrich, Dietmar Czernich and Franco Ferrari, 'General Report' in Friedrich Rosenfeld, Dietmar Czernich and Franco Ferrari (eds), *Due Process as a Limit to Discretion in International Commercial Arbitration* (Kluwer Law International, 2020)

Rosenfeld, Friedrich Jakob, 'Chapter 8: Country Report: Germany' in Friedrich Rosenfeld, Dietmar Czernich and Franco Ferrari (eds), *Due Process as a Limit to Discretion in International Commercial Arbitration* (Kluwer Law International, 2020)

Scherer, Maxi, 'Effects of Foreign Judgments Relating to International Arbitral Awards: Is the "Judgment Route" the Wrong Road?' (2013) 4(3) *Journal of International Dispute Settlement* 587

Scherer, Maxi, 'Long-Awaited New French Arbitration Law Revealed' on Kluwer Arbitration Blog (15 January 2011), http://arbitrationblog.kluwerarbitration.com/2011/01/15/long-awaited-new-french-arbitration-law-revealed/?print=print

Scherer, Maxi, 'New York Convention: Violation of Due Process, Article V (1)(b)' in Reinmar Wolff (ed.), *New York Convention: Convention on the Recognition and Enforcement of Foreign Arbitral Awards of 10 June 1958: Commentary* (C.H. Beck • Hart • Nomos, 2012)

Schill, Stephan W, 'General Principles of Law and International Investment Law' in Tarcisio Gazzini and Eric De Brabandere (eds), *International Investment Law: The Sources of Rights and Obligations* (Brill, 2012)

School of International Arbitration at Queen Mary University of London and White & Case, '2015 International Arbitration Survey: Improvements and Innovations in International Arbitration' (Queen Mary University of London and White & Case, 2015)

School of International Arbitration at Queen Mary University of London and White & Case, '2018 International Arbitration Survey: The Evolution of International Arbitration' (Queen Mary University of London and White & Case, 2018)

Schreuer, Christoph, 'The Interpretation of Treaties by Domestic Courts' (1971) 45 *British Yearbook of International Law* 255

Settem, Ola Johan, *Applications of the 'Fair Hearing' Norm in ECHR Article 6(1) to Civil Proceedings: With Special Emphasis on the Balance Between Procedural Safeguards and Efficiency* (Springer, 2016)

Shaw, Malcolm, *International Law* (Cambridge University Press, 7th ed., 2014)

Shaw, Malcolm N (ed.), *Rosenne's Law and Practice of the International Court: 1920-2015* (Brill, 5th ed., 2016)

Siems, Mathias, 'Bringing in Foreign Ideas: The Quest for "Better Law" in Implicit Comparative Law' (2014) 9 *Journal of Comparative Law* 119

Siems, Mathias, *Comparative Law* (Oxford University Press, 2nd ed., 2018)

Skouteris, Thomas, *The Notion of Progress in International Law Discourse* (TMC Asser Press, 2010)

Slaughter, Anne-Marie, 'A Global Community of Courts' (2003) 44(1) *Harvard International Law Journal* 191

Slaughter, Anne-Marie, 'Judicial Globalization' (2000) 40 *Virginia Journal of International Law* 1103

Slaughter, Anne-Marie, *A New World Order* (Princeton University Press, 2004)

Slaughter, Anne-Marie, 'A Typology of Transjudicial Communication' (1994) 29 *University of Richmond Law Review* 99

Sloss, David L, 'United States' in David Sloss (ed.), *The Role of Domestic Courts in Treaty Enforcement: A Comparative Study* (Cambridge University Press, 2009)

Sloss, David L, 'Domestic Application of Treaties' in Duncan B Hollis (ed.), *The Oxford Guide to Treaties* (Oxford University Press, 2nd ed., 2020)

Smith, Gordon, 'Comparative Analysis of Joinder and Consolidation Provisions under Leading Arbitral Rules' (2018) 35(2) *Journal of International Arbitration* 173

Smits, Jan M, 'Comparative Law and Its Influence on National Legal Systems' in Mathias Reimann and Reinhard Zimmeremann (eds), *The Oxford Handbook of Comparative Law* (Oxford University Press, 2nd ed., 2019)

Solomon, Dennis, 'Interpretation and Application of the New York Convention in Germany' in George A Bermann (ed.), *Recognition and Enforcement of Foreign Arbitral Awards – The Interpretation and Application of the New York Convention by National Courts* (Springer, 2017)

Sornarajah, M, *The International Law on Foreign Investment* (Cambridge University Press, 3rd ed., 2010)

Spiermann, Ole, 'The History of Article 38 of the Statute of the International Court of Justice: "A Purely Platonic Discussion"?' in Samantha Besson and Jean d'Aspremont (eds), *The Oxford Handbook of the Sources of International Law* (Oxford University Press, 2017)

Stampa, Gonzalo, 'The Prague Rules' (2019) 35(2) *Arbitration International* 221

Stone, John Henry Dingfelder, *Court Interpreters and Fair Trials* (Springer, 2018)

Strong, SI, 'Research in International Commercial Arbitration: Special Skills, Special Sources' (2009) 20(2) *American Review of International Arbitration* 119

Tang, Zheng Sophia, 'Chapter 5: Country Report: China' in Friedrich Rosenfeld, Dietmar Czernich and Franco Ferrari (eds), *Due Process as a Limit to Discretion in International Commercial Arbitration* (Kluwer Law International, 2020)

Tanzi, Attila, 'Conclusions: Testing General Principles of Law in International Investment Law: Between Principles and Rules of International Law' in Mads Andenas et al. (eds), *General Principles and the Coherence of International Law* (Brill, 2019)

Tao, Jingzhou and Mariana Zhong, 'Resolving Disputes in China: New and Sometimes Unpredictable Developments' in Peter Quayle and Xuan Gao (eds), *International Organizations and the Promotion of Effective Dispute Resolution* (Brill & Nijhoff, 2019)

The IBA Arbitration Guidelines and Rules Subcommittee, 'The Report on the Reception of the IBA Arbitration Soft Law Products' (International Bar Association, September 2016)

The IBA Conflicts of Interest Subcommittee, 'The IBA Guidelines on Conflicts of Interest in International Arbitration: The First Five Years, 2004-2009' (2010) 4(1) *Dispute Resolution International* 5

Thirlway, Hugh, 'The Law and Procedure of the International Court of Justice 1960-1989: Part Eleven' (2001) 71(1) *British Yearbook of International Law* 71

Thirlway, Hugh, *The Sources of International Law* (Oxford University Press, 2nd ed., 2019)

Train, François-Xavier, 'Interpretation and Application of the New York Convention in France' in George A Bermann (ed.), *Recognition and Enforcement of Foreign Arbitral Awards – The Interpretation and Application of the New York Convention by National Courts* (Springer, 2017)

Trakman, Leon E, 'Aligning State Sovereignty with Transnational Public Policy' (2018) 93(2) *Tulane Law Review* 207

Trechsel, Stefan, *Human Rights in Criminal Proceedings* (Oxford University Press, 2005)

Tzanakopoulos, Antonios, 'Domestic Courts in International Law: The International Judicial Function of National Courts' (2011) 34(1) *Loyola of Los Angeles International & Comparative Law Review* 133

Tzanakopoulos, Antonios, 'Judicial Dialogue as a Means of Interpretation' in Helmut Philipp Aust and Georg Nolte (eds), *The Interpretation of International Law by Domestic Courts* (Oxford University Press, 2016)

United Nations Commission on International Trade Law, Secretariat Guide on the Convention on the Recognition and Enforcement of Foreign Arbitral Awards (2016)

Vadi, Valentina, *Analogies in International Investment Law and Arbitration* (Cambridge University Press, 2015)

Verbist, Herman, 'Challenges on Grounds of Due Process Pursuant to Article V(1)(B) of the New York Convention' in Emmanuel Gaillard and Domenico Di Pietro (eds), *Enforcement of Arbitration Agreements and International Arbitral Awards: The New York Convention in Practice* (Cameron May, 2008)

Verdier, Pierre-Hugues and Mila Versteeg, 'International Law in National Legal Systems: An Empirical Investigation' (2015) 109(3) *American Journal of International Law* 514

Vogenauer, Stefan, 'Sources of Law and Legal Method in Comparative Law' in Mathias Reimann and Reinhard Zimmermann (eds), *The Oxford Handbook of Comparative Law* (Oxford University Press, 2nd ed., 2019)

Waibel, Michael, 'Principles of Treaty Interpretation Developed for and Applied by National Courts?' in Helmut Philipp Aust and Georg Nolte (eds), *The Interpretation of International Law by Domestic Courts* (Oxford University Press, 2016)

Waincymer, Jeff, *Procedure and Evidence in International Arbitration* (Kluwer Law International, 2012)

Walsh, Thomas W and Ruth Teitelbaum, 'The LCIA Court Decisions on Challenges to Arbitrators: An Introduction' (2011) 27(3) *Arbitration International* 283

Wolff, Reinmar (ed.), *New York Convention: Convention on the Recognition and Enforcement of Foreign Arbitral Awards of 10 June 1958 Commentary* (C.H. Beck • Hart • Nomos, 2012)

Wouter, Jan, et al., *International Law: A European Perspective* (Hart Publishing, 2018)

Wouters, Jan, 'Conclusions: The Role of General Principles in a Multi-layered Legal Setting' in Mads Andenas et al. (eds), *General Principles and the Coherence of International Law* (Brill, 2019)

Zhu, Lei and Yongping Xiao, 'Article V(1)(b) of the New York Convention in China: Applying the Due Process Defense Without the Doctrine of Due Process' (2019) 49 *Hong Kong Law Journal* 57

Zweigert, Konrad and Hein Kötz, *An Introduction to Comparative Law* (Tony Weir trans, Oxford University Press, 3rd ed., 1998)

1966 (2) *Yearbook of the International Law Commission*

1999 IBA Working Party and 2010 IBA Rules of Evidence Review Subcommittee, 'Commentary on the Revised Text of the 2010 IBA Rules on the Taking of Evidence in International Arbitration' (2011) 5(1) *Dispute Resolution International* 45

刘贵祥，沈红雨 [Guixiang Liu and Hongyu Shen]《我国承认和执行外国仲裁裁决的司法实践述评》[Judicial Practice of the Recognition and Enforcement of Foreign Arbitral Awards in China] (2002) 79(1) 《北京仲裁》*Beijing Arbitration* 1

高晓力[Gao Xiaoli]《中国法院承认和执行外国仲裁裁决的积极实践》[Positive Practice of Chinese Courts in Recognizing and Enforcing Foreign Arbitral Awards] (2018) 5《法律适用》*Journal of Law Application* 2

Table of Cases/Awards

Table of Treaties/UN Documents

African Charter on Human and Peoples' Rights, adopted 27 June 1981, 1520 UNTS 217 (entered into force 21 October 1986), 70

American Convention on Human Rights, opened for signature 22 November 1969, 1144 UNTS 123 (entered into force 18 July 1978), 70

Charter of Fundamental Rights of the European Union (entered into force 1 December 2009), 11, 70, 94, 114

Comments of the Representative of the Egyptian Government, Mr Osman: Summary Record of the Sixth Meeting, E/AC42/SR6, 4, 46

Convention for the Protection of Human Rights and Fundamental Freedoms, opened for signature 4 November 1950, 213 UNTS 221 (entered into force 3 September 1953), 70, 94, 114

Convention on the Execution of Foreign Arbitral Awards, open for signature 26 September 1927, 92 LNTS 301 (entered into force 25 July 1929), 29, 149

Convention on the Recognition and Enforcement of Foreign Arbitral Awards, open for signature 10 June 1958, 330 UNTS 3 (entered into force 7 June 1959), 1, 26, 46, 61, 63, 66, 67, 73, 96, 134, 189

Convention on the Recognition and Enforcement of Foreign Judgments in Civil or Commercial Matters, concluded 2 July 2019, 97

Convention on the Settlement of Investment Disputes between States and Nationals of other States, opened for signature 18 March 1965, 575 UNTS 159 (entered into force 14 October 1966), 96

European Convention on International Commercial Arbitration, opened for signature 21 April 1961, 484 UNTS 349 (entered into force 18 October 1965), 96, 113

Final Act and Convention on the Recognition and Enforcement of Foreign Arbitral Awards, E/CONF.26/8Rev.1 (10 June 1958), 74

Human Rights Committee, *Views: Communication No 1347/2005*, 90th sess., UN Doc. CCPR/C/90/D/1347/2005 (23 July 2007), 101

Human Rights Committee, *Views: Communication No 1510/2006*, 95th sess., UN Doc. CCPR/C/95/D/1510/2006 (30 March 2009), 101

Table of Legislation

Table of Institutional Rules/Soft Laws

INTERNATIONAL ARBITRATION LAW LIBRARY

1. Moshe Hirsch, *The Arbitration Mechanism of the International Center for the Settlement of Investment Disputes,* 1993 (ISBN 07-923-1993-1).
2. Aida B. Avanessian, *Iran-United States Claims Tribunal in Action,* 1993 (ISBN 18-533-3902-4).
3. Isaak I. Dore, *The UNCITRAL Framework for Arbitration in Contemporary Perspective,* 1993 (ISBN 18-533-3573-8).
4. Vesna Lazić, *Insolvency Proceedings and Commercial Arbitration,* 1998 (ISBN 90-411-1115-8).
5. Joachim Frick, *Arbitration in Complex International Contracts,* 2001 (ISBN 90-411-1662-1).
6. Katherine Lynch, *The Forces of Economic Globalization: Challenges to the Regime of International Commercial Arbitration,* 2003 (ISBN 90-411-1994-9).
7. Christoph Liebscher, *The Healthy Award: Challenge in International Commercial Arbitration,* 2003 (ISBN 90-411-2011-4).
8. Hamid G. Gharavi, *The International Effectiveness of the Annulment of an Arbitral Award,* 2003 (ISBN 90-411-1717-2).
9. Abdulhay Sayed, *Corruption in International Trade and Commercial Arbitration,* 2004 (ISBN 90-411-2236-2).
10. Gabrielle Kaufmann-Kohler & Thomas Schultz, *Online Dispute Resolution: Challenges for Contemporary Justice,* 2004 (ISBN 90-411-2318-0).
11. Christopher R. Drahozal & Richard W. Naimark (eds), *Towards a Science of International Arbitration: Collected Empirical Research,* 2005 (ISBN 90-411-2322-9).
12. Ali Yeşilirmak, *Provisional Measures in International Commercial Arbitration,* 2005 (ISBN 90-411-2353-9).
13. Christian Bühring-Uhle, *Arbitration and Mediation in International Business,* second revised edition, 2006 (ISBN 978-9-041-12256-8).
14. Bernard Hanotiau, *Complex Arbitrations: Multi-party, Multi-contract and Multi-issue – A Comparative Study,* Second Edition, 2020 (ISBN 978-94-035-1261-7).
15. Loukas A. Mistelis & Julian D.M. Lew (eds), *Pervasive Problems in International Arbitration,* 2006 (ISBN 978-9-041-12450-0).
16. Julian D.M. Lew & Loukas A. Mistelis (eds), *Arbitration Insights – Twenty Years of the Annual Lecture of the School of International Arbitration, Sponsored by Freshfields Bruckhaus Deringer,* 2006 (ISBN 978-9-041-12606-1).
17. Mark Kantor, *Valuation for Arbitration: Compensation Standards, Valuation Methods and Expert Evidence,* 2008 (ISBN 978-9-041-12735-8).
18. Christoph Brunner, *Force Majeure and Hardship under General Contract Principles: Exemption for Non-Performance in International Arbitration,* 2009 (ISBN 978-90-411-2792-1).

19. Loukas A. Mistelis & Stavros L. Brekoulakis (eds), *Arbitrability: International & Comparative Perspectives*, 2009 (ISBN 978-90-411-2730-3).
20. Sam Luttrell, *Bias Challenges in International Commercial Arbitration: The Need for a 'Real Danger' Test*, 2009 (ISBN 978-90-411-3191-1).
21. Monique Sasson, *Substantive Law in Investment Treaty Arbitration: The Unsettled Relationship Between International Law and Municipal Law*, Second Edition, 2017 (ISBN 978-90-411-6103-1).
22. Ileana M. Smeureanu, *Confidentiality in International Commercial Arbitration*, 2011 (ISBN 978-90-411-3226-0).
23. Won Kidane, *China-Africa Dispute Settlement: The Law, Economics and Culture of Arbitration*, 2011 (ISBN 978-90-411-3674-9).
24. Karel Daele, *Challenge and Disqualification of Arbitrators in International Arbitration*, 2012 (ISBN 978-90-411-3799-9).
25. Crina Baltag, *The Energy Charter Treaty: The Notion of Investor*, 2012 (ISBN 978-90-411-3428-8).
26. Alexandra Diehl, *The Core Standard of International Investment Protection: Fair and Equitable Treatment*, 2012 (ISBN 978-90-411-3869-9).
27. Manuel Indlekofer, *International Arbitration and the Permanent Court of Arbitration*, 2013 (ISBN 978-90-411-4766-0).
28. Günther J. Horvath & Stephan Wilske (eds), *Guerrilla Tactics in International Arbitration*, 2013 (ISBN 978-90-411-4002-9).
29. Albert Badia, *Piercing the Veil of State Enterprises in International Arbitration*, 2014 (ISBN 978-90-411-5162-9).
30. Nadja Erk, *Parallel Proceedings in International Arbitration: A Comparative European Perspective*, 2014 (ISBN 978-90-411-5264-0).
31. Simon Vorburger, *International Arbitration and Cross-Border Insolvency: Comparative Perspectives*, 2014 (ISBN 978-90-411-5419-4).
32. Ahmad Ali Ghouri, *Interaction and Conflict of Treaties in Investment Arbitration*, 2015 (ISBN 978-90-411-5417-0).
33. Reto Marghitola, *Document Production in International Arbitration*, 2015 (ISBN 978-90-411-5159-9).
34. Alfonso Gómez-Acebo, *Party-Appointed Arbitrators in International Commercial Arbitration*, 2016 (ISBN 978-90-411-6671-5).
35. Jonas von Goeler, *Third-Party Funding in International Arbitration and Its Impact on Procedure*, 2016 (ISBN 978-90-411-5015-8).
36. Dean Lewis, *The Interpretation and Uniformity of the UNCITRAL Model Law on International Commercial Arbitration: Focusing on Australia, Hong Kong and Singapore*, 2016 (ISBN 978-90-411-6700-2).
37. Stavros Brekoulakis, Julian D.M. Lew & Loukas Mistelis (eds), *The Evolution and Future of International Arbitration*, 2016 (ISBN 978-90-411-7004-0).
38. Rémy Gerbay, *The Functions of Arbitral Institutions*, 2016 (ISBN 978-90-411-6217-5).

39. Maximilian Clasmeier, *Arbitral Awards as Investments: Treaty Interpretation and the Dynamics of International Investment Law*, 2017 (ISBN 978-90-411-8357-6).
40. Tony Cole (ed.), *The Roles of Psychology in International Arbitration*, 2017 (ISBN 978-90-411-5921-2).
41. Pietro Ferrario, *The Adaptation of Long-Term Gas Sale Agreements by Arbitrators*, 2017 (ISBN 978-90-411-8232-6).
42. Jacob B. van de Velden, *Finality in Litigation: The Law and Practice of Preclusion – Res Judicata (Merger and Estoppel), Abuse of Process and Recognition of Foreign Judgments*, 2017 (ISBN 978-90-411-8342-2).
43. Dolores Bentolila, *Arbitrators as Lawmakers*, 2017 (ISBN 978-90-411-8354-5).
44. Giacomo Marchisio, *The Notion of Award in International Commercial Arbitration: A Comparative Analysis of French Law, English Law, and the UNCITRAL Model Law*, 2017 (ISBN 978-90-411-8391-0).
45. Csaba Kovács, *Attribution in International Investment Law*, 2018 (ISBN 978-90-411-9675-0).
46. Mary Mitsi, *The Decision-Making Process of Investor-State Arbitration Tribunals*, 2019 (ISBN 978-90-411-9600-2).
47. Ahmet Cemil Yıldırım, *Interpretation of Contracts in Comparative and Uniform Law*, 2019 (ISBN 978-94-035-1130-6).
48. Beata Gessel-Kalinowska vel Kalisz, *The Legal, Real and Converged Interest in Declaratory Relief*, 2019 (ISBN 978-94-035-1244-0).
49. Maximilian Pika, *Third-Party Effects of Arbitral Awards: Res Judicata Against Privies, Non-mutual Preclusion and Factual Effects*, 2019 (ISBN 978-94-035-1273-0).
50. Yulia Levashova, *The Right of States to Regulate in International Investment Law: The Search for Balance Between Public Interest and Fair and Equitable Treatment*, 2019 (ISBN 978-94-035-0931-0).
51. Flavia Marisi, *Environmental Interests in Investment Arbitration: Challenges and Directions*, 2020 (ISBN 978-94-035-1723-0).
52. Martina Magnarelli, *Privity of Contract in International Investment Arbitration: Original Sin or Useful Tool?*, 2020 (ISBN 978-94-035-2020-9).
53. Xu Qian, *Water Services Disputes in International Arbitration: Reconsidering the Nexus of Investment Protection, Environment, and Human Rights*, 2020 (ISBN 978-94-035-2203-6).
54. Nobumichi Teramura, Ex Aequo et Bono *as a Response to the 'Over-Judicialisation' of International Commercial Arbitration*, 2020 (ISBN 978-94-035-2073-5).
55. Bruno Guandalini, *Economic Analysis of the Arbitrator's Function*, 2020 (ISBN 978-94-035-2265-4).
56. Zena Prodromou, *The Public Order Exception in International Trade, Investment, Human Rights and Commercial Disputes*, 2020 (ISBN 978-94-035-2031-5).

57. Jürg Künzle, *Multiple Contracts and Coordination in International Construction Projects: A Swiss Law Analysis*, 2020 (ISBN 978-94-035-2024-7).
58. Cornel Marian, *The State's Power to Tax in the Investment Arbitration of Energy Disputes: Outer Limits and the Energy Charter Treaty*, 2020 (ISBN 978-94-035-1752-0).
59. Luke Nottage, Shahla Ali, Bruno Jetin & Nobumichi Teramura (eds.), *New Frontiers in Asia-Pacific International Arbitration and Dispute Resolution*, 2021 (ISBN 978-94-035-2855-7).
60. Eva Litina, *Theory, Law and Practice of Maritime Arbitration: The Case of International Contracts for the Carriage of Goods by Sea*, 2021 (ISBN 978-94-035-3035-2).
61. Franco Ferrari & Friedrich Rosenfeld (eds), *Autonomous Versus Domestic Concepts under the New York Convention*, 2021 (ISBN 978-94-035-3173-1).
62. Doğan Gültutan, *Moral Damages under International Investment Law: The Path Towards Convergence*, 2022 (ISBN 978-94-035-4025-2).
63. Simon Foote QC, *The Bona Fide Investor: Corporate Nationality and Treaty Shopping in Investment Treaty Law*, 2022 (ISBN 978-94-035-4185-3).
64. George A. Bermann, *Twilight Issues in International Arbitration: Latent Choice of Law Challenges*, 2023 (ISBN 978-94-035-1746-9).
65. Emmanuel Obiora Igbokwe, *Dealing with Bribery and Corruption in International Commercial Arbitration: To Probe or Not to Probe*, 2023 (ISBN 978-94-035-2066-7).
66. Peter Sester, *Contract Law in International Commercial Arbitration*, 2023 (ISBN 978-94-035-1036-1).
67. Julian Bickmann, *Fact-Finding in International Arbitration: The Emergence of a Transnational* Lex Evidentiae, 2023 (ISBN 978-94-035-1886-2).
68. Giovanna E. Gismondi, *International Environmental Law and International Human Rights Law in Investment Treaty Arbitration: The Contribution of Host States' Argumentation in Re-Shaping International Investment Law*, 2023 (ISBN 978-94-035-3047-5).
69. Fabricio Fortese, *Early Determination of Jurisdiction*, 2024 (ISBN 978-94-035-0268-7).
70. Sabrina Pearson-Wenger, *Good Faith in International Commercial Arbitration: Its Application by Arbitral Tribunals to the Parties' Contract and the Arbitration Agreement*, 2024 (ISBN 978-94-035-0738-5).
71. Charalampos Tagaroulias, *International Investment Law and the Law of the European Union: How Regionalism and Interregionalism Have Shaped the Relationship in the Post-Lisbon Era*, 2024 (ISBN 978-94-035-0708-8).
72. Dan Xie, *Transnational Due Process and Article V(1)(b) of the New York Convention: Grounding Interpretation and Application of the Due Process Defence in the Public International Law Framework for Treaty Interpretation*, 2024 (ISBN 978-94-035-2437-5).

www.ingramcontent.com/pod-product-compliance
Lightning Source LLC
LaVergne TN
LVHW020000031026
849161LV00021B/774